Anthropological Investigations in Contemporary India:
A cross-cultural perspective

OrangeBooks Publication

1st Floor, Rajhans Arcade, Mall Road, Kohka, Bhilai, Chhattisgarh 490020

Website:**www.orangebooks.in**

© Copyright, 2024, Author

All rights reserved. No part of this book may be reproduced, stored in a retrieval system, or transmitted, in any form by any means, electronic, mechanical, magnetic, optical, chemical, manual, photocopying, recording or otherwise, without the prior written consent of its writer.

First Edition, 2024

Anthropological Investigations in Contemporary India

A cross-cultural perspective

C.J. SONOWAL & MILONJYOTI BORGOHAIN

OrangeBooks Publication
www.orangebooks.in

About the Editors

Dr C. J. Sonowal is a renowned anthropologist who is currently attached to the prestigious Tata Institute of Social Sciences in Mumbai. With a wealth of experience in research, teaching, and guiding M. Phil and Ph.D. students, he has published several books and articles in his field. Dr Sonowal's research interests are focused on the study of Indigenous societies, especially on the health and treatment-seeking behaviour of Indigenous people, Tribal Religion, Identity, and Ethnicity. He is a well-respected expert in his field and has contributed significantly to the advancement of knowledge in Anthropology.

Milonjyoti Borgohain is a highly accomplished Anthropologist with a Master's Degree and and PhD in Anthropology. He serves as the Assistant Professor and Head of the Department of Anthropology at Moridhal College, Dhemaji, affiliated with Dibrugarh University, Dibrugarh, Assam, India. Milonjyoti is also the esteemed Editor of Skylines of Anthropology, an International Journal and Academic Research Foundation (ARF, India). He has an impressive publication record in various national and international journals, covering topics such as nutritional health, human growth and development, indigenous health practices, migration, dermatoglyphics, intellectual disability, and more. Milonjyoti has even conducted a minor research project under UGC.

About the Book

The field of Anthropology took a while to gain recognition as a significant academic discipline, even though it had already spread and its potential had been discussed theoretically among hopeful Indian students. It was not until decades later that anthropology was given equal importance to other social and bio-social disciplines. Relying solely on database disciplines like economics, demography, and geography was insufficient for assessing and understanding complex societal issues. Anthropology's interpretive methodology recognises that each human society is unique, providing anthropologists with valuable insight into diverse domains and enabling them to offer appropriate solutions. Through the use of critical theories and the deconstruction of conventional narratives, Anthropology has become a fascinating subject of global interest.

Within this book, readers will find insightful theoretical analyses and detailed micro-level studies that broaden our understanding of pressing contemporary issues through an anthropological lens. Each paper within the book contextualises its findings within the larger societal framework, providing a comprehensive view of the situations being examined. This book's particular strength lies in its emphasis on decolonising anthropological knowledge, exploring the nuances of stigma from an anthropological perspective, highlighting the significance of religion as an ethnic marker, exploring the problems and prospects of writing indigenous ethnohistory of tribes and indigenous people, illuminating food culture through an anthropological lens, examining borderland markets, and exploring the connection of biology and society within the realm of health issues.

Contents

About The Editors v
About the Book vi
Our Contributors x
Preface xiii

1 Introduction 1
   C.J. Sonowal

2 Towards A Method of Decolonising Knowledge: Where Does
   Anthropology Stand? 13
   Sabina Yasmin Rahman

3 Experiencing the Stigma of being 'Suspected': An Anthropological
   Discourse of Lived Experiences of Families of Prisoners 33
   Afiya Khalid

4 Religion as an Ethnic Marker: A Study among the Tai-Khamyangs of
   Assam 52
   Ripunjoy Sonowal

5 Constructing Indigenous History of Tribes: A Study of Historical
   Anthropology with Especial Reference to Sonowal Kachari Tribe in
   Assam 84
   C. J. Sonowal

6 Anthropological Study of Ethnic Food: A Study Among the Dimasa
   Kacharis Of Assam 103
   Kurangana Hazarika
   Anshuman Hazarika

7 Tribal Hinduism Contested: An Autoethnography of Sonowal
   Kacharis of Assam 114
   C.J. Sonowal

8 Impact of COVID-19 on Primary Education: An Anthropological Study in Malayinkeezhu, Kerala 139
   B. Bindu Ramachandran
   Aiswarya. S.V

9 The Cultural Landscape of Borderland Markets: An Anthropological Study of The Assam-Arunachal Borderlands Weekly Markets 154
   Ratna Tayeng

10 The Significance of a Longer Post-Menopausal Phase of Life in Fertility Enhancement and Child Survival: The "Grandmother Hypotheses" Deconstructed 170
   Maitreyee Sharma
   Shabnam Khatoon

11 Caregivers' Response to Health Care Programme on Childhood Pneumonia: An Anthropological Study Among Bhil Tribes 190
   Dr. Prashant Kulkarni
   Dr. Anjali Kurane

12 Risk Factors and Social Determinants of Tuberculosis: An Anthropological Study in The Tea Gardens Of Assam 208
   C.J. Sonowal

13 Influence of Biosocial Factors on Fertility and Child Mortality: An Anthropological Study among the Kabui Naga of Manipur, India 249
   Dr. D.K. Limbu
   Dr. C. Kamei
   Dr. A. Haloi

14 Impact of Supplementary Food and Socio-economic Predictors on Nutritional Status of Children Attending Anganwadis in Bilaspur, Chhattisgarh, India 286
   Manisha Ghritlahre
   Mahua Chanak
   Subal Das
   Kaushik Bose

15 Socio-economic and Reproductive Determinants of Fertility among the Mising Tribe in Dhemaji District of Assam 308
   Dr. Chandika Roy
   Milonjyoti Borgohain

16 Differentials in Hypertension and Anaemia Burden Between the Workers in Abandoned and Operational Tea Plantations: An Anthropological Study in Alipurduar, West Bengal 325
Akash Mallick
Subrata K. Roy

17 Health Care Practises Among the Deshi Muslims: An Anthropological Investigation in Dhubri District, Assam, India ... 354
Suraiya Prodhani
Arifur Zaman

Our Contributors

A. Haloi

1. Sophisticated Analytical Instrument facility, North-Eastern Hill University, India.

Afiya Khalid

2. PhD Scholar, Centre for Study of Social Exclusion and Inclusive Policies, Tata Institute of Social Sciences, Mumbai, 400088

Akash Mallick

3. Assistant Professor, Department of Anthropology, Fakir Mohan University, Odisha.

Anjali Kurane

4. Professor and Head, Department of Anthropology, Savitri Bai Phule Pune University, India.

Anshuman Hazarika

5. Research Scholar, Department of Anthropology, Sikkim Central University, Sikkim.

Arifur Zaman,

6. Associate Professor, Department of Anthropology, Gauhati University, Guwahati, Assam, Pin: 781014.

B. Bindu Ramachandran

7. Professor, Department of Anthropology and Dean, Social Sciences, Kannur University, India.

C. J. Sonowal

8. Professor, Tata Institute of Social Sciences, Mumbai, Former Professor, International Institute for Population Sciences, Deonar, Mumbai. 400 088, India. Selected Professor, Department of Cultural Studies, Tezpur Central University, Assam.

Our Contributors

9. **C. Kamei**
Department of Anthropology, North-Eastern Hill University, India.

10. **Chhandika Roy**
Former Research Scholar, Department of Anthropology, Rajiv Gandhi University, Arunachal Pradesh.

11. **D. K. Limbu**
Professor, Department of Anthropology, North-Eastern Hill University, Shillong

12. **Dr Sabina Yasmin Rahman**
PhD (JNU) Sociology, MA, TISS, Mumbai,
Former Asst. Prof. TISS-Nagaland Campus; JNU, Delhi (Sociology)
Project Head, BOOM Fact Check.

13. **Kaushik Bose**
Professor, Department of Anthropology, Vidyasagar University, West Medinipur, West Bengal.

14. **Kurangana Hazarika**
Research Scholar, Department of Anthropology, Cotton University, Guwahati, Assam.

15. **Mahua Chanak**
Research Scholar, Department of Anthropology, Vidyasagar University, West Medinipur, West Bengal.

16. **Maitreyee Sharma**
Assistant Professor, Department of Anthropology, Dibrugarh University, Assam.

17. **Manisha Ghritlahre**
Research Scholar, Department of Anthropology and Tribal Development, Guru Ghasidas Vishwavidyalaya, Bilaspur, Chhattisgarh.

Our Contributors

Milonjyoti Borgohain
18. Assistant Professor and Head, Department of Anthropology, Moridhal College, Dhemaji, Assam.

Prashant Kulkarni
19. Research Fellow, Department of Anthropology, Savitribai Phule Pune University, India.

Ratna Tayeng
20. Assistant Professor and Head, Department of Anthropology, Dera Natung Govt. College, Itanagar, Arunachal Pradesh.

Ripunjoy Sonowal
21. Assistant Professor, Department of Anthropology, North Gauhati College, Guwahati, Assam.

S. V. Aiswarya
22. Research Student, Department of Anthropology, Kannur University.

Shabnam Khatoon
23. Research Scholar, Department of Anthropology, Dibrugarh University, Assam.

Subal Das
24. Assistant Professor, Department of Anthropology and Tribal Development, Guru Ghasidas Vishwavidyalaya, Bilaspur, Chhattisgarh.

Subrata K. Roy
25. Former Professor, Biological Anthropology Unit, Indian Statistical Institute, Kolkata.

Suraiya Prodhani
26. Research Scholar, Department of Anthropology, Gauhati University, Guwahati, Assam, Pin: 781014

Preface

As I begin writing this introduction, I am filled with a deep sense of joy and reflection. It has been more than thirty years since I began my journey as an anthropologist. I have authored several books, articles, and chapters on a wide range of research topics, but I have never dedicated a book solely to anthropology - until now. It was my co-editor, Milonjyoti Borgohain, a young and vibrant scholar, who encouraged me to undertake this project. Together, we reached out to academics across the country, and after much perseverance, this book has come to fruition. I am incredibly grateful to Milonjyoti for his unwavering support and shared vision. The content of this book, which delves into the evolution and significance of anthropology, is sure to intrigue and captivate the readers.

As an individual who has pursued anthropology for over three decades, I have observed that contemporary to my student life, this field was often chosen by students when other options, such as PCM or economics, were not as accessible. Despite the prevalent belief that job opportunities were scarce for anthropology graduates, many female students persisted in pursuing this field. On a lighter note, our female classmates revealed that their priorities differed from those of their male counterparts, as some were more focused on marriage after obtaining their degree or placed less emphasis on finding a job.

In the past, students exhibited a somewhat lukewarm dedication to anthropology, leaving scant opportunities for graduates to delve into research and training. However, the last two decades have witnessed a remarkable transformation in anthropology, which now stands as a key player among other social sciences. This leap forward was achieved by surmounting initial hurdles such as lack of recognition, limited job prospects, and scarce resources for research and training. Furthermore, the notion of anthropology as a less marketable field has been contested, further propelling its growth.

Preface

The academic discipline of anthropology has faced several obstacles along its journey. The two primary factors that have contributed to its backlog are its methodology of knowledge production, which heavily relies on qualitative data collection and analysis, and the perception of anthropology as a less marketable field. The time-consuming and intensive process of qualitative data analysis has made it challenging to meet the demand for faster conclusions typically associated with quantitative data. Additionally, the lack of resources and support due to the perception of anthropology's marketability has hindered its progress even further.

Moreover, due to its colonial roots, anthropology has traditionally focused more on the study of rural and tribal cultures, often overlooking urban issues and contexts. This historical bias has influenced the discipline's theoretical and methodological rigour, which has been perceived as relatively weaker compared to other social sciences. However, anthropology is on the cusp of a transformation, and there is an increasing recognition of the need for a broader perspective that encompasses urban issues and contexts. This evolution instils optimism about the future trajectory of anthropology.

However, the limitations of all quantitative data-based disciplines like economics, demography, geography, and several others became apparent when they could not fully realise their expectations in the development domain. The significance of human values, perceptions, subjective aspects of human nature and action, and their consequences in the development domain became evident. Anthropological knowledge emerged as one of the few solutions in such cases, armed with century-long insights into human nature and society. The importance of anthropological knowledge has now been recognised nationally and globally. Anthropology has also embraced technological advancements in data collection, data processing, and interpretation of larger data, both qualitative and quantitative. This recognition of anthropology's role in development is sure to enlighten people about its significance.

Anthropology is a field of study that includes a vast range of research-based and review publications, each with distinct merits. However, there has been an ongoing subtle debate regarding the authenticity of these works and their alignment with anthropology's explicit agenda. The essential question in this context is what precisely constitutes an interpretation and discourse as anthropological. Diverse opinions and perspectives have justified a scholarly contribution as anthropological. However, one universal characteristic of any anthropological matter is the revelation of meaning-making through the actions, reactions, behaviour, and performances of the observed or anthropological subjects involved. The observer or researcher should not impose their views without context. The researcher's primary responsibility is to reveal the worldviews of the observed in the context under which the observed find meaning in their actions and reactions.

Throughout the creation of this edition, the authors were consistently encouraged and motivated to integrate this fundamental principle into their analysis, interpretation, and conclusions. As the book's editors, we made a concerted effort to infuse anthropological elements into the text and showcase a diverse array of papers from across the country. Ultimately, our goal is to ensure the reader's satisfaction, which we believe will be the ultimate measure of our success.

1

Introduction

C.J. Sonowal

Part I

Anthropology Matters

The fusion of "Anthropos" and "Logos" was intended to define Anthropology as the scientific study of mankind. However, the precise nature of anthropology may not be immediately apparent. To put it simply, anthropologists explore people and their connections with the natural world, animals, and other humans. Over time, these relationships have become increasingly complex, posing challenges for anthropologists to navigate. Despite these challenges, anthropology remains an invaluable tool for understanding the intricacies of human interactions, highlighting its importance and relevance in our world today.

Over the past two centuries, Anthropology has not only expanded its knowledge base but also evolved significantly. As the name suggests, this field of study is dedicated to understanding the complexities of human beings, the most intricate biological entity on our planet. Anthropologists have broadened their scope of inquiry to encompass a wide range of biological, environmental, socio-cultural, and physical factors that shape human behaviour and relationships. What began as a colonial pursuit to learn about other cultures has transformed into a respected academic discipline within the social and biological sciences. According to Eric Wolf (1964, 84), anthropology offers a uniquely humanistic approach to science. Its interpretive nature also sets it apart from other social sciences, allowing for relatively unbiased analysis.

Through an anthropological lens, things that were once familiar may appear unfamiliar. At the same time, the opposite may also be true as we recognise the underlying similarities in human social and cultural life. Anthropological research has evolved from focusing solely on exotic cultures to examining familiar ones as exotic research locations and studying non-traditional societies within modern state systems. The complexity of human societies has increased due to migration, climate change, economic crises, and the free flow of transnational ideas. Contemporary anthropologists use interpretive research methods to understand modern societies and continue to ask fundamental questions. Although anthropology is often considered the foundation of social sciences, it does not claim to solve all of humanity's problems. However, it equips researchers with the necessary skills and knowledge to competently address complex issues and understand the social relations that shape humanity, society, and the state, underscoring its relevance and importance.

The field of Anthropology is divided into four primary subdisciplines: biological (formerly known as Physical) Anthropology, Archaeology, Linguistic Anthropology, and Cultural Anthropology. Within these subdisciplines, additional areas of specialisation continue to expand. This edition offers an introduction to Cultural and Biological Anthropology, with brief reflections provided in the following paragraphs.

It is widely recognised that social and cultural anthropology evolved from the need of colonial administrators to comprehend the societies they were colonising. Likewise, physical anthropology was inspired by the quest to understand human evolution and locate the elusive connection between humans and primates. Over time, these two core branches of anthropology expanded as new ideas and requirements emerged. The expanding scope of physical anthropology necessitated a shift to biological anthropology, while cultural anthropology branched out into several interconnected subfields.

The field of biological anthropology explores the biological variations, adaptations, and evolution of humans. Physical anthropology, which preceded biological anthropology, originated in the eighteenth century and initially concentrated on physical differences among humans. In the past, physical anthropologists attempted to classify and rank human beings based on anatomical disparities influenced by the concept of race. However, modern anthropologists acknowledge that all humans belong to the same species, Homo sapiens sapiens. Despite varying physical appearances, factors such as environment, diet, activities, and genetics account for differences among individuals.

Biological Anthropology has significantly expanded in scope over time, now including six subdisciplines: primatology, palaeoanthropology, molecular anthropology, bioarchaeology, forensic anthropology, and human biology. The primary focus of biological anthropologists is to answer questions related to human beings' place in nature, their unique characteristics, the origin and evolution of humans, and the migration and variations of humans worldwide. However, it is important to note that the distinction between biological and cultural anthropology is limited to disciplinary discourse. For humans, biology and culture are inextricably linked, and biological anthropological discussions cannot ignore cultural references. Consequently, physical anthropologists emphasise bio-social investigations and explanations to recognise and address these interrelations.

Cultural anthropology is an expansive field within the larger realm of anthropology. While social anthropology is often considered a distinct area of study, the two are closely intertwined, given that culture is an inherent aspect of human society. The primary distinction between the two lies in their respective areas of investigation: social anthropology delves into the organisational structure and behaviour of human beings. In contrast, cultural anthropology explores the significance of actions within a complex whole. Given its vast scope, cultural anthropology encompasses nearly every facet of human life and their interactions with both tangible and intangible elements of the world around them.

Cultural anthropology stands out among other social sciences due to its broad scope and distinct methodology. Anthropologists rely on various methodological tools such as cultural relativism, ethnography, auto-ethnography, participant observation, and interpretive research to understand and analyse local life-worlds on their own terms. Through the lens of cultural relativism, anthropologists strive to interpret the behaviours and actions of individuals within their respective societies, with an emphasis on the meaning those individuals attach to their actions.

This approach rejects the notion of ranking cultures along a high-low or modern-primitive dichotomy, recognising that every culture is unique.

Anthropological research relies heavily on ethnography as an indispensable tool. Anthropologists engage in immersive fieldwork to collect qualitative data in various ways. This method is time-intensive but crucial, as it requires the researcher to gain familiarity with the field situation and the people. Participant observation is one of the unique ways that anthropologists collect data in ethnographic fieldwork. Through participant observation methods, intensive interviews, and a significant amount of time spent in the field, researchers gather subjective and qualitative data from the people they study. Anthropologists employ an interpretive method to analyse field situations, which allows them to uncover the meaning behind the observed population's acts, behaviours, expressions, and perceptions. This way, researchers attempt to understand the inherent meaning-making of the behaviour and actions of the people under study. Through this process, anthropologists can make visible the reality that would otherwise remain invisible or seen in another way. Anthropologists acknowledge that some of the most essential things in life, culture, and society cannot be measured.

Anthropology sheds light on the natural causes and scope of differences among humans, both in terms of society and biology. Through a culturally neutral perspective called cultural relativism, anthropology provides insight into the diversity of human culture and physicality, enabling us to understand better and engage with people from different backgrounds. In today's world, where technology has brought us closer together than ever before, this outlook is crucial for successful interaction with the many social, cultural, and physical domains we encounter globally.

Despite the current global climate, many communities and individuals are turning to their ancestral or reconstructed cultural roots as a way to assert their existence and distinctiveness in the larger world. A sense of perceived threat from the ever-expanding reach of global influence has fuelled this trend. Anthropological research and analysis can help to create a new narrative that highlights the unique histories and perspectives of indigenous peoples, making them more visible in the face of global dominance.

Anthropology is a powerful tool for understanding both ourselves and the complex web of cultural exchange and competition that characterises our world. By exploring what it means to be human, anthropology provides valuable insights into the human experience and the challenges we face in a rapidly changing global landscape.

As globalisation continues to be a topic of much discussion, social researchers question the colonial constructs of research methods used to study non-European societies and disagree with the narrative set to represent and depict these societies. Anthropological accounts, in particular, are under scrutiny for their undeniable genesis to colonialism and colonial viewpoints and interests. To address this, a group of present-day social scientists are exploring the decolonisation of research methodology by adapting to an indigenous way of researching while studying and representing native societies. This perspective has led to the inclusion of auto-ethnography in social research, occupying a significant place in anthropological investigations. However, challenges for anthropologists have increased as primordial and perceived primordial characters such as ethnic identity, religion, language, common historical traditions, shared homelands, class, caste, and communities are aggressively linked with politics of nationalism and existential discourses. To mitigate these issues, anthropologists must enrich their theoretical groundings, methodological expertise, and practical engagement with social justice and inherent human values.

According to Dr Agustín Fuentes of the University of Notre Dame, anthropology is an essential field of study that seeks to understand and serve humanity. Through exploring the reasons behind societal systems and crises such as healthcare access and inequality, anthropology helps us learn from our past and make informed decisions for the future. By examining both historical and present-day trends, we gain valuable insights into what works and what does not in society. Furthermore, anthropology encourages us to see beyond traditional narratives and embrace the diverse realities that exist within our world. Ultimately, this understanding leads to greater inclusivity and tolerance.

Introduction

Part II

This book is a compilation of chapters written on human beings' socio-cultural and biological aspects from an anthropological perspective. The editors have tried including papers from different geographical localities and on diverse subjects. The chapters may be divided into two broad categories - papers containing purely social and cultural aspects and papers containing bio-social components. A brief introduction of the chapters has been arranged as follows:

One of the contributors to the academic domain's decolonisation of knowledge production is Dr Sabina Yasmin Rahman. Her chapter focuses on decolonising anthropology and raises thought-provoking and critical questions. The decolonisation project challenges the dominant section of social science researchers and the Western power structure of knowledge production. This structure has historically favoured European or Western academics and their interpretations and generalisations of non-Western territories. The resulting theories were often imposed or propagated as universal without recognition of the knowledge producers from non-Western or colonised areas.

The origin of Anthropology is closely tied to colonialism, as the vast majority of theories, concepts, and evidence were gathered from colonised countries around the globe. Additionally, the research methods employed by colonial anthropologists often resulted in a macro-narrative that was ethnocentric and placed the Western world at the top of the social hierarchy. Unfortunately, this legacy still lingers in the field of anthropology today. However, there are now many voices calling for a decolonisation of knowledge and knowledge production, urging us to re-think, re-interpret, re-narrate, and re-construct our understanding of the world. Dr Sabina has been instrumental in this effort, offering critical insights and examples from around the world, including India.

Afiya Khalid, a PhD research scholar, explores the topic of stigma experienced by Muslim family members of those accused and imprisoned for terrorism in her paper. The paper critically examines the subjective generation and objective experience of social stigma faced by the victims. Anthropologists have not extensively discussed stigma within the academic domain, particularly its association with various identities such as gender, religion, community, economic status, and locality.

Stigma is a collection of negative beliefs that a society or group holds about a particular thing. This feeling of disapproval often leads to unfair discrimination and exclusion of individuals. People who are stigmatised are often viewed as having a "spoiled identity" based on stereotypes or negative perceptions that are different from societal norms. These definitions help us understand the inherent characteristics of stigma beyond just psychological viewpoints. Anthropologists' understanding of individual and social characteristics and relationships can aid in comprehending the genesis, progression, and consequences of stigma at both individual and social levels. Through the recording and analysis of narratives from family members of Muslim terror-accused individuals, the author provides valuable insight into identity-related social stigma among the minority community in a particular locality in Uttar Pradesh, India. The author's research methodology is well-conceived and expertly applied in her study.

Ripunjoy Sonowal has authored a chapter titled "*Religion as an Ethnic Marker: A Study Among the Tai-Khamyangs of Assam*." In this chapter, the author delves into the religious practices of the people, highlighting how Buddhism has played a significant role in promoting a peaceful and harmonious way of life through religious education and training. The author also notes the presence of a unique blend of local animistic practices and global religious influences, such as Buddhism, among the people. This cultural diversity fosters an environment where individuals can engage in cultural and political discourse while accommodating new ideas that enter their domains through various channels.

C.J. Sonowal draws scholars' attention to exciting and crucial aspects of indigenous populations and tribal societies, which have been a core domain of ethnography and cultural anthropology. His writing under the title "*Constructing Indigenous History of Tribes: A Study of Historical Anthropology with Especial Reference to Sonowal Kachari Tribe in Assam*" delves into the question of why indigenous and tribal societies are interpreted as non-temporal or ahistorical societies. Relating the detachment of events in tribal society as the subject matter of historical anthropology, the author brings forth a very genuine and integral context of anthropology often ignored or neglected by mainstream anthropologists. To contextualise the core issue, the author starts with the definition of history, the changing perspective of history dealing with human activities temporally and spatially and some theoretical and critical aspects of the relations between history and anthropology.

The concept of historical anthropology is then introduced, which is a subfield of anthropology that utilises social and cultural anthropology methodologies to challenge traditional historical narratives by examining historical societies. It shows how historical anthropology focuses on the temporality of people's cultural practices and beliefs rather than solely on contemporary cultures or historical events. The author also discusses briefly the transformation of myth to history as a complex process that presents history as a series of transformations without any specific timeline. It shows that in tribal and indigenous societies, the memory of the past is recorded in various forms of culture and folklore, some of which are concrete and chronological.

The article discusses the challenges of recording the history of indigenous and tribal communities from their own perspective. For instance, the oral traditions of these societies often cyclically present events, making it difficult to establish a linear chronology. Additionally, the mainstream historical accounts worldwide often overlook the history of indigenous communities, focusing instead on the narratives of dominant cultures. The text emphasises the importance of oral traditions in preserving the history of these communities and the need to transform timeless, horizontal data into specific, vertical accounts that reflect the chronology of events. Furthermore, it highlights the lack of representation of Adivasi or tribal communities in modern state archives and how tribal societies have been viewed through the lens of others. The term "tribe" was coined by colonial ethnographers. Overall, the text calls for a more inclusive and accurate approach to documenting the history of indigenous communities.

In their paper, "*An Anthropological Study of Ethnic Food: A Study among the Dimasa Kacharis of Assam,*" Kurangana Hazarika and Anshuman Hazarika emphasise the significance of the "Anthropology of Food" and shed light on the food habits and customs of the Dimasa society. The authors reveal that the Dimasa tribe's food habits are deeply rooted in their local beliefs, traditions, customs, and taboos, and certain food practices serve as ethnic markers within the tribe.

The candid revelation of the pensive thought of being a Tribe and being something undefined to himself has emerged as a discourse on "autoethnography" for the author CJ Sonowal. His chapter titled *"Tribal Hinduism Contested: An Autoethnography of Sonowal Kacharis of Assam"* demonstrates how, being an anthropologist, he can immerse in the field as an observed (anthropological subject) and experience the phenomena while using reflexology, he can observe and interpret the experiences he has experienced as a subject or observed. The chapter explains the various stages in social sciences in terms of the search for truth or research. Further, the author deals with the theoretical aspects of autoethnography, and as a subject of observation or study, he revisits his childhood experiences and adult interaction with his significant others and counters the alien cultural components he and his fellow tribes are destined to follow. His reflection on the past has produced several thought-provoking questions and situations that the author or the researcher that follows has to explain or answer.

The chapter titled "Impact of Covid-19 on Primary Education: A Study in Malayinkeezhu Village, Kerala", by Bindu Ramachandran and S. V. Aiswarya, sheds light on the challenges faced by students amidst the pandemic. The paper highlights the prevalence of feelings of loss, sadness, loneliness, and uncertainty among students, regardless of whether they attended classes online or in person. The lack of face-to-face interactions with teachers during online classes was identified as a significant contributing factor. The authors also note that the absence of regular classes has had a negative impact on primary school students' foundational knowledge.

In his paper "*The Cultural Landscape of Borderland Markets: A Study of Weekly Markets on The Assam-Arunachal Borderlands,*" Ratna Tayeng delves into the significance of markets located at the border of two states with distinct ethnic groups with varying cultural practices and material foundations. Through his research, Tayeng highlights the historical past and tradition of interdependence between the people on either side of the border and sheds light on the cultural underpinnings and centuries-old memories that exist amidst the modern market system.

Maitreyee Sharma and Shabnam Khatoon have co-authored a unique chapter titled "The Significance of a Longer post-Menopausal Phase of Life in Fertility Enhancement and Child Survival: The "Grandmother Hypotheses" Deconstructed". The "grandmother hypothesis" suggests that elderly women can enhance their fitness by acting as caretakers for their grandchildren. By providing care and support during pregnancy, childbirth, and childcare, grandmothers enable mothers to have more offspring. Consequently, women with a genetic disposition for longevity would eventually have a more significant number of grandchildren, who would also inherit the genes for longevity. The article highlights various biosocial factors that could be used to evaluate grandmothering empirically across different human cultural groups. The authors also reveal that research is scarce on this topic.

In their research on the *Caregivers' Response to Healthcare Programme on Childhood Pneumonia: An Anthropological Study Among Bhil Tribes*, Prashant Kulkarni and Anjali Kurane shed light on the implementation process and outcome of a health program designed for under-five children. The study examines the health beliefs and treatment-seeking behaviour of caregivers within the Bhil tribes by analysing the decision-making processes related to pneumonia care. Through 25 in-depth interviews with healthcare providers and implementing entities, as well as 107 caregivers of children under five, the authors reveal that socio-cultural beliefs, nutrition practices, and traditional healers all play a role in the success of the health program. The authors also highlight the challenges posed by private practitioners who manage childhood pneumonia cases in parallel with the health program.

The chapter authored by C.J. Sonowal, titled "*Risk Factors and Social Determinants of Tuberculosis: An Anthropological Study in the Tea Gardens of Assam*," holds significant anthropological value in examining the health and treatment-seeking behaviour of a marginalised population group, namely the tea garden workers of Assam. This includes a specific focus on the incidence of Tuberculosis within the tea gardens of Assam, which is identified as one of the deadliest diseases and commonly referred to as the "disease of the poor." India has the highest yearly incidence of TB in the world, and along with biomedical determinants and risk factors, social determinants increase the risk of exposure to TB germs and after-exposure effects on a population. It has become increasingly clear that intervention in social determinants is necessary to complement the curative TB control regimen, as the latter alone has been unable to control TB effectively. Despite the presence of a TB monitoring mechanism, there remains a high TB burden in the tea gardens of Assam. This paper explores the extent of risk factors and social determinants among the tea garden worker population, which may help inform policy planning for controlling TB in Assam's tea gardens.

D.K. Limbu, C. Kamei, and A. Haloi have investigated the impact of various biosocial factors on fertility and child mortality rates among rural and urban populations of the Kabui Naga in Manipur in their chapter titled "*Influence of Bio-Social Factors on Fertility and Child Mortality among the Kabui Naga of Manipur, India*," The study analysed data from 434 ever-married women between the ages of 15 and 49, with 174 participants from the Imphal West district and 260 from the Tamenglong sub-division. Utilising SPSS 16 software, the data was processed and analysed with a significance level of 5%. The study identified key biosocial factors such as the mother's age at marriage, age at first childbirth, birth interval, family structure, maternal education, and household income that impact fertility and infant and child mortality among the Kabui Naga. Furthermore, the findings highlighted the critical implications of India's rural-urban divide on fertility and child mortality rates.

In a research paper titled "Impact of Supplementary Food and Socio-economic Predictors on Nutritional Status of Children Attending Anganwadis in Bilaspur, Chhattisgarh, India", Manisha Ghritlahre, Mahua Chanak, Subal Das, and Kaushik Bose have found the 48.7% of children suffered from stunting, 46.3% were underweight, and 28.8% suffered from wasting. The research also highlighted a significant correlation between the receipt of supplementary food provided by ICDS and improved height-for-age, weight-for-age, and BMI-for-age metrics. Additionally, the study found that children who did not receive regular supplementary food provided in Anganwadi centres had poorer nutritional status than those who received regular food.

In their paper titled "Socio-economic and Reproductive Determinants of Fertility Among the Mising Tribe of Assam in the Dhemaji District," Chandika Roy and Milonjyoti Borgohain highlight the social factors that impact the fertility rates of Mising women. The study discovered that a woman's age is directly correlated with her fertility levels. Additionally, the research revealed that women in the tribe typically experience menarche between the ages of 14-16, get married between 15-18, and have their first child between 18-21.

According to research conducted by Akash Mallick, titled "Differentials in Hypertension and Anaemia Burden between the Workers in Abandoned and Operational Tea Plantation: An Anthropological Study in Alipurduar, West Bengal ", tea workers face significant economic uncertainty that puts them at risk for health conditions such as high blood pressure and low haemoglobin levels. The study found that both male and female workers had similar mean blood pressure levels, but the prevalence of hypertension was higher among the former group. Similarly, the prevalence of anaemia was found to be more than 70% for males and 88% for females. The workers' age and educational level were also found to be significant factors in determining their risk for hypertension and anaemia.

In their joint paper, Dr Arifur Zaman and Suraiya Prodhani delve into the healthcare practices of Deshi Muslims in the Dhubri District of Assam, India. Deshi Muslims in Assam are indigenous people who converted to Islam in the past, and they differentiate themselves from Muslim people who migrated from East Pakistan and Bangladesh by using the term Deshi, meaning "belonging to the country." Using an anthropological perspective, the authors describe the two interactive worlds of Deshi Muslim society in relation to health perception and treatment-seeking behaviour. The study suggests that Deshi Muslims follow traditional healthcare practices similar to those of indigenous tribal groups, likely due to their origin being linked to the local indigenous tribal people of the region. The acceptance of modern healthcare facilities varies among Deshi Muslims depending on their proximity to urban areas and accessibility to modern healthcare services. However, the constant service of grassroots-level health workers like ASHA has influenced women to seek modern healthcare. The authors explore the relationship between nature, culture, and humans, highlighting the use of herbs, shrubs, animals, and by-products in treatment.

2

Towards A Method of Decolonising Knowledge: Where Does Anthropology Stand?

Sabina Yasmin Rahman

Introduction

The *Encyclopaedia Britannica* describes "decolonisation" as the process by which colonies become independent of the colonising country. The *Cambridge Dictionary* describes it as the process in which a country that was a colony in the past (controlled by another country) becomes politically independent: the process of getting rid of colonies. In the academic domain, the concept is primarily used to denote a process where the academic ideas propagated by the Europeans are disavowed or contended in an attempt to replace or enhance them with local or indigenous thinking contextualised to the local situations of past and present. Thus, when we talk of decolonisation in the academic sense, especially within the social sciences, we are really talking about the decolonisation of knowledge.

In a more specific sense, we can term it epistemic decolonisation or epistemological decolonisation, questioning and critiquing the perceived hegemony of the "Western knowledge system", as Dreyer (2017) coined it. By this term, Dreyer referred to the institutionalisation and development of scientific knowledge in Europe, flaring to other parts of the world as part of Western modernity and its continuation in present-day scholarship. However, while using the term, Dreyer was aware of the gross simplification of the century-long development of science and the great multiplicity of epistemological, ontological, methodological and axiological constellations within this knowledge system in the Western world. The idea of decolonisation of knowledge has been accepted in a variety of subjects, including in the epistemology of philosophy, science, history of science, and essential categories in the social sciences.

Decolonisation of Knowledge

Generally speaking, the decolonisation of knowledge seeks to inquire about the historical mechanisms of knowledge production and how they are based on colonial and ethnocentric perceptions of the Western mind, as Heleta (2018) maintains. Dreyer regurgitated that the Western knowledge system was positioned to legitimise Europe's colonial expedition, establishing colonial rule and infusing the forms of civilisation that the colonisers carried with them. Based on its apparently universal (broad-based) quality, the knowledge produced by the Western system could proclaim superiority over the knowledge produced by other systems. Ivanovic (2019) maintains that the colonised were repressed by the colonisers, restricting them from colonised forms of knowledge production, the modes of production of meaning, their symbolic universe, the model of expression and the objectification of subjectivity.

Linda Smith (2012) attributes the profound turmoil experienced by colonised people to Imperialism and colonialism, which severed their connections to their histories, landscapes, languages, social relations, and ways of thinking, feeling, and interacting with the world. While colonialism may have disappeared legally and politically from historically colonised territories, its legacy endures in many 'colonial situations' where individuals and groups continue to be marginalised and exploited. Enrique Dussel (2019) finds the origin of the theme of epistemological decolonisation among a group of Latin American thinkers. For him, epistemological decolonisation is structured around the notions of coloniality of power and trans-modernity. Walter Mignolo (2007) credits this to the ingenious work of Peruvian sociologist Anibal Quijano, who explicitly linked the coloniality of power in the political and economic spheres with the coloniality of knowledge. As observed by Mignolo, Quijano's critical deliberation on problematic areas like post-colonialism, subaltern studies, and postmodernism helped develop epistemological decolonisation.

The contention between colonial and decolonial knowledge production is that generally, the conception of ideas such as "truth" and "facts" are believed or claimed to be Western constructs and universal, an idea which is also infused by the Western tradition of thought. As Naude (2017) maintains, the dominant trend is that the Western knowledge system has become a norm for global knowledge, and its methodologies are projected as the only ones deemed appropriate for use in knowledge production. This perceived hegemonic approach towards other knowledge systems ultimately has reduced epistemic diversity and established the Western system of knowledge production as the centre of knowledge, suppressing all other knowledge forms. To this dominance, the scholars of decolonisation maintain that the notions of truth and fact are "local" since human societies and culture are varied, and thus, what is "discovered" or "expressed" in one place or time may not be applicable in another. Thus, instead of "knowledge", Gordon (2014) proposes to use "knowledges" to stress the fact that the modes of knowledge production and notions of knowledge are widely diversified. Internalising the view that the modern foundation of knowledge is territorial and imperial, rooted in European modernity, and moulded by a macro narrative, Mignolo & Tlostanova (2006) see the epistemic decolonisation as an extensive philosophical caricature to re-establish the geo-political locations of theology, secular philosophy and scientific reason. Ndlovu-Gatsheni (2020) maintains that epistemic decolonisation also affirms the modes and principles of knowledge produced at the local level, which were denied or ridiculed by the pomposity of Christianisation, civilisation, progress, development and market democracy.

The Colonial Link to Anthropological Knowledge Production:

The etymology of "Anthropology" derives from the Greek ***anthropos*** ("human") and ***logia*** ("study"). Anthropology is the study of people everywhere-present, near past, and antiquity. The beginning of anthropology was profoundly tangled with Western expansion and the exploration of the non-Western world, setting a long-term objective to unearth universal laws about human nature. Anthropologists, sponsored mainly by the colonial administration, primarily derived these laws from the study of the newly discovered 'primitive' societies.

Anthropologists, often finding themselves in a moral quandary, were tasked with supplying information to aid Western efforts to control the non-Western world. They perceived themselves as impartial scientific observers, documenting 'primitive' lifestyles before they vanished or became Westernized. However, their role as intermediaries, attempting to mitigate the impact of Western political domination and economic exploitation, implicated them in the colonisation process. They played various roles, such as providing scientific justifications for colonial policies, documenting indigenous cultures for Western consumption, and serving as intermediaries between the colonisers and the colonised. However, anthropology also served a practical purpose to supplement the Western man's self-knowledge (Diamond, 1964, p. 432; Worsley, 1964, p. 11).

Fieldwork has been anthropologists' characteristic tradition, carried out mainly in colonised territories where the subjects of the anthropological study were devastated physically, economically, culturally, and socially by the colonisers. Levi-Strauss (1966:126) describes the historical setting of anthropology under the colonial clutch by saying that during this time, millions of innocent human beings have had their resources plundered; their institutions and beliefs were destroyed, whilst they themselves were ruthlessly killed, thrown into bondage, and contaminated by diseases they were unable to resist. The role of anthropologists was significantly affected by his membership in the dominant group – the coloniser. The anthropologist, like the other Europeans in a colony, occupied a position of economic, political, and psychological superiority vis-a-vis the subject-people.

Little attention was paid to the fact that the benefits gained were based on the exploitation of the natives. This unique treatment was accorded to the colonial anthropologist, not because of superior accomplishments or contributions valued by the native people but simply because the anthropologist was a member of the group in power and perpetual dominance. Gough (1968:404) notes: "We tended to accept the imperialist framework as given, perhaps partly because we were influenced by the dominant ideas of our time, and partly because at the time there was little anyone could do to dismantle the empire." The dominant political interests of the times not only blinded many anthropologists to the implications of their position but also influenced them, apparently unconsciously, to justify the prevailing colonial social system.

Maquet (1964) postulates that in their theoretical orientations, anthropologists working in Africa at different periods unconsciously supported the political and administrative goals of their own countries vis-a-vis the groups studied. He attempts to show how, during the colonial era, unilineal evolutionism developed an image of the "savage", which seemed to justify colonial expansion, and how, between World War I and World War II, structural-functionalism focused on the health and holistic integration of traditional cultures and the disruptive effects of industrialisation, at a period when Western rule was beginning to be undermined by educated radical African urbanites advocating change.

Through stressing the moral inferiority of the Africans at an earlier period and the dangers of rapid change at a later one and emphasising the difference between Europeans and Africans throughout, the anthropologist was providing conceptual and theoretical models which were socially useful to the existing colonial system. The landmark anthropological traditions of the colonial period were utmost ethnocentric since these put the Western domain at the top of the hierarchy as the model social system in terms of development, rationality and civilisation. These traditions include the racial classification of human beings on some particular physical characteristics and putting the racial criteria of "Caucasoids" as the superior and fully evolved ones. One can see the ethnocentric distribution of fossil findings and their classification as humanoid to humans territorially. The macro narratives of the evolution and development of human societies were also ethnocentric since Western societies were kept as civilised and fully developed societies. In contrast, the societies from colonised territories were placed at different stages or levels of the evolutionary schemes. Some of the social institutions and sociocultural practices were classified into ethnocentric hierarchies, such as marriage, religious beliefs, and practices.

The most critical aspect of colonial epistemology in anthropology is the narrative set by the anthropologists for the societies they studied. Anthropologists of those days claimed to remain an observer, harmless, non-interfering and neutral by tradition. They were destined to describe what they observed and understood as outsiders, claiming to be objective and not moved by the emotions and meaning-making mechanisms of the studied people in terms of what they act, behave, and believe. Apparently, the studied people hardly have a voice and choice to echo their viewpoints to their significant others – the Western world. Thus, the core anthropological theories like evolution, development, structuralism, functionalism, and theories related to religion and beliefs were designed on the basis of the understanding of the outsiders from the fieldwork carried out by the anthropologists and their general observations and narrated before the world outside.

Deliberating Decolonisation of Knowledge in Anthropology

The accounts of the colonial legacy of anthropology are long enough and concrete as well. It was also a coincidence that lots of theories of the search for truth as the philosophical foundation of social research evolved during these days, which the colonial anthropologists themselves propounded or followed from their contemporaries in other social science fields. Given this upper-handed position of Western scholars over the non-Western academic domain, these theories received universal status. They became the norm for the scientific way of doing research in anthropology as well. As discussed above, the growing concerns for and contentions against many of these Western constructs developed under the colonial regime and territorially Western world have led scholars of the non-Western domain to seek to decolonise, and even reject, the dominant systems of knowledge production and strive to retell the stories of locals in their own terms. As the very foundation of anthropology is based on colonial interests and sponsorships, it is a very challenging task to decolonise anthropology in the true sense since there needs to be a thorough re-writing of non-Western social history and customs.

The task of decolonising had already begun in the late twentieth century with powerful voices such as Ngugi was Thiong'o, Kenyan novelist and post-colonial theorist, calling for *Decolonising the Mind* (1986) and critiquing the politics of the usage of colonial language in the development of post-colonial subjectivities. Churning had already begun within the discipline of anthropology, where core concepts, methodologies, and imaginations of the discipline's future were being interrogated so as to create a more humane anthropology. Many arguments have been made as to how to define best, and practice decolonial anthropology. According to Bolles (2023, p. 519), the original "decolonising generation" attended graduate school in the 1970s and 80s, having since written and trained a new generation of decolonial anthropologists who produced remarkable work in the field. The current decolonising generation is devoted to forging new pathways of imagining what it means to have a decolonised approach to being an anthropologist.

Post-War Global Crisis and Development Of Anthropology

Speaking of the crisis faced by social anthropology in the seventies, Talal Asad (1975) echoed the concerns of other anthropologists who saw the discipline's preoccupation with obtaining and extending knowledge to "primitive" or "preliterate" societies as a matter of serious incompatibility in the post-Second World War period when attainment of political independence by colonised countries, especially in Africa, fundamentally changed the nature of the world in which the discipline – its object and organisational base – existed:

> *"We must begin from the fact that the basic reality which made pre-war social anthropology a feasible and effective enterprise was the power relationship between dominating (European) and dominated (non-European) cultures. We then need to ask ourselves how this relationship has affected the practical pre-conditions of social anthropology, the uses to which its knowledge was put, the theoretical treatment of particular topics, the mode of perceiving and objectifying alien societies, and the anthropologist's claim of political neutrality."* (Asad 1975, p. 17)

He further observed that the shift from "tribal" leaders to a bourgeoisie with nationalistic aspirations in some of these countries led to attempts to recover an indigenous history and denounce the colonial ties of anthropology. Moreover, the seventies and eighties were also a time when neocolonialism was being recognised and spoken about as a corollary to the post-colonial moment, a phenomenon that today refers to the "enduring coloniality of power, political economy, and knowledge" (Harrison, 2016, p-16). Turning the critical lens inwards towards the discipline itself, Asad highlights for his readers the fact of anthropology's rootedness not only in the ideals of enlightenment but also in "an unequal power encounter between the West and Third World."

It is this encounter that enabled the West access to the history and culture of the societies it dominated, thereby making possible the construction of universal understanding that also reinforced inequities between European and non-European worlds and, by extension, between Europeanised elites and "traditional" Third World masses. Moreover, it is this unequal encounter that enabled the one-sided intimacy that made anthropological exercise practicable, which goes into the very heart of the conditions of knowledge extraction and construction of the "other" and arguably the inherent incapacity of the discipline to allow reciprocity:

> *"The colonial power structure made the object of anthropological study accessible and safe – because of it, the sustained physical proximity between the observing European and the living non-European became a practical possibility. It made possible the kind of human intimacy on which anthropological fieldwork is based but ensured that that intimacy should be one-sided and provisional. It is worth noting that virtually no European anthropologist has been won over personally by the subordinated culture he has studied, although countless non-Europeans, having come to the West to study its culture, have been captured by its values and assumption and also contributed to an understanding of it"* (p. 17).

Decolonising anthropology also brings to mind the work of Faye V. Harrison and her 1991 work *Decolonizing Anthropology: Moving Further towards an Anthropology of Liberation,* which focuses on anthropologists of colour and passing the platform to once silenced and marginalised voices to create a paradigm shift within the discipline and pave a new way for the "transformation of anthropology from a Western intellectual tradition to one that embraces the critical intellectual traditions and chronicles the experiences of Third-World people, including native anthropologists" (Moses cited in Harrison 1997, p. v).

As one speaks of decolonising anthropology with renewed vigour in various parts of the postmodern techno-liberal – or "techno-feudal" as some have called it – world, new dimensions to the transformative work that began in the late seventies and eighties are no doubt at play. However, much of the original concerns relating to the unequal distribution of power between the colonial and post-colonial practitioners of the discipline and its various cognates continue to remain in place. Part of the answer as to why such is the case may perhaps be found in the plurality of conceptual, methodological and pedagogical approaches that are to be found in its various specialisations and sister disciplines, so much so that there can be no one coherent or linear way to deconstruct the epistemic journeys that each had undergone, or is bound to undertake, up until this period of the twenty-first century. Nonetheless, there is consensus around the vision that the task of reconstructing a decolonised anthropology must advance the understanding of humankind in all its uniqueness as well as commonality based on democratised points of view.

Disciplinary challenges and professionalisation in India

Within the Indian context, anthropology has its colonial trajectory and attempts to redeem itself towards liberatory ends for its once-colonised subjects. Since archiving and conservation practices, too, vary greatly and are authentic aspects of how unequal power and resource – infrastructure, cultural, material and affective – allocations between the colonial and post-colonial actors make itself manifest in hierarchising the anthropologies (but also other disciplines, especially the social sciences), Uberoi et al. (2007) discuss the scant regard that goes into preserving institutional memory once stalwarts have passed on as follows:

"Once key players have left the scene or the chain of apostolic succession has ruptured, there appear to be few institutionalised mechanisms for preserving professional history. Personal libraries are sold off, destroyed, or gifted to ill-run institutions. Fieldnotes, offprints, unpublished manuscripts, photographs, and correspondence are only fitfully preserved by descendants who tend, soon enough, to tire of their pious responsibility and the endless battle against dust, mould, and bugs. There is no recognised and centralised archive for depositing such materials and no directory of local archives and repositories. Museums and collections enthusiastically started, routinely falling prey to neglect and misappropriation. Even in the university system, one finds that departmental handbooks and syllabi are difficult to locate, and dissertations are often untraceable...Indeed, compared to their

colleagues in other disciplines, it seems that Indian sociologists and social anthropologists are usually afflicted by disciplinary angst." (Uberoi, 2007, pp. 2-3)

Nevertheless, such "disciplinary *angst*" notwithstanding, it must also be acknowledged that the difficult task of carrying over the legacy of building and preserving the disciplinary knowledge from one generation of anthropologists [and sociologists] to the next, given the odds listed above, has only been possible due to the generous donation of time, persistence and the labour of love of dedicated students, colleagues, friends and family. Historically, leading post-independence scholars in India who established university departments like M.N. Srinivas and G.S. Ghurye refused to distinguish between anthropology and sociology and identified as the latter. Early in 2024, we lost a stalwart of Indian sociology, JPS Uberoi, who arguably has made one of the most remarkable contributions to decolonising anthropology and initiated the European Studies Programme at the Department of Sociology, University of Delhi. Speaking of Uberoi, former student and editor of his volume *Mind and Society: From Indian Studies to General Sociology,* Tyabji (2019, p. xi) writes of his supervisor and friend that he offers "the only Indian approach to academic scholarship that has seriously attempted to undertake the swarajist programme of considering modern western civilisation in its entirety from an independent, decolonised, Indian perspective."

According to Baviskar (2023), however, the organisational basis of the discipline in India today is being gradually reshaped by the mutual impact of neoliberal policies and Hindu nationalist agendas. Tracing back the longstanding association that Indian "sociologists-anthropologists", as she refers to them, have had with the State and how involved our tribe has hitherto been in public engagements addressing urgent questions impacting the daily lives of the people, Baviskar (2023, p. 389) writes:

"As part of the tiny English-educated intelligentsia in a developmental state, sociologist-anthropologists have never been shy about offering their opinions, even considering it their duty to do so. However, these considered views have become increasingly ineffectual in winning a wider audience or influencing state policy. Why?

The answer lies in how sociology-anthropology's closeness to the centres of power has shifted over time. Under colonialism, anthropologists were integral to the project of rule, enumerating and fixing the fluidity of Indian society into rigid categories of caste, tribe, village, and religion... Anthropologist-administrators produced classificatory schemas that started as technologies of government but were consolidated into collective identities that have now been internalised in political and social life. This was the acme of anthropology's influence on the subcontinent, its closest alignment with bureaucratic power."

To illustrate this point, she cites the example of Verrier Elwin, whose ethnographic work in the northeast of India called for the tribes to be protected by the State. To this end, Elwin worked closely with Jawaharlal Nehru to draft a policy to grant autonomy to the various indigenous and tribal communities in the North-East Frontier Agency (NEFA, now the State of Arunachal Pradesh). These efforts were, however, quickly forgotten after Independence and its goal to further industrial development, leading to mass displacement and land alienation of tribal communities, the consequences of which are faced by the community members even today. Baviskar also speaks of colonial-era government agencies such as the Anthropological Survey of India (ASI), which may have upgraded to a more politically correct vocabulary for tribes and indigenous communities but remain paternalistic and woefully behind when it comes to representing their interests as well as collective socio-political and environmental aspirations within policies designed under a vision a development that is inherently exclusionary or treats tribes as collateral damage.

At the level of higher education, the disciplines have taken a hit following economic liberalisation. By the early 1990s, social sciences had an established presence in public universities, and the success of affirmative action policies meant that these institutions provided some semblance of social justice along with the promise of employability and upward mobility. However, when university enrolments got better with more representation from the diverse marginalised groups (women, Dalits and Other Backward Classes), talks about market viability and usefulness started entering higher education, and the country witnessed large-scale privatisation of the higher education system under neoliberal policies. According to Deshpande (2022), the share of private universities in total enrolment had risen from 50 to 80 percent in the last 20 years, where public universities experienced budget cuts and permanent faculty recruitments stalled to be filled by temporary teachers as "ad-hoc" or "guest" faculty hired by the semester with low wages and no job security. Furthermore, since the coming of the Hindu nationalist party to power in 2014, the social sciences have come under unprecedented attack. Their resentment is a curious mix of ideological opposition to what has traditionally been considered a Left-leaning enterprise along with a class-based critique of left-liberal politics within academia being elitist, "anti-national", and "anti-Hindu".

Lamenting the impact of these trends on the development of the disciplines and suppression of critical intellectual faculty within the academy, Deshpande (2022) observes:

"In India until now, the intellectual world and the world of power shared something like a doxa [an unspoken cultural framework], no matter how strongly heterodox intellectuals opposed their orthodox rulers. Today, this is no longer true. The ruling class-or those who matter within it- have no regard for the world of ideas as it has been shaped by the institutions (universities, academia, research institutes) nurtured by previous ruling classes. They are interested in only two things-technical expertise that can help them achieve their immediate goals or institutional confirmation of their claim about [Hindu India's] ancient achievements."

The current predicament of the social sciences in India, far from questioning the distortions caused by colonial sensibilities and ways of knowledge construction, seems to be harking back to a pre-colonial order that seeks to reinstate older oppressive social hierarchies that were seeing their gradual undoing due to the modernity and empiricism underlying the intellectual progress and public engagement sociologists-anthropologists have partaken in through the postmodern, post-colonial period. In short, it appears to be a project of decoloniality gone rogue: a neocolonial appropriation cloaked in a specifically constructed and mythologised garb of a pristine golden Hindu past, now in the process of manifesting that which could have been, had it not been for the colonisers and their elite

Westernised left-liberal protégés. However, despite these setbacks – being relegated to a "low status" within the social sciences and enduring systematic attack on the profession, including being slandered as "urban Naxals" – the departments of sociology and anthropology continue to be thronged by students who believe that higher qualifications could help land them a good job or gain the cultural capital of a university degree.

Towards A Method of Decolonising Anthropology

Given the context mentioned above, Baviskar (2023, p. 392) finds hope in the students who she thinks play a critical role in "decolonising disciplinary hierarchies" through their idealism and activism:

"In the Indian context today, their [students'] activism outside the classroom enables us to be sociologists-anthropologists. […] I dwell on them here because, in India at this political juncture, they play a particularly pivotal role in orienting the academy. Situating their politics and appreciating their place-specific significance is to apply anthropological methods to the academy. Anthropologists in the North need to do so, too. Take the very term decolonisation…Few Indian scholars use it… Our hesitation stems largely from the fact that, in India, the discourse of decolonisation has been appropriated by the Hindu Right."

Thus, engagement with students, especially the Dalit, minority and Adivasi students, and their politics emerge as an essential exercise and an important strategy in decolonising the university spaces in the Indian context, as they remain overwhelmingly upper caste and upper class. Deshpande (2022) agrees, as he, much like Ngugi, reiterates the concern over the use of the English language as the preferred medium of communication and accruing social and cultural capital among the elite that generally dominate the academy. Shedding light on the consequent marginalisation and isolation that scholars from oppressed backgrounds experience within academic spaces, Baviskar (2023) further notes:

"When Dalit and Adivasi scholars are hired, they often feel marginalised in the department and the discipline. Short on resources and self-assurance, many study their community since they are familiar with the language, feel comfortable with its milieu, and perhaps care

most deeply about its issues. Unfortunately, this leads them to be typecast as 'native informants,' limited in the range of their work, incarcerated in their ascriptive identity. For Adivasi and Dalit scholars, the first step in decolonisation is to secure a position in the upper-caste Hindu-dominated academy. The second, and even more difficult step, is to develop the confidence of the coloniser and study the Other."

Here, Baviskar is probably referring to the "othered" accumulating their shared resources and collective strength to study not just their peripheralisation but also using education and politics to empower themselves and unpack the dominant "Self"; that is, to write back from the margins instigating the process of decolonisation from grassroots-level up. As summarised by Bolles (2023, p. 519), to begin with, decolonisation would require "taking seriously the critiques and theories of anthropology's peripheral allies." It also involves going beyond the coloniser's point of view and including the frame of reference of those who are or have been the perpetual subjects of study.

Speaking of decolonising or radically reconstructing anthropology, Harrison (2008, p. 1) attempts to offer what she refers to as "a multidimensional strategy or model for transformation based on the notion of "reworking" the field". She further elaborates on how the idea of reworking anthropology "underscores the importance of holism, reintegration and synthesis—*weaving*..." This synthesis informs the manner in which she conceives of the overall project to ultimately "create conditions for a more enriching and enabling analysis and understanding of the human experience" (p. 2). Towards this goal mentioned above, Harrison (2008, p. 2) delineates a list of interrelated objectives, which she believes must be based on "cooperative labour" and, to some extent, be grounded in a critical anthropology of anthropology:

"These objectives can best be described as a call for (1) re-historicizing anthropology (both the researchers and those whom they research), (2) rethinking theory (what it entails and who is authorised to do it), (3) rethinking the cross-pollinating intellectual potential of both interdisciplinarity and interdisciplinarity, (4) rising to the growing challenges of ethically and politically responsible research, and (5) mapping the mediated connections among local and supralocal spheres of culture, power, and political economy as they are being realigned and

restructured in the age of neoliberal globalisation. Other important objectives that also must be met if we are to pursue the critical reconstruction strategy I have in mind are (6) interrogating the ways anthropology is practised in academia and beyond, (7) promoting greater diversity and deepening the democratisation of participation and decision making in the profession, (8) finding more effective ways to link our academic pursuits to urgent issues of public engagement, and finally, (9) developing a commitment to decentering Western epistemologies and to promoting a genuine multicultural dialogue in the study of humanity."

However, Harrison (2008, p. 9) also warns against the liberal tendency within the academy today to co-opt into the disciplinary polyvocal mainstream the more politically charged elements of radical critique that the reconstructive project of critical anthropology entails, and which is indispensable to the meticulous and self-reflexive work of liberating the colonised Self as well as the disciplinary environment:

"The new status quo, made up of liberals/left-leaning scholarship...is no longer reinventing anthropology; it is doing anthropology and enjoying the rewards for having achieved recognition in the field. My very sense of professional identity and my critical vantage, however, are informed by the historical consciousness of one who belongs to a people, both in immediate ethnoracial and broad diasporic senses, still underrepresented in anthropology and academia generally and subjected to ideological othering and nativisation. Given this subaltern positionality, I cannot just do anthropology without being concerned with how the discipline is changing, what these changes mean now, and what they will mean in the long range."

Referring to the rich and diverse noncanonical tradition that lies outside of the Western catalogue that has been the norm in anthropology, Harrison speaks of a "transformed anthropology" that is not limited by the confined of the discipline's institutional and intellectual nodes in the global North. Including the anthropological traditions of post-colonial nations such as India in her discussions, Harrison (2008, p. 11) contends that decolonial anthropology must endeavour to provide further space to the intellectual history and anthropological inquiries that are taking place in the marginalised geographies or among peripheralised groups and demand to be taken seriously:

[...] I see myself as one among those who are producing an "alternative anthropology" (Buck, 2001, pp. 7-8), an anthropology critically reconstructed and reworked to correct and transcend the most problematic aspects of the discipline's colonial history and legacy. The transformed anthropology I envision...would recognise that although the profession's institutional centres have been dominated by British, American, and French axes of authority, the intellectual life of the discipline has extended well beyond the North's major metropolitan centres to a variety of sites, typically devalued as peripheral zones of theory (Appadurai, 1986) around the world. India, for instance, has a rich anthropological tradition, one that has historical ties, of course, to British social anthropology (Srinivas, 1997); however, Indian anthropology has developed an impetus of its own. Besides India, which-as reflected in the Annual Review of Anthropology's recent contents-is beginning to be recognised as an important locus for social anthropology, other national and regional anthropologies merit greater international exposure and study.

Further, echoing Baviskar's (2023) earlier remarks on the discrimination faced by Dalit and Adivasi scholars within the academe, Harrison too alerts us of the racialisation that is rampant and experienced personally by her [and her black colleagues and students] within academia and the field of professional anthropology. Using sociologist Patricia Hill Collins's (1990) understanding of "outsider within locations," she makes sense of the peculiar space black scholars have to occupy to resist and disrupt forms of subjection continuously. From being utilised merely to fulfil diversity requirements for institutional mechanisms to their ordinary attitudes and behaviours being construed differently, black scholars have to constantly expend additional energy to navigate the system so as not to disturb the status quo implicit within academia that continues to be a colonial enterprise. Harrison (2008, pp. 15-16) relates this experience as follows:

"Attributes valued within academia are sometimes construed in racially distorted ways. For example, intellectual competence, normally expected of professors, may become a problem when it clashes with the belief still too commonly held that blacks are less intelligent than whites.

An intelligent black professor may be viewed as an exception to the rule and/or as a target for student-and collegial-resentment and recalcitrance. Her authority in the classroom may be resisted or rejected. [...] Whether we like it or not, race is an enduring principle of classification and organisation within academe, relegating some people to outsides within. Putting coloured people in their place through racially marked circumscription often layered with meanings related to gender and class, may be subtle, but it is, nonetheless, real. In order to negotiate, resist, and adjust to its most humiliating and hurtful forms, racially marked intellectuals often find themselves deploying energy that might otherwise be invested in furthering their scholarship."

Conclusion

From the above discussion, it is possible to surmise that a method of decolonising anthropology must go hand in hand with the laborious task of checking our own attitudes and praxis against colonial biases. It is a conscious reworking and reconstruction of our knowledge base to explore what our intellectual history fragmented by colonial interventions could be without the power hierarchies structured, perpetuated and consolidated to maintain and promote the globalised colonial enterprise that knowledge production and classification are part of. As Bolles (2023, p. 519) succinctly explains:

"Decolonisation comes from a neo-Marxist political perspective, but it also experiments with interpretive and reflexive ethnographic analysis to produce knowledge at the intersection of these approaches. Overall, decolonisation is about bringing to light, subtle aspects of the process that can easily be missed. To decolonise anthropology means to recognise and confront the discipline's colonial legacies, which have led to the marginalisation and exploitation of Indigenous peoples and their knowledge."

A decolonial anthropology is, therefore, not so much an attempt at undoing and, thereby, recapturing the passage of lost time as it is a mode of operating-a manner of using existing cartography interrogatively to trace some original/pre-existent and other, only possible alternative routes to understanding and arriving at what present imaginaries could have been. In doing that, decolonising anthropology has the enormous task at hand of radically reconceptualising the purpose and value of the discipline by forging reciprocal relationships with marginalised and peripherialised communities and ensuring that the research process is designed and developed in ways that do not accentuate power disparities but instead becomes a method to undo the deleterious impact of oppressive power structures. In this way, decolonial anthropology can strive towards its ultimate goal of humanising the discourse within the discipline, both in theory and practice.

References

Asad, T. (1973). *Anthropology and the Colonial Encounter*. London: Ithaca Press.

Baviskar, A. (2023). Decolonizing a discipline in distress. *American Ethnologist* 50: pp. 387–395. https://doi.org/10.1111/amet.13197

Bolles, A. L. (2023). Decolonizing anthropology: an ongoing process. *American Ethnologist* 50: 519–522. https://doi.org/10.1111/amet.13199

Deshpande, S. (2022). The Turbulent Future of Higher Education. *India Forum*, October 12. https://www.theindiaforum.in/education/turbulent-future-higher-education

Diamond, S. (1964). A revolutionary discipline. *Current Anthropology*, 5:432- 37.

Dreyer, Jaco S. (2017). Practical theology and the call for the decolonisation of higher education in South Africa: Reflections and proposals. *HTS Theological Studies,* **73** (4): 1–7 [2, 3, 5]. doi:10.4102/hts.v73i4.4805. ISSN 0259-9422.

Dussel, E. (2019). Epistemological Decolonization of Theology. In Barreto, Raimundo; Sirvent, Roberto (eds.). *Decolonial Christianities: Latinx and Latin American Perspective*. Springer Nature. pp. 25, 26. ISBN 9783030241667.

Gordon, L. R. (2014). Disciplinary Decadence and the Decolonisation of Knowledge. *Africa Development.* **XXXIX** (1): 81–92 [81].

Gough, K. (1968). New proposals for anthropologists. *Current Anthropology*, 9:403-7.

Harrison, F. V. (2016). Decolonizing anthropology: A conversation with Faye V. Harrison, Part I, *Athrodendum*, May 2. https://savageminds.org/2016/05/02/decolonizing-anthropology-a-conversation-with-faye-v-harrison-part-i/

Harrison, F. V. (2008). *Outsider Within: Reworking Anthropology in the Global Age*. Urbana and Chicago: University of Illinois Press.

Harrison, F. V. (1997). *Decolonizing Anthropology: Moving Further toward an Anthropology of Liberation*. Arlington, VA: American Anthropological Association.

Heleta, S. (2018). "Decolonizing Knowledge in South Africa: Dismantling the 'pedagogy of big lies'". *Ufahamu: A Journal of African Studies*, **40** (2): 47–65 [48–50]. doi:10.5070/F7402040942

Ivanovic, M. (2019). Echoes of the Past: Colonial Legacy and Eurocentric Humanitarianism. *The Rest Write Back: Discourse and Decolonization*. BRILL. pp. 82–102 [98]. doi:10.1163/9789004398313_005.

Levi-Strauss, C. (1966). Anthropology: Its achievements and future. Current Anthropology, 7:124-27.

Maquet, J. J. (1964). Objectivity in anthropology. Current Anthropology, 5:47-55.

Mignolo, Walter D. (2007). Delinking: The Rhetoric of Modernity, the Logic of Coloniality and the Grammar of De-Coloniality. *Cultural Studies*, 21, no. 2–3: 449–513.

Mignolo, W. D.; Tlostanova, M. V. (2006). Theorizing from the Borders: Shifting to Geo- and Body-Politics of Knowledge. *European Journal of Social Theory*, **9** (2): 205–221 [205]. doi:10.1177/1368431006063333.

Naude, P. (2017). Decolonising Knowledge: Can Ubuntu Ethics Save Us from Coloniality? *Journal of Business Ethics*. Springer Science and Business Media LLC. **159** (1): 23–37 [23–24]. doi:10.1007/s10551-017-3763-4

Ndlovu-Gatsheni, S. J. (2020). The Dynamics of Epistemological Decolonisation in the 21st Century: Towards Epistemic Freedom. *Strategic Review for Southern Africa*, **40** (1): 16–45 [18, 21, 30]. doi:10.35293/SRSA.V40I1.268.

Ngũgĩ wa Thiong'o (1986). *Decolonising the Mind: The Politics of Language in African Literature*. London: Portsmouth, N.H.: J. Currey; Heinemann.

Uberoi, J.P.S. and K. Tyabji (Ed.) (2019). *Mind and Society: From Indian Studies to General Sociology*. New Delhi: Oxford University Press.

Uberoi, P., N. Sunder, and S. Despande (Eds) (2007). *Anthropology in the East: Founders of Indian Sociology and Anthropology*. New Delhi: Permanent Black.

Smith Linda Tuhiwai. (2012). *Decolonizing Methodologies: Research and Indigenous Peoples*. Zed Books, London.

Worsley, P. (1964). *The third world*. Chicago: University of Chicago Press.

3

Experiencing the Stigma of being 'Suspected': An Anthropological Discourse of Lived Experiences of Families of Prisoners

Afiya Khalid

Stigma is both perceptual and a very influential word or concept, of course, negatively, in human life. The Britannica Dictionary defines "stigma" as a set of negative and often unfair beliefs that a society or group of people have about something. The Cambridge Dictionary defines "Stigma" as a strong feeling of disapproval that most people in a society have about something, especially when this is unfair. The American Psychological Association Dictionary defines "Stigma" as the negative social attitude attached to a characteristic of an individual that may be regarded as a mental, physical, or social deficiency. A stigma implies social disapproval and can lead unfairly to discrimination against and exclusion of the individual.

Erving Goffman (1963), in his seminal work *Stigma: Notes on the Management of Spoiled Identity,* wrote the most established definition of stigma. For him, stigma is "an attribute that is deeply discrediting" that reduces someone "from a whole and usual person to a tainted, discounted one". The stigmatised, thus, are perceived as having a "spoiled identity" (Goffman, 1963, p. 3). Taking the cue from Goffman's initial conceptualisation, Dudley (2000) defined stigma as stereotypes or negative views attributed to a person or groups of people when their characteristics or behaviours are viewed as different from or inferior to societal norms. These definitions helped us understand the inherent characteristics of stigma much beyond only psychological points of view. Thus, the horizon of understanding stigma is relevant in other contexts, such as towards individuals of varied backgrounds, including race, gender, and sexual orientation.

The idea of social stigma and its concept has undergone several changes in its definition and articulation since its first articulation by Erving Goffman (1960). Although in its early stages, the study of social stigma was heavily focused on psychological approaches, Goffman's idea of social stigma is a process based on the social construction of identity. So, according to Goffman, a person who suffers from a stigmatised condition thus passes from —normal to —discredited social status (Goffman, 1963). He includes both social and psychological approaches to stigma, but he primarily focuses more on the psychological elements of stigma and its psychological impacts on the individual. Focusing on the processes by which stigma gets internalised and changes or shapes individual behaviour has created an articulated understanding of the psychology of the stigmatised (Kleiman, 2009). Thus, it has provided a comprehensive understanding of how social life and relationships are changed by stigma. In contemporary times, the field of anthropology has contributed to the discussion by providing a broader understanding of the stigma, which identifies the social processes that occur in a given socio-cultural environment and whose effects can be observed within individual behaviour (Tshaka, 2019). More specifically, illustrations given by Link and Phelan (2001) have included a component of institutionalised disadvantages or structural discrimination placed on stigmatised groups or individuals. It also elucidates the ways the power, socio, and politics shape the divide of stigma in the social milieu.

The social psychological groundwork emphasises the pivotal role of (negative) stereotypes in the process of stigmatisation. Empirical evidence suggests that families can face stereotyping based on their socioeconomic status. Moore (2016, in her thesis conducted in the United States, discovered that wives of incarcerated men perceived societal stereotypes portraying them as uneducated, deviant, and/or gullible. One participant articulated that some individuals in society regarded women in her position as the 'bottom of the barrel' (Moore, 2016, p. 36). Similarly, in the United

Kingdom, Foster (2017, p. 209) observed that 'prisoners' families often grapple with economic challenges, leading to the experience of stigma and shame derived from their socio-economic circumstances. However, Foster did not delve into the intricacies of this aspect of stigma. These findings underscore the imperative to investigate both direct stigma and 'courtesy stigma,' recognising that 'the most profound stigmatisation often occurs at the intersection of multiple forms of exclusion' (Cornish, 2006, p. 465).

The inherent issues related to identity-based stigma have been discussed by some scholars Condry (2007). He notes that women, including partners, mothers, and sisters of incarcerated individuals, often assume the responsibility of caring for the children of those in prison, as evidenced in the works of Condry (2007). The stigma of being the caregiver and the relative of the person in prison always haunts them. Moreover, within the specific context of Muslim communities in Indian jails, an intricately communalised nature of stigmatisation emerges when addressing the circumstances of families with acquitted members. This is notably highlighted in the research conducted by Raghavan and Nair, who explored the overrepresentation of Muslims in Maharashtra jails (Raghavan & Nair, 2013). It stated that a clear link between the criminal justice system and the religious minority, which leads to the overrepresentation of Muslims in the general population compared to their presence in prisons, necessitates an exploration of its underlying causes.

The authors have noted that the heightened prevalence of poverty within Muslim communities is one of the determining factors of such stigmatisation. This economic factor stands out as a crucial element contributing to the observed discrepancy. Furthermore, this study asserts that the manifestation of bias within both societal attitudes and the criminal justice system, particularly evident in law enforcement practices targeting minority communities, serves as another influential factor amplifying the disproportionate incarceration rates.

The enduring impact of religious identity on the post-acquittal phase merits thorough consideration, forming a crucial aspect of the broader academic discourse on the complexities surrounding familial experiences with imprisonment. As stated by Raghavan and Nair (2013), "It has brought into focus the issue of over-representation of the Muslim community in our prisons and examined some of the underlying reasons for this. It majorly points to the larger issue of social exclusion and marginalisation of communities which suffer from structural and systemic discrimination."

More recent anthropological works have focused more on stigma as embedded in moral experience and stigmatised a person as a person's moral status. So, maintaining social status in society depends on meeting the social obligations and norms given by their local environment of social circles. There are different components of stigma, one of which is associating human differences with negative attributes. Crockers and colleagues (1998) put it up very well in their definition of stigma as an attribute or characteristic that conveys a devalued social identity in a particular context. So, in this aspect, stigma carries a label and a stereotype that links a person to the undesirable characteristics that form the stereotypes. These social labels connote a separation of us from them. As a result, the labelled person experiences status loss and discrimination once the cultural stereotype is in its place. In light of this, the conceptualisation of stigma suggests a key determinant of life, from psychological effects and well-being to employment, housing, education, social security, and life itself. The social status of a person put behind a bar is obviously different from that of others who are out of it since it is a negative attribute of society, a punitive consequence of a crime. The depth of stigma of being behind the bar increases along with other attributes like religious affiliation, ethnicity, class structure and contemporary socio-political environment. Notably, the stigma does not contain the person stigmatised. The consequence encompasses its family, relatives and even the locality and the community. It originates from their link to someone in prison and their socially excluded backgrounds (Kotova, 2020).

It is imperative to acknowledge that any in-depth examination of the stigma encountered by families of incarcerated individuals necessitates a nuanced understanding of the distinctly gendered and racialised dimensions inherent in this phenomenon. This identity-specific bias in terms of experiencing stigma is not merely an isolated phenomenon but is deeply embedded in the structural fabric of society and the criminal justice apparatus. The perpetuation of bias within these structural elements compounds the stigmatisation process experienced by Muslim individuals, contributing substantially to their overrepresentation in the prison system.

The argument thus posits that bias operates as a systemic force, intertwining with broader societal structures and influencing the trajectory of individuals within the criminal justice system. This intersectionality becomes particularly pronounced when scrutinising the experiences of families grappling with incarceration and, in some instances, the post-acquittal phases. Consequently, understanding the role of religious identity becomes integral to comprehending the multifaceted challenges encountered by these families. Article 2 (2) of the Covenant covers not only the right not to be subjected to any discrimination or humiliation but also the de facto discrimination. However, families of prisoners do not easily fit into any of the explicitly prohibited grounds of discrimination or humiliation. The social rights committee has paid attention and indicated that the provision may extend to the —social groups that face negative stereotyping and stigmatisation based on their social situation.

The paper addresses the series of manifestations of social stigmatisation that not only falls under the scope of social rights recognised under international law but is also a significant part of the Indian constitution. As illustrated below with the narratives of the families, they have experienced the social stigma which had effects on mental health, the humiliation of children and other people, loss of jobs, inability to access social assistance programmes and threats to privacy and security. Comfort (2009, 2007) states that a variant of this concept is usually utilised in the context of families of people in prison is 'courtesy stigma': the process through which one's identity is tainted by virtue of their association with the stigmatised individual (Goffman, 1963). As a result, this process is a manifestation of negative value judgment, which is the natural starting point for any concept that is inherently negative.

This paper contends that the nature and severity of the alleged crimes significantly shape the experiences of families within the criminal justice system, particularly concerning their interaction with stigma. Through an extensive exploration of stigma's nuanced processes, the study elucidates how the perceived intensity and type of the accused crimes intertwine with the family's engagement with the legal framework. The argument posits that the gravity and nature of the charges contribute profoundly to shaping the family's interactions with the criminal justice system, profoundly influencing their experiences of stigma within societal and legal realms.

The overall aim of the study is to explore the implications of imprisonment on family members, focusing on the stigma attached to their lives. These experiences of stigma among family members of those incarcerated are recurring themes in the literature (Codd, 2008). These stigmatised families have always been treated as the - other and are subjected to a lack of support and hostility (Davies, 1992).

Methodology

This paper is based on a study conducted for MPhil Degree. It delves into the experiences of Muslim families whose members have faced incarceration on terror-related charges. Through in-depth interviews with five family members involved in the cases of the accused (later acquitted), the research centres on unravelling the profound impact of stigma on these families. Using narrative data analysis, the study unveils the intricate ways in which stigma manifests across family, community and the criminal justice system. The findings underscore the profound hardships and social stigmatisation faced by these families due to their association with the accused. It argues that the pervasive stigma not only affects their social lives but permeates into various facets of their existence, encompassing financial strain, mental trauma, compromised mental health, privacy and security concerns, and significantly impacts the education of both children and other family members. The primary activity of any research is to mould the research problem in a methodological structure so that it can be interrogated systematically and sequentially, following a linear as well as cyclical process. Thus, the first and foremost step was to determine the existential nature of the problem on the methodological ground – whether stigma is an objective entity out there, independent of one's perception or belief, or it is merely a subjective entity perceived or created by the people who experience it.

The introduction section discusses that "Stigma" is a subjective entity objectively experienced by a person as a member of a particular category-gender, religion, community, economic class, residence of a particular locality, and so on. Thus, ontologically, it possesses a nominalist character. It does not have any objective existence out there and thus cannot be studied physically by observing or measuring it. Since the existential conditions and the nature and the extent of "Stigma" depend on the personal and, to a great extent, on the structural condition of the society where a person lives, perceiving and experiencing stigma is also conditioned and directed by certain authorities external and internal to the person experiencing it.

Given the multifaceted identity or the conditional existence of "stigma" in human societies, it is essential to logically define the "epistemology" or the way of knowledge production while researching "Stigma". The literature review and the discussion that follows indicate that "Stigma" may be identified, measured and assessed by interrogating two domains: the person who experiences it and the significant others (person and the structural arrangement) whom the victim (one who experiences stigma) identify or perceive as the perpetrators. It necessitates the exploration of various determinants that possibly objectify the grossly subjective entity called "stigma". Along with such exploration, it is also of utmost importance to understand the meaning-making of the significant behaviour, acts, and incidents involved by the victim and the supposed perpetrator.

Responding to this situation, the study employs an exploratory and interpretative approach to delve into the multifaceted phenomenon of stigma experienced by families affected by imprisonment in false terror-related cases. Since the locus of the investigation is highly subjective, both in action and reaction, no law of natural sciences could be used to search for the truth. Indeed, it drew the researcher towards an anti-positivist stand. Thus, a qualitative paradigm was chosen to offer a nuanced understanding of the stigma as moulded by the victims based on perceived or felt discrimination issues, delving into the intricate details and processes underlying its occurrence and the motives of the actors involved. The qualitative case study research design was adopted to navigate sensitive issues and grasp the nuanced experiences of the study participants.

By now, social science researchers are almost sure that in the case of subjective matters, human beings create, act and react willfully in response to some stimuli. Although it is often argued that the narrow and broader social surroundings influence the perception and behaviour of people, indicating a necessity of the determinism paradigm to be employed in social sciences, a deeper insight into social relations always advocates for a voluntarism paradigm where humans are the initiator of their action with free will and creativity, producing their own environment. In this particular case, one can see the influence of the perpetrator on the victims in building their perception and experiencing stigma. However, the victims are not bound to think, perceive and create their world of perception and action in a definite or given way, as may be the case in the determinism paradigm (as we see in positivist research approaches). There is no definite law that directs human action and reactions in this case. Thus, the foundation of the research approach remained voluntarism in totality.

It is imperative that, from the interpretive perspective, human interaction and negotiation form the basis for understanding social life. The researcher assumed a fluidity in the social world, acknowledging the changing views of participants and emphasising the need for careful interpretation in presenting partial understanding. Thus, the case study method was utilised to contextualise the experiences of terror-accused families and later acquitted, shedding light on the social stigma attached to them in both the community and society. In-depth interviews, along with semi-structured interviews, provided a qualitative and in-depth exploration, allowing participants to share their perspectives openly and encouraging the emergence of unanticipated insights. Snowball sampling was employed for participant selection, leveraging existing contacts to reach respondents. The data collection process unfolded in central Delhi and its outskirts, utilising both case studies and semi-structured interviews to capture a rich tapestry of experiences.

Narrative analysis was applied to make sense of the extensive data, identifying common themes and categorising responses within organised themes. The fieldwork experiences emphasised the crucial role of rapport building, ensuring the trust and comfort of participants in sharing authentic experiences. The researcher's identity as a Muslim woman was navigated, balancing insider status within an organisation and mitigating the risk of being perceived as an outsider. Overall, the qualitative methods employed in this study facilitated a nuanced exploration of the stigma experienced by families affected by imprisonment in false terror-related cases. Drawing from the poignant accounts and lived experiences of these families, the study sought to uncover the pervasive and profoundly impactful stigma entrenched within their daily lives. By applying a thematic lens to the collected narratives, the analysis aimed to discern and highlight the multifaceted manifestations of this social stigma as a central focus of investigation. Through this methodological approach, the study endeavoured to bridge the literature on the subject with the nuanced and diverse themes that emerged from the narratives. It aspired to elucidate the profound and enduring effects of social stigma on these families while navigating the broader contexts of incarceration and its ramifications on their lives. In totality, methodologically, the research remained ideographic, where the researcher tried to understand and depict how the individual creates, modifies and interprets the world he lives in.

Every Day of Being "Suspected"

The narratives shared by family members of those accused of terror crimes paint a harrowing picture of their lives under the relentless shadow of suspicion. The overarching theme of being suspected every day permeates their existence, shaping their interactions, choices, and experiences. These accounts pivot from police interactions to societal encounters post-incarceration, unveiling the multifaceted impacts, perceptions, and responses in the wake of a terror-stricken climate. The qualitative analysis of these interviews spotlights a recurring pattern of enduring verbal and, in some cases, physical abuse in their daily encounters. From being labelled derogatory names in public spaces to enduring stares and ostracisation at workplaces, these families recount a litany of humiliations. Their experiences manifest a painful reality of being marginalised and stigmatised solely due to their association with the accused family members. For instance, one of the respondents described this daily stigma of being humiliated and stereotyped, one of the participants (brother of the accused),

> *"People tortured so much. They used to trip me whenever I went on the road. I got scared to walk on roads."*

The narratives vividly capture the insidious nature of this stigma, with respondents recounting chilling instances of societal disdain and prejudice. They endured public humiliation and discrimination, experiencing the weight of being labelled as 'terrorists' or 'anti-nationals' simply because of their unwavering support for their accused family members. The stigma's pervasive nature inflicted profound social, emotional, and economic consequences, fracturing relationships, disrupting housing, and imposing a sense of alienation within communities. This perpetual suspicion, reinforced by societal biases and amplified through media representation, exacerbates their plight. The narratives reveal the painful reality of Muslims being cast as perpetual 'outsiders,' perpetually under the cloud of suspicion. The stigma associated with terrorism not only isolates these families but also engenders a broader societal division between 'us' and 'them,' blurring the lines between individual culpability and community blame. This narrative by one of the respondents shows the by-association stigma families face when dealing with case proceedings.

> *"Once he was sent to jail, the court procedures started. My life continued in this way for five years. I kept meeting him 2-6 times in a month. I had to face many problems to meet him. Moreover, in those five years, I had to bear many taunts. Useless people who do not do anything productive teased me in public. They made fun of me. I tolerated everything. I was helping with the proceedings of the case, and I was tolerating these people, too."*

Negative experiences and responses recounted by the respondents were solely based on the incarceration of family members in terror crimes. They all felt that they were being - suspected‖ due to the fact they were handling the case of their family member. All the respondents experienced the stigma of being attached to terrorism, and it was due to the arrest of family members in terror crimes.

> *"They used to call me "terrorist", "anti-national" and "ghaddar" just for the reason that I was fighting for my brother. They did not wait till the judgment come."*

Moreover, the differential treatment based on the gravity of the alleged crime further underscores the stark realities faced by these families. They recount instances where landlords evicted them upon learning about the accusations through media reports, highlighting the influence of public perception on their everyday lives. The narratives also expose the indirect imposition of stigma by law enforcement, coercing neighbours and relatives to sever ties, reflecting the insensitivity and questionable legitimacy of counter-terrorism measures. In essence, these narratives offer a chilling glimpse into the lived experiences of families ensnared in the web of suspicion, unveiling the profound impact of societal stigma and systemic biases. The theme of being suspected every day emerges as a haunting reality, illustrating the deep-seated challenges and unwarranted hardships endured by these families merely due to their familial association with alleged terror crimes.

Privacy and Security Challenges Amongst Stigmatised Families

The narratives shared by families of terror-accused individuals present a stark portrayal of the threats to their privacy and security resulting from the societal stigma they endure. These families found themselves in a precarious position, often forced to make life-altering decisions due to the pervasive threat to their privacy and security.

> *"I was so shocked; I had no control over my things. The person who lived in my house was behaving like an owner, and I could not do anything. The time was so terrible, but I survived, and my parents did too. However, Maulana was in jail, but me and my family were in the jail from where no one can escape."*

The stories highlighted instances where families faced unwarranted intrusion into their personal lives, primarily through verbal assaults and derogatory comments hurled by neighbours and acquaintances. This intrusion transcended verbal abuse and extended to the sanctity of their homes, as demonstrated by the incident where a tenant withheld rent and openly disparaged the family, linking them to the accused member. This lack of respect for their privacy and security escalated further when the families chose not to report instances of abuse or threats to the authorities. Despite the ordeal they faced, these families exhibited a pronounced reluctance to engage with law enforcement, fearing exacerbation of their situation and a lack of meaningful response from the authorities. The accounts also highlighted a pervasive atmosphere of fear and insecurity that permeated their everyday lives. The families found themselves in a constant state of apprehension, hesitant to take action against those responsible for their torment due to concerns of further retaliation or aggravation of their vulnerable state.

This climate of fear led to a paradoxical situation where maintaining secrecy seemed safer than seeking recourse or support. The families grappled with the dilemma of protecting their privacy while navigating a hostile environment, where disclosing their plight posed a greater risk than enduring the persistent threats and abuse. The narratives elucidate how the stigma associated with supporting accused members of terror crimes encroaches upon the fundamental rights of these families, eroding their sense of privacy and security. Their experiences underscore the deep-seated fear of repercussions and societal exclusion, shaping their choices and influencing their actions within a fraught and suspicious societal landscape. A key characteristic of stigmatisation is secrecy, which can lead to further distress. For many families, the level of fear experienced by the perceived threats involved in disclosing their situation may be greater than the experience of overt hostility (Codd, 2008).

Societal Stigma and Economic Strains

The experience of incarceration within families accused of terror-related crimes echoes far beyond the confinement of the accused individual. One of the most profound impacts manifests in the economic sphere, where the repercussions are felt acutely by these families, often leading to financial instability and hardship. In the aftermath of a family member's arrest, the sudden disruption of income sources becomes a jarring reality. The loss of the primary breadwinner or contributor triggers a domino effect, propelling these families into economic turmoil.

> *"At the time of my brother's arrest, I lost a lot of business. However, people forget such things easily when they can take advantage of the situation. Some people took advantage of me."*

Respondents recounted the abrupt financial shocks, struggling to manage households or businesses, which previously relied on the arrested individual's income.

> *"I have a quality. I am a very hardworking person, and I work with dedication. People took advantage of me. I stitched clothes for people. They earned much more than they paid me. They used to pay me very little, but I used to do it because I thought something was better than nothing. I used to work sixteen hours to earn enough to manage the*

expenses. I worked six hours extra every day to make more money. Then, I used to curtail the needs. That is how I managed five years."

This shift created an unanticipated burden, amplifying financial strain across the entire family. What compounds this economic crisis is the social stigma that attaches itself like an indelible mark upon these families. Codd (2008) defined it as the impoverishment of these families, and individuals supporting them have been described as shadow punishments. Their involvement in defending or supporting the accused member, even within the bounds of legality and familial obligation, invites society's ire and discrimination. The derogatory labels of "terrorist" or "anti-national" are hurled at them, a venomous consequence of their association with the case. The economic repercussions are not confined to mere financial loss. The affected families encounter tangible manifestations of discrimination, eviction threats, and difficulties in sustaining businesses or livelihoods due to persistent societal suspicion and ostracisation.

"My landlord was a Hindu man. He got scared and started living outside. His mother was at home. Neighbours started asking him questions about me and the media. He was so scared! Yes, when he was threatened, he got scared and asked me to vacate the house. I told them that no harm would come to them. I told him that no policeman had come to pay a visit."

Landlords, neighbours, and even workplace interactions become arenas of hostility and mistrust, stripping away the financial stability these families once had. The struggle to make ends meet becomes an arduous feat, with respondents narrating tales of relentless work hours, compromised earnings, and the painful prioritisation of needs. Necessities like food, shelter, and education become challenging to afford, leading to drastic measures such as working additional hours or reducing expenditures to cope with the economic distress. The collateral damage caused by this stigma extends beyond monetary woes. These families encounter impediments in accessing healthcare, resulting in tragedies like the loss of loved ones due to compromised medical care. The intertwining of economic turmoil and societal stigma paints a harrowing picture of the multifaceted adversities faced by these families, underscoring the urgent need for tailored interventions and support mechanisms to address their socio-economic struggles.

Stigma's Impact: Incarceration and Children's Education

Indeed, the incarceration of a family member, especially a parent, significantly impacts children's educational trajectories. Beyond financial constraints, stigma emerges as a prominent factor impeding their academic journey. The stories shared by families reveal how these children, despite their eagerness to pursue education, are abruptly pulled out of school due to financial struggles triggered by a parent's imprisonment.

> *"My children stopped going to school soon after my husband's arrest. My elder son used to study in a private school. He was very intelligent. We had to drop them out of school. After that, my elder brother got distracted and said no to studies. Other children got admission in government schools after a long time with the help of a friend of my husband's."*

The stigma intertwined with incarceration deepens the plight of these children. Instances abound where children, previously excelling in studies, had to abandon their educational pursuits. The distressing tales echo the disruptive nature of parental incarceration on children's educational aspirations. A poignant account narrates how a child's enthusiasm for education waned following their parent's arrest, leading to a stark deviation from academic commitment.

Furthermore, the financial instability inflicted by incarceration creates a tumultuous environment, forcing children to transition to less favourable schooling options. The struggle to secure admission to government schools after a prolonged hiatus reflects the enduring impact of parental imprisonment on the educational continuity of these children. Ultimately, the intersection of stigma and economic strain emerges as a dual force, severely hampering the educational prospects of these children. It is evident that the trauma resulting from familial incarceration not only disrupts their education but also subjects them to societal judgment and stigma, further complicating their academic journey.

Stigma, Incarceration, and Mental Health

The experience of incarceration casts a profound shadow on the mental health of both incarcerated individuals and their families, perpetuating an enduring sense of stigma. While some of the mental health effects are directly linked to the imprisonment itself, many others stem from the enduring emotional trauma, financial strain, and persistent social stigma that persist long after the accused member's release.

"I understand the feeling of vulnerability and suffering. So, I try to help people. Same relatives and people who harassed me. They used me and earned well. I cannot forget those days. I will not ever. My parents have been tortured so much in Orissa, where they live. They were distraught with all the things but assured by the fact that I was doing everything related to the case. Relatives who used to come once in a year stopped going to them."

The weight of stigma looms heavily, pushing families into a realm of chronic stress, depression, and anxiety. Participants described a pervasive sense of fear and trauma that persisted even after the acquittal of the accused family member.

"The level of fear is so intense that if someone comes to call me downstairs, I get scared too much. In our home town in Orissa, people harassed us so much and used to see us in a very heinous way. Due to police enquiry of terror crime in our home town, people become weird and humiliated our parents to a great extent. They used to keep silence."

The ongoing fear of social rejection, humiliation, and ostracisation haunted their daily lives. Chronic stress, depression, and anxiety became unwelcome companions as families grappled with the dual challenge of supporting their incarcerated relatives and sustaining themselves amidst social isolation. Accounts revealed the deteriorating health of family members, attributing it directly to the societal pressure and constant scrutiny from their community due to media coverage of the case. The attached stigma, particularly the association with the heinous crime of "terrorism," exacerbated their isolation, forcing them into self-imposed isolation.

"My health kept deteriorating because of social pressure; a lot of people were asking so many things by looking at media stories of my sister. We are happy; we do not want to remember those traumatic experiences. We want to focus on the present and future. I am scared of meeting people if someone might have the plan to prosecute us again. The question emerges as I meet the new people."

Narratives painted a picture of post-traumatic stress, despair, and anxiety that continued to plague these families. Despite their yearning for healing and stability, the absence of institutional support left them emotionally and financially adrift. The trauma remained largely unaddressed, lingering as nightmares, hopelessness, and deep-seated anxiety about social interactions, hindering their ability to rebuild their lives. The mental effects stemming from stigma endured long beyond the period of incarceration, echoing a silent struggle without avenues for treatment or support to navigate the trauma, grief, and persistent sense of loss.

Navigating Social Stigma: Coping and Support

The response to social stigma following the incarceration of family members for alleged terror crimes has varied among affected individuals, families, and communities. Muslim families subjected to suspicion and stigma reported diverse coping mechanisms, primarily driven by fear, caution, and the desire for safety. These responses included maintaining a low profile, residing in perceived "safe" areas, exercising caution in social interactions, and adopting a reserved demeanour. The pervasive sense of fear and suspicion within the community contributed to internal divisions and mutual distrust among its members. The awareness of Terrorism Laws and their seemingly arbitrary application further intensified the feelings of fear and vigilance. As a result, many individuals felt compelled to limit their activities and interactions, fostering an environment of caution and secrecy. Some respondents, however, chose a different approach, demonstrating resilience amid adversity. Despite the societal stigma, they remained committed to their principles, embracing honesty and transparency in their actions.

"Sometimes, I used to meet people who would help me with things for my brother. I should not lie about them. They did not give me much money. However, they gave me a few thousand. I still meet those people. I still call them. Some people wanted to meet. I told them to come to the court to meet. Moreover, they used to come to meet my brother at the court. If there was fear among people, there were helping people, too."

They recounted instances where they received support and acknowledgement for their commitment to seeking justice for their incarcerated family members. These individuals defied the norm of laying low and instead engaged with their communities, advocating for truth and justice. However, others expressed the impact of such stigma on personal relationships and social interactions. They highlighted the shift in dynamics within their social circles, with relatives and acquaintances distancing themselves due to the associated stigma. Nevertheless, amidst the negativity, these individuals also found solace in the supportive gestures from certain individuals and organisations, which served as a beacon of hope during trying times. These varied responses to social stigma underline the complex interplay between fear, resilience, social ostracisation, and the pursuit of justice. While some individuals chose to maintain a low profile and navigate cautiously through society, others stood firm, advocating truth and seeking support amid the stigmatisation. The narratives reflect the nuanced ways individuals navigate societal pressures, preserving their integrity while enduring the ramifications of stigma.

Conclusion

Throughout this study, the multifaceted impact of incarceration on families entangled in terror crime accusations has been extensively explored. The intricate web of challenges these families face spans various dimensions, encompassing social stigma, economic strain, threats to privacy, mental health repercussions, and the navigation of stigma-laden social interactions. The resounding theme that emerges from this examination is the pervasive and profound effect of social stigma. It permeates the fabric of daily life, influencing various facets, such as the dynamics within communities, the treatment received from others, and the overall well-being of individuals. This stigma, fueled by the accusations and incarceration of a family member, looms more significant than the challenges of meeting basic needs or ensuring privacy and security. Moreover, the exploration into coping mechanisms reveals a pervasive strategy: silence. Within the oppressive atmosphere of suspicion and ostracisation, maintaining a low profile appears to be the preferred approach. Families find solace in remaining reticent, navigating the complexities of stigma while silently working towards the release of their incarcerated member and striving to reclaim their tarnished reputation. Beyond the overarching theme of stigma, other critical aspects come to light. Financial hardships, educational disruptions for children, mental health strains, and the erosion of privacy significantly compound the adversity faced by these families. The economic strain resulting from the loss of income sources exacerbates the already burdensome situation. Children's education is disrupted, mental health issues emerge, and the erosion of privacy amplifies the distress experienced. In essence, this comprehensive analysis underscores the multifaceted and enduring challenges faced by families affected by terror-related incarcerations. It accentuates the overarching influence of social stigma while acknowledging the profound and lasting impacts on various aspects of life. The pervasive silence adopted by these families while navigating the intricate interplay of challenges stands as a testament to their resilience in the face of immense adversity.

References

Comfort, M. (2007). Punishment beyond the legal offender. *Annual Review of Law and Social Science, 3*, 271-296.

Comfort, M. (2009). Doing time together: Love and family in the shadow of the prison. Chicago, IL: University of Chicago Press.

Condry, R. (2007). Families shamed: The consequences of crime for relatives of serious offenders. Abingdon, UK: Willan Publishing.

Condry, R., Kotova, A., & Minson, S. (2016). Social Injustice and Collateral Damage: The Families and Children of Prisoners. In Y. Jewkes, J. Bennett, & B. Crewe (Eds.), *Handbook on Prisons.* Abingdon: Routledge.

Cornish, F. (2006). Challenging the stigma of sex work in India: Material context and symbolic change. *Journal of Community and Applied Social Psychology, 16*(6), 462–471.

Codd, H. (2008). In the shadow of prison: Families, imprisonment, and criminal justice. Portland, OR: Willan Publishing.

Crocker, J., Major, B., & Steele, C. (1998). Social Stigma. In S. Fiske, D. Gilbert, & G. Lindzey (Eds.), *Handbook of Social Psychology* (Vol. 2, pp. 504–53). Boston, MA: McGraw-Hill.

Davies, J. (1992). War memorials. *The Sociological Review, pp. 40*, 112–128.

Dudley, J. R. (2020). Confronting stigma within the services system. *Social Work*, 45:449–455.

Foster, R. G. (2017). *Half in/Half Out: Exploring the experiences of the families of prisoners in a Scottish prison visitors centre* (Doctoral dissertation, University of Glasgow). Retrieved from https://pdfs.semanticscholar.org/c187/ad51333d4e3a26a96b3f33954b47ea275c8b.pdf

Goffman, E. (1963). *Stigma: Notes on the Management of Spoiled Identity*. Englewood Cliffs, N.J.: Prentice-Hall.

Kleinman, A., & Hall-Clifford, R. (2009). Stigma: A social, cultural and moral process. *Journal of Epidemiology and Community Health, 63*(6), 418-419. https://doi.org/10.1136/jech.2008.084277

Kotova, A. (2020). Beyond courtesy stigma: Towards a multi-faceted and cumulative model of stigmatization of families of people in prison. *Forensic Science International: Mind and Law, p.* 1, 100021. https://doi.org/10.1016/j.fsiml.2020.100021

Link, B. G., & Phelan, J. C. (2001). Conceptualizing stigma. *Annual Review of Sociology, pp. 27,* 363–385.

Moore, H. (2016). *Prison wife stigma: An exploration of stigma by affiliation and strategic presentation of self* (Master's thesis, Kansas State University). Retrieved from https://pdfs.semanticscholar.org/3b8d/145572b5637faa881133f0c0c11351d5d84b.pdf.

Raghavan, V., & Nair, R. (2013). A Study of the Socio-Economic Profile and Rehabilitation Needs of Muslim Community in Prisons in Maharashtra. Mumbai: Centre for Criminology and Justice School of Social Work, TISS.

Tshaka, A. & Oyelana, A. A. (2019). Mitigating the Effects of Father Imprisonment on the Family: A Study of Social Work Intervention Strategies in Raymond Mhlaba Local Municipality in Eastern Cape. *J Hum Ecol*, 68(1-3): 157-173.

4

Religion as an Ethnic Marker: A Study among the Tai-Khamyangs of Assam

Ripunjoy Sonowal

Introduction

Religion is a universal and pervasive institution in human society. It is an ancient form of human culture, a set of beliefs and practices generally held by a group involving adherence to codified rituals. Durkheim (1915) described religion as "a unified system of beliefs and practices relative to sacred things, that is to say, set apart and forbidden, beliefs and practices which unite into one single moral community, called a church, all those who adhere to them". Religion is the most elusive of all the manifestations of man's intellectual and social life. The beliefs, thoughts and actions with which religion is concerned could be found at all levels of culture – primitive or civilised. Man's *religious quest* makes him restless beyond satisfying his basic physical needs. Hence, the Biblical saying is that man *cannot live by bread alone*. Religion, according to Majumdar and Madan (1996), "is the human response to the apprehension of something, or power, which is supernatural and super sensory. It is the expression of the manner and type of adjustment affected by a people with their conception of the supernatural". Religion plays a significant role in a man's life in society. It helps in achieving psychological adjustments and peace of mind. Moreover, it is one of the sources of morality. Religion is a system of beliefs, emotional attitudes, and practices employed by a group of people to attempt to cope with the ultimate problems of human life. It involves some emotional bond that binds the individuals together. Kingsley Davis (1966) remarks that "religion helps to integrate not only the society but also the personality". Religion plays the most crucial part in maintaining social cohesion and equilibrium. Religion furnishes a concrete reference for the values and a rallying point for all individuals who share the same values. It provides a means for constantly renewing common sentiments through its collective rituals. Firth (1961) said that "religious rites unite the members of the society in common assembly under an aegis which cannot be easily disputed, and so reaffirm their solidarity and enforce social interaction".

The study of the religious practices of the different ethnic communities of North East India represents an ideal topic for contemporary anthropological research. However, comprehensive studies in this direction have remained limited so far. The Tai-Khamyangs are a small Tai-Buddhist tribe of Assam. The available and accessible literature on the Khamyangs mainly discusses their material culture, ethno-medicine, and a few aspects of their socio-cultural life. Their religion, religious life, and other critical aspects are seldom discussed. Against this backdrop, an attempt has been made in the present paper to discuss briefly *Theravada* Buddhism as practised by the Tai-Khamyangs. Their pre-Buddhist faith and worship, as well as the different religious festivals (Buddhist and pre-Buddhist) celebrated by the people, are also briefly described. The paper also briefly discusses the notion of religion shaping their identity, existence and cultural plurality, as well as the recent changes observed in different aspects of their religion.

The Tai-Khamyangs

The Tai-Khamyangs or Khamjangs, popularly known as Shyams, are a section of the outstanding Tai stock. 'Tai' is a generic term meaning 'the Free' or 'Free Men' that represents a significant branch of the Mongoloid population of mainland Southeast Asia. Grierson (1966) states that "its members are to be found from Assam too far into the Chinese province of Kwangsi and from Bangkok to the interior of Yunnan". Khamyang is a Tai word; Kham means 'gold', and Yang or Jang means 'to have'. So, etymologically, the term Khamyang stands for the people from the Land of Gold. The Tai-Khamyangs migrated to upper Assam from North Myanmar via the Patkai hills towards the end of the 18th century AD. Today, they are a distinct scheduled tribe of the state, with their unique culture and tradition. In Assam, they are recognised as a scheduled tribe

(Hills; *Man*-Tai speaking group) by the constitution of India. They are small in number, with a total population of around 3600 individuals. At present, the Tai-Khamyangs predominantly reside in the Upper Assam region - in Disangpani, Chalapothar, Moniting, Bongaon and Rahan Shyam villages in Charaideo district; Powai Mukh village in Margherita, Tinsukia district; in Balijan, Betbari and Na-Shyam villages near Titabar in Jorhat district; and Rajapukhuri Shyam village in Golaghat district. Besides, there are some small settlements in places like Da Chuk, Kasupather, Gidingpather, Hofai and Bordum in the Namsai district of Arunachal Pradesh. Linguistically, they belong to the Tai linguistic group, which is a subgroup of the Tai Kadai language family. The Tai-Khamyangs, except those residing in Powai Mukh and Gidingpather, do not use the Tai language. They speak Assamese and use Assamese script. However, many Tai terms are still retained in their vocabulary. Their society is divided into nine exogamous clans (*Phan*) - *Thaomung, Chaohai, Chaolun, Chaolek, Tungkhang, Wailong* (also known as *Bailong*), *Panngyok, Phaalik,* and *Chaosong*. They are patrilineal, patriarchal and patrilocal. The rules of tribal endogamy and clan exogamy concerning marital alliances are followed. However, marriage with other Tai groups and with other Assamese communities is permitted and accepted by society. Women enjoy a relatively high position in the society. Agriculture is the main occupation of the Khamyangs. They are traditionally pile dwellers.

Materials and methods

The study was conducted in two ancient Tai-Khamyang villages, Chalapothar and Disangpani, in Charaideo district, Assam. The villages were established around 1869 and 1875, respectively. These are the oldest among all the Khamyang villages in Assam and, hence, are the main cultural centres of the Tai-Khamyangs. Standard anthropological methods, i.e., observation, extensive personal interviews and discussions, were used during fieldwork to generate the required mass of data from the key informants' viz. the *Bhante* (senior monk), the novices and temple boys of the Buddhist monastery, and select elderly villagers (both male and female). The collected data was systematically organised to draw a clear picture and presented in the following paragraphs.

Results and Discussion

The Tai-Khamyangs refer to the Supreme Being as Phra, who is omniscient, omnipotent and omnibenevolent. They regard Lord Buddha as the almighty God or *Phra*. The Tai-Khamyangs are devout followers of *Theravada* or *Hinayana* Buddhism. The two main sects of Buddhism are *Mahayana* (its teachings believe in public salvation; the followers emphasise the superhuman qualities of the Buddha) and *Hinayana* (its teachings believe in self-salvation; focuses on the ethics and moral discipline taught by the Buddha). The Khamyangs usually identify the two sects as *Mahajan* and *Hinjan*. In Tai-Khamyang manuscripts, *Theravada* Buddhism is known as *Tra-Stratow*. For centuries, *Theravada* Buddhism has been the predominant religion of Sri Lanka and the Southeast Asian countries of Myanmar, Cambodia, Laos, Thailand and Vietnam. *Theravada* Buddhism originates in India; it is the oldest surviving form of Buddhism in the world, founded after the 3rd Buddhist Council held around 250 BCE at Asokarama in Pataliputra, supposedly under the patronage of Emperor Ashoka. *Theravada* means 'the doctrine of the elders' (Gellner, 1990), 'the Teaching of the Elders, or 'the Ancient Teaching'. This school of Buddhism attempts to preserve the teachings of the Buddha in the Pali language (a non-literary ancient Indian vernacular dialect derived from Sanskrit and serving *Theravada* Buddhism as the language of the scriptures and sermons; it is also the language that the Buddha used during his life). *Tripitaka*, the sacred religious text of Buddhism, is the principal tenet of this sect. The practice of Buddhism, a highly doctrinal and metaphysically advanced religion, by the Tai-Khamyangs is a matter of great value, i.e., the believers have assimilated the metaphysical spirit to a high degree. They follow all the rituals detailed in their holy texts and are deeply guided by the various precepts of Lord Buddha's teachings.

The Tai-Khamyangs have been professing *Theravada* Buddhism since a significantly earlier period. They must have adopted *Theravada* Buddhism after the Tai/Shan principalities located in Upper Myanmar came into contact with the Burmese Bagan Kingdom (849-1297), where *Theravada* Buddhism was the main religion. King Anawrahta invited many Mon, Indian and Sinhalese *Theravada* Buddhist monks to Bagan to propagate and reform *Theravada* Buddhism in his kingdom (*Htin Aung, 1967).* Later, Burmese kings of the Taungoo dynasty (1510-1752) and the Konbaung dynasty (1752-1885) continued to promote *Theravada* Buddhism in the traditional manner of a Dharma King (*Dhamma-raja*). This included patronising monastic ordinations, missionaries, scholarship and the copying of scripture, as well as establishing new temples, monasteries and animal sanctuaries (Harvey, 1925; Leider, 2004). This sustained state support allowed *Theravada* Buddhism to penetrate the rural regions of the country. By the 18th century, village monasteries were a common feature of every Burmese village, and they became the main centre of education (Lieberman, 2003). Mong (2004) states that since the 11th century A.D. the Burmese had adopted Buddhism, and the Tai also must have been influenced by Buddhism since then. Burmese king Bayinnaung (1551-1581) sent Buddhist monks to the Tai states, and the Tai rulers were ordered to follow these monks. Hence, from these historical accounts, it can be inferred that the Tai people adopted *Theravada* Buddhism many centuries ago. The oral history of the Tai-Khamyangs says that they brought the faith along with them when they immigrated to *Saumarapitha*, i.e., erstwhile eastern Assam from North Burma in the late 18th century, and established Buddhist temples having regular priests. Except for the Tai-Ahoms, the other Tai groups were *Theravada* Buddhists before they arrived in Assam and maintained their faith till today (Mishra & Sahai, 2007).

The Tai-Khamyangs believe that the universe is comprised of three different types of beings, viz. *Phan-Kon, i.e., humans; Phan-Phi, i.e., spirits; and Phan-Sang,* i.e., the world of gods. They are highly aware of the karmic consequences (*Karma-phala*; fruit of action) of their actions in daily life. They believe that an individual's present state depends on the kinds of works carried out during the current life, and based on that, an individual attains a good rebirth and higher state of being. As per the Buddha's teachings, to attain *Nirvana* (salvation), one must 'earn merit' (*Punya*) in life, and it is essential to preserve the merit for the next birth and improve *Kamma* (*Karma*) – the concept of action, work, or deed, and its effect or consequences. The Tai-Khamyangs believe that there are both good and bad aspects of *karma* and that their work or actions in the present life would influence their future effect, i.e. good deeds contribute to good *karma* and happier rebirths. In contrast, evil deeds contribute to bad *karma* and bad rebirths. Merit can be earned through charity, i.e., offering

Dana - giving something to someone who most needs it. It signifies the most pious and virtuous act of the donor. So, the people regularly offer *danas* to the monks through food, robes, and articles of daily need. Besides, they render their services in cash and kind in the construction, renovation and maintenance of the village Buddha *Vihar*. Donating *Tankhon* and Buddha idols and images to the *Vihar* is done by the people with extreme devotion. It will be relevant to note here that *Theravada* Buddhism among the Tai-Khamyangs has become, through the centuries, so amazingly blended with some aspects of earlier animism or pre-Buddhist (or extra-Buddhist) indigenous beliefs and practices that it is impossible to segregate the pure elements. They have become more syncretic and synthesised. The outcome of the process is the assimilation of numerous benevolent and malevolent spirits and local deities, as well as the synthesis of customs, rituals, and so forth. *Theravada* Buddhism among the Tai-Khamyangs is highly influenced by the Burmese/Myanmar tradition of the religion. Also, it has many similarities with the *Theravada* Buddhism of Southeast Asia. It was informed that, earlier, monks from Myanmar made occasional visits to the Buddha *Vihars* of Tai-Khamyang villages in Assam to impart religious teachings. *Theravada* Buddhism forms an integral part of the life and culture of the Tai-Khamyangs. The socio-religious life of the people significantly circles the Buddha *Vihar* (*Bodh Vihara*), the precepts/virtues of the Buddha, the Buddhist monks (*Bhikkhus*) and the monastic life. The pre-Buddhist faith and traditional worship also occupied an essential place in their socio-religious life.

The Buddha *Vihar*

The Buddha *Vihar* (Temple/Monastery), called *Kyong* or *Chong* in Tai, is the principal place of worship of the Tai-Khamyangs and where all the community-level socio-religious activities are held. The Buddha *Vihar* reflects the twin role of the Buddhist *Sangha*, i.e., to provide the best possible condition for individual development and to teach the *Dhamma/Dharma* to humankind. Every Khamyang village possesses a Buddha *Vihar*, which is generally located in a central place of the village and built in a way that distinguishes its structural design from the rest of the village houses and other adjoining structures. The *Vihar* land is the village's property. The Buddha *Vihar* compound is impressive, and proper cleanliness and hygiene are always maintained. A Buddha *Vihar* means all the buildings enclosed within the walls of the sacred compound. Each *Vihar* complex consists of one large, well-crafted, spacious, and well-lit prayer hall/temple with a unique architectural design (that resembles Buddhist temples of Myanmar or Thailand), which is elaborately decorated; a concrete structure in the form of a small shrine called *Kyong-phra* which is meant for the ritualistic bath of the Buddha's idols (*Kyong-phra* consists of a long boat with a magnificently carved dragon head or a simple wooden boat and a small empty decorated shrine); *Sima-ghar* (place for ordination ceremony; *ghar*: Assamese word meaning a house), living quarter for the monk/s called as *Bapu-ghar* (*Bapu*: the Assamese word for monk); dormitory for the novices (*Sarman*) and temple boys (*Mung-jang*); and separate accommodations - *Kuti* for visiting monks and *Pusi* for visiting nuns. There are also sheds with platforms (*Sarap*) that the male and female devotees (*Upasak* and *Upasika*), generally the old and aged ones, use while observing certain religious functions. A small library also forms a part of the *Vihar*. The *Vihar* also has a kitchen and a small dining hall. Occasional guests are suitably accommodated in the *Vihar's* guest house (*Sala*).

An impressive entrance gate (presence of the Buddhist *Torana* - free-standing ornamental or arched gateway for ceremonial purposes, and decorated with the *dharma chakra* - the wheel of dharma, and floral and ornamental patterns), beautiful golden coloured pagoda/*stupa* (*Kongmu-kham*), Ashoka pillar (*Chow-tengta*), temple bell (*Kese*), a well (*Nong*), and the sacred *Pipal* or Bodhi tree (*Ficus religiosa* Linn.; *Tun-pothi*) are the other notable essential features of the *Vihar*. Varieties of fruit plants and numerous flower and ornamental plants (grown in the flower garden: *Chiun-mokya*) are also grown within the *Vihar* compound. The *Vihar* also has a scrubby area with medicinal plants and herbs. The *Vihar* boundary is well-fenced with bamboo and concrete walls. Further, the Buddha *Vihar* also acts as a traditional school where the novices learn about Lord Buddha's teachings under the senior monk's guidance. It also serves as a public place where villagers relax, exchanging news and knowledge. Customarily, it is a place of worship and spiritual solace, a seat of learning, a book depository, a way farers inn, a local clubhouse, a bank, a vault, and a site of numerous country fairs and festivals (Chu, 1968). Inside the prayer hall, in its sanctum sanctorum, many Buddha idols (made of marble stone, silver, bronze, brass and wood) of different sizes are kept on an elevated altar (*Plang*) in front of which regular prayers are offered by the monks as well as by the villagers. The idols are kept in an arranged order, i.e., the big life-size idols are placed in the middle position, while the other idols are kept in a sequential order in the left, right and front line according to their size. Some idols are donated by devotees, who mostly bring the idols from Myanmar or Thailand. On the occasion of the donation, a special ceremony called *Poi-Lu-Phra* (donation of Buddha idol to the temple) is organised in the *Vihar*. The Buddha idols of the *Vihar* always face towards the east. It was stated that the reason for the same lies in the fact that Lord Buddha received enlightenment or perfect insight under the Bodhi tree by facing this direction. The front of the altar is reserved for the monks to deliver sermons and religious teachings. Embroidered prayer flags (*Tan-khon*) were hand-woven by the villagers and donated to the Vihar on different occasions, and photographs depicting different aspects of the life of Lord Buddha are hung on the walls of the prayer hall. The villagers widely donate *Tan-khon* during Buddhist festivals and religious ceremonies, seeking merit, welfare, long life, quick recovery from illness, and remembrance of their dead relatives and friends. A good collection of valuable books and manuscripts (*Phulik*) on Buddhism (written in English, Assamese, Pali and Tai languages) can be seen in the *Vihar* Library. The manuscripts include, among others, sacred religious texts like *Pitaka* (*Tripitaka*), *Dharmapada* and *Jataka*. It is a pious tradition among the monks and novices to preserve these holy texts in the *Vihar*. The lay devotees sometimes donate books and sacred manuscripts on Buddhism to the *Vihar* library. The ceremony held to mark such occasions is called *Pustaka dana*. Interested persons can read the various books in the *Vihar* but cannot borrow them.

Apart from regular visits to the Buddha *Vihar*, the Tai-Khamyangs also offer prayers to Lord Buddha at the family level as a part of their daily routine. Every Khamyang household has a place of worship - a high-raised platform or altar built in the eastern direction where all the family members offer daily prayers to Lord Buddha every morning and evening. The altar consists of a large wooden shelf for the necessary prayer materials, particularly the Buddha idol and image, a bell metal vase containing fresh water and flowers (*Mokya*) to honour the Buddha, a few columns of Holy

Scripture, candles (*Simi*) and incense sticks (*Hom*). Food offerings are also placed here; however, food is offered only in the morning prayer. The daily household prayer (*Khamcing; Buddha Vandana*) is usually brief and simple, which only expresses reverence to the *Triratna* or the three gems viz. the Buddha, the Dhamma and the Sangha. Prayers are recited in Pali. In their daily prayers at home, a Khamyang devotee requests the almighty Lord Buddha to free him/her from woes, scourges, enemies, and misfortunes and help them attain *Nirvana*- a true Buddhist's ultimate goal. Among the elderly villagers, one respected person is selected as a *Pathek* (*Chao-chere*), who plays an essential role in all the religious functions and ceremonies of the village. A *Pathek* is well-versed in the culture and tradition of the people and holds his position till his death. He possesses sufficient knowledge about all Buddhist religious matters. He is entrusted with reading the *Mongolsutra* (a manuscript of cultural and religious importance) during the household religious ceremonies. Besides, he is the person who has to formally inform the monks about the purpose of the various religious occasions.

Precepts of the Buddha

Pancha Sil/Sila (Five Precepts)

The Khamyangs of all age groups observe the Buddha's basic five moral precepts for an ethical life called the *Pancha Sil*. The precepts are essential to liberating oneself from suffering and are practical instructions to support one's daily conduct while advancing to enlightenment. The people usually receive these precepts from the monks during different religious functions organised in the Buddha *Vihar* around the year. Besides, during different religious ceremonies organised at the household level, the precepts are administered to the family members as part of the ritual. Each percept is first recited by the presiding monk and then repeated by the devotees. When reciting the precepts, the devotees must sit in a humble posture by having their hands joined palm to palm in front of the chest and the legs folded behind. In the *Theravada* tradition, the precepts are recited in a standardised fashion, using the Pali language. The recitation of the *Pancha Sil* is as follows -

1. **Panatipata Veramani Sikhapadam Samadiyami**
   - (I vow to observe the rule of abstinence from taking a life.)

2. **Adinnadana Veramani Sikhapadam Samadiyami**
   - (I vow to observe the rule of abstinence from taking what is not given.)

3. **Abrahmacariya Veramani Sikhapadam Samadiyami**
   - (I vow to observe the rule of abstinence from lustful misconduct/sexual activity.)

4. **Musavada Veramani Sikhapadam Samadiyami**
   - (I vow to observe the rule of abstinence from telling a lie.)

5. **Suramerayamajja pamadatthana Veramani Sikhapadam Samadiyami**
   - (I vow to observe the rule of abstinence from taking liquor and other intoxicating substances.)

The recitation ends with the last word, Samadiyami, being uttered and the devotees bowing their heads and raising their joined hands to the forehead.

Asta Sil (Eight Precepts)

The elderly villagers above 50 years must follow three more precepts besides the five basic precepts. The two sets of precepts are called *Asta Sil* (Eight precepts). On every Buddhist holy day, interested older adults go to the Buddha *Vihar* early in the morning before sunrise to receive the *Asta Sil* from the monk. They carry with them prayer items like flowers (nicely put in a *Paan* – small bamboo wicker), candles, incense sticks, puffed rice (*Khao-pook*), fruits, as well as food for the monk(s) of the *Vihar*. The people first pray to Lord Buddha by lightening the candles and incense sticks and offering gifts in front of the high pedestal where the Buddha idols are kept. Then, the devotees hold the flowers between their hand palms in front of their chests and recite the eight precepts one by one after the monk. The three additional precepts are:

1. **Vikalabbhojana Veramani Sikhapadam Samadiyami**
   - (I vow to observe the rule of abstinence from taking food at the wrong time, i.e., in the afternoon.)

2. **Nacca-gitavadita-visukadassna Veramani Sikhapadam Samadiyami**
   - (I vow to observe the rule of abstinence from dancing, singing, music, and visiting entertainment shows.)

3. **Mala-gandha-vilepana-dharana-mandana-vibhusanatthana Veramani Sikhapadam Samadiyami**
   - (I vow to observe the rule of abstinence from wearing garlands, using makeup perfumes, wearing ornaments and body decorations.)

Dasa-sikka-padani (Ten Precepts)

The *Dasa-sikka-padani* (Ten precepts) are followed rigidly only by the monks and novices, who are members of the Buddhist Sangha. They led the monastic life and recited the ten precepts at any time, wearing yellow robes with shaved heads, which set them apart from the other lay Buddhists of the village (Sarmah, 2001). The remaining two precepts are–

1. **Uccasayana-mahasyana Veramani Sikhapadam Samadiyami**
   - (I vow to observe the rule of abstinence from lying in a high or luxurious sleeping place.)

2. **Jatarupa-rajata-patiggahanna Veramani Sikhapadam Samadiyami**
   - (I vow to observe the rule of abstinence from accepting gold and silver).

The Monk and the Monastic Life

The Buddhist Monk (*Bhikkhu*) is an ordained male in Buddhist monasticism. In *Theravada* Buddhism, the lives of all Buddhist monastics are governed by a set of rules called the *Patimokkha* (Ariyesako, 1998).

Their lifestyles are shaped to support their spiritual practice, i.e., to live a simple and meditative life with minimum necessities, only enough to sustain themselves and attain Nirvana. The Buddhist Sangha aims to form the "community of consciousness" and give the *bhikkus* an ideal condition for "continued conditioning of consciousness away from individualism in all the ordinary, everyday actions of life" (Ling, 1973). Among the Tai-Khamyangs, every lay male community member is expected to enter the monastic life as a novice, at least for three months when he is young and long before his marriage. Persons who had served the Buddha *Vihar* as a novice or monk enjoy a respected and honourable position in their society. However, there is no compulsion on the parents to send their sons to the *Vihar* for training and to lead an ascetic life. An interested boy who intends to become a novice (*Sarman*) and a monk must start training by serving as a temple boy (*Mung-jang*) at 9 or 10 years old. The temple boy/s serves the *Vihar* as attendants to the monks. They perform manual work like cleaning the *Vihar* and its courtyard, fetching water, preparing tea, and going to the village shop and weekly market. Monks do not possess money, but these disciples may receive it from the devotees and spend it for the monks' requirements. In addition, the temple boy/s has to assist the chief monk in his day-to-day work in the monastery and perform his religious functions like reading and reciting holy books and praying to Lord Buddha. In the process, he acquires an excellent knowledge of the same. However, along with these activities, he has to continue with his regular education, i.e., either exclusively in Pali or in combination with the regular formal education provided in schools and colleges. A temple boy may leave the *Vihar* and return to lead everyday village life after obtaining formal permission from the senior monk of the *Vihar*.

A temple boy is upgraded to the position of a *Sarman* when he is under 20 years of age and can read and write Pali scripts, recite all the Buddhist precepts and understand the main principles of Buddhism. The people call a *Sarman Horu Bhante* (junior monk) or *Chow-sang*. A temple boy is elevated to the position of a novice in an elaborate investiture ceremony called *Sarman tula* or *Poi Chow-Sangkham*. The chief monk of the village Buddha *Vihar* selects the auspicious day of the ceremony. It is attended by the monks and novices from monasteries of other Tai-Khamyang villages. For the ceremony, the boy's father collects the following eight articles called *Asta parikkhara* - one *Changkan* (a piece of yellow cloth about 2 meters long and 1.5 meters wide), one *Khampeng* (yellow cloth), one *Cipic* (a begging bowl), one *Mittha* (a razor), one *Pha sat nang* (a piece of white cloth for filtration), one *Ongkachet* (a yellow upper garment, one *Khi-mai* (needle and thread) and one *Tong-mai* (a stick). After the bath, the boy is adorned with colourful costumes and ornaments (that represent the princely garments of Prince Siddhartha) and then seated on an elevated bamboo platform, and the guests offer him gifts. An elaborate feast is also arranged for all the guests. After that, he is carried by his father and other older adults on their shoulders and seated on a bamboo chair with an umbrella fixed on its back (representing the throne). Two bamboo poles are fixed on the two sides of the chair to carry it on the shoulders. Then, in a big procession, the prospective *Sarman* is taken through the village and finally to the *Vihar*. He puts aside his princely garments, shaves his head, and wears a white loin cloth. He then approaches the assembled monks, taking with him the yellow robes, candles and incense sticks, and bows down three times before the chief monk, seeking permission to enter the monastic life as a disciple of the Buddha. He presents the *Asta parikkhara* to the chief monk, who in turn advises him how to follow the life of a novice, recites the ten precepts to him, and then formally hands back the *Asta parikkhara*. The new *Sarman* then takes up his begging bowl, kneels before the assembled monks and bows three times in reverence for being allowed to serve as a *Sarman*. He has to lead a straightforward life and follow a strict code of regulations in the *Vihar*. Being an apprentice to become a future monk, a *Sarman* continues to practice his daily religious duties, study the Buddhist scriptures and the *Suttas*, and learn the Dhamma under the guidance of the senior monk. The objective of being a monk/*bhikkhu* is to understand the meaning of one's life and the condition of life in order to lead oneself towards Nirvana, the state of enlightenment. The principle of the practice is the elimination of "self" or individual existence, which is the cause of every human condition. The monastic life does not eliminate a *Sarman's* right to maintain relations with his family of orientation, travel and go to the market to make purchases. He can do it with the due permission of the chief monk of the *Vihar*. He may even be allowed to stay in his parent's house for a few days whenever any situation demands. However, he must remain within the village during fasting and not venture outside.

The monks are the most revered persons in the *Theravada* Buddhist societies. In the religious hierarchy of the *Theravada* Buddhist world, a senior monk's position is superior to all. Among the Tai-Khamyangs, a monk is popularly called a *Bhante*, *Bhikkhu* (as in Pali), or *Bapu* (in Assamese). They also sometimes use the Tai term *Chao-mun* to address a monk. A Buddhist monk or *Bhikkhu* is, by definition, a sharer, living on alms and having no permanent abode. They have been an essential part of the Buddhist Trinity called the *Triratna* (Singh, 2013). The rules and regulations of the Buddhist principles more strictly govern the life of a monk. Apart from following the ten precepts, the *bhikkhus* are submissive and obedient to the principles of *Vinaya Pitaka*, which contains 227 training rules for the *Bhikkhus*. Every Tai-Khamyang village must have a *Bhante* to perform the various religious ceremonies. He is regarded as an indispensable part of the village. In the socio-religious life of the Tai-Khamyangs, the *Bhante* and the young novice/s occupy a dignified and respectable position. They are paid homage to by all members of society irrespective of age. They are not counted in the social division of the Tai-Khamyang community as they have abandoned their worldly life. They wear a yellow/amber coloured robe called a *Chivar*, and their heads are always shaved. All the villagers oblige the *Bhante* by providing all the necessities of sustenance. On a rotation basis, he is provided with cooked food daily in the morning before noon by the villagers collectively or by every village family; besides, he is provided with robes and medicines. The *Bhante* is a knowledgeable person who is well-versed in the Pali script and has profound knowledge of Buddhism. He is also an expert in Buddhist astrology. The *Bhante* plays a crucial role in reminding the people about their religious duties and the philosophies of the Buddha. He participates in and conducts the village's various community-level religious functions and ceremonies. Depending on age, experience, and seniority, a monk can be categorised as Sthavir, Mahasthavir, Ther, or *Mahather*.

Celebration of Buddhist Holy Days and Festivals

The Tai-Khamyangs celebrate several holy days and festivals (*Poi* - is the Tai word meaning festival) in different periods of the year. They consider the four days of each lunar month, i.e., the new and full moon days and the eighth day after each of the days mentioned above, as holy days. The people collectively celebrate these four holy days as *Uposatha* days. *Uposatha* days are times of renewed dedication to Dhamma practice, observed by the lay followers and the monastics. On the holy days, all the Khamyang people assemble in their village, Buddha Vihar, early in the morning and collectively pray to Lord Buddha, the Dhamma and the Sangha in the presence of the senior *Bhante* and other monks. In front of the Buddha idols in the prayer hall of the *Vihar*, the devotees light candles, burn incense sticks, and offer flowers, food and gifts (*Dan/Dana*) articles, besides listening to sermons by monks and participating in meditation sessions. The people also pay homage to the monks by offering alms, food, and other items that are needed for daily living to earn merit. The monks bless the devotees and administer the moral precepts of *Pancha Sil* and *Asta Sil*. Some of the important religious festivals and ceremonies of the people are briefly described here:

Poi Sang-Ken:

It is the traditional New Year festival or the annual spring festival of the Tai-Khamyangs and other Tai Buddhist communities of North East India. Considered the most important festival of the Tai people, it is publicly celebrated in the Buddha *Vihars* of all Tai-Khamyang villages annually from the 13th to the 15th of April with great religious fervour and much pomp and gait. *Poi Sang-Ken* starts on the day of *Sankranti* in April (*Nuean Ha*), the fifth month of the year of the Tai Luni-solar calendar. It is celebrated in the last days of the old year, and the New Year begins on the day just after the end of the festival. *Poi Sang-Ken* festival is rich with symbolic traditions; it also means 'cleansing with fresh water' (water is considered the symbol of peace and purity) – the Buddha, the Dharma and the Sangha. On the first day of the festival (called *Poi Hap*), all the Buddha idols and the sacred manuscripts and religious books of the *Vihar* are ritually washed. At an auspicious time according to the *Sangcret* (i.e., the Tai *Panjika* or Tai astrological daily calendar and almanac that comes from Mandalay every year), the monk, the pathek and some of the villagers take down the idols from the alter of the prayer hall, carry them out of the *Vihar* in a procession (traditional musical instruments are played and puffed rice and flowers are showered at the Buddha idols by the villagers during the procession), and are placed inside the *Kyong-Phra*, decorated with colourful papers and flowers, for the next three days for the ceremonial bathing (*Chon-phra*).

A specially designed rotating wooden fountain (*Kungpan*) with small hollow pipes and a wheel fixed in its centre is made to perform the ceremonial bathing ritual. It is placed inside the *Kyong-Phra* and connected to the wooden boat (*Hang-hoe*) so that when water is poured into the boat, the wheel starts rotating owing to the pressure of the water. The rotating wheel thus helps sprinkle the water over the Buddha idols kept in the *Kyong-Phra*. All the villagers bring clean water from the nearby river, pond or wells to pour over the idols, and the process has to be repeated three times. Before pouring, flowers are put in the water in order to make them scented. This water, which has washed the Gods, is collected as holy water by the devotees. The sacred manuscripts and religious books are placed on a table next to the *Kyong-Phra* window. A rope holds them together, one end of which is positioned outside the *Kyong-Phra*. The people pour water over the rope three times, thus performing the ritual washing of the Dharma. For the ceremonial bathing of the Sangha, the people pour water three times on the feet and the folded hands of the monk/s, offer gifts and flowers and take their blessings for good luck, good health, peace and harmony throughout the year. Water is also poured on the feet of elders and parents, seeking blessing from them. The sacred *Bodhi* tree, the pagoda, and all other monuments within the *Vihar* premises are also given ceremonial wash by splashing water on it. The people pray (*Kham-sin*) by offering flowers, lighting candles (Simi-tong), and burning incense sticks in the *Vihar*. The Buddha *Vihar* campus is beautifully illuminated with candlelight and colourful lanterns, creating a serene and peaceful ambience, and the villagers in their homes do the same. On the third day, at an auspicious time, according to the *Sangcret*, the Buddha idols are reinstalled at the original altar of the *Vihar*. The traditional musical instruments, namely *Konglung* (Large drum), *Yammong* (Medium-sized hanging gong), *Pai-Seng* (Cymbals), *Pee* (Flute) and *Kese* (Bronze bell) are played on the occasion, along with performing their traditional dance and songs.

During the festival, as a traditional ritual, all the villagers, especially the young boys and girls, splash small buckets full of clean water on each other and passers-by. This symbolises spiritual purification in order to begin the New Year free from impurities and the washing away of one's diseases, sins and bad luck; it also fosters unity and provides amusement and merrymaking. Hence, it is also widely known as the Festival of Water (*Poi San-Nam*), and the Tai-Khamyangs also call it *Pani Bihu* in Assamese. The people also prepare traditional foods from glutinous rice and make offerings to earn merit in the Buddhist New Year. On the last day, devotees take *Pancha Sil* or *Ashta Sil*, according to their age and vows. After the final prayer, everyone in the village gathers for a community feast. *Poi Sang-Ken* is also celebrated at the individual level; people clean their houses, pray to Lord Buddha for the well-being of their family, bow and show respect to their elders, and serve delicious food and present new clothes to them. Donations are made to the *Vihar* and the needy. *Poi Sang-Ken* festival, thus, celebrated with great devotion and enthusiasm, marks a farewell to the old year and a warm welcome to the New Year.

Poi Mai-Ko-Chum-Fai:

Mai-Ko-Chum-Fai (*Mai:* wood; *Ko:* to place one above the other; *Chum-Fai:* to burn) means the burning of wood placed in a pile. It is celebrated on the *night of Purnima* in the month of *Magh* (*Noun Sam*; Jan-Feb) to mark the success of the new harvest. During the festival, young boys of the village collect firewood and construct a *Meji* on the river bank or in an open field suitably selected near the village. It is constructed by piling the firewood horizontally, one above the other crosswise, up to a height of about 8-10 meters. The shape of the *meji* is triangular, which tapers at the top and is supported by long bamboo poles from all sides to prevent it from falling. The *meji* is decorated with colourful paper. In the evening, all the villagers gather near the *meji* with flowers, incense sticks, candles, and rice packets as offerings. The *Bhante* conducts the prayers and administers *Panch Sil* to the people. After that, an elderly villager sets fire to the *meji* at the summit with the help of a long bamboo pole. All the villagers propitiate the *meji* fire called *Phi-Fai* (*Phi:* spirit/deity; *Fai*: fire), meaning the fire spirit. Firecrackers are burst as an amusement. The celebration is concluded with a community feast where the newly harvested rice is cooked.

Poi Noun-Houk:

Buddha *Jayanti* or Buddha *Purnima* is celebrated as *Poi Noun-Houk* among the Tai-Khamyangs. It is celebrated on the full moon, *Uposatha* day of the *Vaisakha* month according to the Buddhist calendar to commemorate the birth, enlightenment and death of Lord Buddha. Incidentally, all three sacred events of the Buddha's life occurred on the same day. On the day of the festival, early morning, all the villagers gather in the Buddha *Vihar* for a mass prayer. The *Bhante* hoists the World Buddhist flag, keeping in solidarity with the World Fellowship of the Buddhist Sangha. The festival begins by pouring water onto the sacred Bodhi tree, under which Gautama Buddha attained enlightenment and became the Buddha. The people pray by offering flowers to the Buddha idol of the monastery and light candles and incense sticks. The Monk of the *Vihar* is gifted with articles of daily use by the villagers. A community feast is also organised on the festival day. For the same, the village youths, on the previous day of the festival, collect rice, vegetables and other items necessary for the feast from every village household.

Barsha Bash (Poi-Chatang)/Monsoon Fast:

It is an essential religious occasion in which the Buddhist monks and the followers of the Eight Precepts fast for three months from the full moon day of *Aahar* (June-July) to the full moon day of *Aahin* (September-October). On the occasion, the elderly villagers visit the village of *Vihar* and hold regular prayers. The starting day of *Barsha Bash* is called *Poi Khaw-Wa,* and the ending day is called *Poi Akwa* – where the union of the Buddhist monks gather in a particular place in the village and pray to the Buddha to forgive them for their faults.

Poi Kathin:

Also called *Kathin Chivar Dan,* celebrated within the month of October-November before the conclusion of the *Prabarana Purnima,* means offering of the sacred yellow robes. This festival commemorates the Buddha's first sermon to his five disciples. Among the various gifts offered to the monks, all the *Theravada* Buddhists world over, including the Tai-Khamyangs, consider that the gift of a new *Chivar* (monk's robe) that is weaved in their looms with much hardship (*kathin*) is the most prominent symbol of sacrifice, through which one can achieve salvation. Hence, a day before the festival, some women and girls from the village who are expert weavers gather at a common place and weave the *Chivar* for the *Bhante* (and for the *Sarman/s*) of the Buddha *Vihar* in a single night. The festival is also held centrally in one of the Khamyang villages to which monks from other Buddha *Vihars*, as well as people from other villages, are invited. Early in the morning on the day of the festival, all the villagers go to the Vihar with gifts of new robes, fruits, and foods prepared in their respective homes, as well as other necessary items for the monk/s' day-to-day needs. They assemble on the Vihar ground, standing in a single line with their gifts and food items. After that, the monks, in order of their seniority, walk out of the temple in a procession with their begging bowls. The villagers put their gifts and food items in the monks' begging bowls one by one. The filled-in bowls are emptied into other bigger containers by a few elderly villagers assisting the monks. Thus, in this manner, everybody avails the opportunity to make their offerings to the monks. The senior most *Bhante* distributes the *Chivars* among the monks. In addition, the people tie their offerings like books, pens, currency notes, biscuits, candles and incense stick packets onto a handmade *Kalpataru* (wishing tree) with strings considered auspicious and pray for their wishes to be fulfilled. Prayer sessions are held in the *Vihar* during the ceremony, seeking peace, progress, and prosperity for the people. The ceremony of releasing floating lamps (*Poi-Phong*) is organised in the evening.

Poi Lu-Phra:

It is the festive occasion in which a person or a family or the entire village collectively donates an idol of Lord Buddha to the village *Vihar* to fulfil some special wish or earn merit. On an auspicious day, generally on *Purnima*, the Monk and *Vihar's* novices, the village headman, and other senior villagers arrive at the donor's place where the idol is kept. The monk sprinkles holy water on the idol and moves the same to the *Vihar* in a procession. After reaching there, the idol is first moved around the main worship hall three times. After that, it is ceremoniously placed along with other idols and statues of Lord Buddha on the main altar. The occasion is marked by prayers and lighting candles and incense sticks.

Poi Leng:

Poi Leng is one of the most important festivals in Tai-Khamyang. It is celebrated on the occasion of a prominent monk's death (e.g., one with the rank of *Mahather*). The Tai word *Leng* means a chariot. In this ceremony, a chariot is made from wood, which is beautifully decorated with colourful patterns and designs to carry the corpse of the deceased monk. The cremation ceremony is marked by the pulling of the chariot by the villagers, religious prayers and discussions, an exhibition, and the traditional game of tug-of-war. The pulling of the chariot and the game of tug-of-war between the men and women of the village is an integral part of the celebration. *Poi Leng* festival plays a significant social role as it unites the Tai-Khamyangs under one umbrella, and strong social solidarity is seen among the people during the celebration.

Pre-Buddhist Faith and Traditional Worships

It is not easy to ascertain the religious affiliation of the Tai-Khamyangs before the advent of Buddhism. Initially, until the arrival of Buddhism, the Tai followed animism and were spirit worshippers. They believe that natural geographic features surrounding their life are protected by spirits or seemingly supernatural forces, or in other words, the tutelary gods, for example, the spirit of the rice fields, rivers, forests, bamboo groves, mountains, the house spirit who protect their dwellings, the territorial or village spirit on whom the survival and safety of the village ultimately depend, as well as the spirits of their ancestors. The power of spirits is all-pervasive, and everything in the physical world is controlled by one spirit or the other. The relationship of the villagers to these spirits is one of reverential fear, dependence, submission and propitiation (Namchoom & Lalhmingpuii, 2016). These spirits often interact with the world of the living, and if appeased and respected by the people, they can bring them luck and prosperity. At times, they are also supposed to protect the people. However, if angered or disrespected, they are believed to cause harm and bring about hardships and loss for the offender. The guardian spirit of the village is celebrated and propitiated with communal gatherings and food offerings. The prayers offered to the different spirits not only give the people hope but also provide them with the strength to face the challenges they may be facing in their lives. As mentioned earlier, *Theravada*

Buddhism among the Tai-Khamyangs is amazingly blended with some aspects of earlier animism or pre-Buddhist (or extra-Buddhist) indigenous beliefs and practices. The successful amalgamation of the traditional elements and practices with Buddhism over the centuries has enriched their religious configuration. Thus, the Tai-Khamyangs still believe in and worship several *primordial* malevolent and benevolent spirits (*Phi*), including the spirits of their ancestors.

One of the most notable rituals in this category is the *Phi-Su-Moung* or *Moung-Phi* worship. *Phi-Su-Moung* is the village's guardian spirit worshipped on the following day or after seven days of *Poi-Sang-Ken* in April. He is the only spirit who is accorded special worship collectively by the villagers. It is generally believed that if this benevolent spirit is not appropriately worshipped, there might be an epidemic outbreak and unnatural deaths in the village. For ritual worship, the Tai-Khamyangs construct a pyramid-like structure - *a* stupa (*Chaitya*) of sand and clay, having eight round steps and a wooden crown on its top at the village's main entrance. Every step of the *Chaitya* is decorated with coloured prayer flags. A bamboo fence is erected encircling the *Chaitya*. The villagers offer flowers, puffed rice, light candles, and incense sticks at the *Chaitya*. The *Bhante* administers *Pancha Sil* and *Asta Sil* to the villagers and prays for the welfare of the village. The next day, in the monastery, an elevated bamboo platform is constructed where a basket of sand is placed. On it, a pot of water, leaves of a mango tree, some *Dubori bon* (*Cynodon dactylon*) and a bundle of thread are kept. By touching the thread, the *Bhante* recites some holy verses. All the villagers collect a small portion of the above items, which are believed to have possessed magical powers during the ritual to protect the village and the households. The sand and water are sprinkled around the household compound to ensure safety from evil spirits. A piece of the holy thread is also placed horizontally at the main entrance of the village in order to prevent evil forces from entering the village.

The Tai-Khamyangs generally believe that the world is full of various types of malevolent spirits, and they are a cause of great concern for the people due to the kinds of suffering they can inflict on human beings. Some of them are very vindictive and harm people at the slightest pretext. There is always a danger that they may offend one spirit or the other at some point or the other. A highly fierce spirit called *Mota Khetor* is believed to be responsible for miscarriages and female sterility. It is said that the spirit kills the fetus in the womb of the mother within 2-3 months of pregnancy. In the event of such cases, curative measures involving herbal as well as magico-religious and spiritual means of treatment are provided by the traditional medicine man. The magico-religious and spiritual means of treatment include rituals performed in order to propitiate the spirit and seek relief from the misery caused (Sonowal & Baruah, 2011).

The *Khwan/Khon-Khao* worship is another vital ritual celebrated at the family level. *Khon-Khao* means the soul of the rice, represented by a female deity - *Nang Khon-Khao*. The rice soul is ceremonially propitiated by the female members of every Khamyang family in December-January after the annual harvest. The rice soul is believed to reside in the paddy's last sheaf, left in the field tied in a bundle. So, it is ceremonially brought to the family granary from the field on an auspicious date. An elderly lady of the family goes to the paddy field with a sickle and a new hand-woven *Fa-chet* (traditional Tai-Khamyang *Gamucha, a thin,* coarse cotton towel). Meanwhile, two banana plant saplings are erected near the door of the granary, and inside the granary, on a bamboo tray, powdered rice cakes and a pot of water are kept to welcome the khon of rice. The last sheaf of the paddy is carefully cut and placed on the *Fa-chaet* along with some of the scattered paddy pods collected from the field. Then, it is carried to the house by the lady on her head, and the same is kept inside the granary. Propitiation of the soul of the rice is akin to the propitiation of the Goddess of wealth. It is believed that if the soul is satisfied with the family, it enjoys a good harvest and never faces any financial crisis. The Calling of *Khwan* or *Hong Khwan* is another crucial traditional ritual observed by the Tai-Khamyangs. The *khwan* can be described as a person's 'inner-self', 'soul' or 'individual spirit'. It is believed that a person's soul (spirit) will be destabilised or even lost when he/she is in a bad situation or experiences misfortune such as having an accident or being harmed, or it may leave the body to protect itself from potentially damaging situations, either emotional or physical. Whenever the *khwan* is lost, the sufferer undergoes severe depression and becomes susceptible to diseases and unexplained morbid conditions. In such situations, the ritual of *Hong Khwan* (i.e., to call or bring back) is performed to fetch the soul of an individual from wherever it may be roaming back to the body and thus re-establish maximum health. The elderly womenfolk of the village perform it.

Ancestor (*Mae-dam*) worship is a significant pre-Buddhist sacred ritual of the Tai-Khamyangs. It is related to the idea of the soul living forever; after one's death, his/her soul would leave the body, become a god and return to heaven where the ancestors live. They believe that if the family members and close relatives observe the ritual of ancestor worship, the dead ones, particularly the parents and grandparents, come down to the earth to bless their offspring and accept their offerings. A family-level ceremony, it is ritually observed annually during *the Poi Sang-Ken festival* on the first day of the New Year to honour and offer solace to the departed souls, allowing them to attain peace in the afterlife. Early in the morning, the family members, usually led by the eldest son, perform Tang-som (post-cremation funeral ritual) by offering food items, fruits, water and flowers and lighting candles at the *Kong-mu* (a small pagoda-shaped structure) constructed in the eastern direction outside the house. All the family members pray to seek blessings from the spirits of their ancestors for a peaceful, happy and prosperous life. The ceremony is also known as the *Kong-mu Phi-han* ceremony. However, the people abandoned the ceremony's sacrificial practices - the slaughter of fowls and the use of rice wine, long back as they were followers of Buddhism. The Tai-Khamyangs believe that the house spirit (*Phi-Haun*) resides in the central post/pillar (facing the eastern direction) of their houses, which they call *Phi-Lum-Khuta*. Hence, during the *Poi Sang-Ken* festival, on the first day of the New Year, the people, with great devotion, wash the *Phi-Lum-Khuta* and pray by offering a *Fa-chaet* along with food items prepared from steam-cooked glutinous rice (*Khao-hai*), fruits, flowers, and water at the foot of the main post. Some Tai-Khamyangs, at the family level, worship Lord Indra, the god of the sky, who is called Shakra-*de* by the people (Bailong, 2021). He is considered an important deity in Buddhism, and he rules the 33 gods. *Mangkala* is another family-level ritual celebrated usually at the beginning of the Buddhist New Year. Early in the morning, a family prays to the Almighty and wishes for an *auspicious* year with plenty of good fortune, health and happiness. The *Pathek* administers *Mongolsutra* (*Prik*) verses to the family members. All the fellow villagers are invited to the ceremony.

The pre-Buddhist folk religion of the Tai-Khamyangs can be conjectured as polytheistic and animistic. The people believe in multiple *primordial* spirits and regional deities, which can be termed tutelary gods, and have continued worshipping them generation after generation, apart from the tenets of *Theravada* Buddhist philosophy. The traditional non-Buddhist beliefs and practices exist alongside the primary religion they profess. The Buddhist beliefs and practices are considered to be superior and the predominant belief system of the villagers; hence, they belong to the sacred world. The belief in spirits, on the other hand, is regarded as profane; hence, they must be kept apart from the Buddhist beliefs and practices (Namchoom & Lalhmingpuii, 2016). The syncretism of the traditional beliefs and practices with *Theravada* Buddhism forms the essence of present-day Buddhism among the Tai-Khamyangs. In the traditional rituals and ceremonies, which are not purely related to *Theravada* Buddhism, the monks generally do not participate. Singh (2013) mentioned that while performing their traditional ceremonies, the Tai people do not involve the Buddhist monks. *Chow-Mo*, the conventional priest, performs such ceremonies and rituals in the presence of the villagers. The Tai religious hymns (*Kham-Tra*), mainly from the pre-Buddhist period and recorded in old manuscripts, are chanted in a specific manner during the traditional religious ceremonies. These manuscripts are not kept in the *Vihar* but are well-preserved by the village priests in their homes.

The Notion of Identity, Existence and Cultural Plurality

Buddhism plays a significant part in shaping the identity, existence, and cultural plurality of the Tai-Khamyangs. The people are the strict followers of *Theravada* Buddhism. The Khamyangs have been Buddhists for a long time before they migrated to Northeast India from the Shan State area of northern Myanmar many centuries ago. Since then, they have never been willing to convert to any other religion. As a result, there exists no known Christians or Muslims among the Tai-Khamyangs of India. Therefore, whenever someone identifies as a Tai-Khamyang or simply from the surname itself, like Shyam, Chowlu, Thaumung and Pangyok, he/she is always supposed to be a Buddhist. Religion is invariably one of the crucial markers of the identity of the Tai-Khamyangs. All the socio-cultural activities of the people have been genuinely religious. The different festivals and holy days celebrated by the Khamyangs revolve around the principles and teachings of the Buddha. Buddhism supports the Khamyangs in sharing a great community spirit and allows harmonious living. The community celebrates all socio-cultural and religious festivals. The link between religion and identity among the Tai-Khamyangs is seen, particularly in the celebration of *Poi-Sang-Ken* - the traditional New Year/Spring festival (according to the *Theravada* Buddhist calendar and in line with the *Theravada* Buddhist world) with great devotion and in a more grandiose way instead of celebrating *Poi Pee-Mau*, which is the original New Year of the Tai people. *Poi Pee-Mau* seems to be celebrated with lesser fanfare locally in the Khamyang villages in November-December (according to the Tai calendar). Thus, the essence of celebrating *Poi Sang-Ken,* hoisting the World Buddhist flag during Buddha *Jayanti*, as well as celebrating the other Buddhist festivals, religious ceremonies and worship, not only reflects the intrinsic values of their culture and tradition but also helps to create a sense of identity, unity, the feeling of brotherhood and mutual understanding among all the members, across all works of life of the Tai-Khamyang community.

The Tai-Khamyangs (along with the other Tai Buddhist tribes of Northeast India) show a sense of fellowship with the *Theravada* Buddhist countries of Southeast Asia, particularly Myanmar and Thailand. The Tai or Shan are the largest minority population of Myanmar, whereas, in Thailand, the Thai/Tai are the dominant ethnic group in Central and Southern Thailand (Siam proper). Religion is one of the significant factors, besides the similarities in language and cultural traits, that connect the Khamyangs with the Tai people of these nations. The influence of the Burmese tradition of Theravada Buddhism and the village Buddha Vihars (both old and newly constructed ones) have a profound impact on the cultural landscape of Assam and are visible in the form of art and architecture as well as in people's daily way of living. Historically, there have been religious and spiritual contacts in the form of visits by Buddhist monks from Myanmar to the Tai-Khamyang villages in Assam. In recent years, religious contacts and cultural exchanges between the Tai-Khamyangs and the people of Myanmar and Thailand have seen a slight increase as researchers, scholars, academicians, tourists, and pilgrims from both sides have started visiting each other's places more often. Moreover, in October 2019, the Royal Thai Kathina (*Chivara Dana*) ceremony was held in the Chalapothar Buddha *Vihar* under the aegis of His Majesty the King of Thailand. It is worth mentioning that this is the first Royal Thai *Kathina* ceremony held in a Tai-Khamyang village, thus highlighting the people's shared religious and cultural traditions.

The Tai-Khamyangs, although a lesser-known *Theravada* Buddhist tribe of Assam, with its microscopic population, have maintained their ways of life, tradition and culture. They have not undergone assimilation to the extent their brethren, the Tai-Ahoms, have gone. Buddhism has been inculcating religious commitment and providing a sense of purpose among the Khamyangs. The village community funds traditionally maintain the Buddha *Vihars* of the Tai-Khamyang villages. Repairing or adding to a religious building has always been considered an act of merit among Buddhists since the good done in this life will give future benefits in the next life. The Khamyangs, therefore, seek to repair their Buddha *Vihars* and maintain them in as perfect a condition as possible. Repairing and maintaining a *Vihar* building is considered a way of keeping Buddhism alive. It is considered the duty of a good Buddhist and a contribution or act of great merit that one can make in this present life.

Animals have always been regarded in Buddhist thought as sentient beings. Earlier, sacrificing animals was practised by the Khamyangs as part of their different pre-Buddhist rituals - to show loyalty and worship and calm the supernatural beings. Since Buddhism was introduced, the people have abandoned the sacrificial part of their pre-Buddhist rituals; they do not perform any sacrifice. The concept of animal sacrifice or any other form of sacrifice was never preached or propagated by Buddha. The first of the five precepts bans the taking of life. From the beginning of Buddhism, there were regulations intended to prevent the harming of sentient beings in the animal realm for various reasons. It is relevant to note here that the Tai-Khamyangs eat both fish and meat (but abstain from eating beef), although they never kill them. They buy chopped pieces of fish and meat from the nearby markets. In Buddhism, meat is permitted if it is not deliberately slaughtered for the consumer if the consumer has not seen or heard the animal being killed. Buddhism as a religion is also a way of life, a philosophy that one follows. So, if one wants to eat meat, one can. Unlike the other indigenous Assamese ethnic groups (including the Tai-Ahoms) who have the traditional practice of preparing different types of rice beer for local consumption as well as using it in their numerous magico-religious and sacrificial rituals, the Tai-Khamyangs refrain entirely from taking/using any alcohol – including rice beer. Observant Buddhists typically avoid consuming alcohol as it violates the fifth of the five precepts, the basic Buddhist code of ethics, and can disrupt mindfulness and impede one's progress. Nonetheless, many Khamyang people drink alcohol; however, taking alcohol within the village periphery or in the public festivals/occasions organised in the village is strictly barred.

Many pluralistic ethos are observed in the Tai-Khamyang culture and society. Because Buddhism forms a crucial aspect of their identity, the people are not barred from a pluralistic attitude toward religious beliefs. The predominant opinion among the people is that many religions can be true, rather than that theirs is the one 'true religion'. The Tai-Khamyangs not only peacefully co-exist with the ethnic Assamese communities but also place strong expectations of integration on members (rather than assimilation). For example, the Khamyangs celebrate the Assamese Bihu festival with much enthusiasm. In addition, they also celebrate the festivals of Diwali and Holi, which the Hindus, Sikhs, and Jains more commonly celebrate. There are no religious restrictions on praying, meditating, or participating in a ritual performance at a Hindu temple, in an Assamese Namghar, or any other place of worship. Interestingly, Bihu and modern Assamese songs are generally played in the festivals of the Khamyangs, and the younger generation is quite proficient in them. Although open to and influenced by Hinduism and the Assamese culture, the Khamyangs have never deviated from their traditional religious beliefs and practices. Many non-Buddhist guests come to attend the various Buddhist festivals and indigenous ceremonies celebrated by the Khamyangs. All these guests are provided with excellent Tai-Khamyang hospitality. Hospitality to others is a central theme in Buddhism. The idea of hospitality prescribes that one should offer one's home, food, and other resources to the needs of others – particularly those who do not share one's nationality, culture, language, or religion. This idea carries with it a demand to respect the other in his/her differences and, thus, has been traditionally an example of cultural pluralism. The resilience and adaptability nurtured by religious pluralism among the Tai-Khamyangs have enriched their unique culture.

Some Observed Changes

Change is a continuous process; it is the unchangeable law of nature. As a part of nature, society is not an exception to this external law. With time, specific inevitable changes have occurred virtually at all levels of religious beliefs and activities. Some of these changes are modest in scope; others are radical. In this fast-paced world, with the rapid advancements of communication and other technologies and sciences and the trend towards increased religious freedoms, the Tai-Khamyang society has also undergone several changes in the sphere of religion. Owing to decades of interaction and association with the neighbouring Assamese and other Hindu caste communities, the Khamyangs, particularly the younger generation, actively take part in many Hindu festivals like Holi, Durga Puja, Diwali, Vishwakarma Puja, Saraswati Puja and Shiva-Ratri. Most notably, like any other indigenous ethnic group of Assam, the Tai-Khamyangs celebrate the three Bihus *viz*. Bohag or Rongali *Bihu*, Kati or Kongali *Bihu* and Magh or Bhogali *Bihu with full enthusiasm* - festivals uniquely Assamese and associated with agriculture, particularly rice cultivation.

Changes are also observed in the construction of the prayer hall/temple of the Buddha *Vihar*. Earlier, the Tai-Khamyangs constructed their Buddha *Vihars* using locally available bio-resources like wood, bamboo, and *Toko* leaves (*Livistona jenkinsiana* Griff.) for thatching; these were humble cottage *Vihars*. The temple was traditionally built on a raised floor (*Chang*). Later, the *Vihars* were constructed in typical Assam-type structures (sometimes with concrete walls made of brick and cement) with roofs made of GI sheet. However, in recent times, the temples and other structures of their Buddha *Vihars* have been renovated or rebuilt, adopting impressive architectural designs which resemble Burmese-style Buddhist monasteries. The temple structures display multiple ornamental roof tiers; two or three tiers are most often used. Additionally, a decorative multi-tier spire is placed on the main roof of the prayer hall. It does not serve any utilitarian purpose but marks the structure as a sacred space; this ornamental crown is also widely seen in the Buddhist temples of Burma and is known as *hti,* which translates to an umbrella (Das, 2021). The imposing *Kongmu Kham* (Golden Pagoda) of Chalapothar Shyam village *resembles the* Shwedagon Pagoda in Myanmar. Expert artisans are also brought in from Myanmar to construct the *Kyongs*. As the villages do not have a purposely built community hall, the ground floor of the newly built temples doubles up as a community hall and cultural centre for all the villagers, where they hold official meetings and organise cultural programmes.

A *Vihar* traditionally does not have a kitchen, as monks do not cook food for consumption. However, a small kitchen is found in the *Vihar* compound, and it is used mainly by the temple boys. It is used chiefly for preparing hot water and tea for guests. Regarding monastic life, it was observed that the members of the younger generation who are well educated, by and large, nowadays do not show the desired interest in entering monkhood and leading an ascetic life. Changes are also observed in the household place of worship. Earlier, the families had their place of worship in a small temple built within the household compound or in a separate room. However, nowadays, as the traditional Tai-Khamyang stilt houses (known as *Houn Haang*) are being gradually replaced by modern Assam-type concrete houses and RCC buildings, the scarcity of space has led the people to have their place of worship in a specified corner of their living room. Further, images and idols of Hindu Goddesses like Laxmi and Saraswati are considered auspicious to keep and worship at home. The Tai religious hymns/*mantras* chanted during folk religious ceremonies and used in various magico-religious rituals are gradually declining. Most knowledge holders have expired due to old age, and the younger generation cannot read and write the Tai script. Hence, it is not easy to pass on the knowledge of religious texts from one generation to the next.

Conclusion

Theravada Buddhism plays a vital role in the socio-cultural life of the Tai-Khamyangs of Assam. It is the most potent and most sustained uniting force among the people. The Tai-Khamyangs are strict followers of *Theravada* Buddhism and have kept their religious identity intact. The pre-Buddhist or extra-Buddhist animistic beliefs and practices, i.e., spirit worship as well as worship of some regional deities that have survived until the present day among the Khamyangs have suitably co-existed with the *Theravada* Buddhist beliefs and rituals and have been accepted as a part of the religion; However, they take a subsidiary position to the Buddha. Buddhism has adapted and responded to different cultures and social climates. In spite of this co-existence, the Tai-Khamyangs maintain a definite boundary between the two different religious domains in terms of practices. They have *Theravada* Buddhism at their heart and are one of the most devout Buddhist communities in this part of the world. *Theravada* Buddhism and the Tai-Khamyangs are inseparable. The socio-cultural and religious life of the Tai-Khamyangs significantly circles the Buddha *Vihar*, the precepts/virtues of the Buddha, the Buddhist monks and the monastic life. Most people follow the Five Precepts to ensure they live a morally good life, eliminate suffering, and achieve enlightenment. The celebration of the various Buddhist festivals, religious ceremonies, and worship reflects the intrinsic values of their culture and tradition. It helps to create a sense of identity, unity, brotherhood and mutual understanding among all the members of the Tai-Khamyang tribe. Evidence from the existing data implies that religion has positively helped the Tai-Khamyangs with their identity formation, existence, and cultivation of their culture's pluralistic ethos. Barring a few material changes, there seems to be no significant change in the people's religious outlook, responsibilities, beliefs and practices. In today's modernisation and worldwide development, the Tai-Khamyangs successfully preserve and follow the *Theravada* Buddhist philosophy and adapt it for continuity in an organised and institutionalised form. The present paper opens the scope for further in-depth anthropological studies on topics such as studying the pre-Buddhist or extra-Buddhist faith and spirit worship practices of the Tai-Khamyangs, among others.

Acknowledgement

The author is very much thankful to all the respondents for participating in the study and sharing their valuable information.

References

Ariyesako, Bhikkhu. (1998). *The Bhikkhus' Rules: A Guide for Lay People. The Theravada in Buddhist Monk's Rules*. Sanghaloka Forest Hermitage, Kallista, Australia. Available from: http://www.buddhanet.net/pdf_file/bhkkrule.pdf

Bailong, C. (2021). *Tai-Khamyang Buranji (Chitou Tai-Khamyang)*. Guwahati: Purbayon Publication.

Chu, V. (1968). *Thailand Today: A Visit to Modern Siam*. New York: Crowell Publishing.

Das, A. (2021). *Theravada Buddhist Monasteries of Arunachal Pradesh: A Study of Art and Visual Culture*. Available from: https://map.sahapedia.org/article/Theravada-Buddhist/10435

Davis, K. (1966). *Human Society*. New York: Macmillan Co.

Durkheim, E. (1915). *The Elementary Forms of Religious Life*. New York: Oxford University Press.

Firth, R. (1961). *Elements of Social Organization*. London: Walts and Co.

Gellner, D.N. (1990). Introduction: What is the Anthropology of Buddhism about? *Journal of the Anthropological Society of Oxford*, 21(2), 95-112.

Grierson, G.A. (1966). *Linguistic Survey of India.* Vol. II. Delhi: Motilal Banarsidas.

Harvey, G.E. (1925). History of Burma: From the Earliest Times to 10 March 1824. London: Frank Cass & Co.

Htin Aung, M. (1967). *A History of Burma*. New York & London: Cambridge University Press.

Leider, J.P. (2004). Text, Lineage and Tradition in Burma: The Struggle for Norms and Religious Legitimacy under King Bodawphaya (1782-1819). *The Journal of Burma Studies*, 9: 82–129.

Lieberman, V.B. (2003). Strange Parallels: Southeast Asia in Global Context, c. 800-1830, Vol. I: Integration on the Mainland. Cambridge: Cambridge University Press.

Ling, T. (1973). The Buddha: Buddhist Civilization in India and Ceylon. London: Temple Smith.

Majumdar, D.N. & Madan, T.N. (1996). *An Introduction to Social Anthropology*. Noida: Mayoor Paperbacks.

Mishra, N. & Sahai, S. (Ed.) (2007). *Indo-Thai Historical and Cultural Linkages*. New Delhi: Manohar Publishers.

Mong, S. K. (2004). *History and Development of the Shan Scripts*. Chiangmai: Silkworm Books.

Namchoom, V. & Lalhmingpuii, C. (2016). Theravada Buddhism and Traditional Religion in Lathao: A Tai Khampti Village in Arunachal Pradesh. *The Journal of North East Indian Cultures*, 3(1): 42-58.

Sarmah, P. (2001). Change and Continuity among the Tai-Khamyangs of Assam. Digboi: Priyam Publications.

Singh, B.K. (2013). The Tai-Khamtis: Historical and Sociological Perspective. Guwahati: EBH Publishers.

Sonowal, R. & Barua, I. (2011). Ethnomedical Practices among the Tai-Khamyangs of Assam, India. *Studies on Ethno-Medicine*, 5(1):41-50.

5

Constructing Indigenous History of Tribes, A Study of Historical Anthropology with Especial Reference to Sonowal Kachari Tribe in Assam

C. J. Sonowal

Excavating the Roots and the Nature of History

The word "History" comes from the Greek word "historía," which means knowledge gained through investigation. This makes it a structured study and documentation of human activity that includes past events and the recollection, discovery, organisation, presentation, and interpretation of these events. Historical sources like written documents, oral accounts, art, and physical artefacts, as well as ecological indicators, are utilised to gain knowledge (Arnold, 2000). However, there have been ongoing debates and discussions about what form history should take. From a scholastic and laypeople's viewpoint, history is commonly viewed as the tales of kings and rulers, their voyages, political relationships, wars, and administration. People seldom come across descriptions of ordinary folks' daily lives and reflections of their social existence in traditional history. The portrayal of specific population groups may be affected by the historians' and their sponsors' varied interests. Notably, conventional history has barely included the history of indigenous populations.

The Interplay between Anthropology and History: A Complex Relationship

Throughout their development, history and sociocultural anthropology have progressed alongside one another. During the early stages of sociocultural anthropology, historical explanations were favoured, with ethnographic materials being viewed as historical documents. However, with the advent of functionalism and structuralism, an ahistorical or antihistorical perspective was adopted, leading to the crystallisation of the following distinctions.:

➤ The time of the savage pertains to anthropology, while contemporary time belongs to sociology, and the past belongs to history.

➤ According to the terminology used by Claude Levi-Strauss, anthropology is concerned with "cold" societies without a history; historians study "hot" societies or the history recorded in writing; archaeology and ethnography deal with cultures without a writing system.

➤ Anthropologists are interested in cultural reproductions, invariants, systemic explanations, and synchrony since historians are interested in change perceived as cause-effect relationships, chronology, and diachrony (Pomian, 2006, pp. 199-202).

Historical anthropology is a domain of knowledge creation that utilises social and cultural anthropology methodologies and objectives to examine historical societies. It is a contested idea, and its interpretation varies across academia, as some consider it equivalent to cultural history, the history of mentalities, ethnohistory, microhistory, or history from below. Jean-Claude Schmitt (2008) acknowledges that the field of historical anthropology has been enriched by the critical contributions of anthropologists such as Arnold van Gennep, Clifford Geertz, Emile Durkheim, Jack Goody, Lucien Lévy-Bruhl, Marcel Mauss, and Victor Turner.

Historical anthropology has seen significant growth since its inception in the Annales school, founded by Marc Bloch and Lucien Febvre in 1929. This school introduced a groundbreaking approach to history, championed by Fernand Braudel, which shifted the focus from studying leaders to ordinary individuals and from politics, diplomacy, and wars to subjects like climate, demography, agriculture, commerce, technology, transportation, and communication.

Historical anthropology, like anthropology, has faced criticism for its perceived biases and partiality. It is often seen as an unintentional tool of domination by Europeans and Americans over non-Western societies. However, since World War II, reflexive approaches have led to more nuanced developments in the field. This has attracted Anglo-American historians to the 'historical anthropology' banner, marking a significant shift in the field's trajectory.

Historical anthropology is a captivating subfield of anthropology that delves into the complexities of human societies and cultures throughout history. It studies the evolution of cultural practices, beliefs, and values, offering a comprehensive understanding of how our past has shaped our present. By examining the influence of various historical factors, including economic, political, and social changes, historical anthropology can help us understand the roots of contemporary cultural practices and beliefs. Additionally, it sheds light on the ways in which different societies have interacted with each other, the global interconnectedness of human history, and the impact of cultural exchange on societies and cultures. Furthermore, historical anthropology can provide insight into how human societies have adapted to and coped with major historical events, such as wars, pandemics, and natural disasters.

The Genesis of Historical Anthropology

The field of historical anthropology can be traced back to Franz Boas's ideas. He believed that a comprehensive understanding of human societies required an appreciation of their historical development. Marcel Mauss, a French anthropologist, further emphasised the significance of studying the historical context of cultural practices and rituals. He argued that external factors significantly impact their evolution.

Thus, historical anthropology's essential characteristics and uniqueness differentiate it from other anthropological and historical discourses. It focuses on the temporality of people's cultural practices and beliefs rather than solely on contemporary cultures or historical events. It employs diverse multidisciplinary approaches to collecting data and includes historically marginalised groups in its study domain.

Ethnographic investigation in the field often encounters the constant transformation of historical events, including considerably recent ones, into mythical history, which becomes a model history in place of History. This transformation, known as 'ethnological eternity', poses a significant challenge for ethnographers as myths cannot be examined and questioned. When one sees ethnography as a-historical, it appears that the sociocultural processes studied by ethnologists are repeatable and reversible; therefore, in ethnological cultures, the present is not different from the past, and events are predictable; nothing here happens for the first time and once only; events are a realisation of permanent patterns (Levi-Strauss, 1966). This is one of the reasons why researchers hardly find the history of tribal and indigenous people on their own merits, as the knowledge and the epistemology of studying and presenting these societies are based on ethnographic accounts of non-locals. Thus, the tribal societies are called a-historical societies.

Anthropological studies of societies, particularly indigenous and tribal ones, suggest that these societies have a stable and systemic structure that persists over time and space. This also supports the idea that these societies are self-sufficient, self-controlled, and homogenous, making them resistant to change. Such reconstruction of societies has kept alive the myth of "peoples with a history" and the concept of "ethnological eternity." Similarly, Ludwik Stomma (1986) argues that folk-type cultures are closed cultures, determined by their isolation in space, class, and awareness, and that they transform history into myth.

Some scholars argue that historical context is crucial in understanding societal changes and events. However, others feel that a culture's historical background cannot fully explain why people participate in political movements or violent invasions. Historians have shifted their focus from leaders to the masses, and some believe that this has made history too similar to ethnology, sacrificing sociology and other exact sciences. According to Le Goff, this has led to a critical acceptance of specific theories, procedures, and topics. Hermann Bausinger, a German ethnologist, believes that folk-type cultures are complex systems that are intertwined with their historical context. These cultures are also connected to broader sociocultural, economic, and political systems. Bausinger believes that relying solely on methodological principles to interpret culturally evolving phenomena, especially those that originate from other cultures, is illogical. He also notes that these societies' social orders and arrangements may appear static and simple to outsiders, but they are subject to historical change.

The transformation of myth to history is a complex process that presents history as a series of transformations without any specific timeline. According to Sahlin, every culture has its own history, and native histories cannot be described in the same way as classical history since they are the practice of myths and the product of local discourses. The memory of the past is recorded in various forms of culture and folklore, some of which are concrete and chronological. In contrast, others focus on historiosophical content that presupposes the existence of a transcendental ultimate goal of history, which is the meaning of world history. In hierarchical societies where the ruler is considered divine, history is qualitative, not quantitative, and the ruler is both a prerequisite for the existence of a community and the foundation of the system that determines whether the community will continue or cease to exist. In such societies, no single historical knowledge exists. Rules have their dynastic traditions, genealogies, ceremonials, epics, legends, etc., while the others live apparently outside history.

The Problems and Prospect of creating Indigenous History of Tribes

Recording the history of indigenous peoples from their own perspective can be a difficult task, as history is typically organised around time. This can create a challenge in indigenous societies, where time is not always a central aspect of folk narratives. As a result, these societies are often seen as lacking in historical significance. Tribal leaders prioritise the preservation of traditions and customs over recording the accounts of rulers or chiefs, as any deviation could undermine the tribe's values. Therefore, oral traditions play a prominent and enduring role in these societies, with actions remaining significant even if the timing is less critical. The main challenge in documenting history through these narratives is to transform timeless, horizontal data into specific, vertical accounts that reflect the chronology of events.

The mainstream historical accounts worldwide often overlook the history of indigenous communities. The term "tribe" was coined by colonial ethnographers and has been a topic of debate since then. However, the unique socio-cultural characteristics of these communities cannot be denied. Some people assume that tribal societies are isolated and separate from others, but they have always interacted with non-tribal cultures. In fact, there have been many instances of give-and-take relationships between tribes and non-tribal societies. Some tribal communities even established kingdoms and were identified as Kshatriyas, separating themselves from their fellow people and society. The geographical and geophysical situation of these communities compelled them to keep a relative distance from others and live a distinct cultural and economic life with political autonomy. This may be why tribal communities in the plains, who share similar economic pursuits, have embedded socio-cultural components of non-tribal societies to a great extent. However, the history of tribes is often viewed through the lens of others, not the tribes themselves. Furthermore, the only way to learn about tribes is through the literary domain, which the elite has dominated. As a result, the history of tribes that are known today differs from what they believe it to be. In recent years, tribal or folk narratives have become a powerful source of writing tribal history, encompassing their culture, past, and endless encounters with their surroundings.

The task of documenting the histories of Adivasi or tribal communities is a challenging one due to their lack of representation in modern state archives. These communities are usually only mentioned in state records as objects of counter-insurgency and policy, and it is rare to find accounts of them in critical interpretations of texts, particularly religious ones. Unlike the history of caste and untouchability, which can be traced through religious traditions, Adivasis and tribes cannot claim alternative archives and histories of their own. Neither literature nor religion is available at a similar scale for these communities. However, there are conventional ethnographic accounts of Adivasis and tribes. In recent decades, self-reflexive forms of fieldwork and anthropological writing have improved our knowledge of their lives and histories. Nevertheless, these accounts are still insufficient for writing the history of tribes in their own right.

When studying tribes as a historical entity, scholars must consider the issue that arises due to the modern origin of the term "tribe". The term originated from imperial governmental technologies, and in colonial records, tribes were defined as people who lived in hills, forests, and frontiers and were socially and materially segregated from "society". In this context, "society" refers to entities with evolved religions, such as Hinduism and Islam, as well as complex stratifications like class and caste. In contrast to the characteristics of "society", tribes were portrayed as non-monetized, egalitarian, and primordial communities in a romanticised image from the late eighteenth century onwards.

India's hill and forest communities were not stateless or outside of history, nor were they entirely non-hierarchical and egalitarian, as some argue. Instead, they were actively involved in matters such as kingship, land and forest politics, tribute relationships with other groups, specialised occupations, and even commerce and warfare. Indian society was complex, consisting of diverse ethnic, linguistic, sectarian, and territorial communities. In the 20th century, Dalits expressed their democratic aspirations through questions of representation, while Adivasis focused on issues of autonomy. Despite extensive research on representation, there has been little exploration of autonomy's meaning in democratic theory.

Dr B.R. Ambedkar had a different approach to defining the idea of minorities in India's federal democracy. He believed that the Dalit minority should be defined based on social marginalisation rather than religious, cultural or national distinctions. According to him, tribes did not have enough representation in the Indian population to stand as a political constituency on their own. Ambedkar believed that Hinduism was caste-ridden, and the concept of purity and pollution ruled it. As a result, Hindus had failed to civilise the tribes of India. The tribes were considered outcasts and polluting, leading to their exclusion from mainstream society. This exclusion, according to Ambedkar, was justified as the tribes remained "savage" and irrational, often living a life of criminality. Therefore, Ambedkar believed that the tribes could be excluded from current deliberations about a future constitution.

According to scholars, tribal societies and their way of life are closely connected to their ecological surroundings. These societies usually practice a combination of individual ownership, communal property, and village rights and often inhabit forested and hilly areas instead of cleared plains. During the colonial era, these communities were deemed incompatible with modern property and productivity systems. Consequently, colonial rulers attempted to "civilise" tribes by settling them and transforming them into productive peasants. However, many tribes claimed their lands and forests based on "unverifiable" and "irrational" grounds, such as being the first settlers and clearers of the land or considering it the home of their gods and ancestors.

Understanding the Adivasi and tribal movements for autonomy requires delving into the intertwined histories of land rights, ecological politics, and territorial autonomy. However, establishing autonomous zones within the nation and its economy might not be feasible, given the weak grounds for the notion of homeland and sovereign territoriality (Ghosh & Sengupta, 1982). The concept of land needs to be reimagined through two perspectives: ecology, including the forest, field, minerals, water, and animals, and specific modes of habitation and relation to such land, as evidenced by Adivasi histories. These modes of habitation and relation involve political, cultural, symbolic, and spiritual investments made by diverse peoples. By viewing land as both territory and ecology, one can understand that so-called tribal society and agrarian peasant society worked in indispensable interaction with each other, as Sumit Guha suggests. During colonial "modern" times, agricultural and forest land became labelled as modern and primitive, civilised and wild, respectively (Skaria, 1997).

Historians who specialise in tribal history face a challenge when writing about tribal history. This is because the social category of tribes did not exist in the past in the way that it is currently perceived. To tackle this issue, these historians have developed two strategies. The first strategy involves arguing that the concept of tribes is not an ancient or primitive phenomenon but rather a modern one. They assert that tribes were portrayed as "primitive" in order to create a social context against which other societies could be viewed as "modern". Therefore, the term "primitive" does not refer to an actual historical past but rather a logical one. In this way, "primitive" does not mean "before modern" but instead establishes the existence of an opposite kind of society, which is "modern". However, this view tends to diminish the historical significance of tribal societies.

Indigenous historians seek to uncover folk narratives that depict a distinct type of past-one that differs from textual documents and archaeological sites. To recreate the narratives of tribal pasts in the tribal subject's voice, historians have adopted an alternative approach to studying memory and myth, combining it with ethnological fieldwork in contemporary society. This allows them to utilise their narratives alongside the ancestor's stories, tribal lore, and field conversations.

While "caste" was a construct of the colonial era, rewriting Indian history from a Dalit perspective was possible because of terms such as varna and jati and subjects such as the shudra and the antyaja, which were commonly mentioned in ancient and medieval texts, enabling a long history of caste in India. However, for modern tribal categories, no analogous figure or term existed in tradition. Therefore, it is impossible to conceive of a long history of tribes in such cases. The tribe or the Adivasi, therefore, remained a presentist figure in both political and academic discourse, attributed to memory but with no history.

Chatterjee argues that a deep history of people currently known as tribes and Adivasis is indeed possible. However, such history can only be written if scholars first abandon the modern colonial categories of tribe and aborigine. One must approach this history as the "history of territory" inhabited by various communities engaged in complex interactions, some of which were later isolated and reconstructed as tribes. In other words, Chatterjee demonstrates that there is indeed a long history of peoples now known as tribes, but that history is not solely a history of tribes. It is the history of alternative geographies in which people referred to as tribes figure centrally, not as tribes, but as part of a complex political configuration of diverse social and ethnic groups.

Additionally, the Adivasi community has faced challenges in developing a robust political theology or a vibrant poetic-mythic tradition that could serve as a powerful counter to dominant world religions like Hinduism and Christianity. In contrast, similar traditions can be found among the Dalits and Australian Aborigines. Despite the fact that Adivasi culture predates both of these religions, their limitations have left the Adivasi people caught in the middle of a religious tug-of-war between these global belief systems. As a result, the Adivasi community is often viewed as passive, lacking a theological foundation and engaging only in discrete forms of worship and celebration.

The Distortion and Falsification of Social Reality of Tribes

The Adivasi community lacks a strong political theology or a rich poetic-mythic tradition that could serve as a counter to dominant religions like Hinduism or Christianity. This is in contrast to the Dalits and Australian Aborigines who have such traditions. Despite the fact that Adivasi culture predates both Hinduism and Christianity, these limitations have resulted in the Adivasi people being caught in the middle of a religious tug-of-war between these global belief systems. As a result, the Adivasi community is often seen as passive, lacking a theological religion, and only engaging in discrete forms of worship and celebration.

One can observe a similar trend of Hinduisation in the history of the Ahom and Koch Kings. In academic articles, this author has discussed the distorted history of locals in detail. This distortion is not limited to people only, as people also see the Hinduisation of geographical entities like rivers, water bodies, hills, and forests. For example, the creation story of Brahmaputra has been Hinduised, and it is considered a less pure and sacred river. It is important to note that all our kings, chiefs, and natural bodies have been given a lower status than mainland Indian kings and natural bodies in terms of blood purity and legend of origin. The pristine Ahom predecessors, Khun Lung and Khun Lai, were portrayed as the sons of Lord Indra (pure blood) and Sama (an impure blood woman on earth). The Koch dynasty is said to have originated from the offspring of Lord Siva (pure blood) and a local woman (wife of Haria Mech, who was of impure blood as she was a member of a local tribe). Even Narakasura was born to Lord Vishnu (the supreme god) with the Goddess Earth while she was menstruating (thereby considered impure).

It is worth noting that tribal oral tradition, which includes folksongs, proverbs, and mythological tales, has been influenced by both non-local and Hindu elements. This makes it difficult to differentiate between local and exotic aspects and assert what remains as our authentic historical heritage. The impact of distorted history has already taken root in tribal collective consciousness, shaping their perception and narratives of the past and potentially hindering our ability to explore the genuine components of our folk history. Thus, placing indigenous historians in the context of folk traditions presents a formidable challenge.

Emotional Aspects While Dealing with Indigenous Tribal History

The connection between emotion and historical writing has long been a powerful force, shaping the very content of history itself. At times, some people seek to be portrayed in a way that differs from their true identity, whether it be their affiliation with a particular group or their territorial ties to loved ones. Additionally, there is a concerning tendency to view the works of foreign writers as the gold standard. However, in rigorous, scientific, historical endeavours, emotions must be kept at bay.

Writing Indigenous Tribal History is a Global Movement

Over the years, there has been a concerted effort to preserve the unique cultures of indigenous and folk communities. Mudrooroo Narrogin (1990) provided a critical analysis of "Aboriginality" in Australia using postmodern reasoning, examining the complexities of indigenous identity. Various writers, such as Kevin Gilbert (1988), Justine Saunders (1989), Jack Davis et al. (1990), Archie Weller (1986), and Eric Willmot's Pemulwuy (1987), have boldly proclaimed that Aboriginal literature reflects the experiences of a threatened minority and serves as a means of preserving their culture. However, post-colonial Aboriginal historians, such as Gay Raines (1991) and Nelson (1990), have highlighted the challenges they face in navigating their past through colonialist historical narratives and striving to salvage their histories from distortions and denigrations to make them relevant to their people. Bethwell A. Ogot (2009) has noted that the Western notion of linear history does not apply to the Aboriginal idea of Dreaming, which exists outside of time. Similarly, African folk history writers have encountered similar challenges, with David William Cohen (1985) pointing out that external voices heavily influence the representation of Africa's past and present, raising concerns about Africans' ability to shape their history in the face of external forces.

In his book, Mudimbe (1994) argues that the way Africa is typically portrayed in media is more revealing about the people doing the portraying than it is about Africa itself. He suggests that the portrayal of Africa is often a reflection of the biases, preconceptions, and prejudices of those who create and disseminate such representations. Similarly, Levy-Bruhl (1923) argued that primitive societies have irrational intellectual content and behaviour. This idea has been widely criticised and questioned, as it fails to acknowledge the complex and sophisticated cultural systems of so-called "primitive" societies.

Donald L. Fixico (2009) contends that writing about the history of American Indians requires comprehensive knowledge of Indian culture and thought, an idea known as "writing from home." This approach emphasises the importance of being connected to the community and culture being written about to understand and represent it accurately and authentically. Calvin Martin (1992) explains that American Indian mythic thinking is distinct from other forms of perception and experience. He argues that myths are not merely fanciful stories but rather embody deep cultural and spiritual meanings that are often overlooked by those who view them from outside the culture.

Finally, Dee Brown (1970) encourages readers to consider the value of the American Indian perspective, particularly in understanding the complex history of relations between Indians and non-Indians in the United States. He argues that the Indian perspective can provide unique insights and perspectives that are often missing from mainstream historical accounts.

The Stand of Indian Initiatives

The history of tribal groups and Adivasi in India is a subject that poses a significant challenge for historians due to their invisibility in modern state archives. This is despite the fact that these groups were actively involved in kingship, land and forest policies, and tributary relationships with other social groups. Scholars who have taken up this subject, such as Banerjee, Guha, Davis, Skaria, Chatterjee, and Choksi, have delved into the intricacies of these relationships and the complexity of social divisions beyond the caste-tribe dichotomy.

Moreover, the tribes in India have been associated with world religions like Hinduism and Christianity, which have caused them to lose their original belief systems. However, classic Hinduism and Christianity have also incorporated folk traditions, which have resulted in regional variations that add to the complexity of writing tribal history in the present. Thus, the study of tribal history requires a nuanced understanding of the multiple factors that have influenced the development and changes in the social, cultural, and religious practices of these groups over time.

Contextualising the Temporal and Spatial Domains of Sonowal Kacharis

The Sonowal Kacharis are a tribe located in the Brahmaputra valley of Assam, India. With a population of 253,344, they are the fourth-largest tribal group in Assam. They are believed to be the earliest known inhabitants of the region, with no history of migration and share Mongoloid racial characteristics, suggesting an East Asian origin. Along with other Kachari groups and the Bodos, the Sonowal Kacharis contribute to a total tribal population of nearly three million in the state. The Sonowal Kacharis lack a hierarchical political system, and scholars believe they remained a village-based peasantry while being subjects of the Ahom kings from the 13th to early 19th century.

The Sonowal Kacharis have experienced significant changes in their social and cultural traditions, leading to the loss of their language and the acceptance of Vaishnava traditions. However, they have not entirely abandoned their traditional beliefs and practices. The introduction of the Vaishnavite tradition brought new religious and social practices that were unfamiliar to the Sonowal Kacharis, leading to the loss of their primary deity, "Baitho," and religious mediator, "*Gojai*." Some individuals took pride in the mythical connection between the Kshatriyas of mainland Indian Epics, such as the Mahabharata, and their people. However, some Sonowal Kacharis are now revisiting their past and present through their own stories and narratives, recognising that their traditional social reality has been distorted.

Writing a tribal history can be a challenging task, mainly due to the limited availability of artefacts. In the context of the Sonowal Kacharis, several research questions need to be addressed to produce a comprehensive tribal history. These include exploring how the myths and cosmogonies of Sonowal Kacharis depict their origin, migration, and existence in space and time. It is also essential to determine to what extent these mythological stories can be related to physical entities of the Sonowal Kachari physical domains such as land, forest, hills, and other natural bodies.

Furthermore, it is necessary to investigate whether the oral traditions of Sonowal Kacharis exhibit their social, cultural, economic, and political life and their relations with other neighbouring societies. Available narratives and written documents of surrounding populations can be used as artefacts to establish relationships with them in the historical past. Various kinds of administrative records can also be used to gain insights into the project. Google Earth can be employed to record the population growth, migration, and settlement of Sonowal Kacharis with the help of census records, GIS, and Geopolitical transitions.

Anthropometric data such as inter-ethnic genetic similarity and the difference between neighbouring populations can be used to gather information. Archaeological evidence, art forms, and material culture can be analysed to establish the ethnohistory and cultural affinity of the Sonowal Kacharis. It is essential to separate stories already infused by the so-called others relating to the Kachari tribes, in general, and the Sonowal Kacharis, in particular. Finally, it is crucial to draw a boundary between "us" and "others" from the available and dominant versions and perceptions while analysing the data.

Availability and Authenticity of and Access to Historical Artifacts of Sonowal Kacharis

It is truly inspiring to see the dedication of indigenous writers from the Sonowal Kachari Society who have taken the initiative to create written works on a variety of issues that affect their community. In the past, some writers and activists even conducted field-based inquiries to gather information. The Sonowal Kachari Autonomous Council has also contributed to the promotion of such writing. Most of these publications delve into the social and cultural aspects of the Sonowal Kacharis, covering topics such as *Haidang Geet, Baitho Puja*, folk songs like *Bihu* and *Huchari*, and various rites, rituals, and ceremonies. However, there is limited information available on the historical accounts of the Sonowal Kacharis. Only a couple of books provide such accounts, which are primarily based on secondary evidence from the Ahom Chronicles. It is worth noting that the migration history, settlements, and historical events unique to the Sonowal Kacharis share many similarities with neighbouring communities like the Deori, Chutiya, Moran, and Ahoms.

It has been noted that the Sonowal Kachari tribe is mentioned only minimally in the current districts of Dibrugarh and Tinsukia despite nearly half of the tribe's population residing there. According to the tribe's folktales and mythical narratives, the Sadiya region was home to Kachari settlements in prehistoric and historic times. The available explanations and narratives suggest that the Chutiya kings ruled Sadiya until 1523 AD and that the Deori tribe also has several memories indicating their presence in Sadiya during the same period. During this time, Sonowal Kacharis lamented in their folksongs about the lost land of Sadiya at the behest of Sadia Khowa Gohain. These overlapping accounts render the past historical accounts of Sonowal Kacharis uncertain and ambiguous. It remains unclear why Sonowal Kacharis do not share a spatial linkage or a contagious territorial existence with other Kachari groups in the region if they are the same population as Dimasa Kacharis.

The *Haidang geet*, a famous folksong of Sonowal Kacharis, mentions Lord Siva and Parvati several times. However, it is uncommon for Siva to be the primary god among the tribes of Assam. Although Siva's presence is widespread among India's indigenous populations, many of these groups may not be recognised as tribes. The Nataraja form of Lord Siva was created in South India, and the story of Boli Raja is particularly significant in Kerala. People celebrate Onam as their national and New Year's Day, believing that Raja Boli visits the earth on that day from Patal Lok. Lord Siva is often considered the god of non-Aryans, the indigenous people. Therefore, it is vital to investigate how the concept of Lord Siva became prevalent among Sonowal Kacharis and how people associated Baitho with Lord Siva. Researchers also need to consider what sources they have to support or clarify our claims and knowledge of these indigenous groups.

It is important to address the issue of religious conversion and transition among Sonowal Kacharis. Sonowal Kachari's inclination towards Vaishnavism has significantly damaged their ethnohistorical components over the years. However, the story and history of their submission to Vaishnavism are mythical and unproven. It is doubtful that any of their enthusiastic writers have ever attempted to interact with the Aoniati Satra or searched in the *Guru Charit Puthis* about the record of Sonowal Kachari's conversion to Vaishnavism.

The intrusion of Rama, Srikrishna, Rukmini, Usha, Lakshmi, and Parvati in their folk narratives, folksongs, proverbs, and beliefs has dramatically affected the historicity of the Sonowal Kacharis. There is also a lot of contention about the term Kirata for Sonowal Kacharis and Kirata Sanskriti for Sonowal Kachari cultural practices. This is because there is disagreement about the location of the territory called Pragjyotishpura, as the descriptions made in Ramayana and Mahabharata about the Pragjyotishpura do not fit with the location of Assam or the northeast.

Ptolemy and the 7th-century Chinese Buddhist monk Xuanzang, or Hiuen Tsang, did not describe Assam as Kamrupa. Therefore, the existence of Kirata as a similar population mentioned in the epic Mahabharata and some Puranas may not be the same population that is known to people now as the Kacharis and other tribes. Thus, it is essential to delve deeper into these issues to discover their origin and establishment. When writing authentic and indigenous history, one cannot unquestioningly believe or include narratives as authentic since those were written in the past and written by some elites.

The queries and discussions above are critical for those who wish to write an authentic and scientific history of any tribe or indigenous population, including Sonowal Kacharis. The researchers in this domain are fortunate enough to have the reconstructed social histories (*Buranji*) of local ethnic groups such as the *Chutiya Jatir Buranji*, *Moran Janagusthir Buranji*, and hosts of writings on Deori culture, origin, and establishment. Furthermore, researchers may have easier access to critical discussions on Ahom's relation with other populations they ruled or had relations with. Several other resources mentioned above will immensely help researchers write tribal national and indigenous history, which is devoid of the dominance of elites of vested interests and imaginations.

References

Ambedkar BR. (1947). 'States and Minorities, 1947', Dr Babasaheb Ambedkar Writings and Speeches (BAWS), vol. 1, pp. 381–449.

Arthur, K. (1985). Fiction and Rewriting of History. *Westerly*, 1, pp. 55

Banerjee Prathama. (2016). Writing the Adivasi: Some historiographical notes. *The Indian Economic and Social History Review*, p. 53, 1: pp. 1–23.

Bethwell A. Ogot. (2009). Rereading the History and Historiography of Epistemic Domination and Resistance in Africa. *African Studies Review*, 52(1): 1–22.

Calvin Martin. (1992). In the Spirit of the Earth: Rethinking History and Time, Baltimore, MD: Johns Hopkins University.

Choksi Nishant. (2014). 'Scripting Autonomy: Script, Code, and Performance among Santali Speakers in Eastern India', unpublished thesis, University of Michigan.

Cohen, D. W. (1985). Making Social History from Pirn's Doorway. In Oliver Zunz (ed.), *Reliving the Past: The Worlds of Social History*, Chapel Hill: The University of North Carolina Press.

Dark, E. (1990). The Timeless Land. Sydney: Collins, Angus & Robertson.

Dee Brown. (1970). Bury My Heart at Wounded Knee: An Indian History American West. New York: Holt, Rinehart.

Donald L. Fixico. (2009). American Indian History and Writing from Home: Constructing an Indian Perspective. *American Indian Quarterly*, 33(4): 553–560.

Elizabeth A. Ten Dyke, 'Anthropology, Historical' in Encyclopaedia of Historians and Historical Writing, ed. by Kelly Boyd (Chicago: Fitzroy Dearborn, 1999), pp. 37--40 (p. 38).

Evans-Pritchard. (1937). *Witchcraft, Oracles, and Magic among the Azande*. Oxford: Clarendon Press. Fage, J. D. 1981.

Gay Raines. (1991). Aboriginal Writing as a Reassertion of Cultural Identity. *Antipodes*, 5(2): 01-106.

Gilbert, K. (1977). *Living Black: Blacks Talk to Kevin Gilbert*. Melbourne: Penguin Australia.

Guha, S. (2013). Beyond Caste: Identity and Power in South Asia, Past and Present, Leiden, 2013.

Hountondji, Paulin. (1983). African Philosophy: Myth and Reality. Translated by Henri Evans with Jonathan Ree. Bloomington: Indiana University Press

Indrani Chatterjee. (2013). Forgotten Friends: Monks, Marriages, and Memories of Northeast India. New Delhi: Oxford University Press.

Jean-Claude Schmitt (2008). *"Anthropologie historique"*. Bulletin du Centre d'Études Médiévales d'Auxerre (Hors-série n° 2). Cem.revues.org. doi:10.4000/cem.8862. Retrieved 2015-08-17.

Lévi-Strauss, Claude. (1966). *The Savage Mind*. Chicago, Illinois: University of Chicago Press. p. 219. ISBN 0-226-47484-4. OCLC 491441

Levy-Bruhl, L. (1923). *Primitive Mentality*. Boston: Beacon Press.

Mudimbe, V. Y (1994). *The Idea of Africa*. Bloomington: Indiana University Press.

Narogin, M. (1990). Writing From the Fringe: A Study of Modern Aboriginal Literature. Melbourne: Hyland House.

Pomian, K. (2006). *Historia*. Nauka wobec pamieci [Sur l'histoire]. Transl. by H. Abramowicz. Lublin: Wydawnictwo Uniwersytetu Marii Curie-Sklodowskie.

Saunders, J. (1989). *Plays From Black Australia*. Sydney: Currency.

Shoemaker, Adam. (1990). *Black Words, White Page*. St. Lucia: U of Queensland P.

Skaria, A. (1997). Shades of Wildness Tribe, Caste, and Gender in Western India. *Journal of Asian Studies*, Vol. 56 (3), 1997, pp. 726–45.

Sonowal CJ, (2020). *Social Exclusion: A Discourse on Tribal Societies in Assam*. Akansha Publishing House, New Delhi.

Sonowal CJ. (2008). Indian Tribes and Issue of Social Inclusion and Exclusion. *Studies of Tribes and Tribals*. 6:123-34

Sonowal CJ. (2010). Quest for Identity, Autonomy and Development: The contemporary trends of Ethnic and Tribal Assertion in Assam (Vol. 2). Akansha Publishing House, New Delhi.

Sonowal CJ. (2011). The democracy of exclusion of tribal India through inclusive policies. *The Eastern Anthropologist*, 64:383-399.

Sonowal CJ. (2014). Religion and Ethnic Reconstruction among the Tribes of Northeast India. Akansha Publishing House, New Delhi.

Sonowal CJ. (2017). History of Religion of the Indigenous population of Brahmaputra Valley. In, S Sengupta (ed). Gyan Publishing House, New Delhi.

Sonowal CJ. (2021). Mythology, Cultural Expansionism and Nationbuilding in India: An Anthropological Interpretation. In, NK Gogoi and M Sharma (Ed.). *India's North-East, Contribution of Anthropology*. Dibrugarh University.

Sonowal CJ. (2022a). The Making of the Lesser Hindus through Mythology in Assam'. *Pragyajyoti*, 2019-2020: 4-12.

Sonowal CJ. (2022b). Investigating the Process of Social Exclusion and Inclusive Policies: A Research Study Guideline with Special Reference to Tribes of India'. In, M. Talukdar and A Baruah (Ed.). *Current Research Trend: A Multidisciplinary Bouquet*, Duliajan College, Dibrugarh.

Willmot, E. (1987). Pemulwuy: *The Rainbow Warrior*. McMahon's Point, NSW: Weldon's.

6

Anthropological Study of Ethnic Food A Study Among the Dimasa Kacharis of Assam

Kurangana Hazarika
Anshuman Hazarika

Introduction

Food is a prerequisite for attaining good health and maintaining adequate growth and body equilibrium (ICMR, 1997). The choice of food is deeply related to an individual's affordability and access to food and is mainly influenced by the cultural practices of his living environment (Palta, 2001). However, natural resources, climate, and other aspects of the geographical and physical environment also significantly impact food habits. However, again, the eating habits of a specific community rely not only on the resources present in that particular habitat but also on how and to what extent those resources are used. The way they use food depends on their culture, too.

Food is a vital part of culture, reflecting a region's history and identity and passed down through traditions and rituals. It unites communities during gatherings and celebrations, maintaining unique culinary heritages and sparking fusion cuisines as cultures interact. Culture is an inclusive and powerful foundation that affects all food choices. People classify the foods in the same ways that exist in their culture, subculture, and ethnic groups to select the food that is favourite and acceptable for them. (Haghighian Roudsari et al., 2019). Food often carries deep symbolism, and even within a single culture, regional variations create diversity. Ethnic food fosters cultural exchange, community bonds, and social transformation by celebrating diverse cuisines, promoting understanding, and offering economic and educational opportunities, contributing to a more inclusive society. Food has recently been used in various fields, such as public relations and public diplomacy. Studies assert that food has the potential to change the public perception of a nation's image. (Karaosmanoğlu, 2020). It has historically facilitated cultural exchange and serves as a form of artistic expression. Food preserves and expresses cultural heritage, fosters social bonds, and plays a significant role in defining cultural identity, making it a dynamic aspect of human society. Food has always been much more than a source of body nourishment. It plays a significant role in the social lives of human groups. Social systems and culture are major determinants of what we eat. The choice of food is deeply related to the lifestyle of an individual and the place in which he is living (Rao et al., 2006).

The anthropology of food as a distinct subfield within anthropology began to gain recognition and prominence in the mid-20th century. While the study of food and culinary practices has always been a part of anthropological research, it was in the mid-20th century that it began to be more systematically and explicitly studied as a focused area of research. For anthropologists, food and foodways offer uniquely powerful windows to understand individual cultures and societies, mainly when they are situated in the context of global and historical flows and connections. The ethnographic methods of participant observation are ideally suited to grasping the material processes and the symbolic meanings surrounding the production, distribution, and consumption of foods (Tierney et al., 2012). While anthropologists have extensively examined the ritual and symbolic importance of food, there is a gap in understanding how the biological properties of specific foods influence their role in regulating human behaviour, promoting health, and supporting religious worship. Spiritual practices are closely tied to the physical act of consuming food, and the dietary preferences of followers not only reflect their faith but also serve as guidelines for their spiritual well-being (Waldstein, 2018).

In particular, the food of Assam, as of any other place, is primarily influenced by its climate, soil, and vegetation. This northeastern state of India is mainly agrarian. Rice is the staple diet, and the ordinary people of Assam eat it daily. The traditional foods of the tribal people are straightforward, and they use these in traditions and festivals (Bareh, 2001). These traditional foods are not only rich in nutrients but are also used to cure several diseases. (Singh and Sureja, 2006). Diversity in traditions and cultures among different communities in Assam has resulted in many food productions. These are slowly gaining recognition in the urban world for their immense benefits.

It is often stated that food habits seldom or never change and are difficult to change (Mishra et al., 2002). However, with time and the acculturation process, tribes naturally tend to replace their food origins, traditional eating patterns, and food elements. The present study searches for the original and traditional food habits and customs of the Dimasa-Kacharis of Assam. It also aims to underscore the importance of preserving cultural food heritage and understanding how these practices evolve.

The People

The Dimasa inhabit Assam and Nagaland states in Northeastern India. Dimasa mythology says they are the children or descendants of a big river, meaning the Brahmaputra. 'Di' means water, 'Ma' means big, and 'Sa' means children. Dimasa Kachari is mainly found in the present-day Dima Hasao District (Old name "North Cachar Hills" or "N. C. Hills") of Assam. They also have a sizable population in Cachar, Karbi Anglong, Nowgong (Hojai, Hailakandi, and Karimganj districts of the Assam State and also Dimapur and Jiribam regions of Nagaland and Manipur states, respectively. The Komorakata Village is about 7 km west of Hojai Railway station in Hojai district, Assam. It is connected through National Highway 19.

Objectives of the Present Study

The prime objective of the study is to understand the food habits and customs of Dimasa Kacharis, who resides in Komorakata village, Hojai district of Assam. The study also attempts to highlight the deep connection between the food, culture, and tradition of the tribe, shedding light on various aspects of their dietary practices.

Methodology

The study was conducted in Komorakata village of Hojai district, Assam. The village was selected based on a larger homogenous Dimasa population in the Hojai district. A total of 50 households were randomly selected for data collection. Structured and unstructured interview techniques were used to gather information from the respondents to accomplish the present study. Persons with traditional knowledge and who are currently practising the production of ethnic foods were interviewed. A few case studies were recorded of preparing various traditional dishes. Information about food habits included a daily meal pattern, general food habits, method of cooking food, food habits in different physiological conditions, alcoholic practices, food customs on different occasions, information on socially prestigious and restricted foods, etc. The secondary sources were collected from available books, journals, and electronic and non-electronic sources.

Food Habit Of The Dimasa Tribe

Daily Food

The people of Komorakata village mainly depend on rice as the main staple diet. They eat rice as their primary daily food, with other subsidiary diets: vegetables, fish, egg, dal, and potato. Rice made from *Bara* paddy is a delicacy for the Dimasas. They produce a kind of alkali by burning the trunk of the plantains. They use this alkali in curries of different types. Alkali curry with dried fish is a favourite delicacy for the people of Komorakata village. Vegetables grown in the kitchen garden, tender vegetables, and other eatables, including roots procured from the neighbouring forest and hills, supplement their staple diet. Rice with vegetable curry, chillies, dried fish, and occasionally with meat are generally taken. Fish for domestic consumption is caught in rivers, streams, and ponds. Dried fish is brought chiefly from the local weekly market.

The favourite beverage of the Dimasas is rice beer called the *Judima*. The Dimasa women make rice beer at home with locally available rice and other ingredients. Notably, Dimasas are not habitual drinkers. During festivals, feasts, weddings, and death ceremonies, rice beer is used.

The Dimasa people of Kumorakata village also have bamboo shoots called *Miya*. A kind of rice powder called *Hon* is also eaten. The curry of *Hon* is called *Hon Samlai*. These people eat three main dishes with rice: Alkali or khar dishes and *Mudru* or boiled vegetable dishes. They also eat a kind of cocoon called *Endi* cocoon, called *Lodama*, in the Dimasa language.

Religious Food

In times of religious practices, the villagers have slightly different kinds of foods. The Dimasa people stay without food on many religious occasions in the name of gods and goddesses. On the day of "Shiva Ratri", at the end of the day, after performing "*Shiva puja*", they have "*Mah Prasad* " *and khisari*, which contain rice, dal, and vegetables.

They sacrifice animals like goats, ducks, pigeons, and hens on certain occasions. In the name of God, a little rice beer is offered and sacrificed, and the remaining portion is cooked with *hon* or rice powder and made as a curry without adding turmeric and other spices. Ripe bananas are distributed with '*mah prasad*'. Their traditional *Judima* is a must with any food, even on religious occasions.

Food on Festive Occasions

In this Dimasa village, the villagers celebrate various festivals from time to time. So, they have various foods for different festive occasions. On special festive occasions, the villagers prepare exceptional food. Some of their food habits according to particular festive occasions are mentioned below-

    i.   As an agricultural festival, the Dimasa people of Komorakata village celebrate the Bihu festival. Hono is served along with other traditional dishes. It is a fatty food made by grinding roasted parboiled rice. It is mainly eaten with milk and sugar. Another thing they eat is *Honpher*. It is called *pitha*, a rice cake or pancake, a thin flat cake prepared on a frying pan. They eat fried rice, which is called *piao*. It is eaten with tea. Dimasas also eats a special rice called Makham Mabreng during the Bihu festival.

ii. In worship, a kind of fast food made from powdered rice is eaten with silkworms. They eat fried silkworms. As a drink, they have their traditional drink, '*Judima*', which is made from rice powder called *Hamartoma*.

iii. In marriage ceremonies, the Dimasa people prepare various foods. On the day of marriage, the bride and the groom are not allowed rice or a heavy diet. They can have only light food like milk, tea, and curd. They can have food after performing the social rites. On the other hand, at the feasts, both vegetarian and non-vegetarian foods are arranged. *Judima* or rice beer must be in the diet. They also offered rice and beer to their souls and goddesses on that day. They offer intoxicants like tobacco and Biri to the villages. All these arrangements are made according to the ability of the family. Some traditional Dimasa foods arranged in the marriage ceremony are - *Jhoudi, Jukaop* and *Juharo*.

iv. In case of the death of a person, in the Dimasa group of people, the household performs the funeral ceremony. Members of the dead one's descent group are considered impure and observe some customs within them. The people of the household and relatives eat only boiled food for 12 days from the day of death. They can only have fruits in the daytime. When stars come out, only they can have other food. On the 13th day, the household organises a feast. The villagers came and joined the feast. On that day, they started to have non-vegetarian food. The duck's meat is cooked for the elders, and mutton is for other villagers. Fish is also cooked. A kind of new leaf is cooked named *Imprimido*. A sour rice powder named Sawkha Hon is cooked. All the villagers eat rice powder and cane fibre dishes to prevent witchcraft from spreading in the community. *Joo* or *Judima* is a must, along with all the traditional dishes in the Dimasa community of Komorakata village. Pork is strictly prohibited in such social ceremonies.

Medicinal substances

The villagers of Komorakata village use medicinal leaves to cure diseases. Dimasa people used tamarind to cure colds and flu. They boil some raw tamarind and drink the boiled water to get relief. They boil red ants and drink that water to cure pox. They use the roots of a grass named *Doukhajyao khelong* to cure toothache. Dimasa people use onion or *barbule* in case of burn injury. Dimasa people use the oil from hornbills when bones break. Red grass, Nikhil, and gamboges are eaten to cure dysentery. The task of the elephant is grinding and massaging if someone gets injured. The Leaves of Tulsi are used to cure cough. They use ' *Bhedai lata*', pudina, and Haldi for stomach pain.

Restriction of Food in Particular Period of Woman's Life

There are some particular periods for all women in which they enter into restrictions regarding their food habits. These particular periods may be their puberty and menstruation or the period of delivery. During menstruation, females are prohibited from eating hot and sour food, i.e., eggs, meat, or sour and spicy food.

In the Dimasa community, after the child's delivery, they eat a kind of food named *Thakong Kufu*. After childbirth, she should not have sheat fish (*borali fish*), duck meat of duck Pontiusus chola (*puthi fish*), pumpkin, and rice cakes for three months. After seven days of childbirth, *Laikonthai*, a kind of banana, *Nagren*; dry fish, *Lodama*; silkworm, *Toudi*; eggs are mixed and fried together, called *Gomdengba*, and fed to the new mother. *Toubehengiva*, or chicken curry, is cooked by an older woman. Dimasa women fast for the whole day of marriage.

Taboos Related to Food

The Dimasa people of Komorakata village maintain some food taboos. In Komorakata village, people do not eat beef and pork. Beef is strictly prohibited among them, and pork is not used in any social ceremonies. When a death occurs in a family, all the family members only take boiled food for several days. During most of the prohibitions, the villagers did not know why. However, they follow these prohibitions according to their tradition and customs.

Judima

Judima is a traditional ethnic rice wine associated with the Dimasa people of Assam. It received a geographical indication tag in 2021. The whole process for Preparing Judima Is completed in two stages:

1. Making Rice Starter Cakes, and
2. Preparation Of Rice Wine;

The process starts with the locals preparing a starter cake called Hamao. The starter cake is prepared from the bark of the plant *Thembra*. The bark is dried, chopped into tiny pieces, and crushed to powder. This powder is mixed with rice flour and water and made into dough. The starter cake is kept dry for three to five days, strained, and used for drinking. The taste depends on how long it takes to keep. The longer the time, the better it tastes.

Method of Cooking and Preparation of Food

The villagers of Komorakata have used various methods for cooking or preparing food. These methods are boiling, roasting, steaming, frying, raw, and drying.

Boiling: Food ingredients are put into boiling water and boiled until edible. Examples include rice, eggs, potatoes, and pulses.

Roasting: The ingredients are cooked before a fire or plugged into hot ashes. Small fish, potatoes, and brinjal are prepared using the roasting method.

Frying: First, mustard oil is heated in the frying pan. Then, the food ingredients are put into the pan, cut into small pieces, and washed. A ladle stirs them from time to time. When the food becomes edible, it is brought down from the oven. This method is used to cook fish, meat, eggs, and vegetables.

Steaming*:* Food ingredients are cooked by steam, which is produced by boiling water in a kettle or an earthen pot. When the pot's boiling water has begun to produce steam, the ingredients are hung inside the mouth of the pot, which is tied by cloth. If possible, the mouth is closed by a stopper. "Tekeli Pitha" and "Urahi pitha," small fish, are cooked using this method.

Raw: The villagers of Komorakata prepared some food, mainly from vegetables, without cooking. These raw foods are tomato, spinach, cabbage, and various fruits.

Some vegetables that are locally available in the homes of Dimasa are:

i. *Alusoe* – It is a kind of flower that tastes bitter

ii. *Soukha*- The upper part of the cane

iii. *Miphrai*- A traditional leafy vegetable used by Dimasa.

iv. *Lehedia*- Lehedi leaf.

v. *Miyawashi*- Bamboo shoot.

vi. *Pokadai*- This is found in paddy fields.

vii. *Thoukha*- A kind of bitter seed used in other dishes.

viii. *Mokong kereng*- Tern leaf vegetable.

ix. *Theklao*- Hibiseus sabdariffa (Tengamora)

x. *Khungathai*- Brinjal like tree.

Conclusion

The food habits of the Dimasa tribe of Assam are deeply related to their lifestyle and are influenced by many socio-cultural and economic factors. Most of the Dimasa families of the village were nonvegetarian and followed a two-time-a-day meal pattern. Like every other tribal community, Dimasas also has a system for preparing and preserving food. Rice is the staple food of the Dimasa. The favourite beverage of the Dimasas is rice beer called the *Judima*. However, it is worth remembering that the Dimasas are not habitual drinkers. During festivals, feasts, weddings, death ceremonies, etc., rice beer is freely used. However, at other times, only a limited quantity is used for everyday domestic consumption.

With time, the tribe has also adapted to new food habits. The change occurred in almost every society and Komorakata village. However, Judima's recent getting a GI tag is significant to their food habits. It is, therefore, essential to document the traditional foods and related habits of the Dimasa tribe. Notably, the younger generation of the tribe is not very much exposed to their traditional food habits.

It is essential to recognise that the evolving food habits of the Dimasa community are shaped by a complex interplay of cultural, environmental, economic, and social factors. Each tribal group has its unique history and context, and their food habits may evolve in distinct ways based on their specific circumstances and priorities. The future scope of studying the dynamics of food in the Dimasa community is extensive. It has the potential to contribute to cultural preservation, health improvement, sustainable development, and much more. It requires a collaborative and culturally sensitive approach, respecting the autonomy and rights of the community and recognising the value of their traditional knowledge and food practices.

References

Bahadur, K.P. (1978). *Caste Tribe & Culture of India*, Ess Ess Publications, New Delhi.

Bareh, H.M. (1984). *Encyclopaedia of NEG region. I. Arunachal Pradesh.* Mittal Publication: New Delhi. pp. 2–233.

Bhattacharya, P.C. (1983). B*oro and Dimasa: A comparative study.* Bulletin of the Tribal Research Institute, pp. 170–179.

Bordoloi, B.N. (1984). *The Dimasa Kacharis of Assam.* Tribal Research Institute, Assam, Guwahati.

Bordoloi, P. (2005). *Jana-Kristi.* Folklore Society of Assam, Guwahati.

Danda, D. G. (1977). *Among the Dimasas of Assam.* Sterling Publishers, New Delhi.

Haghighian Roudsari, A., Vedadhir, A., Rahmani, J., & Milani Bonab, A. (2019). Explaining the barriers and facilitators of ethnic and traditional food choices from the viewpoints of women. Journal of Ethnic Foods.

Karaosmanoğlu, D. (2020). How to study ethnic food: senses, power, and intercultural studies. Journal of Ethnic Food.

Nath, M., Dutta, B.K & Hajra, P.K. (2011). *Medicinal Plants Used in Major Diseases by Dimasa Tribe of Barak Valley.* Assam University Journal of Science & Technology: Biological and Environment Sciences, Vol. 7 November.

Rao, K.M, Kumar, R.H., Venkaiah, K., Brahmam, G.N.V. (2006). *Nutritional status of Saharia- A primitive tribe of Rajasthan, India.* J. Hum. Ecol., 14(3). pp.117-123.

Singh, Anamika & Singh, Ranjay & Sureja, Amish. (2007). *Cultural significance and diversities of ethnic foods of Northeast India.* Indian journal of traditional knowledge. 6(1). pp. 79-94.

Tierney, R. K., & Ohnuki-Tierney, E. (2012). *Anthropology of Food.* The Oxford Handbook of Food History. Oxford University Press.

Thaosen, S.R. (1962) '*Dimasa Kachari*' in *Asomor Janajati,* P.C. Bhattacharya (ed.), Gauhati: Asom Sahitya Sabha.

Waldstein, A. (2018). *Anthropology of Food.* The International Encyclopedia of Anthropology, Hilary Callan(ed.), John Wiley & Sons, Ltd.

7

Tribal Hinduism Contested
An Autoethnography of Sonowal Kacharis of Assam

C.J. Sonowal

Introduction

Autoethnography is an emerging field in social science research. It has gained prominence as a methodological perspective of looking at social reality through the lens of the observed, where the researcher himself is a subject. This unique approach allows for a more personal and subjective understanding of the social phenomena under study. Anthropology, as a subject matter related to human society, is closely associated with autoethnography. Venturing into the domain of autoethnography requires prior insight into various philosophical understandings of the search for truth in social science research. As an anthropologist, I have conducted a lot of ethnographic studies. However, it is my first autoethnographic account using my own tribe and myself as the observed one. Since it is a relatively new field, I would like to delineate all possible aspects related to autoethnography as a methodological tool. I have organised the discussion in the following manner:

First, I revisit the basic philosophy of research as a tool to uncover truth while understanding social reality. A discussion of the definitions and characteristics of ethnography follows this. Third, I delve into autoethnography and its unique features. Fourth, I share my deeply personal experiences as a member of the Sonowal Kacharis tribe, a community with its own distinct cultural practices and beliefs. These narratives are then interpreted and explained. Finally, I justify my writing as an autoethnographic account, highlighting its relevance in understanding the Sonowal Kacharis tribe and their social reality.

The Search for Truth in Understanding Social Reality

Human beings experience lots of events or occurrences in and around them. Pushed by human instinct, they try to comprehend or internalise why and how those events happen. In some cases, their query ends with some simple solution or answers, whereas, in some cases, they seek a more acceptable answer using specific ways. This search for understanding or knowledge may be termed a search for truth. The search for truth has given rise to various domains of science and philosophy – from the belief and practices in supernatural beings and religious beliefs and practices to intricate scientific inquiries. Thus, the basic steps in research are - experience, reasoning and research.

Experiencing certain events is not a simple phenomenon since a person's experience is moulded or guided by specific inherent ideas or knowledge, so it becomes subjective. Further, certain authorities always influence and determine how a person should or must experience certain events. It limits the acquiring truth since authority defines norms of experiencing and understanding the nature of phenomena. For instance, the social positioning of a person greatly influences how they experience events. A wife may experience a violent act perpetrated by her husband differently from a similar act perpetrated by someone other than her husband. The list thus goes on.

The search for truth involves reasoning, which is the process of trying to understand why things happen. There are two main ways to explain the reason for something: inductive and deductive reasoning. Inductive reasoning involves looking at individual events of a similar nature and coming to a conclusion based on that information. On the other hand, deductive reasoning involves relating personal experiences to generally accepted or known consequences of similar events. This requires the observer to have prior knowledge of similar situations or conditions. Inductive reasoning moves from specific events to a general conclusion, while deductive reasoning moves from general principles to specific conclusions. Inductive reasoning is mainly used for theory building, while deductive reasoning is used for testing and refining theories. However, contemporary social research often combines both approaches as needed.

When someone searches for the truth or conducts social reality research, they are essentially trying to find a conclusion based on evidence. This involves suggesting hypotheses, logically developing them, and interpreting scientific findings. This process is known as research, which is the systematic, controlled, empirical, and critical investigation of propositions about the presumed relations among natural phenomena. However, not all researchers follow the same principles.

Natural science research differs from social science research because the laws of behaviour of natural phenomena cannot be applied to social sciences. This is because people and their behaviour differ greatly from each other and insensate natural phenomena. Therefore, different conceptions of social reality, the individual, and social behaviour arise. The four components of social reality are ontology, epistemology, human nature, and methodology. Ontology deals with the question of the existence of any issue as defined at the beginning of the research. This could be about a particular term, perception, belief, structure, or anything else. Three basic inquiries are involved with the ontological perspective of the subject matter of any research:

a) Is the subject matter under study external to an individual or a product of individual consciousness?

b) Whether the subject matter under study is an objective or a result of individual cognition (Subjective)?

c) Is the subject matter under study a given (out there) in the world, or does one's mind create it?

From these inquiries, we may obtain a binary of assumptions. In one situation, we may find that objects (the subject matter) have an independent existence and are not dependent on the knower, which is a realist perspective. In another situation, assumptions may suggest that objects of thought are mere words; there are no independently accessible things constituting the meaning of a word, which creates a nominalist perspective.

Epistemology deals with the production and obtaining of knowledge. Three basic enquiries related to epistemology are:

a) What are the nature and forms of knowledge?

b) How can the knowledge related to the subject matter be acquired?

c) How do we communicate knowledge acquired from other human beings?

There are two different perspectives on the epistemology of research. The first perspective considers knowledge as objective, tangible and difficult to obtain. In this case, researchers must be observers and use natural science methods, which is known as the positivist perspective. This type of research is quantitative. The second perspective views knowledge as personal, subjective and unique. Here, researchers are involved with their subjects, and they reject the natural science approach. This approach is known as anti-positivist or interpretive. Research is all about understanding how humans respond to different situations. Therefore, it is essential to assume how humans react to various situations. In summary, there are two dominant ways people may respond to certain situations.

a) Humans mechanically respond to their environment - as a product of the environment and controlled by the environment. Thus, people's social reality may be studied and concluded by studying the environment (material and non-material) where people interact. This approach leads to determinism from a research perspective.

b) Humans initiate their own actions with free will and creativity, producing their environment. According to this assumption, there is heterogeneity in people's experiences and responses to a similar situation. Therefore, it cannot be generalised. It leads to interpretive inquiries and assumes human nature under voluntarism.

The three essential components of research are ontology, epistemology, and methodology. These components are interrelated, with ontology determining epistemology, which in turn determines methodology. When the subject matter's ontology is objective, the epistemology is positivist, and the researcher takes the stand of determinism. This means that the researcher tries to find the regularity and laws of the relationship between variables or factors that influence human responses. The methodology then becomes nomothetic, analysing the relationship and regularities between selected factors to discover general laws. On the other hand, when the ontology of the subject matter is subjective, the epistemology becomes anti-positivist, and the researcher takes the stand of voluntarism. This means that the researcher tries to study the unique behaviour of humans as the initiators of their actions with free will and creativity. The methodology then becomes ideographic, where the researcher tries to understand how the individual creates, modifies, and interprets the world they live in.

In any scientific research, the paradigms that need to be discussed are essential. For Denzin and Lincoln, paradigms are "an interpretative framework and a net that contains the researcher's epistemological, ontological and methodological premises" (2003: 33). In qualitative research, the paradigms generally used may be seen as "positivist and post-positivist", "constructivist-interpretive", "critical", and "feminist-post-structural". These paradigms have evolved through questioning, refining, and rejecting the previous ones on specific points of contrast and contentions. However, Brewer (2000) classifies the epistemological approaches to ethnography as "positivist", "humanist", "post-modern", and "post-post-modern". Over time, ethnographers have been taking more interest in critical approaches to study and analyse social reality and challenge the status quo. The expansion of epistemological approaches in ethnography is the consequence of such increasing interest.

Defining Ethnography

Etymologically, 'ethnography' is derived from the Greek word "*ethnos*", meaning folk, people, the nation, and "*grapho*", meaning "I write". Thus, **Ethnography may be defined as a descriptive study of a particular human society (or culture) or a methodological approach to** such a study. As a norm, ethnographic discourse requires one's all-embracing revelation to surroundings or settings that are intrinsic or appropriate to the anthropologist's study object in the culture and everyday life of the subjects of his study.

Ethnography as a subject matter and methodological perspective has emanated from anthropology. Scientific ethnography emerged with the extensive fieldwork-based research of Bronisław Malinowski, a British anthropologist, who did extensive fieldwork in the Trobriand Islands of Melanesia (*c.* 1915). Margaret Mead, an American anthropologist, followed his tradition and did extensive fieldwork in Samoa (1925). Typically, ethnography is a research method used by cultural anthropologists. It also refers to the written text used to report that research. For Denscombe (1998), "ethnography is a description of peoples and cultures and understanding things from the point of view of those involved rather than explaining things from the outsider's point of view (pp. 68-9)." Offering a closer view of ethnography, Brewer (2000) defines ethnography as "the study of people in naturally occurring settings or 'fields' capturing their social meanings and ordinary activities in a systematic way or research methods (p. 6)." Burgess (1982: 15) points out the involvement of ethnographers in unstructured fieldwork or field research, which may be flexible and open-ended. Similarly, Hammersley (1990:1-2) proposes the five features to identify ethnographic field research, which primarily deals with the contexts of the study, the data collection methods and the units of analysis.

Dealing with ethnography is incomplete without the reference to the views of Malinowski (1922: xvi). He points out that the core components of ethnographic study are to "deal with the totality of all social, cultural and psychological aspects of the community because they are so interwoven that no one can be understood without taking into account all the others." Thus, an ethnographer is often engrossed in the field context for an extended period, explores the social environment or culture and produces a detailed sketch of it. The ethnographers also aim to relate how situations, lives and meanings are lived rather than just observing and reporting what occurs. In contrast to a linear and predetermined structured path of investigation, as seen in other scientific approaches, an ethnographer adopts a flexible cyclical pattern.

Dealing with Autoethnography:

Defining Autoethnography

After defining ethnography, it becomes clear that "Autoethnography" deals something with the self (auto) with ethno (the nation, people, the society) and the graphy (writing it down). It is about how one relates the self to the people and society to which one belongs through social and cultural experiences. Thus, Sparkes (2000, 21) defines it as "the personalised accounts that draw upon the experience of the author/researcher to extend sociological understanding." Pelias (2003, 372) says, "It lets one use oneself to get to culture."

The Philosophical and theoretical foundations for autoethnographic methods

Postmodernism challenges the dominance of positivism and shows that knowledge can be gained and shared in various ways. According to Vidich and Lyman (2000: 60), the post-modern research approach questions assumptions in both qualitative and quantitative methods and urges researchers not to rely solely on established values, theories, perspectives, and prejudices as study resources. The post-modern era has facilitated the adoption of critical theories, such as feminist theories, in academic research and has opened up a new range of research strategies. Bochner (2001) suggests that there has been a critical discourse in scientific traditions that places less emphasis on established rationality, objectivity, and truth, with a focus on increasing the power of social research to have a moral effect rather than just a methodological one. In this regard, the statement made by Stivers (1993) is significant. According to the author, the idea of universal truth is merely a dream of power over others that cannot be achieved through research. Alternative knowledge production processes that are free from established processes better serve the purpose. Autoethnography is one such process.

Conventional ethnography took a positivist stance where the ethnographer had to remain detached from the culture under study to avoid disrupting it. Therefore, ethnographers would not get emotionally involved, and the observed would not know what the ethnographer went back to say to other people. In contrast, critical ethnography advocates immersing oneself in the field and being part of the culture. For critical ethnographers, this does not disrupt the culture because objective truth is not attainable anyway. We are always biased because we can only understand culture through our bodies, our own lenses, and our worldviews to interpret. However, critical ethnographers try to immerse themselves within these cultures and are reflexive by examining their biases. They can acknowledge and challenge them to be more open and understanding.

Autoethnography intensely depends on "self-reflexivity" – attending to one's positioning in the interpretation of others. It is disclosing one's personal, social and cultural location. Some of the questions asked by an autoethnographer to himself are: What are his motives, why does he want to understand something, and what is the worthiness of telling the story to other people? What is his position? It is essential to look at the preconceived understanding one brings when one is situated in a culture. Since such understandings can influence the interpretation of the behaviour of the "observed", including the self and identity consciousness, it is essential to check how he would have behaved if there were no such understandings. Based on the story, the researcher has to understand who he/she is and what not. The story must tell the rules of others, physically or emotionally present there. The researcher must relate to others who have to understand themselves through the researcher's story. When one is doing autoethnographic work, telling his/her personal stories in relationships with others, it is very important to allow both people to identify with the researcher.

The Research Setting:

The Entry Point of The Researcher

Having this background insight about doing autoethnography will allow me to introduce my research setting. My adoration for knowing my people and culture steadily increased since I started taking an interest in social and cultural anthropology as a student of the subject. My first step in re-examining my traditional domain started when I studied the Kumar community next to my native village as a field setting for my MSc dissertation. It opened my eyes to how inexperienced I was about my next neighbours with whom I had personal and social interaction since childhood; I played and studied with those friends, cultivated in the same field and contested for scarce resources. My second experience was meaningful for my enthusiasm to study my people when I read a report on Sonowal Kacharis written by a Master's degree student. It shocked me with its misstated details about our life and society. These experiences led me to consider conducting my PhD research on my tribe. After joining TISS, Mumbai, I have written research-based books and articles on tribes, including my tribe. However, those were different from the reflection of self-experience with the culture. In a true sense, this is my first attempt to write an autoethnography in brief with some limited but very close-to-my-heart experiences.

Looking Back at the Traditional Domain of the Researcher

Let me situate in the context of the study. I was born to a Sonowal Kachari couple in a village, a forest village in the Dibrugarh district. Since I realised, I had spent my childhood solely swimming in the stream, running by my home, working in the paddy field, herding cattle, collecting firewood from the nearby forest, and playing with my schoolmates in the playground and also in the jungle. I remember collecting wood from the forest to make "*Meji*" (a wooden and bamboo-made structure to be burnt during *Magh Bihu*, a harvest festival). I remember collecting the bark of the *Tora* (Alpinia nigra) plant from the marshy land inside the jungle well before the occasion of *Bohag Bihu* (the spring festival) to make ropes and fasten it to our cattle on the occasion of *Goru Bihu* – the festival for cattle. I also remember following the rules and the obligation we had to follow while collecting the bark of the Tora plant so that it would not get contaminated.

Similarly, we had to be attentive to the rules related to collecting certain herbs for the *Goru Bihu*, such as *Makhiloti* (Flemingia) and *Dighloti* (Litsea salicifolia). We collected those plants before a crow could caw at dawn from a distance, from where one could not hear the sound of the *Dheki* (a wooden implement used to dehusk paddy) of our village. I also remember how we used to predict the general weather conditions of the year to come, just observing whether the cattle in the cowshed were sleeping or standing the morning of the *Goru Bihu* day. We could predict whether the coming year would benefit us by engaging in egg fights on the same day. We were also concerned with the well-being of our cattle for the coming year. We made new ropes from the tender barks of the *Tora* plant, smeared them with the paste made of black gram and turmeric, decorated them with the flower of the *Tongloti* (Eupatorium cannabinum) plant, and tied the cattle with it on the night of Goru Bihu. Thus, we had to be conversant and attached to all these rules, practices and beliefs. It needed a perfect plan and execution. Bihu was not simply a festival for us; it was our lifeline.

We were not lone human beings there. On the one hand, we were scared of the spirits residing in gloomy trees, especially at night and noon, since disturbing them would invite misfortune and illness. However, on the other, the supreme being, the *Bathow* (though he was seldom approached), protected us. Besides, our village deity, *Gatigiri*, whom we used to revere on the occasion of the new year (during spring festival) and every occasion of village-level religious functions and ceremonies, was there to take care of our well-being. We all had our family deities who were watchful of us around the year, for good and evil. Without their quiet permission or reporting them, our parents never left for outlying places or took someone unwell to doctors. We knew where the spirits lived; we could diagnose the causes of illness one suffered from the knowledge we inherited from our forefathers.

Our economy used to pivot around the act of cultivation. We used to choose varieties of paddy according to our requirements. We needed *Bora* rice to prepare liquor for festivals and offer to our ancestors on certain occasions. We cultivated *lahi* rice because it ripened earlier than other rice varieties, and harvesting became easier. It also serves to fill the gap between two main crops. We cultivated *Sali* rice because it was resistant to severe weather, it was heavy, and we could preserve them for a long. The straw of Sali rice was also extended and strong enough to be used as thatch to cover our roofs. Our granaries were not simply the storage of crops. Instead, those were places where the deity of fortune and wealth resided. So, it was a sacred place, and we had many restrictions and rules entering and using it.

Specific rules governed us. We had our clan and family lineages. Marriage was strictly prohibited within these groups. The whole lineage, and if known, whole clan members would be polluted when a child took birth in any family within these groups. So also the death case. Cooperation and help were obligatory for lineage members to be offered to the deceased family. However, in case of another occasion, the village folks are the help at hand. It was the amiable invitation or request that mattered for physical help people offered to the needy, not the price or compensation. No "outsider" knew about our clan, lineage, laws and responsibilities. Importantly, no nonnatives came to suggest our duties and told stories about our origin and establishment and our relationship with the universe, the sky, water, air and fire. Our folksongs and other oral traditions reminded us through daily utterances and occasional performances. We had our priests, orators, and medicine men who specialised in their field. Our priests and orators could relate us with the non-human domains, and we did not need outside specialists.

The Antagonistic Dualism of the Researcher's Traditional Domain:

So far, the story I have narrated looks smooth and rosy. However, there have been wrenches in it. We have a "*Namghar*" (village monastery) in the village. It is a sacred place where my people, the elders, recite a religious text. It is called *Kirtan* (which means reciting or singing prayers to the god). However, it was not the meaning we conceived. I, and my fellow folks, did not understand and could not connect it to our life and surroundings (I am sure most elders reciting and following the orator were in a similar position to me). It glorified some powerful beings called Rama, Krishna, Brahma and Vishnu and conveyed how they slew the demons and oriented local people about religion and righteousness. It talked about the Ganges, Yamuna, the Himalayas, the sea and sages, the heaven and the *devatas* living in places unfamiliar to us. People hardly knew how these gods and goddesses were connected to our lives, where these sacred rivers and tall mountains were located, what heaven looked like, and why we would know and herald these entities. The gods, deities, and spirits we knew and interacted with never lived in *Namghar*. We did not worship them there.

Then, what did we think of the significance of *Namghar*, and why did we perform rituals there? For my friends and me, rituals in *Namghar* meant the delicious *Mithoi* (sweet and spicy ball-shaped food item made of rice cake mixed with black pepper and *Gur*), sugarcane and coconut pieces (which were scarcely available in my place). Interestingly, yearly, we had at least three feasts and rituals in *Namghar*. These feasts were attractive for two reasons: we used to get Mithoi, and we got to eat meat and black gram dishes and enjoyed it with our male family members, friends, and elders in the open field in the open field front of the *Namghar*. Every abled member of the village got one or the other duties to accomplish that occasion. Importantly, this feast had nothing to do with what the religious text revealed through the recitation of the orator. The swan, duck, and fish we ate there were offered to the gods and deities we knew and had relations to our lives and work.

Reciting *Kirtan* had also spread to our homes. Our parents used to organise rituals where the *Kirtan* was recited. However, we had to go to a non-tribal astrologer or foreteller to see for a legitimate date to perform it, and also what were the things we had to offer in the name of the god we did not know well. We had to offer curd and rice-made items like *Kumal chawl* (breakfast item made of rice) early in the morning as soon as the reciting *Kirtan* finished. In no traditional rituals did we offer any milk product. However, the day that followed was commemorated ardently, slaughtering ducks and fishes in the name of our family deities and ancestors. Our ancestors, at least up to nine generations, never left us alone in the mortal world. They were vigilant for good and against bad. For their service, we only had to offer them food and drink on every momentous occasion, like when we took to food from new crops, celebrated *Bihu*, or performed any rituals. The ninth goes for eternal rest when a new member joins them (by death).

I remember our parents paying religious taxes *(kar bhar)* to the *Satra* - a religious institution of the Vaishnava religious faith in Assam. The *Pachani* (lower-level disciples and workers of Satra Institution) used to come to a nearby village to collect such taxes from the villages where the disciples of the Vaishnava religious faith resided. One person from each village was responsible for accumulating the tax – in cash and handing it over. In return, he was given a small clay bar called "Mritika Mati". A little dust from this clay was mixed with water to prepare holy water (*Shanti Pani*) to purify us from the impurity we gathered and the sin we committed, thereby becoming pure enough to live a usual life. In the Vaishnava faith, drinking holy water was mandatory to get purified.

My maternal uncle was an efficient and recognised orator of Vaishnavite religious texts in our village and was also authorised to keep the holly clay bars. During my childhood, I used to infiltrate the boundary between the sacred and the profane, opening the religious texts covered with a red cloth and reading the same without taking a holy bath. For this unauthorised adventure, I was punished too. Interestingly, one day, my maternal uncle entered our dining room where I was eating. He addressed my mother as elder sister and asked her to look at the holy clay bars he was carrying with him from the *Satra* representatives. As usual, I was more excited than my mother. I stood up from my *pira* (a wooden seat we used to sit on) and held a piece of the holy clay bar with my hand. I saw that there were imprints of human feet. I asked my uncle what it was, and he answered it was the sole of the *Gosai* – the head of the Satra. The immediate issue was not about the imprints; instead, it was my unholy act of touching the holy clay bar with my unclean hands. The clay bars were powerful enough to evade the impact of my innocently induced impurity; however, I was not strong enough to escape the punitive action for my innocent, unholy act.

What about our school life? We started the day with *Slokas* and prayers. As soon as the teacher came, we started the *Sloka* (the eleven vows of Mahatma Gandhi) – "*Ahimsa, Satya, Asteya, Brahmacharya, ...*". Then our prayer starts, mainly consisting of lyrics pleading Vishnu, Krishna, and Rama to show us light, emancipate us, praise god and his incarnations in different forms and acts and so on. Finally, we concluded our morning prayer with the Sloka - *Asato Ma Sad-Gamaya……. Om Shaantih, Shaantih, Shaantih.* Indeed, we uttered them erroneously without knowing the meaning and significance of these philosophically heavy cognitions. However, we did not bring anything back home from school except the books and some textual knowledge. Our world back home was based on learning from our surroundings – material and non-material. Moreover, there were no traces of those entities we uttered in the school.

These were the memories of my childhood when I was very much traditional, living in my village. However, I had to come out of the closet of the traditional womb for better and higher study, to the Government Boy's Higher Secondary School, then to DHS Kanoi College and finally to Dibrugarh University for my Master's degree and beyond. The day-to-day contexts and the contrasts of traditional life mattered to me less than before. However, entering the field of Anthropology acted as a resurgent wave in me to interpret the dualism I used to live in, in social, cultural, religious and worldviews.

Though the list of narratives is far more extensive, for the sake of this paper, I will conclude the contexts with two exciting experiences of mine, which are relatively recent. In 2013, my loving mother expired. So, I was in my father's native village for a few days, mingling with the fellow people there and preparing for the death rites. There, again, I needed the holly water since my mother died, and we became socially impure. I was informed that nowadays, the holly water is provided by a Brahmin priest, not by a person assigned by the Satra since the Satras are now not keen enough to collect religious taxes from tribal villages. It was about the story of my dear deceased friend "Kusha", who once was asked to bring the holy water (Shanti Pani) from that priest. There was a tradition of offering a token amount of Rs. 1.25 to the person for the holy water. However, Kusha lost the 25-paisa coin on the way. The priest told him to give him the exact amount lest he could not give him the holy water. My dear friend innocently tried to settle the issue by advising the Brahmin that he could provide him with holy water equivalent to one rupee.

The other story was related to my mother's death rite. We had two options: use the service of a Brahmin priest or a Sonowal Kachari Priest, a *Medhi*, whom the *Gosain* of *Satra* authorises to conduct death rituals. My elder brothers preferred a Brahmin priest to the *Medhi*. As a tradition, we had to perform a ritual on the bank of a small natural stream near our home. When offering homage to my mother, the Brahman priest wanted to know our *Gotra* (clan). I told them that we do not have a *Gotra*, but we have lineage and clan (Vansha). He said, "Okay, tell me the name. I said, *"Khatuwali"* (my lineage name). The priest said, "No, there is no such *Gotra* in the Hindu ritualistic text". So, he could not chant that name, and the offerings would not reach my mother unless we uttered a valid *Gotra* name. There was no way out. So, the priest declared that our *Gotra* was the "*Kashyap Gotra*" (a clan name prevalent in Hindu religious texts) from that moment. So, the job was accomplished. Then he directed us to utter the name of the river Ganges every time we put something in the stream's water in the name of my deceased mother. As I inquired why we should name the Ganges when we were putting the offerings in the local stream, the priest informed me that only the river Ganges had the power and authority to carry the offerings to the deceased soul.

The Researcher's Encounter with Reflexology – *the interpretation of the social reality*:

Having narrated my smooth and contentious traditional domain, I will now try to make my auto (Self) narrative an ethno (cultural) graphy (writing). Let me start with my memories related to our cultural aspects. The narratives show that celebrating *Magh Bihu* was intimately related to our cultural ecology. There were two parts, one at the family level and the other at the village level. Our families prepared for the festival with lots of eatables and drinks that took at least 15 days of preparation. We, the young ones, used to collect wood from the forest, cut the *nora* (straw of the paddy plant) and construct the tent suitable to stay the nights at least 15 days before the festival amidst the paddy field and planning to celebrate the festival with all possible means. It was also our concern to finish harvesting well before the festival day, and for the boys, the concern was to help each needy family carry the paddy bundles to the granaries before dusk. Serving the night riders at the tent with rice cake, duck meat, locally brewed liquor, and other eatables was the moral duty of the efficient women cook of the families. So, the availability of *nora* in the paddy field, collection of wood from the nearby forest, collection of bamboo from some selected bamboo grooves, and above all, freeing the youth from harvesting activities were intimately related to crop cycle, ecology and culture.

The preparation for the annual festival of Bohag Bihu held a different significance for each age group within our community. As the festival approached, the surrounding flora and fauna served as a natural reminder of the occasion. The Bihu phul, a stunning orchid, began to bloom along the banks of the nearby stream, while the Bihuti charai, a seasonal bird, filled the air with its joyful song. Finally, the sweet and unmistakable voice of the cuckoo could be heard in the distance, gradually drawing closer to our village. All of these natural phenomena served to help us prepare for the upcoming celebrations.

The Goru Bihu celebration, part of the larger Bohag Bihu festivities, was a complex affair steeped in tradition and ritual. It involved a wide array of activities, each with its own set of beliefs and practices. These customs and practices were essential to our unique community and gave our world a rich and complex character.

In reflecting on the attributes of our community, which we now refer to as the "Sonowal Kachari" tribe, it is clear that our festivals were not just occasions for merrymaking and celebration. Instead, they were an integral part of our daily lives. The flora, fauna, and natural world around us, as well as our crops, our means of production, our cattle, and even our gods and forefathers, were all interrelated. Above all, we had our own way of understanding the value we placed on all of these aspects of our social and cultural lives, which was unique to our community.

I missed two crucial points that I needed to reflect on. Bohag is a season which makes people passionate and hopeful. People start doing new things, and boys and girls plan for their conjugal lives and exchange love and affection during this Bihu. Interestingly, many girls and boys elope with their dear ones during this season. Elopement marriage is widely practised among the Sonowal Kacharis. Their folk songs (including Bihu songs) are full of such indications. Further, the *Huchari*, a kind of chorus sung during *Bohag Bihu* mainly by the adult people among Sonowal Kacharis, illustrates the people's social and cultural life, norms, practices and history. It differs from the Huchari songs sung and performed by other Assamese communities in Assam.

As my primary focus is to elucidate the socio-religious domains of Sonowal Kacharis through the lens of Hinduism, I argue that Sonowal Kachari's religious practices are explicitly different from those we call a Hindu society. Most practices and values attached to *Bihu* as a national festival of the greater Assamese community might be a diffusion from traditional societies like the Sonowal Kacharis. Reflecting on the dual domain of belief and practices we lived in, I have many unresolved contentions. As mentioned in my narratives, we had many gods and goddesses. We had compassionate ones to protect us; however, they punished us if we disturbed or disobeyed. As one can observe, they did not have any link or relations to the supernatural beings introduced by the Vaishnava and Hindu religious entities. It is still unclear to me (I believe, for all my fellow people) why our ancestors had to be imbibed with the idea of the presence of those entities which in no way were related to our social, cultural, economic and religious life and necessities. Why did our forefathers agree to pay the religious tax to the Satras for providing us with a religious tradition we did not understand and internalise? Some yet-to-be-proved narratives explain how and why the Sonowal Kacharis embraced Vaishnavism in the late 19th and early 20th centuries. Some of them are based on mythical stories that are hard to believe.

Nevertheless, these stories summarise that the non-traditional religious *gurus* (preachers) proved superior to the Sonowal Kachari *gurus*. Moreover, a few stories also indicate how these alien *gurus* were treacherous enough to fool the tribal consciences and establish the superiority of their aura and faith over the tribal traditions. I believe that societies like the Sonowal Kacharis needed to interact with non-tribal societies in social and cultural domains, and they had to show that they were not inferior to others. Since the Sonowal Kachari social and cultural traditions were a mismatch, incorporating the Vaishnava tradition, a dominant religious faith in Assam, might have helped them to reveal their identity as civilised beings. The record of Satra reveals that the tribal disciples were not pure enough to enter the main assembly halls owing to their tribal identity, food habits and lifeways.

However, my people were independent of the philosophy and rules of other societies. Nor were the goods infused by the Vaishnava gurus ruling our traditional world. Our rivers, forests, lands, crops, weather, everything, were managed by our pristine gods. Then, I believe the Vaishnavite traditions brought us a sense and belief of an extra shield of protection. The structural form, like the Namghar, the holy books, the *Kirtan* and *Bhagavata,* and the easy way of performing the Vaishnavite rituals attracted our people. It was an extra shield of protection when our parents could not find a cause for some bad things happening; they used to go to a foreteller or astrologer, who usually happened to be a Brahmin or Mahanta (lesser than the Brahmins in social status). They also kept some ideas about our traditional practices. So, seeing the context, they maintained a balance between the two traditions and advised performing Vaishnavite rituals with a trace of traditional ones. Dualism thus prevailed with ease and meaning. Other than that, our people had nothing to do with the exotic religious beliefs and the exotic gods.

Coming back to the holy water and the clay bar with the foot imprints of the *Gosai,* I am emotionally disturbed and academically enthusiastic to reflect on it. We had a traditional practice of using cow dung mixed with water and sprinkling it in our house in and out with a few stripes of *Dubari* (Bermuda) grass (Cynodon dactylon) to purify our houses in the event of birth and death. Further, on the occasion of *Bihu*, we sprinkled the water with freshly ground rice powder. Taking a sip of holy water prepared from the clay bar with the foot imprints of the *Gosain* seems to be accepting the supremacy of the Satra over the tradition and becoming subject to it having no valid reason. It is quite intriguing why the entire Sonowal Kachari people became so weak socially and morally that they had to be purified by the Satra, which is in no way related to their life and culture. Why did the Sonowal Kacharis think or perceive that they became so impure that only the holy water of the Satra could purify them? Why did they not continue with their traditional way of getting purified? Had there not been the Satras, who would have made them pure? If this is Hinduisation, I do not see any difference between Christianization and Hinduization in India. The inherent meaning and function of religion, then, also has to be defined afresh. My dear poor friend Kusha might have thought logically about the value of the holy water in terms of money he had to pay since the concept of such impurity and the means of purification could not penetrate his tribal mind. It was an alien idea imposed without relating to the cultural ecology of our people.

Being Sonowal Kacharis, did we have a religion at all? I am still trying to understand the typical definition of religion and the phenomena I observe among societies which they call a religion. Hindu religious texts talk of "*Dharm*" and "*Adharm*" (Religious and irreligious). The Hindu gods were born as epic heroes like Rama, Krishna, Parasurama, and many more to establish righteousness among those who knowingly or unknowingly could not follow the righteousness on earth. The Hindu epics are full of stories about how the epic heroes killed or subdued the demons (or, say, the native heroes) who were against righteousness and established the desired civilisation. The universal truth about the religious expansion is that Christianity and Hinduism did not accept that there was civilisation outside their religious domain. Thus, the history of world religion depicts the spread of civilisation (religion) as a divine act, sometimes accomplished in coercive or treacherous ways. I want to position Satra as an agency that looks at the Sonowal Kacharis as an uncivilised lot. As a divine duty, it took all possible ways to teach and give us civilisation. According to our folk narratives, the body of our religious *guru, Gojai,* was treacherously burned at the behest of the *Gosain,* and he advised our people to keep the Vaishnava religious text on his symbolic burial. To date, two raised platforms of soil are kept in the *Namghar*, each having four extended limbs symbolising the burials of *Gojai* and his helper *Monai;* both were the pristine priests of our Supreme god Baitho. We call this altar *Tiphai.* Vaishnavite religious texts *Kirtan* and *Bhagavata* are kept in these two structures placed on wooden stools called *thoga*. Now, many of our people look at this arrangement as the dominance of Satra on tradition.

Further, the literature produced for and by the Sonowal Kachari people equated our supreme god, Baitho, with the Hindu God Lord Siva, making the merger of the Sonowal Kacharis into Hindu identity smoother, at least at perceptual levels. This process is similar to how the Christians converted a large chunk of tribal people to Christianity in the northeast and mainland India (Sonowal, 2014; Eaton, 1997). A similar strategy was also used to Hinduise the Ahom dynasty. I have already mentioned the Kshatriyaisation process of Kacharis of lower Assam, linking them to the epic hero Bhima and his son Ghotatkocha (Sonowal, 2008, 2014, 2017, 2021). However, amidst all these contentious events and perceptions, the critical question is, "Who defines righteousness and the criteria for civilisation? How do the agencies get the authority to decide who should possess what cultural component?

Now, I will come to my new identity assigned by the Brahmin priest during my mother's death ritual. All these past fifty years, I had no problem living a dignified life, having social interactions and cultural representation. However, when I wanted to penetrate the civilised world and give the departed soul of my mother an assured place in eternity, as perceived by my Vaishnavite conscience, I needed the gate pass, an identity given by and acceptable to the perceptually civilised domain. I was in a dilemma about carrying forward the new clan identity, "*Kashyap Gotra*," since my people hardly knew anything about it. They would outrightly have excluded me from the rules, values and moral obligations attached to kinship and clan organisations had I declared that my clan had been changed. Such an act would have betrayed my entire community and forefathers. What great thing have I done by changing my clan identity, undermining and devaluating the identity and dignity of my forefathers, becoming a Vaishnavite and inviting the Brahmin priest? Can it be a Sonowal Kachari religion? Is it really a character of civilised Sonowal Kachari? Being critical, absolutely not. I should not be such a Hindu.

I am also uncomfortable with the narrative that only the Ganges can purify, and only the holy water body can. All the small and big rivers in my locality (or the state of Assam) have been great for me. These are our economic resources, our lifelines, and they live in our hearts and culture. We have songs, lullabies, stories, and gods and goddesses related to them. Above all, we have the mighty Luhit (the Brahmaputra). Then why could these so important water bodies not be pure enough to purify us? Why should we know or utter the name of a river that has no physical or mythological connection with our life and culture? Who has constructed the domain of purity, power, and authority that intends to control our lives? Indeed, not by any of our people.

I have written somewhere about the status of the Brahmaputra in the Hindu mythological domain (Sonowal, 2021). We observed the "Nomami Brahmaputra" (organised by the Government of Assam) festival, which aimed to enhance Assam's tourism industry. However, probably only a few people know why pilgrimage could not develop along the bank of the mighty Brahmaputra, unlike the Ganges and many other rivers in mainland India. Let me mention here that the Brahmaputra is a cursed river according to Hindu mythology. It is destined to carry dirty things around the year except for the day of "Ashokastami" when a part of the Ganges flows through it. Thus, we see pilgrims in Parasuram Kund on that very day. Like the natives, the natural entities are also uncivilised and impure here to be eligible to serve any divine purpose to their people.

Hurriedly, I peep into my schooling days in the village. I narrated the prayers we had to recite. It has been evident by now that the heavy philosophical burdens and the gods and goddesses we used to name were the Hindu Gods, and we did not know how they were related to us. However, the young minds and hearts were formally infused with these components in the schools. Back home or on the way to and from school, we had to be concerned about our known deities and spirits. Our traditional entities had never been the contents of any prayer or discussion in the school. The practices we followed in school infused in our tender minds a sense of inferiority since our parents did not know about those prayers, the stories we learnt in school, and our gods and goddesses had a limited range of domains to control or influence our life whenever we are out of the traditional closet.

Contextualising the Findings and Understandings:

Were the Sonowal Kacharis backward Hindus?

Now, I directly land into the contention whether the Tribes in India are Hindus or were they Hindus before converting to another religion. Amidst several perceptions, G.S. Ghurye's (1959: 19) concept of designing the tribes as the "imperfectly integrated classes of Hindu society" or the "backward Hindus" has far-reaching implications in Indian politics. It seems that Right Wing Hindu organisations (also having a substantial influence on Indian Politics) have internalised his theory about the Tribes. The contemporary Ant-Conversion Bills and the drive for "*Ghar Wapsi*" (coming back home for converts to the Hindu fold) are the impacts of these perspectives when looking at tribal societies in India. Ghurye's project was based on the presence of a sufficient number of cultural components in a tribal society similar to Hindu culture. He designed those tribal societies as Hindu, with the majority components similar to the Hindu culture. However, there has always been a question of to what extent Hindu components are initially Hindu. Studies have shown that towards its periphery, the classic or core Hindu traditions dilute and imbibe lots of local (non-Hindu) components. Thus, it is always important to focus on the reference point to examine who integrates whom. Indeed, in the case of Sonowal Kacharis, the infusion of Hindu components was non-essential and trivial in terms of their day-to-day utility and existence. It has been a superficial umbrella based on an imported idea of purity and civilisation.

Is the Researcher Successful in his Search for Truth?

Now, let me reflect on the methodological aspects of what I have done. Contrary to the childhood experiences I narrated here, my reflections on these experiences have been a continuous process. I agree that the personal quality of reflecting on events makes a difference. My fellow friends were not equally exposed to the significant others I was exposed to. They were also not into the social sciences as well. My present reflection was undoubtedly different from those days when I was a local. Importantly, my people had to continue many traditions that had no significance to them, lest it might affect them badly. Tribal people always have a fear of the unknown. Since the Vaishnavite tradition was all about an unknown entity, they had to continue it, although they were unable to find the link between their necessity and appeasement. So, they needed a non-traditional foreteller to show the link or the reasons. These were some of the factors or authorities that influenced my way of experiencing the events throughout my life. Coming to the use of ontological and epistemological perspectives for the interpretation, I reflect on the following:

I narrated about Sonowal Kachari traditions, gods, goddesses, identity and many other perceptual entities. My ontological perspective is based loosely on realism since, for me, all these entities were hard and given out there. Those were independent of my feelings and experiences. Thus, I built my epistemology on cause-effect relationships. Despite perceptual (say, the existence of God, identity, traditions), the entities affected our lives physically and socially.

Subsequently, I have presented the behaviour of my people under determinism with a certain amount of fluidity since our socio-cultural beliefs and practices were like a mechanical response to the geophysical environment and cultural ecology. People were hardly ready for new ideas or questions in the socio-cultural domain. Thus, the culture complex was relatively static. To a great extent, I was in a comfortable position to use the lens of my people while interpreting the experiences and events since I belonged to the community and the experiences were mine. However, I acknowledge the individual heterogeneity in experiencing as the authority or factors influencing my experiences differed from others. I was trying to be critical by roaming between the two worlds we were concerned about and bringing in instances and records of reasons and linkages of events and thoughts. I also tried to reveal the shortcomings and necessity for change, preservation and continuity in cultural components and the meaning they make for our people.

Thus, I believe that I have produced an autoethnographic account. Because I did not simply narrate the events; instead, I tried to situate them within the social and cultural life of the Sonowal Kacharis as the experience of a person who belonged to that society. The graphy (description or writings) was about my (self or auto) experiences of the events I felt, touched, internalised and reasoned those experiences. I experienced them as a member of the Sonowal Kachari society; therefore, I interpreted them as situating myself as a member of the society and experiencing those events. I adopted both evocative and analytical frameworks within my autoethnographic account since I wanted to make my account interpretive as well as critical. However, the crucial problem with autoethnography was that I re-entered my traditional domain with lots of exposure to the philosophical domain and critical deliberation on ethnicity, identity and ethnic reconstruction and representation. Such understanding inspired me to conclude or justify my reflection without much deliberation on what and how I was experiencing the events when I was not what I am now. Probably, I am not able to empty my preconceptions.

Conclusion

Autoethnography is an emerging field evolving steadily. It is an opportunity and a challenge for ethnographers who want to interpret the societies immersing themselves in the field. It has opened the scope for the social and cultural anthropologists who conventionally deal with the societies otherwise studied and presented by the colonial anthropologist or native anthropologists through the lens of colonial constructs. Tribal and indigenous societies are some of such societies where autoethnography as a research methodology has a great scope to unravel the untold, unrepresented and distorted stories about the people there. India's northeast is an emerging field for autoethnographers.

Though I have used autoethnography as a research methodology to reflect on my experience and interpret my narratives as an insider, one can also do autoethnography on a society other than its own. It is all about reflecting on the experience of the self and situating oneself in the social context of the observed. It is all about observing the self as an observer and being one of those about whom one studies. At best, autoethnography as a methodological tool can help social scientists uncover societies' distorted meanings and bring the social reality closer to the audience.

References

Bochner, A. P. (2000). Criteria against ourselves. *Qualitative Inquiry*, 6(2), 266–272. https://doi.org/10.1177/107780040000600209

Brewer, J. (2000). *Ethnography*. Buckingham: Open University Press.

Burgess, R. (1982). *Field Research: A Source Book and Field Manual*. London: Allen and Unwin.

Denscombe P. (1998). The Good Research Guide for Small Scale Social Research Projects. Buckingham: Open University Press.

Denzin, N. K., & Lincoln, Y. S. (2000). Qualitative methods: Their history in sociology and anthropology. In *The Handbook of Qualitative Research*. Sage.

Eaton, R. M. (1997). Comparative history as World History: Religious conversion in modern India. *Journal of World History*, 8(2), 243–271. https://doi.org/10.1353/jwh.2005.0063

Hammersley, M. (1990). *Reading Ethnographic Research*. London: Longman.

Malinowski, B. (1922). *Argonauts of the Western Pacific*. London: Routledge.

Pelias, R. J. (2003). The Academic Tourist: An Autoethnography. *Qualitative Inquiry*, 9(3), 369–373. https://doi.org/10.1177/1077800403009003003

Sonowal, C. J. (2008). Indian tribes and the issue of Social Inclusion and exclusion. *Studies of Tribes and Tribals*, 6(2), 123–134. https://doi.org/10.1080/0972639x.2008.11886586

Sonowal, C. J. (2014). Dynamics of Religion, Ethnic Identity and Changes in Northeast India. In C. J. Sonowal (Ed.), *Religion and Ethnic Reconstruction among the Tribes of Northeast India* (pp. 58–116). Delhi: Akanksha Publishing House.

Sonowal, C. J. (2017). History of Religion of Indigenous Populations of Brahmaputra Valley. In S. Sengupta (Ed.), *Contemporary Anthropological Research in Eastern and North Eastern India* (pp. 121–144). Delhi: Gyan Publishing House.

Sonowal, C. J. (2021). Mythology, Cultural Expansionism and Nation Building in India: An Anthropological Interpretation. In N. K. Gogoi & M. Sharma (Eds.), *India's North-East: Contribution of Anthropology* (pp. 47–70). Dibrugarh University, Dibrugarh.

Sparkes, A. C. (1996). The fatal flaw: A narrative of the fragile body-self. *Qualitative Inquiry*, *2*(4), 463–494. https://doi.org/10.1177/107780049600200405

Sparkes, A. C. (2000). Autoethnography and narratives of Self: Reflections on criteria in action. *Sociology of Sport Journal*, *17*(1), 21–43. https://doi.org/10.1123/ssj.17.1.21

Stivers, C. (1993). Reflections on the role of personal narrative in social science. *Signs: Journal of Women in Culture and Society*, 18(2), 408–425, https://doi.org/10.1086/494800

Vidich, A. J., & Lyman, S. M. (2000). Qualitative methods: Their history in sociology and anthropology. In *Handbook of qualitative research* (2nd ed., pp. 37–84). Thousand Oaks, CA: Sage.

8

Impact of COVID-19 on Primary Education: An Anthropological Study in Malayinkeezhu, Kerala

B. Bindu Ramachandran
Aiswarya. S.V

Introduction

Kerala's social development and quality of life interventions are indisputably inspiring. The state supports a high quality of literacy, with nearly all children receiving primary education. Thiruvananthapuram, the capital city of Kerala, had long sought to establish a planned system of primary education that included school facilities, scheduled hours, uniforms, exams, and printed textbooks. Christian missionaries also contributed significantly to the progressive growth of education in Kerala. Both urban and rural areas have almost an equal distribution of learning facilities.

The COVID-19 pandemic has caused significant setbacks in education worldwide. The pandemic has forced the closure of all educational facilities and initiated offering blended learning and virtual classes as an alternative strategy to maintain the learning environment. Significant challenges were present in the case of primary-level children. Classes were cancelled, exams at various levels were postponed, and the admissions and recruitment processes were delayed.

According to UNESCO reports, almost 1.6 billion children have been wedged by the COVID-19 epidemic, which has interrupted schooling in more than 150 countries. As a result, several nations implemented remote learning in some capacity. Although virtual learning methods continue to promise, students from economically disadvantaged groups face significant difficulties due to a lack of access to digital equipment.

Prior research on online learning has rarely studied the viewpoints of younger children or their parents, which has primarily concentrated on the opinions of parents, teachers, and students in tertiary education. This study, including observations from teachers and parents, examines the pleasure, apparent efficacy, and preference of primary school students for online learning during the pandemic.

Study Area and People

The study was conducted among primary school children (class I to VII) in the village of Malayinkeezhu in the Thiruvananthapuram district of Kerala. A survey was conducted (both online and offline) among the parents of primary school children in this village, irrespective of the educational institutions where they study. Since they cooperated well, the researcher could take interviews along with the survey. Required data regarding the impact of online learning on primary school children in this village was also collected from the teachers of Government Lower Primary Schools, Malayinkeezhu. Almost 105 parents participated directly in this survey and gave their opinions on the questions. For further clarification, an interview was also conducted among several private tuition teachers in and around the village.

Materials And Methods

The influence of COVID-19 on students' access to high-quality primary education in Kerala's Malayinkeezhu village is examined here. Initially, a detailed search was conducted with the help of secondary sources to understand the emerging trends in online education worldwide, particularly in Kerala. The impacts of online learning (both positive and negative), the opinions of primary school children regarding their acceptance of the unique learning environment, and suggestions of parents as well as teachers were made as part of the study. Since this is an anthropological study, research methods about the discipline were followed in every stage of the study. Discussions were done comprehensively with school staff to assess their preferences, perceptions, and valuable suggestions. A survey among 105 individuals randomly selected from the study village constituted the study sample, and data were collected mainly through questionnaire surveys that were done both online and offline and via unstructured interviews. The online personal survey of parents and teachers of primary class students aged 6 – 12 years in the village of Malayinkeezhu consisted of two segments, and the data of interest were:

- The practicalities of teaching and learning from home for parents and teachers during pandemic lockdown.
- The mental well-being of parents and teachers supporting learning from home during the lockdown.
- The positive and negative effects of online learning on primary school children.

The present study brought forward the facts and suggested remedial measures to rectify the inadequacies to a certain extent. Both primary and secondary data were collected to understand the positive and negative effects of the pandemic-induced lockdown on primary education in the village of Malayinkeezhu. Personal interviews of students and parents of the locality were taken as part of the primary data collection. Secondary data was collected from government sites in the state education department.

Malayinkeezhu government primary schools were visited to collect data regarding students' learning outcomes before and after the pandemic. Questionnaires were prepared in advance after considering the respondents' capacity. Statistical tools such as simple, multiple-bar diagrams and graphs were used for data presentation.

Study Design: Cross-sectional descriptive study with a quantitative approach.

Sample Size:

A random selection of primary school children's families was done in the Malayinkeezhu village, so we got a sample size of 105 individuals. The researchers opted for the non-probabilistic selection of the people considering the following inclusion criteria:

1. Those who are the parents or teachers of primary school children
2. Willing to participate.

Nature and Sources of Data:

Primary data was collected from the primary school children, their families, and teachers of Malayinkeezhu government primary schools regarding their learning methods, accessibility to digital platforms, and learning outcomes post-pandemic. Secondary data was collected through documents from the education department and the relevant offices.

Data Collection Tools and Technique:

For data collection, a questionnaire cum schedule for participants was designed to extract the information mentioned above. A separate schedule was prepared to gather basic information about the pandemic-induced impacts of learning. Face-to-face interviews were conducted in the field with the parents of primary school children.

Method of Analysis:

After collecting all primary data, it was analysed using a holistic and comparative approach. The aim was to fulfil the objectives mentioned. Statistic tools like bar graphs and pie charts were used. The outcomes were shared with the participant community and related institutions. Also, an online questionnaire survey was conducted among the parents and teachers of primary school students through Google online platforms between July and August 2022.

Research Questions

a) What is the pandemic's impact on school children's education?
b) What difficulties do schoolchildren face in online learning?
c) How much time is spent on daily online learning routines, such as the average time spent on online study (hours) /day, the medium of instruction, and the average time spent on self-study (hours)/day?

d) How can the online learning experience be used to assess satisfaction levels among students, teachers, and parents?

The survey was conducted in a transparent, informed set-up, and consent was obtained from the individuals for participation. No individual was forced against their will, and no identifying information was collected.

Data Analysis and Results

Impact of the Pandemic on Education

On January 30, 2020, after COVID-19 had started to blow out, the World Health Organization (WHO) avowed the outbreak as a Public Health Emergency of International Concern. National authorities worldwide have introduced travel restrictions, lockdowns, and occupational hazard measures in reaction to this issue. Pre-schools, schools, and universities have been closed internationally or locally in 172 nations, affecting more than 98.5% of the world's student population (UNESCO, 2020).

Teachers have been appreciative of modifying their methods of instruction and relying more and more on digital technology due to the rapid shift from traditional schooling to home education. They had to develop innovative ways to work using video conferencing and internet resources because they had little to no experience in remote learning. Along with developing these new skills, teachers had to learn how to keep kids motivated and interested while creating a secure setting where primary students could keep developing. The introduction of digital technologies for educational access was augmented through the pandemic. Educational institutions accepted blended learning and encouraged students' and teachers' technological receptiveness. Online group meetings and webinars make up for missed social and educational events, but students' and teachers' enthusiasm has declined.

The pandemic's rapid shift to online learning has provided the parents of young children affected with new opportunities and unexpected issues. Given these particular circumstances, it is critical to examine parents' attitudes toward online learning and the extent of their preparation for engaging children in online learning. The survey revealed that as many as

92% of the respondents preferred the offline learning method, compared to nearly 8% of respondents who preferred online learning.

The parents frequently encountered challenges because of a lack of time, technological issues with remote learning, and doubts about their teaching skills and expertise. Some students with particular learning difficulties suffered from the situation's worsening effects:

a) Safety
b) Save travel time
c) Affordable
d) More time for extra-curricular activities
e) Flexible schedule and environment
f) Self-disciplinary skills

The data on the difficulty children faced in online education was collected by asking the children direct questions in front of their parents. Eighty percent of children reported that they face difficulty in learning through online mode. Many children have been forced to learn in front of screens over the past two years due to the dangerous scenario brought on by the worldwide pandemic. From the study, it is understood that although teachers, staff, and school administrators made noble efforts-many of whom rapidly created online lessons, remote-teaching plans, and practical methods for satisfying kids' basic needs-challenges remained.

The shift to online learning has had consequences for students and teachers, who were instructed to modify the curricula and help their students adjust to the new learning environment. Parents and educators were more attentive than before, and many wondered whether the transition to online learning would have long-lasting effects on students who leave the classroom. Due to the far-reaching change in work life and the additional responsibility of supporting their child's educational needs, most families experienced disruption in their family environments, and many of their established routines have also changed. Due to the rapid expansion of screen technologies (such as tabs and smartphones), parents have expressed their ambiguity over whether mobile gadgets could benefit or harm their children.

The following are the major problems highlighted by the parents of primary school students:

- They are worried about their kids' potential academic deterioration due to school and online learning inconveniences.

- Parents worry that their kids spend too much time on screens.

- Parents worry about their kids' ability to sustain relationships with friends and classmates.

- The mental health of children was also a worry for parents.

According to the opinion of the surveyed population, traditional classroom learning offers minimal distraction, individual attention, hands-on practice, and more interaction and engagement with peers and teachers. To understand the impacts in detail, the researcher conducted online and direct surveys to analyse which learning method is widely accepted among the parents of primary school children. Despite the safety that online learning provides amidst the pandemic-ridden world around, the researchers came across the following disadvantages faced by primary school students, their parents and teachers:

a) Technical Issues:

Students experienced issues with launching virtual learning platforms and other online platforms, creating difficulty in online classes. Due to their limited familiarity with technology, elementary students encountered technical difficulties in online classes. The speeds with which they enrolled in the course and participated in all live sessions were significantly influenced by their ability to access the internet effectively. The internet was not sufficiently accessible or affordable since data packages are expensive compared to people's income. The rural population of the village surveyed lacked proper network connection; hence, they do not find online learning a viable option for primary school children. Failure in the network hampers the continuation of classes, making it difficult for students and teachers.

b) Lack of Technical Knowledge:

Many parents and primary school students struggle to use smartphones or even the most basic computer programmes. Moreover, they find resolving technical issues challenging. Some parents intermittently lack basic technological knowledge in logging into the system, participating in live classes, submitting assignments, and communicating with teachers.

c) Communication Issues in Online Learning:

Parents highlight the lack of communication skills as another problem. When learning online, the absence of group study and discussion usually does not happen, resulting in the absence of students' confidence to write clearly to understand the purpose of their assignments and distancing due to lockdown constrained some children to talk to their teachers and peers. Lack of interest, low technological proficiency with Apps and video calls, or an inability to communicate effectively in live chats, emails, or text messages are some of the issues identified among the students in the research population.

d) Virtual Engagement Challenge:

In-person communication is challenging for students who have trouble grasping topics. Even though teachers used to interact with the students through live sessions, presentations, recorded videos, and lectures, along with communicating through direct calls, some students opined that they felt detached emotionally. These students frequently fail to clear their doubts and face difficulty conversing directly with their teachers and friends.

e) Challenges Teachers Face:

Since most still teach in traditional classrooms, not all teachers know about online learning and its procedures. They felt it challenging to alter their teaching style. Teachers opined that student easily get distracted and lose concentration during live sessions. Occasionally, teachers could worry about the chance of missing online classes. They believe there are possibilities for misappropriation while writing online exams and presentations.

f) Affordability:

Online education requires two things:

i. A gadget (Smartphone, tablet or computer)

ii. A stable and high-speed internet connection

Money and access to resources are required to avail of the above facilities. Parents who cannot afford these or do not have access to smartphones, tablets, or laptops with an internet connection found difficulty accessing online education. This means parents without a steady income experienced difficulty managing their children's online classes.

From this survey, the researchers realised that even poor households with meagre income greatly value their children's education. Hence, they replaced their 3G mobile phones with 4G, assuring better online education for their children. Some of them even took loans from Self Help Groups (Kudumbashree) and Cooperatives to purchase laptops and tablets to ease the difficulties faced by their children during online learning.

g) Prolonged Screen Exposure:

Most kids spend more time watching screens when they have to stay home because of the pandemic. According to earlier studies, increased screen usage among pre-schoolers is linked to attention and self-regulation issues. Other unfavourable effects of excessive screen use and sedentary activities include sleep issues and the beginning of myopia. Blue light exposure in the evening inhibits melatonin production, affecting sleep onset and shortening sleep duration. The parents, who must manage their demanding employment obligations while working from home and their parenting responsibilities and home-schooling their children during the epidemic, were also in grave danger due to this predicament.

h) Health Issues:

Reports from the field show health issues due to prolonged online classes. These include eyesight problems, backache, headache, fatigue and insomnia. Unlike in classrooms, children are not required to follow proper ergonomics at home. Parents complained about their children's obesity either as a result of the accessibility of junk food at home or as a result of a lack of outside physical activity. Due to muscle tightness brought on by inactivity, parents are anxious about their children's ability to compete in sports when they resume playing. Lack of exercise, inadequate nutrition, and insufficient exposure to sunlight are additional factors that lead to calcium and vitamin D deficiency.

i) Lack of Peer Interaction:

Effective learning is built on long-term relationships between students and teachers. Their lack of social connection expressively obstructs students' satisfaction. Teachers believe that lack of social interaction in online classes during the pandemic has a significant psychological impact on students and teachers, including fear of aloneness, untimely use of mobile devices, and reduced fear of academic evaluations. Lack of social interaction has had several adverse effects, including the fact that students become bored with their studies, develop bad attendance habits, misuse technology, and lose focus.

j) Keeping Children Focused:

Generally, children did not use their computers or laptops for schoolwork in pre-pandemic time. They used these devices to watch videos and play games. The parents report that because of this, children find it challenging to focus on their studies when it is done on a computer.

k) Disruption of Routine Activities:

When children are young, having a schedule benefits them. The epidemic has significantly altered the concept of having a regular schedule. Due to inconsistent school schedules, internet pleasure, and a lack of time for tasks, most families are confused. According to several studies, children who spend much time watching screens have disturbed sleep patterns. It is a fairly common problem today because children must spend nearly eight or nine hours in front of a screen. The average amount of sleep needed by children between the ages of eleven and eighteen is seven hours. To solve this problem once and for all, promote non-screen time before bed.

A youngster should engage in reading, breathing exercises, board games, and other activities before bed and avoid watching television or online videos. It will assist students in creating a more wholesome sleep schedule. It is essential to realise that schools are also adjusting to this new normal.

Fixing a new routine is necessary because if there is ample time for domestic tasks, recreational activities, extra-curricular activities and online studies, children can clearly understand when to pay attention and relax.

Outdoor games are familiar and routine practices found among rural children. Before lockdowns, children spent ample evenings and weekends playing in the open grounds. However, with the onset of online and hybrid classes, these children are now devoid of their leisure time, though forcefully. 60% of the parents in this study opined that their children are not getting enough time for outdoor games and leisure time. It hindered children's physical activities and indirectly hampered their psychological health and development.

l) Misuse of the Internet and Social Media:

Screen time has increased at an extraordinary rate due to the pandemic outbreak. More and more families were turned to digital solutions to keep their children engaged during school closures and severe containment measures. However, not all kids have the tools, knowledge, or abilities to stay safe online. Spending more time on virtual platforms could make youngsters more vulnerable to online sexual exploitation and training. Lack of in-character interactions with friends and peers recommended them to risk-taking behaviours and lifted their risk of turning into the goal of cyberbullying.

m) Hampers Personality Development:

Prolonged screen time induces stress and burnout, directly impacting their emotional intelligence and further degrading their academic development and overall personality. The sudden switch from traditional classroom instruction to online learning has upset the kids' psychological balance. Parents and teachers fear students' feelings and emotions, which require a specific academic performance.

n) Work Management Issues with Parents:

Despite favourable circumstances, it is a reality that all parents want their children to do well in school. However, the change has proven challenging for many families. Accessibility problems have disproportionately affected lower-income families because they might not have access to two necessities for online learning: high-speed internet and a computer. Parents could help their children by spending time with them and ensuring they remain focused on their studies. It is not required to assist them daily -maybe only for a week. Children learn to focus daily for a set amount of time in this way. This further streamlines their daily activities and dramatically boosts their output during online classes.

Most children surveyed had special private tuition or were taught by their mothers at home. Since most fathers worked away from home or abroad, mothers played a significant role in educating their children. More than half are homemakers or part-time workers, and only a handful are full-time employees. So, more participants can save time educating their kids and taking care of their regular homework and activities.

Even individuals with less extreme reactions and many of their parents reported experiencing more unfavourable emotions throughout the pandemic. Additionally, throughout the 2020–21 academic year, parents, administrators, and teachers from all over the nation identified social and emotional distractions because of the most significant issues affecting their students, particularly those learning at home. Concern has also been expressed regarding children more likely to experience abuse at home due to the pandemic.

Even though online education has become the most significant progress in education, some areas of study have not yet caught up with this trend. There is no way to avoid the importance of extra-curricular activities in a child's education. Extra-curricular activities aim to provide children with a secure environment to freely express themselves and apply the academic concepts they have learned. Sports, the arts, music, and dance can improve a child's mental and physical health.

Parents can now book online sessions for their kids to entertain extra-curricular activities like singing, dancing, and even sports through many game-changing portals. Therefore, kids will not lack in any areas of their education in this way. Online learning is considerably more complex than traditional schooling. It demands far more focus and time, and it has a much more significant negative impact on the health of the student and teacher. In the study area, most schools had chosen a schedule that offered the children plenty of breaks to combat this. The 10-10 policy, which calls for 10 minutes of instruction followed by 10 minutes of break, is used in several schools. While this could be advantageous, it might impact a child's schedule and lessen their time for extra-curricular activities. Using breaks as an opportunity for work is one way to address this. For instance, they ask the child to complete a task that does not include a screen when taking a break. They can keep up with their homework while taking the breaks they need and deserve.

This study additionally reveals the disadvantages of being unable to contain different students and teachers, even when attending a web class. Students who study online will not accumulate the vital communication abilities that may be received through private interactions. Other damages reported include lack of motivation, loss of self-discipline, and the aspiration to take a look. The Ineffectiveness of technology, the issue of coaching principles to students, and the social isolation resulting from online getting to know are different bad results of online learning highlighted by teachers and parents.

Observations

It is observed from this study that to succeed in an online programme, students must be well-organised, self-motivated, and time-efficient. At the pandemic's beginning, maintaining one-on-one contact and regular check-ins between teachers and students in a virtual context was especially difficult for rural and village schools. Many students' mental health has suffered from more than a year of shocking loss, sadness, loneliness, and uncertainty, which has worsened the difficulties they experience in the classroom, whether they are taking classes online or in person. There was very little face-to-face interaction between students and teachers when learning online. The study revealed that many primary school students missed classes, which impacted their understanding of the basics.

Today, with enormous technological advancements, teachers can educate their students with online equipment while they cannot interact with them individually or specifically with their difficulties. Online chats, e-mails, and video conferencing are different manners of conversation amongst students, peers, and instructors that promote interpersonal engagement and reduce emotions of isolation.

KITE VICTERS is a State-owned, free-to-air children's educational television channel operated by Kerala Infrastructure and Technology for Education under the Department of General and Higher Education. It comprises scheduled classes mainly targeted at elementary school students who experienced difficulties accessing online classes. Teachers are indispensable, irrespective of the available technology or learning method. Professional development for teachers must be done traditionally, and support must be provided for creating pedagogical and digital tools to facilitate effective in-person and online teaching.

More research and analysis are required about the application of sound pedagogy in online teaching and learning. To continue supporting students, including those who have chosen not to attend classes or are unable to attend due to personal health concerns, distance learning has subsequently been in force until the end of the academic year. The other field of research and development focuses on developing user-friendly technologies to enable advanced, inspired, and collective online training. It would help the teaching-learning system to prepare for such uncertainty in the future.

References

Arnott L., Yelland N. (2020). Multimodal life worlds: Pedagogies for play inquiries and explorations. *Journal of Early Childhood Education Research,* 9(1):124–146.

Franklin, T. O., Burdette, P., East, T., & Mellard, D. F. (2015). Parents' role in their child's online learning experience: State education agency forum proceedings series. (Report No.2). Retrieved from Lawrence, KS.

Garbe, A., Ogurlu, U., Logan, N., & Cook, P. (2020). Parents' experiences with remote education during COVID-19 school closures. *American Journal of Qualitative Research,* 4, 45– 65. https://doi.org/10.29333/ajqr/8471.

Ho, C.S., Chee, C.Y. & Ho, R.C. (2020). Mental health strategies to combat the psychological impact of COVID-19 beyond paranoia and panic. Ann Acad Med Singapore, 49(1).

Karalis, T. (2020). Planning and evaluation during educational disruption: lessons learned from the COVID-19 pandemic for treating emergencies in education. European Journal of Education Studies.

Khalil, R., Mansour, A.E., Fadda, W.A. et al. (2020). The sudden transition to synchronised online learning during the COVID-19 pandemic in Saudi Arabia: a qualitative study exploring medical students' perspectives. *BMC Med Educ* 20, 285. https://doi.org/10.1186/s12909-020-02208-z.

Lee, M., & Figueroa, R. (2012). Internal and external indicators of virtual learning success: a guide to success in K-12 virtual learning. *Distance Learning*, 9(1), 21–28.

Ni, A. Y. (2013). Comparing the effectiveness of classroom and online learning: Teaching research methods. *Journal of Public Affairs Education*, 19, pp 199–215. https://doi.org/10.1080/15236803.2013.12001730.

Nouwen M., Zaman B. (2018). Redefining the role of parents in young children's online interactions. A value-sensitive design case study. *International Journal of Child-Computer Interaction,* 18:22. doi: 10.1016/j.ijcci.2018.06.001.

Schmid, R. F., Bernard, R. M., Borokhovski, E., Tamim, R. M., Abrami, P. C., Surkes, M. A., Woods, J. (2014). The effects of technology use in postsecondary education: A meta-analysis of classroom applications. *Computers & Education*, 72, 271– 291. https://doi.org/10.1016/j.compedu.2013.11.002

Smith S.J., Burdette P.J., Cheatham G.A., Harvey S.P. (2016). Parental role and support for online learning of students with disabilities: A paradigm shift. *Journal of Special Education Leadership,* 29(2):101–112.

Van Lancker, W. and Parolin, Z., (2020). COVID-19, school closures, and child poverty: a social crisis in the making. The Lancet Public Health, 5(5), pp. e243-e244.

Zalaznick M. (2019). Online service intends to expand pre-K access. (EQUITY) *District Administration,* 55(8):12.

9

The Cultural Landscape of Borderland Markets: An Anthropological Study Of The Assam-Arunachal Borderlands Weekly Markets

Ratna Tayeng

Introduction

This paper is based on ongoing research on the weekly markets along the Assam-Arunachal border. These weekly markets are different from other markets in many respects. It is a marketing system where, on a particular day of the week, traders display their commodities in a specific place. The commodities sold and bought in these markets range from small objects of daily use to vegetables, clothes, toys, beads, and electrical gadgets, and the cost of most of these goods is comparatively cheaper compared to the price of similar commodities sold in traditional markets. Theodore C. Bestor (2001) noted that marketplaces vary enormously. They differ according to the local, regional, or global scope of production, distribution, or consumption of the goods and services they trade. Alfred Gell (1982:427) noted, "In non-industrialized societies, markets are arguably central in the understanding of the social system as a whole".

Many scholars worldwide have studied the socio-economic implications of the weekly market. Anthropological studies of markets analyse them as nodes of complex social processes and generators of cultural activity as well as realms for economic exchange (Bestor,2001). According to

Kishore Dash (1996: 185), "This is perhaps the most attractive field of research for social scientists in South-East Asia at present," but "less studied in anthropology" (Ramirez, 2014: 100). Anthropologists with long-term field research can offer a solid corpus of local-level analyses, including detailed studies on the types of commodities traded, the economic impact on local communities, and the social dynamics within these markets, of the dynamic economic relations and transformation in the northeast.

The history of these weekly markets in the Arunachal borderland is as old as the expansion of the British Empire in the early 19th century. However, there were some trade centres along the foothills, where traders from the hills and plains met and used to exchange their goods in the past before the British came to the area. Nonetheless, due to the absence of a money economy, the commodities were exchanged according to the bare needs of individuals, families and villages (Mantche, 2018). Sikdar (1982) states, "Trade in the foothill plains was conducted through an organised market system at the duars. The duars, or passes, through which the tribes came down to the plains, were managed by officers known as Duarias. The first commercial venture at Sadiya was undertaken under the initiative of David Scott, agent to the governor-general, as early as 1826. Besides the periodical markets, annual fairs were held in Udalguri and Doimara (Sikdar 1982:18 & 21).

Trade flourished with the active encouragement of the British authorities. They thought pacifying the people and establishing peace in the entire region was imperative. They realised the importance of commercial intercourse in enhancing their relationship with the hill people, as they needed their essential requirements from the plains. Once the tribes became dependent on the plains for their requirements, it would give the British government a better chance to exert political influence over the hill tribes. With these aims, they wanted to organise annual fairs in the Assam-Arunachal borderlands that continued from the Ahom period. There used to be 35 fairs and duars for traditional Trade, connecting Assam during British and pre-British times. Among these 35 duars, the Udalguri, Sadiya, and Doimara markets were the largest, where Arunachalee and Assamese used to trade and barter.

People in the Arunachal foothills had apparent reasons to contact and trade with those in the Assam plains. Firstly, it is one of the most inhospitable places for farming due to the rugged mountains and, secondly, the unavailability of essential articles of daily consumption in the hills. Therefore, the British government felt that effective and organised trade fairs would help the hill people cater to their needs. Thus, Darrang, Udalgiri, north Lakhimpur, Sadiya, and Margherita developed into trade marts. The tribal people, through transactions at these fairs, came to appreciate the value of money and were lured to these marts by urges of profit ()

Such a commercial relationship was more marked with the Abors (present-day Adis) of the Sadiya Division. It was so because three passes (Duar) were opened at Sadiya, Kobo, and Dola (Gogoi, 1958). The Abors brought Jangphai, cotton, ginger, chillies, beetle leaves, and musk pods; they took salt, cloth, and other necessities from the plains. Cosh (1837) writes, "These people (hill tribes) descend to their markets at Sauddia only in the cold weather and depart to their snows as soon as the Simala tree puts forth its blossoms" (Cosh, 1837, p. 144). Not just Abors, "the Miris, Mishmis, Khamptis, and Singphos also used to bring pepper, unit, ginger, wax, ivory, cotton, Mishmi-teeta, which they exchanged for glass, beads, clothes, salt and money. The fairs were conducted based on a barter and exchange system that proved beneficial both for the Assamese and the Arunachalees and mutually benefited them" Basu (1970: 191).

Sadiya Market in the 19th Century

"The Sadiya market fair catered to the needs of the Arunachal tribes like the Adis, Mishmis, Khamptis, Singphos, Noctes, and Wanchos. They came to the plains by crossing the rivers and through different passes. European planters from Tezpur and Mongoldoi and traders from Dibrugarh and Lakhimpur frequented the Sadiya fair" (Assam Secretariat Record Foreign Proceeding, June April 1877, No. 15). The government made police arrangements to maintain peace at the fair sites. The government provided the usual accommodation to the hill people by constructing temporary sheds. The essential items were rubber, wax, Mishmi-teeta, Mishmi cloth, Adi cloth, elephant tusks, baskets, and mats. The import articles were Eri-cloth, beads, iron, broad-cloth, opium, buffalo, cattle, salt, tea, and sugar. In 1874, 20 mounds of rubber and 110 mounds of wax were sold by the hill tribes, which amounted to Rs 6,000 and Rs 4,400, respectively (Ibid). Regarding exports from Assam, the Eri cloth and salt amounted to Rs 1,800 and Rs 1,120, respectively (Ibid).

Contemporary Weekly Markets along the Assam-Arunachal borders

As mentioned earlier, these markets do not open every day. These markets open once or twice a week. The trader who opens a shop at the market in the morning closes it in the evening. The goods sold in these markets are small, as people only visit to sell and purchase their daily needs. The most critical weekly markets along the Assam-Arunachal boundary are Harmoty Sunday Market, Silapathar Friday Market, Sunday Jonai Bazaar, Friday Paglam Bazaar, and Santipur Friday Market.

People buy a variety of things for everyday use from these weekly markets. Here, they buy all products they do not manufacture themselves. They regularly purchase salt, oil, ornaments, and clothing. As every commodity is now valued in terms of money, the transactions are predominantly in cash, and the barter system is almost non-existent.

Interestingly, beads are the most popular item for these weekly markets. Almost all markets have bead shops, which keep all the Arunachal tribes' beads in their shops. Buyers from Arunachal are primarily women; some buy for domestic purposes, while most buy for business purposes. Women buy beads at wholesale prices and sell them in the state at a higher price. The Nyishis, the Apatanis, and the Adis are the regular customers. The bestselling season for beads is from December to April. The main agricultural products available in these weekly markets are paddy, mustard, potato, radish, brinjal, cabbage, tomato, beans, chilli, onion, ginger, turmeric, pineapple, orange, lemon, banana, betel nut, and betel leaves. Producer farmers depend on these markets not only to dispose of their products for cash but also to procure agricultural inputs and other non-farm products that are not produced locally.

The Cultural Landscape of Borderland Markets

Pale Jonai Tuesday Bazar, Assam

Piglet and local herbs at Paglam Bazaar

Table 1 Weekly Market Places in border areas of East Siang and Dhemaji

Name of the Market	Participant Villages	Location of the market	Items available	Day of Market	Traders
Mer Bazar	Mer, Gadum, Paglam, Namsing, Seram, Borguli, Bijari,	Arunachal Pradesh, East Siang	Vegetables, Meat, Fruits, Basketry, Brass utensils, Iron Utensils,	Sunday	Traders are mainly from Assam. Most of the vegetable

Name of the Market	Participant Villages	Location of the market	Items available	Day of Market	Traders
	Bomjir, Dambuk		Leather goods, Aluminum Utensils, Earthen utensils, Egg and livestock, Wooden utensils, Stationery goods, Clothes, Umbrella, Mosquito nets, Fishing nets of various kinds, Rice, Atta, Dal, Jungle products such as honey		s come from Arunachal villages.
Paglam Bazar	Mer, Gadum, Paglam, Namsing, Seram, Borguli, Bijari,	Dibang Valley, Arunachal Pradesh	All sorts of local commodities are available: earthen utensils,	Friday	Traders are mainly from Assam

The Cultural Landscape of Borderland Markets

Name of the Market	Participant Villages	Location of the market	Items available	Day of Market	Traders
	Bomjir, Dambuk		rope, meat, Tobacco, Tomato, Reed Broom, Betel nut and leaves, mats, dao, plough, axe, and spade.		
Jonai Bazar	Ruksin, Rayang, Poklung, Debing, Depi, Ngorlung, Niklok, Mikong, Maknang, Linka, Leku etc	Dhemaji, Assam	Cosmetics, blankets, dress materials, mats, semi-precious stones, bicycle parts, mobile accessories, dairy products, cement, processed food items, sanitary goods, wooden furniture, herbal roots,	Daily	Traders are only from Assam.

Name of the Market	Participant Villages	Location of the market	Items available	Day of Market	Traders
			household utensils, and electric appliances		
Pale Bazar	Ruksin, Rayang, Poklung, Debing, Depi, Ngorlung, Niklok, Mikong, Maknang, Linka, Leku etc	Ruksin, East Siang, Arunachal Pradesh	Vegetables, household items, meat, fruits, betel leaf, betel nuts, fish, bamboo, and bamboo-made materials, piggery, gamchha, Dao, plough, axe, spade, chisel, handicraft items	Tuesday	Traders are only from Assam; most vegetables come from Arunachal villages.
Leku Forest Bazar Market	Ruksin, Rayang, Poklung, Debing, Depi, Ngorlung, Niklok,	Leku, East Siang, Arunachal Pradesh	Fresh vegetables, Fruits, Garlic, Onion, Chilies, bamboo,	Thursday	Traders are mainly from Assam. Most of the

The Cultural Landscape of Borderland Markets

Name of the Market	Participant Villages	Location of the market	Items available	Day of Market	Traders
	Mikong, Maknang, Linka, Leku etc		Minor Forest products, fishing instruments, lungi, Dao, plough, axe, spade, chisel		vegetables come from Arunachal villages.
Debing Bazar	Depi, Moli, Ruksin, Rayang, Debing	Debing, East Siang, Arunachal Pradesh	Fresh vegetables, Fruits, Garlic, Onion, Chilies, bamboo, Minor Forest products, fishing instruments, lungi, Dao, plough, axe, spade, chisel	Friday	Traders are mainly from Assam.

Source: Fieldwork

Since opening many such weekly markets in the region, they have supplied all the essential commodities in the nearby villages. Neighbouring villagers sell whatever is in season. Not only neighbouring villagers but also villages from far-flung areas visit this market. There are several reasons why people visit this market. One reason is that everything is cheaper in Assam due to the region's lack of transportation and communication facilities. These markets are heaven for Arunachal since the state has no industries.

Some people purchase materials for resale, but most purchase them for daily consumption. Some people visit these markets to purchase herbal medicines and moonstones. Many folk therapists in the locality are specialists in treating infertility, broken bones, jaundice, malaria, dysentery, and typhoid. They come to visit these markets. There is also a cattle market where one can sell and buy cows, goats, and pigs.

Some people even go to these markets specifically to look for and pick agricultural labourers if they are available there. Most of the agricultural labourers working in the adjoining border areas of East Siang are from bordering villages in Assam. Often, these labourers are engaged on a contract basis. The monthly contracts range from Rs 3,000 to 5,000. Not only in the agricultural field, but they are also invited to or engaged in fencing the bamboo garden, kitchen garden, ginger field, and cutting wood. Many are also engaged in house and road construction work. Apart from men and women, petite girls aged 10–20 are kept as housemaids in many Adi families.

Table 2 Prices of crafts and implements in the weekly market

Sl. No.	Name		Material used	Price (in Rs.)
	Local Name	English		
1.	Egin	Basket	Bamboo	500/-
2.	Epo	Winnowing fan	Bamboo	400/-
3.	Ebar	Basket	Bamboo	100/-
4.	Epu	Mat used for storing grain	Cane and Bamboo	1500/-
5.	Ebong	Kind of parasol	Bamboo, Tokow leaves	300/-
6.	Tali	Haversack for men	Cane	1000/-
7.	Nangal	Plough	Wood and Iron	1500/-
8.	Moi	Leveller	Wood	500/-

9.	Kacchi	Sickle	Iron	100/-
10.	Ageing	Axe	Iron and Bamboo	300/-
11.	Pakur	Spade	Iron and Bamboo	200/-
12.	Kurpi	Blade for wedding	Wood and Iron	100/-
13.	Dola	Basket	Bamboo	200/

Table 3 Prices of crops and fruits in the weekly markets

English Name	Local Name	Quantity	Price In Rs
VEGETABLES:			
Brinjal	Bayom	1 kg	20/-
Ginger	Take	1 kg	20/-
Pumpkin	Asitapa	1kg	10/-
Tomato	Aying tumpuluk	1kg	15/-
Local onion	Dilap	1 kg	20/-
-	Papuk	1	10/-
-	Onyin	25 grams	10/-
-	Marshang	25 grams	10/-
Coriander	Ori	5 grams	20/-
Lady's finger	Bendi	1 kg	20/-
Cucumber	Makung	1 kg	30/-
Gourd	Par	1 piece	15/-
Bitter guard	Kerela	1 kg	20/-
Pulses	Peron	1 kg	20/-
Country bean	Rondol	1 kg	20/-
Fern	Takang	25 grams	10/-
Mustards	Tusut petu	10 grams	10/-

English Name	Local Name	Quantity	Price In Rs
	Tulang petu	,,	10/-
	Tugap petu	,,	10/-
-	Kasiang kopi	1 kg	20/-
-	Kosana kopi	1 kg	20/-
Papaya	Omri	1 piece	10/-
Colocasia	Enge	1 kg	20/-
Sweet potato	Singgio engine	3-4 piece	20/-
Chili	Mirsi; sibol, simuk, pettang mirsi etc	5 grams	10/-
	Man mirsi	,,	20/-
Soyabean	Ronyang	50 grams	60/-
FRUITS:			
Jack fruit	Belang	One piece	10/-
Lichi	Lisu	10-15 grams	30/-
-	Bogori	25 grams	10/-
Guava	Mudurang	1 kg	10/-
Sugarcane	Tabat	1 kg	30/-
Mango	Tagung	1 kg	120/-
Pineapple	Takobelang	1 kg	70/-
Lemon	Nimbu	1 kg	20/-
Betel Nut	Tamul	1 kg	100/-
Betel Leave	Pan	1 kg	20/-
Banana	Kopak	10 pieces	20/-
-	Lokyo	10-15 piece	10/-
-	Sumpa	Two pieces	5/-

English Name	Local Name	Quantity	Price In Rs
-	Belam	Three pieces	15/-
-	Komker	10 pieces	10/-
Orange	Tasing	Five pieces	20/-
-	Rabab Tasing	One piece	10/-
Pears	Naspoti	1 kg	20/-
Coconut	Narikol	1 kg	50/-
-	Bureng	1 kg	20/-
Plum	Plam	1 kg	20/-
Wild Walnut	Angke	1 kg	20/-
Star Fruit	Kordoi	1 kg	20/-
Amla	Amloki	1 kg	20/-
Watermelon	Kumrung Makung	1 kg	40/-
Tamarind	Imli	1 kg	50/-

The rates of different kinds of handicrafts and forest produce (vegetables and fruits) are given in the table. The rates generally vary concerning demand and supply. Also, the rate of commercial crops and fruits differs from season to season, depending upon the production quantity. Excess products are sold at cheaper rates. Generally, the rates also come down in the afternoon if the sellers do not get the sales required for working long hours. However, whatever rates are prevalent in weekly markets are significantly lower than in traditional markets.

Paglam Bazaar: A famous weekly Market:

Paglam Bazaar

Paglam Bazaar is one of the oldest weekly markets in Arunachal, bordering Assam. It used to be the nodal centre of market-related activities for the entire Mebo and Dambuk area before completing the Ranaghat Bridge in Pasighat. This weekly market was established at the Arunachal Pradesh border checkpoint, a convenient location for locals from both Assam and Arunachal to congregate. It is situated in the Lower Dibang Valley District, 50 km South of Dambuk and 95 km from Pasighat.

Paglam market starts at 6 a.m. and closes at around 4 p.m. Marketing is most effective in the morning. The attendance at this market ranged from 500-1000 people. The market opened once a week, i.e., on Friday. The vendors are mostly from Assam, Dhola and Dibrugarh areas. It is through these traders that goods reach border villages. These traders buy their things in bigger towns like Dibrugarh, Dhola, Silapathar, Lakhimpur, and Dhemaji. Some people from the neighbouring villages also put up shops in this weekly market. The traders who put up their shops in Paglam Bazaar also travelled to nearby weekly markets. They set up shops in different weekly markets and return to the same place once a week.

Regrettably, this market still lacks adequate facilities. Most sellers sell their products in the open air without a storage facility. As a result, the sellers face many troubles during the rainy season. People living in Paglam and neighbouring villages pay Rs 5 to 8 thousand for one bag of cement if available. People must travel an unmotorable road to reach Pasighat and Roing, which is only possible in winter.

Conclusion

Based on general observation, Arunachal borderlands, from the very early days, had some economic relations within and across the borders. The trade fairs organised by the British government benefited the hill tribes and the people of the plains of Assam. The tribes from the hills attended the fairs to dispose of their surplus products and procure their essential requirements. In return, the people of Assam benefitted by procuring the precious forest products that had come to the market sites. Lila Gogoi (1958) writes, "During the pre-British period, these foothills of Assam and Arunachal Pradesh were symbolised as grounds for economic exchanges and mutual dependency between the hills and plains". Some even settled in the foothill plains for more effortless living, establishing a communication link between the hills and the plains. It not only paved the way for social and cultural contact with the outside world but also enabled the tribal society to mark an end to their geographical isolation.

Today, borderland people sell their products in these weekly markets. As a result, these weekly markets play a significant role in the economy of border people. These markets also serve as a centre for socio-political communication. People's stories from the Assam-Arunachal borderland show that, for all practical purposes, boundaries do not matter. It is more so because the people who have lived along the boundary engage in particular occasions, influence cultures, and facilitate exchange between people. It is a place where mixed people share memories, and these memories can be identified in the form of festivals like Bihu, Ali-Aye Ligang, Diwali, and Durga Puja, where lots of cultural exchange takes place by participating in the festivals. The administrative boundary of the state does not stand in the way of the rational choice of markets for an economic transaction. The Arunachal people sustained all markets along the Assam-Arunachal border. After all, markets do not differentiate customers based on citizenship. These have acted as exchange agents and role models to bring and sustain harmony among various communities in the border region.

References

Adams, Robert McC., J. M. Adovasio, Burchard Brentjes, H. Neville Chittick, Yehudi A. Cohen, Rolf Gundlach, Frank Hole, William H. McNeill, James Mellaart, Janice Stargardt, Bruce G. Trigger, Gary A. Wright and Henry T. Wright, (1974). Anthropological Perspectives on Ancient Trade, Current Anthropology, Vol. 15. No. 3, pp. 239–258.

Basu, N.K. (1970). Assam in the Ahom Age, Calcutta, p-191.

Bestor, T. C. (2001). Markets: Anthropological Aspects, International Encyclopedia of the Social & Behavioral Sciences, 9227–9231.

Cosh, J., M. (1937). (1975). Topography of Assam, New Delhi: SanskaranPrakashak.

Dash, K. C. (1996). The Political Economy of Regional Cooperation in South Asia, Pacific Affairs, Vol. 69, No.2 (Summer, 1996), pp-185-209.

Gell, A. (1982). The Market Wheel: Symbolic Aspects of an Indian Tribal Market, Man, Vol. 17, No. 3, pp. 470–491.

Gogoi, L. (1958). The Age-Old Amity of The Hills and The Plains, in Parag Chalma, 1958, The Outlook (ON N.E.F.A., Assam Sahitya Sabha), Jorhat, Assam.

Luthra, P. N. (1971). North-East Frontier Agency Tribes: Impact of Ahom and British Policy, Economic and Political Weekly, Vol. 6, No. 23 (Jun. 5, 1971), pp. 1143-1145+1147-1149.

Mantche, Chow Chandra (2018). A note on the trade of the Khamtis of Arunachal Pradesh

during pre-colonial and colonial period, Research Guru: Online Journal of Multidisciplinary Subjects, Vol. 12, Issue-3, pp. 214-223.

Ramirez, P. (2013). People of the Margins: Across Ethnic Boundaries in North-East India, New Delhi: Spectrum Publication.

Sikdar, S. (1982). Tribalism vs Colonialism: British Capitalistic Intervention and Transformation of Primitive Economy of Arunachal Pradesh in the Nineteenth Century, Social Scientist, Vol. 10, No. 12 (Dec. 1982), pp. 15–31.

10

The Significance of a Longer Post-Menopausal Phase of Life in Fertility Enhancement and Child Survival: The "Grandmother Hypotheses" Deconstructed

Maitreyee Sharma
Shabnam Khatoon

Menopause Defined

Menopause is the permanent cessation of menstruation for 12 months brought on by an oestrogen depletion and is not a pathology (Peacock & Ketvertis, 2022) and is often identified one year following the last menstrual period (Col et al., 2009). Caucasian women in developed countries attain menopause between 50.1 and 51.5. (McKinlay, 1996; median 51.3; Col et al., 2009). According to some research, Latina (Gold et al., 2001; Alvarado, 1988) and African American (Bromberger et al., 1997) women experience natural menopause roughly two years earlier than white women. The average age of menopause of an Indian woman is 46.2 years, much less than their Western counterparts (Ahuja, 2016). Women's ovarian follicle counts tend to decline as they age. Granulosa cells of the ovary, which were the significant producers of estradiol and inhibin, start declining gradually (Peacock & Ketvertis, 2022). Follicle-stimulating hormone (FSH) and luteinising hormone (LH) synthesis rise due to the lack of inhibition from oestrogen and inhibition of gonadotropins. Because LH is eliminated from the blood more quickly, FSH levels are typically greater than LH. The hypothalamic-pituitary-ovarian axis is thrown off track as oestrogen levels drop. Because of this, endometrial growth fails, leading to irregular menstrual periods (Peacock & Ketvertis, 2022).

Contextualising the longer post-menopausal phase in Human females

Why female humans experience a long post-reproductive phase after menopause has long piqued the curiosity of evolutionary biologists and anthropologists. The distinct post-menopausal phase of life that distinguishes humans from other primates may have coevolved with our remarkable longevity (Hawkes et al., 1998). Nearing the end of their maximal life span, chimpanzees in captivity often reach menopause at around 52 years of age (Videan et al., 2006; Kim et al., 2012). Chimpanzees and shorter-lived monkeys, which likewise experience definite menopause in captivity, have no post-reproductive phase in natural populations (Clarkson et al., 2016). Primates like the chimpanzees that need extended maternal care for their offspring show an early end of fecundity like humans. However, reproductive senescence almost overlaps with the timing of their death. Only human females tend to have a long gap between menopause and the timing of death. Why is it so? The answer to this question will be attempted in this paper by considering various pioneer studies done in this field. Humans can live up to about 100 years, but fertility in women universally ends in about half that period, much before other bodily frailties do (Pavelka & Fedigan, 1991).

The question is how this distinctively human "post-reproductive" aspect of life history came to be favoured by natural selection. Various physiological and sociocultural studies predict that this long phase of the gap has an evolutionary significance. G.C. Williams (1957), the first to postulate this, stated that elderly women should stop having children at an advanced age to minimise the adverse consequences and concentrate on the existing children. By doing this, they would minimise the risks of ageing that come with reproduction and remove a potential threat to the survival of their present offspring (Williams, 1957). Grandmothers and other forms of social capital have played an essential role in the evolution of the extended post-reproductive phase of human life history, which can be described in terms of its "inclusive fitness" (Hawkes et al.,1998). Other studies stated that even though many primates share food with their offspring (Feistner & McGrew, 1989), only human mothers give their weaned children a significant portion of their diets. By doing this, women can make use of resources that their children cannot access but that they can acquire quickly. Deeply buried tubers are a year-round mainstay for some hunter-gatherers (Hawkes et al., 1989; Hawkes et al., 1997). Mothers can go foraging by keeping the weaned children with the grandmothers who, after menopause, do not generally have young children, thus increasing the fertility of their daughters or other fecund closed females in the household.

Ageing mothers who stopped becoming fertile and focused all of their reproductive energy on ensuring the survival of their already-born children would produce more offspring than those who continued to have high-risk pregnancies with infants that were unlikely to survive the mother's death (Hawkes et al., 1998). The female reproductive system in humans ages more rapidly than any other system in the body (Moghadam et al., 2022). Oocyte and primary follicle loss start prenatally at an astounding pace (Finch et al., 2000; Krysko et al., 2008). One million oocytes are present at the birth of a baby girl, out of an initial 7 million at 20 weeks of gestation, and the loss continues postnatally. Throughout a human reproductive lifetime, only around 350 oocytes-or roughly 1/20,000th of the initial 7 million possible eggs-could be ovulated (Finch, 2014). Apoptotic processes unique to the ovary are involved in the mechanisms of oocyte attrition. According to others, eliminating damaged oocytes with chromosomal abnormalities or malformed mitochondria by oocyte attrition is an evolutionary adaptation (Krakauer & Mira, 1999). Primary oocytes are confirmed to be prone to damage as they age because the rise in maternal age is directly associated with chromosomal abnormalities in the foetus (Sadler, 2011).

Contextualising the Longer post-Menopausal Phase, Human Evolution and Adaptation

One of the early assumptions was that menopause should not occur since there should not be any selection for survival following the cessation of reproduction, according to the traditional life-history hypothesis (Cant & Johnstone, 2008; Williams, 1957). The argument is that grandmothers' involvement enables mothers to have more children. Therefore, women genetically predisposed to live longer would eventually have more grandchildren who would also inherit the genes for longevity. Numerous hypotheses exist which state the existential significance of menopause in humans. These hypotheses can be categorised as adaptive and non-adaptive (Brent et al., 2015; Nattrass et al., 2019; Peccei, 2001). According to adaptive theories, post-reproductive life is based on inclusive fitness (Brent et al., 2015). As a result, an older female needs to reduce her reproduction in favour of boosting the reproductive success of her kin (Johnstone & Can't, 2010), focussing on the action of natural selection on human populations.

In contrast, non-adaptive hypotheses contend that menopause is merely the result of a physiological trade-off that favours early reproduction (Wood et al., 2000). Early reproductive cessation has the advantage of enhancing adult daughters' and nieces' fertility as well as the survivability of their descendants. On the other hand, the new approach of the grandmother hypothesis explained human longevity and the long post-reproductive lifespan in women (Hawkes et al., 1998). According to this hypothesis, grandmothers cause a wide range of human traits, including younger weaning ages, longer childhoods, longer life expectancy, and more children than hominoid relatives (Hawkes et al., 1998). The availability of weaning foods, which young juveniles cannot supply for themselves but which caring grandmothers can provide for them, has prompted a shift in diet to account for these varied features. The new grandmother hypothesis emphasises longevity as the outcome of inclusive fitness, whereas the old grandmother hypothesis examines the advantages of early reproductive cessation to invest in offspring reproductive success. Saha and her team (2022) demonstrated that grandmothering may have played a significant role in the evolution of specific genes that support a powerful immune system and resistance to ageing-related cognitive decline.

In contrast to the idea of "antagonistic pleiotropy," which holds that natural selection does not take place in old age (Williams, 1957; Byars & Voskarides, 2020), one current explanation for such prolonged post-reproductive survival is late-life kin selection of grandmothers and other elderly caregivers of helpless young. Specific derived gene variants exist only in the human genome and not the genomes of any other "great apes" and directly or indirectly affect post-reproductive, late-life cognition

(Schwarz et al., 2016). According to Hawkes (2016), this was viewed as genomic confirmation of the evolution of post-menopausal human longevity. A more extended period of growth and maturation must have occurred over the past 2 million years due to a relative and absolute increase in brain size (Charnov et al., 2001). The selected factors causing this growth are yet unknown. However, they may be ecological, social, and technocultural, or more likely blends thereof, with language playing a significant role as a distinguishing trait of our species without a clearly defined age of origin. It also led to changes in our genus' anatomy and life history that may have occurred long before Homo sapiens, possibly dating back to the origin of the genus Homo (Saha et al., 2022). Compared to existing great apes, our species has a shorter interbirth interval, which may have significantly influenced grandmother assistance for the young. Grandmothering and post-reproductive elder mothering would have significantly impacted the transmission of knowledge and norms, which in our species are critically dependent on language ability and have no known analogue in any other species (Saha et al., 2022). It is a fallacy to believe that women today with longer life expectancy live post-menopause because the life expectancy of humans is more significant than it was during our evolutionary history (Fausto-Sterling, 1992). The main reason for lower longevity in the past was high death rates at every younger life stage, not deaths due to ageing (Hawkes & Jones, 2005).

From Hypothetical Domain to the Real-Life Situations

Some claim that the longer lifespan in post-industrial societies is an artefact rather than an adaptation, explaining this phenomenon (Weiss, 1981). Most mothers can, however, live until their mid-forties in horticultural and hunting and gathering communities, where life expectancy at reproductive age is higher (Lancaster & King, 1985; Howell, 1979). There is a good chance that most women who reached childbearing age experienced menopause long before the Industrial Revolution. An anthropologist named Kristen Hawkes extensively researched the Hadza people, a community of hunter-gatherers in northern Tanzania who consume many wild foods, including berries and tubers, when Hawkes discovered the first concrete evidence supporting the grandmother hypothesis. Hawkes highlighted how the support and assistance of grandmothers in a subsistence economy and childrearing allowed their daughters to have additional children. Hadza women generally work long hours foraging, grandmothers the longest. The data strongly support the idea that older women harness extra tubers for their younger female kin to help them save energy when foraging, thus saving time for the daughters to rear and bear additional children.

It is implied that most of what older women acquire is passed on to younger women due to their high tuber income and weight fluctuation patterns across age categories. The fact that older women lose weight more quickly than younger women may mean that older women are not just spending reproductive effort but are paradoxically increasing it as "post-reproductive" as their reproductive potential drops (Hawkes et al., 1989). They also mentioned that the local ecology may involve differences in the fitness-related costs and benefits of foraging in different communities. For example, two elements of the regional environment may be significant! Kung situation. First, the Kalahari's seasonal high temperatures and water shortage may place elderly women under relatively harsh circumstances, lowering their foraging return rates and raising their survival costs (Blurton et al., 1978). This is in contrast to what Hawkes et al. (1989) saw among the Hadza. In addition, babysitting appears to involve far more active monitoring among the! Kung than it did among the Hadza may be due to extreme environment (reasons not confirmed).

The childcare available in foraging communities plays a significant role in the foraging income of the younger daughters. So, seniors may get the most extraordinary increment in inclusive fitness through increased babysitting (Hawkes et al., 1989). Children in the Hadza community were active foragers (Blurton Jones et al., 1989), and older women had high foraging productivity (Hawkes et al., 1989). However, young children are too little to be very efficient at digging the deeply hidden tubers that are year-round staples. Their mothers' foraging efforts influenced the weight increase in children. However, after the birth of her next child, that linkage disappeared, and the gains of the weaned youngsters were dependent on the foraging of the grandmothers (Hawkes, 2003). Thus, the idea is that grandmothers can help gather food and feed children before they can eat on their own, allowing mothers to have additional children. Without grandmothers, the likelihood of a mother giving birth to a child already two years old is substantially lower since, unlike other primates, humans cannot feed and care for themselves right away after weaning. The older child must suffer due to the mother's need to prioritise the new baby.

However, grandmothers can address this issue by serving as additional caretakers and acting as allomothers. The "grandmother hypothesis," put forth by Hawkes in 1997, claimed that the unappreciated evolutionary significance of grandmothering could explain menopause. According to Hawkes, grandmothering contributes to "a full range of social capacities that then serve as the foundation for the evolution of other distinctly human traits, including pair bonding, larger brains, acquiring new skills, and our propensity for cooperation" (Hawkes 1997, pp. 551-577). Even though the idea is inconclusive, the new mathematical data adds yet another significant piece of evidence. Before the woman had another child, Hawkes discovered a correlation between children's growth and their mother's foraging activity. She said their development was related to "grandmother's work." It might facilitate anthropologists' understanding of the evolution of humans and female longevity.

As a result, a grandmother promotes the conception of more children, passing along more copies of her genes to succeeding generations. According to one idea, grandmothering helped genes associated with slower ageing in women than their ancestors spread in prehistoric times, increasing predicted lifespans. It was generally thought that the males accumulated food for their families during hominid evolution, but much evidence proves that they used to bring back the hunt at their sites. Stone tools and bones of multiple large animals in early archaeological sites can seem hard evidence that ancestral hunters brought their kills home to provision their mates and offspring. While at sites, it was the women and elderly grandmothers who helped scrape and push out the bone marrow from the large bones. This notion of Isaac (1978) is supported by Hawkes (2022), While this idea remains controversial. Fox et al. (2010) discovered that a grandmother's effect on her grandchildren changes depending on how closely related they are to each other on the X chromosome by especially examining child mortality in the first three years of life. They found that the presence of a paternal grandmother in all seven populations they studied had a harmful effect on grandsons because her presence was linked with increased mortality. However, a recent study (Chapman et al., 2018) discovered that grandsons' survival is increased in the presence of a maternal grandmother more than a paternal grandmother and that granddaughters' survival is higher than grandsons' in the presence of a paternal grandmother. The central hypothesis, however, that paternal grandmothers would increase granddaughter survival more than maternal grandmothers was not supported, which reduced the overall strength of the hypothesis as provided by Fox et al. (2010).

Contentions and Agreements with Grandmother Hypotheses

According to the "grandmother hypothesis," based on these implicit fitness justifications, post-reproductive life results from the adaptive advantages of supporting offspring's reproductive efforts by caring for grandchildren's food and safety (Hawkes et al., 1998). However, these supportive advantages are arguably insufficient to explain how reproductive cessation evolved in the first place (Can't & Johnstone, 2008; Lahdenperä et al., 2012). Although Sievert acknowledges grandmothers' crucial responsibilities in raising their children and grandchildren, she does not believe that this is why women continue to live through menopause and the reproductive years. The fact that women are born with all the eggs they will ever need made it possible for our species to have post-fertile grandmothers in the first place.

Fish, amphibians, and most reptiles produce eggs throughout their lives. Therefore, their females never go through menopause or experience post-menopausal symptoms. Chapman et al. (2019) observed that the presence of maternal grandmothers 50 to 75 years old boosted the survival of the grandchildren after weaning, demonstrating the fitness benefit of post-reproductive ageing. Co-residence with paternal grandmothers 75 years and older, however, was hazardous to grandchild survival, with those grandmothers who were near death and likely in worse health being notably connected with reduced grandchild survival. They also suggested that the age limitations of gaining inclusive fitness from grandmothering suggest that grandmothering can be selected for post-reproductive longevity only up to a certain point (Chapman et al., 2019). Thus, the explanation and benefits of grandmothering may vary between maternal and paternal grandmothers. Grandmother impacts on grandchild survival varied between maternal and paternal grandmothers (Sear & Coall, 2011)] as well as by the age of the grandchild (Beise & Voland, 2002), demonstrating that help can vary contextually.

One of the recent conclusions was given by Chapman et al. (2019), who stated that grandmothers gain fitness advantages by enhancing grandchild survival, supporting the idea that women's post-reproductive longevity is under positive selection. Importantly, they also discover that grandmothers' advantages over their grandchildren diminish with age and/or the grandmother's deteriorating health (Chapman et al., 2019). Watkins (2021) created a model to address a common criticism of the grandmother hypothesis that human fathers, not grandmothers, are better equipped to be allomothers because of their physical strength and strong financial incentives to support their children. However, the study found that, unlike maternal grandmothers, fathers can never be sure that the children they are raising are their own.

The grandmother hypothesis is shown to be more tenable than a hypothesis that emphasises the contribution of men in the model when paternity uncertainty is considered (Watkins, 2021). In order to better comprehend this pattern, we show that human cognitive capacities, in conjunction with grandmothering, are necessary for its emergence. Indeed, cognitive abilities enable the accumulation of knowledge and experience throughout a lifetime, giving one an advantage when acquiring resources. The extra resources may then be employed to produce more children or passed on to already-born children and grandchildren. Many studies confirm an increase in maternal mortality risk and risk of stillbirth, congenital disabilities and adverse perinatal outcomes with an increase in maternal age at childbirth (Zile et al., 2019; Bouzaglou et al., 2020; Sharma, 2022), which further emphasise that childbearing and childbirth nearing menopause or at the advanced stage are extremely risky and deleterious for mothers as well as child survival. The end of fecundity enables more resources and time to help daughters and grandchildren, thus improving children's fertility and grandchildren's survival (Aimé et al., 2017).

Madrigal and Melendez-Obando investigate grandmother and mother hypotheses to explain why women typically outlive their fertility. The mother hypothesis suggests that early childbearing has a fitness benefit because it allows mothers to focus their energy on their already-born children (Williams, 1957). This hypothesis is based on the premise that life after fertility is not always post-reproductive, similar to the grandmother hypothesis. The investments that increase children's survival in this scenario provide fitness gain. However, the question is, when a mother reaches menopause at 45 to 54 years, the children she produces have already reached maturity, and they can acquire food and livelihood. Caring and assistance are quintessential in infancy, childhood and adolescence. The transmission of moral values of particular societies has to be learned by the children from the peers of the household when the grandparents play the prime role. Sharing care, especially with family members, might prove to be risky. A mother must have faith that all mothers will take good care of the child, including proper nutrition, and will not use the situation to damage the child. Here, she is none other than the maternal grandmother.

Testifying the Grandmother Hypotheses: The Issues

However, how do we testify to the grandmother hypothesis in human societies? Scholars took various variables and aspects from society. Most of the studies about grandmothers' role in the survival of their daughters and grandchildren were ethnographic. Lancy (2014, 2015) and Rogoff (2014), who studied childhood across cultures, noted that formal teaching is uncommon or non-existent in simple societies and through the hominid evolution, and the children mainly learnt by participating and "pitching in" in adult conversation and enculturation by the elders mainly the females in the household. A comparable analogy is language itself. Not because the older generation imparts language to the younger from generation to generation, but infants, toddlers, and children pick up language from the individuals around them as they try to understand what older children and adults are saying and doing and desire to participate in it (Over & Carpenter, 2013).

In the words of Hawkes (2020), "the grandmother hypothesis identifies both a distinctive kind of allomaternal help, reliable daily provisioning, and the socioecology in which supplying it was the consequence of efficient foraging for daily consumption. The particular ancestral allomothering that likely propelled the evolution of the life-history distinctive to our human radiation was the economic productivity of older females." Dimensions that have been/could be taken to understand the effect of grandmothers on fertility and survival of grandchildren are highlighted below:

Chapman et al. (2021) examined whether maternal or paternal grandmother presence (lineage relative to focal individuals) differentially affects two important fitness outcomes of descendants/daughters' fertility and survival, using a pre-industrial genealogical dataset from Finland from the eighteenth to the nineteenth century. In particular, at younger mothers and earlier birth orders, they discovered that the grandmother's presence reduced the time between successive conception and births. Whether maternal grandparents had grandchildren only through daughters, boys, or both, their presence improved the likelihood that the focal grandchildren would survive. They focussed on the variables: age at first reproduction of the daughters, Probability of subsequent births and birth spacing effects, Grandchild survival outcomes, Grandchild survival at different childhood stages and Grandchild survival by lineage exclusivity.

Nenko et al. (2021) highlighted that those grandchildren whose next sibling was born within a close period survived better when the maternal grandmother was present, even though her presence cannot ameliorate the negative impacts of numerous poorer birth conditions. These data show how crucial grandmothers are in recouping the mother's investment in the newborn and helping mothers become pregnant more successfully. They investigated, for the first time, whether grandmothers' presence modified associations between adverse birth status and survival up to 5 years of age, whether *(i)* firstborns, *(ii)* twins, *(iii)* children born within 24 months after their sibling, and *(iv)* children followed by a short interval (i.e., their younger sibling was born within 24 months) survived better when either their maternal, paternal, or both grandmothers were present. In addition, they evaluated whether illegitimate children survived better when the maternal grandmother was present.

Beise (2004) exclusively selected those children in the data sample for whom information about both grandmothers was available. These selections resulted in the primary data sample for calculating child mortality rates and survival. In addition to the grandmother, they also included in the model the survival status of the mother, the father, and both grandfathers to control for any other kin effect.

Sear, Mace, and McGregor (2000) discovered that maternal grandmothers are the only living relatives (apart from mothers) who significantly enhance children's nutritional condition, which is reflected in improved survival rates for children with maternal grandmothers. There is evidence that the maternal grandmother's reproductive status affects the children's nutrition, as shown by the fact that young children grow taller in the presence of non-reproductive grandmothers than in the presence of grandmothers who are still actively reproducing. Both height and weight models included the child's age, the mother's body mass index (BMI, weight (kg)/height (m2)) as covariates, and the child's sex and village as constant factors. The height model also included covariates for the mother's and father's height to control for familial influences on height.

In the research article "Kinship Organisation and the Impact of Grandmothers on Reproductive Success among the Matrilineal Khasi and Patrilineal Bengali of Northeast India, in Grand Motherhood: The Evolutionary Significance of the Second Half of Female Life", Leonetti et al. (2005) documented the effect of a grandmother's presence on the reproductive success of their daughters of reproductive age in two different communities of Northeast India. They collected data on daughters' reproductive histories, grandmothers' current residential status, health status and work-activity capability. Various anthropometric measurements were collected to determine the health and adiposity of the mothers and the nutritional and growth status of the grandchildren in households with grandmothers. Maternal grandmothers in the matrilineal Khasi society were found to have a profound effect on lowering the infant mortality of their daughters.

The emergence of a broad range of social abilities that serve as the building blocks for the evolution of other distinctly human characteristics, such as our propensity for cooperation, pair bonding, larger brains, and acquiring new skills, was learnt from the elderly members in the households and the society. Here, a researcher can take into account the meanings of rites and rituals being done by the maternal/paternal grandmothers for the proper growth of the foetus in the daughter's womb during the different periods of gestation, period of stay in the house of the son-in-law when her daughter is pregnant, child caring by the grandmother when the new mother is healing after childbirth or when she dies during childbirth, storytelling to the grandchildren which is a powerful way of imparting moral values and life skills, caring the child in the absence of the mother and enabling mothers to have more children. Child survival and health in households with grandmothers and without, maternal health during pregnancy and lactation, and duration of breastfeeding are some of the variables that can be considered.

Many studies and literature done so far did not provide the needed attention to the role played by the grandmothers in a daily pattern of livelihood and how they care for the grandchildren when the mothers go out to harness livelihood and also when the mother dies during childbirth leaving behind other infants and children who need special care from the allomothers.

Conclusion

The role of a grandmother in enhancing the reproduction and survival of her children is crucial for the biological and socio-cultural propagation of the human species. However, at present, the joint family system is disintegrating at all levels, even in developing countries and in most simple societies. As a result, the aged grandparents are deemed lonely, and the grandchildren are devoid of their quintessential love and enculturation process. Grandmothers gain life experiences by rearing their children, providing essentials, engaging in ethnomedicinal practice, and imparting moral values through stories and societal phrases. These are extremely important for understanding the unpredictable environment and can be used as survival strategies in times of distress. Post-menopausal grandmothers significantly impact the survival of generations after them, benefiting their genes and their children's bio-culturally. Studies on human forager communities have confirmed that staying near a grandmother can lead to solid family bonding, reduced child mortality, and healthy and safe childbirth. According to a computer simulation, the grandmother effect alone can increase a species' longevity to less than 60,000 years. The grandmother's role is assumed to be remarkable when mothers marry young and when the number of working women is high in a community. In this contention, grandmothers are massive learning institutions for households and an essential social asset that should be considered when developing programmes for young children. Unfortunately, nowadays, they are mostly neglected, and their knowledge is considered outdated and non-beneficial.

References

Aimé, C., André, J. B., & Raymond, M. (2017). Grandmothering and cognitive resources are required for the emergence of menopause and extensive post-reproductive lifespan. *PLoS Computational Biology*, *13*(7), e1005631. https://doi.org/10.1371/journal.pcbi.1005631.

Ahuja M. (2016). Age of menopause and determinants of menopause age: A PAN India survey by IMS. *Journal of mid-life health*, *7*(3), 126–131. https://doi.org/10.4103/0976-7800.191012.

Alvarado, G., Rivera, R., Ruiz, R., Arenas, M., & Rueda, D. (1988). Características del patrón de sangrado menstrual en un grupo de mujeres normales de Durango [The characteristics of the menstrual bleeding pattern in a group of normal women from Durango]. *Ginecologia y obstetricia de Mexico*, *56*, 127–131.

Beise, J. (2004). The Helping and the helpful grandmother - The Role of Maternal and paternal grandmothers in child mortality in the 17th and 18th-century Population of French Settlers in Quebec, Canada.

Beise, J., & Voland, E. (2002). A multilevel event history analysis of the effects of grandmothers on child mortality in a historical German population (Krummhörn, Ostfriesland, 1720-1874). *Demographic Research*, *7*, 469-498.

Blurton Jones, N.G, & Sibly, R. (1978). Testing adaptiveness of culturally determined behaviour: Do Bushman women maximise their reproductive success by spacing births widely and foraging seldom? In: N. Blurton J and V. Reynolds (Eds.), *Human Behaviour and Adaptation,* Society for Study of Human Biology Symposium, No. 18, London: Tylor and Francis, pp. 135–58.

Blurton Jones, N.G., Hawkes, K., O'Connell, J.F. (1989). Modelling and measuring costs of children in two foraging societies. In: Standen V & Foley RA (Eds.), *Comparative socioecology of humans and other mammals,* pp. 367–390. London, UK: Basil Blackwell.

Bouzaglou A, Aubenas I, Abbou H, Rouanet S, Carbonnel M, Pirtea P & Ayoubi JMB (2020). Pregnancy at 40 Years Old and Above Obstetrical, Fetal, and Neonatal Outcomes. Is Age an Independent Risk Factor for Those Complications? *Front. Med.* 7:208. Doi: 10.3389/fmed.2020.00208.

Brent, L. J. N., Franks, D. W., Foster, E. A., Balcomb, K. C., Cant, M. A., & Croft, D. P. (2015). Ecological Knowledge, Leadership, and the Evolution of Menopause in Killer Whales. *Current Biology*, 25(6), 746–750. https://doi.org/10.1016/j.cub.2015.01.037.

Bromberger, J. T., Matthews, K. A., Kuller, L. H., Wing, R. R., Meilahn, E. N., & Plantinga, P. (1997). Prospective study of the determinants of age at menopause. *American Journal of Epidemiology*, *145*(2), 124–133. https://doi.org/10.1093/oxfordjournals.aje.a009083.

Byars, S. G., & Voskarides, K. (2020). Antagonistic pleiotropy in human disease. *Journal of Molecular Evolution*, 88(1), 12–25.

Can't, M. A., & Johnstone, R. A. (2008). Reproductive conflict and the separation of reproductive generations in humans. *Proceedings of the National Academy of Sciences of the United States of America*, *105*(14), 5332–5336. https://doi.org/10.1073/pnas.0711911105.

Chapman, S. N., Jackson, J., Htut, W., Lummaa, V., & Lahdenperä, M. (2019). Asian elephants exhibit post-reproductive lifespans. *BMC Evolutionary Biology*, *19*(1), 1-11.

Chapman, S. N., Lahdenperä, M., Pettay, J. E., Lynch, R. F., & Lummaa, V. (2021). Offspring fertility and grandchild survival were enhanced by maternal grandmothers in a pre-industrial human society. *Scientific reports*, *11*(1), 3652. https://doi.org/10.1038/s41598-021-83353-3.

Chapman, S. N., Pettay, J. E., Lummaa, V., & Lahdenperä, M. (2018). Limited support for the X-linked grandmother hypothesis in pre-industrial Finland. *Biology letters*, *14*(1), 20170651. https://doi.org/10.1098/rsbl.2017.0651.

Charnov, E. L., Turner, T. F., & Winemiller, K. O. (2001). Reproductive constraints and the evolution of life histories with indeterminate growth. *Proceedings of the National Academy of Sciences, 98*(16), 9460-9464.

Clarkson, T. B., Meléndez, G. C., & Appt, S. E. (2013). Timing hypothesis for post-menopausal hormone therapy: its origin, current status, and future. *Menopause (New York, N.Y.), 20*(3), 342–353. https://doi.org/10.1097/GME.0b013e3182843aad.

Col, N. F., Guthrie, J. R., Politi, M., & Dennerstein, L. (2009). Duration of vasomotor symptoms in middle-aged women: a longitudinal study. *Menopause (New York, N.Y.), 16*(3), 453–457. https://doi.org/10.1097/gme.0b013e31818d414e.

Fausto-Sterling, A. (1992). *Myths of Gender*. Revised edition. Basic Books, New York.

Feistner, A & Mcgrew, Wi. (1989). Food-sharing in primates: a critical review. Perspect Primate Biol. 3.

Finch C. E. (2014). The menopause and ageing, a comparative perspective. *The Journal of Steroid Biochemistry and Molecular Biology*, pp. *142*, 132–141. https://doi.org/10.1016/j.jsbmb.2013.03.010.

Finch, C. E., Kirkwood, T. B., & Kirkwood, T. (2000). *Chance, development, and ageing*. Oxford University Press, USA.

Fox, M., Sear, R., Beise, J., Ragsdale, G., Voland, E., & Knapp, L. A. (2010). Grandma plays favourites: X-chromosome relatedness and sex-specific childhood mortality. *Proceedings. Biological sciences, 277*(1681), 567–573. https://doi.org/10.1098/rspb.2009.1660.

Gold, E. B., Bromberger, J., Crawford, S., Samuels, S., Greendale, G. A., Harlow, S. D., & Skurnick, J. (2001). Factors associated with age at natural menopause in a multiethnic sample of midlife women. *American Journal of Epidemiology, 153*(9), 865–874. https://doi.org/10.1093/aje/153.9.865.

Hawkes, K. (2003). Grandmothers and the evolution of human longevity. *American Journal of Human Biology, 15*(3), 380–400.

Hawkes, K. (2016). Genomic evidence for the evolution of human post-menopausal longevity. *Proceedings of the National Academy of Sciences, 113*(1), 17–18.

Hawkes K. (2020). Cognitive consequences of our grandmothering life history: Cultural learning begins in infancy. *Philosophical Transactions of the Royal Society of London. Series B, Biological Sciences*, *375*(1803), 20190501. https://doi.org/10.1098/rstb.2019.0501.

Hawkes, K., & Jones, N. (2005). Grandmotherhood: the evolutionary significance of the second half of female life. New Brunswick: Rutgers University Press.

Hawkes, K., O'Connell, J. F.& Blurton Jones, N. G. (1989). Hardworking Hadza grandmothers. In: V. Standen & R. Foley (Eds.), Comparative socioecology: the behavioural ecology of humans and other mammals, London: Blackwell Scientific Publ., pp. 342–366.

Hawkes, K., O'Connell, J. F., & Blurton Jones, N. G. (1997). Hadza women's time allocation, offspring provisioning, and the evolution of long post-menopausal life span. *Current Anthropology*, 38(4), 551–577.

Hawkes, K., O'Connell, J. F., & Jones, N. B. (1989). *Comparative socioecology: the behavioural ecology of humans and other mammals.* London: Blackwell Scientific Publ.

Hawkes, K., O'Connell, J.F., Jones, N.G., Alvarez, H., & Charnov, E.L. (1998). Grand mothering, Menopause, and the Evolution of Human Life Histories. Proceedings of the National Academy of Sciences of the USA 95 (3): 1336–39.

Hawkes, K., & Smith, K. R. (2009). Brief communication: Evaluating grandmother effects. *American Journal of Physical Anthropology*, *140*(1), 173–176. https://doi.org/10.1002/ajpa.21061.

Howell, N. (Ed.). (2017). *Demography of the Dobe! Kung*. Routledge.

Isaac, G. (1978). The food-sharing behavior of protohuman hominids. *Scientific American*, *238*(4), 90–109.

Johnstone, R. A., & Can't, M. A. (2010). The evolution of menopause in cetaceans and humans: The role of demography. Proceedings of the Royal Society B: Biological Sciences, 277(1701), 3765–3771. https://doi.org/10.1098/rspb.2010.0988.

Kim, P. S., Coxworth, J. E., & Hawkes, K. (2012). Increased longevity evolves from grandmothering. Proceedings. *Biological sciences*, *279*(1749), 4880–4884. https://doi.org/10.1098/rspb.2012.1751.

Krakauer, D. C., & Mira, A. (1999). Mitochondria and germ-cell death. *Nature*, *400*(6740), 125-126.

Krysko, D. V., Diez-Fraile, A., Criel, G., Svistunov, A. A., Vandenabeele, P., & D'Herde, K. (2008). Life and death of female gametes during oogenesis and folliculogenesis. *Apoptosis*, *13*, 1065-1087.

Lahdenperä, M., Gillespie, D. O., Lummaa, V., & Russell, A. F. (2012). Severe intergenerational reproductive conflict and the evolution of menopause. *Ecology Letters*, *15*(11), 1283-1290.

Lancaster, J, & King, B. (1985). An evolutionary perspective on menopause. In: Brown J, &Kerns V (Eds.), *In Her Prime: A New View of Middle-Aged Women*. South Hadley, Massachusetts: Bergen and Garvey Publishers. pp. 13–20.

Lancy, D. F. (2014). The anthropology of childhood: Cherubs, chattel, changelings. Cambridge University Press.

Lancy, D. F. (2015). Teaching is so WEIRD. *Behavioral and Brain Sciences*, pp. *38*, 31.

Leonetti, D. L., Nath, D.C., Hemam, N. S., & Neill, D. B. (2005). Kinship organisation and the impact of grandmothers on reproductive success among the matrilineal Khasi and patrilineal Bengali of Northeast India. In: E. Voland, A. Chasiotis & W. Schiefenhövek (Eds.), *Grandmotherhood: The evolutionary significance of the second half of female life*, pp. 194–214. New Brunswick: Rutgers University Press.

McKinlay, S. M. (1996). The normal menopause transition: an overview. *Maturitas* 23, 137–145. doi: 10.1016/0378-5122(95)00985-X.

Moghadam, A. R. E., Moghadam, M. T., Hemadi, M., & Saki, G. (2022). Oocyte quality and ageing. *JBRA assisted reproduction*, *26*(1), 105–122. https://doi.org/10.5935/1518-0557.20210026.

Nattrass, S., Croft, D. P., Ellis, S., Can't, M. A., Weiss, M. N., Wright, B. M., Stredulinsky, E., Doniol-Valcroze, T., Ford, J. K. B., Balcomb, K. C., & Franks, D. W. (2019). Post-reproductive killer whale grandmothers improve the survival of their grand offspring. *Proceedings of the National Academy of Sciences of the United States of America*, 116(52), 26669–26673. https://doi.org/10.1073/pnas.1903844116.

Nenko, I., Chapman, S.N., et al. (2021). Will granny save me? Birth status, survival, and the role of grandmothers in Historical Finland. *Evolution and Human Behavior*, 42, (3), pp. 239–246.

Over, H., & Carpenter, M. (2013). The social side of imitation. *Child development perspectives*, 7(1), 6-11.

Pavelka, M. S., & Fedigan, L. M. (1991). Menopause: A comparative life history perspective. *American Journal of Physical Anthropology*, 34(S13), 13-38.

Peacock K, &Ketvertis KM. (2022). Menopause. In: StatPearls [Internet], *Treasure Island* (FL): StatPearls Publishing.

Peccei, J. S. (2001). Menopause: Adaptation or epiphenomenon? *Evolutionary Anthropology: Issues, News, and Reviews,* 10(2), 43–57. https://doi.org/10.1002/evan.1013.

Rogoff, B. (2014). Learning by observing and pitching into family and community endeavours: An orientation. *Human Development*, 57(2-3), pp. 69–81.

Sadler, T. W. (2011). *Langman's medical embryology*. Lippincott Williams & Wilkins.

Saha, S., Khan, N., Comi, T., Verhagen, A., Sasmal, A., Diaz, S., Yu, H., Chen, X., Akey, J. M., Frank, M., Gagneux, P., & Varki, A. (2022). Evolution of Human-Specific Alleles Protecting Cognitive Function of Grandmothers. *Molecular Biology and Evolution*, 39(8), msac151. https://doi.org/10.1093/molbev/msac151.

Sear, R., Mace, R., & McGregor, I. A. (2000). Maternal grandmothers improve nutritional status and survival of children in rural Gambia. *Proceedings. Biological sciences*, 267(1453), 1641–1647. https://doi.org/10.1098/rspb.2000.1190.

Schwarz, F., Springer, S. A., Altheide, T. K., Varki, N. M., Gagneux, P., & Varki, A. (2016). Human-specific derived alleles of CD33 and other genes protect against post-reproductive cognitive decline. Proceedings of the National Academy of Sciences, *113*(1), 74-79.

Sharma M. (2022). Pregnancy outcomes of adolescent and adult mothers belonging to the Adi-Minyong tribal population of Arunachal Pradesh. *J. Indian Anthrop. Soc.* 57(2): 158–176.

Videan, E. N., Fritz, J., Heward, C. B., & Murphy, J. (2006). The effects of ageing on hormone and reproductive cycles in female chimpanzees (Pan troglodytes). *Comparative Medicine*, *56*(4), 291–299.

Watkins A. (2021). Reevaluating the grandmother hypothesis. *History and philosophy of the life sciences*, 43(3), 103. https://doi.org/10.1007/s40656-021-00455-x.

Weiss, K.M. (1981). Evolutionary perspectives on human ageing. In: Amoss PT, &Harrell S, Eds.0, *Other ways of growing old. Stanford*, CA: Stanford University Press, pp 25–28.

Williams, G. C. (1957). Pleiotropy, Natural Selection, and the Evolution of Senescence. *Evolution*, 11(4), 398–411. https://doi.org/10.1111/j.1558-5646.1957.tb02911.x.

Wood, J., O'Connor, K., Holman, D., & Brindle, E. (2000). The Evolution of Menopause by Antagonistic Pleiotropy. *Homo*, 51.

Zile, I., Ebela, I., & Rumba-Rozenfelde, I. (2019). Maternal Risk Factors for Stillbirth: A Registry-Based Study. *Medicine (Kaunas, Lithuania)*, *55*(7), 326. https://doi.org/10.3390/medicina55070326

11

Caregivers' Response to Health Care Programme on Childhood Pneumonia: An Anthropological Study Among Bhil Tribes

Dr. Prashant Kulkarni
Dr. Anjali Kurane

Introduction

Early childhood years are an essential foundation period in the development of an individual. Under-five children not only constitute a large group but are also a vulnerable or high-risk group. The risk relates to growth, development, and survival. The first five years are full of health hazards. Since they are a high-risk group, under-five children are exposed to many environmental factors leading to diseases (Ansari et al., 2008). India accounts for about 26 million children born yearly, and children aged 0-6 years have a 13% share of the total population (*Health-UNICEF*, 2019). The child health programmes developed targets to improve child survival and address factors contributing to infant and child mortality (*Child Health: National Health Mission*, 2019). As per the National Health Policy -2017, the child health programmes aim to reduce the under-five mortality rate from 36 (in 2017) to 23 by 2025. Child mortality causes prematurity, low birth weight, pneumonia, and diarrheal diseases. (Ministry of Health & Family Welfare, 2017). UNICEF reports that a child dies due to pneumonia after every 39 seconds. In India, mortality due to pneumonia accounts for approximately one-fourth of the deaths of children under five. Moreover, almost all these deaths can be prevented.

The National Family Health Survey-5 reflects a decrease in neonatal mortality rate (NNMR) from 29.5 to 23.3, Infant Mortality Rate (IMR) decreased from 40.7 to 35.2, and Under-five mortality rate from 49.7 to 45.7(*NFHS-5 Factsheet India*, 2019). The government of India put forth the agenda of child survival and development to achieve the overall development of society (MOHFW, 2014). As per Census 2011, the share of children (0-6 years) accounts for 13% of the total population in the Country, and about 12.7 lakh children die every year before completing five years of age. Eighty-one percent of under-five child morality take place within one year of birth, which accounts for nearly 10.5 lakh infant deaths, whereas 57% of under-five deaths take place within the first month of life, accounts for 7.3 lakh neonatal deaths every year in the Country (Government of India, 2015). It is estimated that 2.1 million children in India die before age five (*WHO-India*). As per WHO-2012 estimates, the causes of Child Mortality in the age group 0-5 years in India are (a) Neonatal causes (53%), (b) Pneumonia (15%), (c) Diarrhoeal disease (12%), (d) Measles (3%), (e) Injuries (3%) and (f) others (14%). Print media reported that pneumonia deaths among children under five in Maharashtra increased by 29.7% in three years, and 2781 children succumbed to acute respiratory infection from 2016-17 to 2018-19 (Chakraborty, 2019). Children from the Schedule Tribe population have a 19 per cent higher risk of death during the neonatal period and a 45 per cent greater risk of death in the post-natal period than the rest of the social group. The NFHS-5 report for Nandurbar (2019-21) indicates that the % of all essential vaccinations is 73%. District Level Household Survey, 2014-15, shows that the prevalence of diarrhoea was high in Amravati and Yavatmal districts. In contrast, the prevalence of acute respiratory infection (ARI) was high in Amravati, Yavatmal, Chandrapur, and Nandurbar districts. In addition, the proportion of people seeking advice or treatment for diarrhoea and ARI was low in Nandurbar, Gadchiroli, and Chandrapur districts. In contrast, the proportion of people seeking advice/treatment for ARI was low in Nandurbar, Chandrapur, and Gadchiroli districts. (NRHM, n.d.)

The GOI, WHO, and UNICEF in September 2014 developed an Integrated Action Plan for Pneumonia and Diarrhea (IAPPD) (Yewale, 2014). The integrated Global Action Plan for the Prevention and Control of

Pneumonia and Diarrhoea (GAPPD) formulated a framework with critical interventions to effectively protect children's health, prevent disease, and treat children appropriately. The framework is known as the Protect, Prevent and Treat framework. Integrated Action Plan for Prevention and Control of Pneumonia and Diarrhoea (IAPPD) – IAPPD was launched in 2014 to address the gaps and prevent diarrhoea and pneumonia among under-five deaths. IAPPD has been formulated for four states with the highest child mortality rate (Uttar Pradesh, Madhya Pradesh, Bihar, and Rajasthan). Integrated Management of Neonatal and Childhood Illnesses (IMNCI) is a skill-based training program for medical officers and health staff, viz. frontline workers (ANMs, AWWs, and ASHA workers). It also focuses on improving the health system by making essential drugs available to workers and health facilities, strengthening referral mechanisms, making health providers/workers available at all levels, and facilitating follow-up visits by supervisors. At the next level, the programme focuses on counselling families and creating awareness about promoting healthy behaviours and counselling regarding managing sick children. The programme also focuses on inter-sector collaboration to ensure community ownership and participation (MOHFW, 2019).

The literature review highlights that most of the works on childhood pneumonia have been carried out in the areas of its prevalence, understanding knowledge and attitude of the health workers, the mothers of under-five children, and practices followed by the caregivers of under-five children. The significant hurdles reported in child health policy implementation include the inadequate educational level of caregivers, lack of required access and utilisation of healthcare services, inadequate coverage of health services, incompatible health-seeking behaviour, and the absence of health education strategies. Since a significant section of people still believes in alternative healthcare like faith healing, worshipping the deities, magico-religious practices and traditional medicines, the development of indigenous knowledge of health and wellbeing might be a promising domain of deliberation amidst the dominance of bio-medical paradigms (Bhasin, 2007; Kalita & Kalita, 2014; Kandel et al., 2020). Considering the community's faith in traditional healers, the sensitisation or education of traditional healers needs to be prioritised for early diagnosis and prompt treatment of pneumonia. Various studies have identified a gap in service utilisation, provider practices and family practices in seeking bio-medical care (Cowling et al., 2014; Guindon et al., 2010; Mathew et al., 2011; Kulkarni & Kurane, 2023). Various studies have identified factors that influence the nature and extent to which the social determinants affect people's health. These determinants include inadequate infrastructure facilities, the powerlessness of the stakeholders with the system, chronic hunger or food insecurity, low level of awareness and health-seeking behaviour, lack of attention in the national programmes, absence of tribal people or representatives in shaping policies (Kulkarni et al., 2014; Nandi, 2015; Narain, 2019). Scholars have listed some risk factors directly related to the issue of health. These include exclusive breastfeeding, indoor air pollution, parental cigarette smoking, malnutrition, common co-morbid conditions, living in a crowded house, and keeping domestic animals inside the main house (Berra et al., 2020; Getaneh et al., 2019; Teepe et al., 2010).

In addition, limited studies were found focusing on health system-related issues, exploring the worldviews of local implementers, and addressing socio-cultural norms. There were also few studies on childhood pneumonia in tribal areas. Hence, understanding the status of implementing health programmes and efforts, especially in tribal areas, to achieve the Sustainable Development Goals for preventable diseases like pneumonia is essential.

This research contributes to understanding the implementation processes and outcomes of the health policy/ programmes developed for under-five tribal children, the interaction between the block (Taluka), district health implementers and decision-makers, the tension between public and private choices and responsibilities, and decision-making by the beneficiaries.

The study aims to provide a tribal population-specific anthropological study of under-five children health policy/programme implementation at the micro level, which will enhance understanding of why there are differences between policy/programme and practice, which can inform future decisions regarding the need to make improvements.

Pneumonia is the single most significant infectious cause of death in children worldwide. (*Pneumonia in Children Statistics - UNICEF DATA*, 2019) Pneumonia killed 740 180 children under the age of 5 in 2019, accounting for 14% of all deaths of children under five but 22% of all deaths in children aged 1 to 5. Studies have shown pneumonia, diarrhoea, and sepsis as the underlying causes of child morbidity and mortality. There are identified determinants that influence the health system.

On the other hand, various policies have been adopted to reduce child deaths. Through Integrated Management of Neonatal and Childhood Illnesses (IMNCI), the first attempt has been made to focus solely on managing the newborn. Despite several policies and program provisioning, the accessibility, availability, and affordability of child health care services remain a challenge to the Indian health care system. Therefore, it becomes crucial to understand the problem of under-five children's health among tribal populations to understand the child health problem comprehensively.

The various frameworks of policy implementation research suggest considering context as an essential factor linking actors and content involved in the policy process. Hence, policy implementation research using a micro perspective and ethnographic inquiry of providers/implementers as well as users of policy/programme is best suited to understanding enablers and challenges in implementation. In addition, pneumonia management will be used to understand the implementation process in tribal-dominant areas of the Nandurbar district.

Methodology

The present study was conducted in the Akkalkuwa block of Nandurbar district of Maharashtra. Nandurbar is one of the tribal-dominant districts in Maharashtra, with 69.3% of the tribal population. Two Primary Health Centres were selected randomly, representing plain and hilly areas. The caregivers (n=107) sample was divided across 66 villages of all the sub-centres of two Primary Health Centres, Daab and Ankush Vihir PHCs. Then, the villages under the respective sub-centre were randomly selected, and the sample was distributed across these villages. The caregiver's interview was conducted by selecting every fifth household in the selected sample village.

The focus of the study is to understand programme managers', grassroots workers' and the community's perspective and their compliance with IMNCI strategy. The health system can use the knowledge obtained from this study to strengthen the local health system in the tribal area and help allocate resources for healthcare workers in IMNCI implementation. This study states that all health policy elements are in a contextual framework and are influenced by various contextual and cultural factors. Various approaches/frameworks exist for studying the progress of or monitoring and evaluating the implementation process and outcome. The Consolidated Framework for Implementation Research (CFIR) focuses more broadly on the social and structural patterns and processes that shape providers' attitudes, beliefs, and intentions. The CFIR consists of a list of constructs for individuals involved with the implementation process (Chart 1).

Unstructured in-depth interviews were conducted with stakeholders (public health officials, health workers, medical officers, private healthcare providers, community leaders and traditional healers), grassroots workers (ASHA, AWWs and ANMs) and familial caregivers of under-five children. The caregivers' interviews were conducted to explore the perspective of pneumonia and healthcare services and understand what factors affect the utilisation of health services (policy outcome). These interviews were conducted in the local tribal dialect, i.e., a Bhili language, with the help of a trained local investigator. In addition, the role of local health administrators was considered to understand administrative and management issues. All the caregivers were asked if any of their children under five had pneumonia (based on the symptoms or diagnosis by any health provider) in the last year (from the day of the interview). If reported, an in-depth interview was conducted.

A total of 25 in-depth interviews with stakeholders,107 caregivers of children under five, and 11 in-depth interviews of caregivers of children affected with pneumonia were conducted to understand the implementation process and policy outcomes. All the caregivers were asked if any of their children under five had pneumonia (based on the symptoms or diagnosis by any health provider) in the last year (from the day of the interview); any of such cases were conducted with in-depth interviews.

Ethical Considerations

All the ethical measures were observed in the study. Written consent was sought from all the respondents who participated in the study during face-to-face interviews. A few interviews with district health officials and private providers were conducted telephonically (in the background of the upsurge of COVID-19), so oral consent was sought from them.

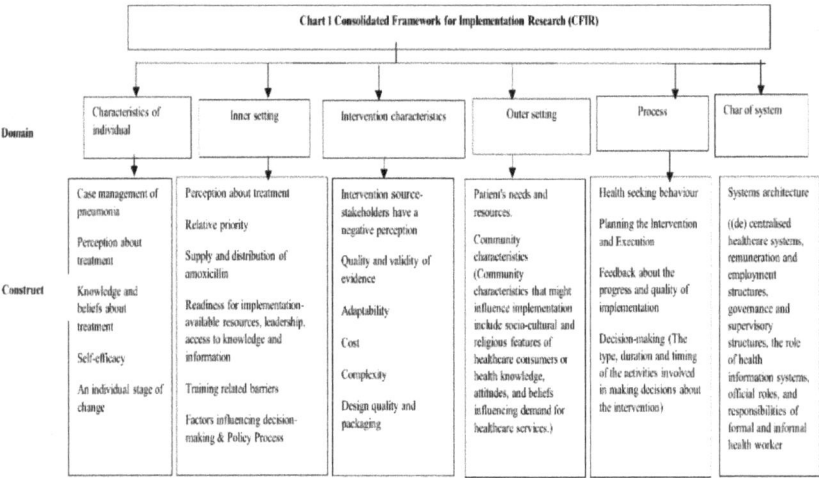

Data Management and Data Analysis

Quantitative data generated from semi-structured interviews with grassroots workers and caregivers were entered into MS Excel software, and a few variables were post-coded based on their free responses. For qualitative data analysis, various codes were developed by re-reading the transcripts. The codes were made in line with the study objectives.

RESULTS

Chart 2: The Profile of the Respondents

Type	Stakeholders (N=25)	Family Caregivers (N=107)
Cadre	Medical officers, district health officials, grassroots workers, community	Except for one, the rest were female.

	representatives, traditional healers, and private providers	
Mean age	Most of them are from the 36-50 years age group	More than half 18-25 years age group
Marital status	Not Applicable	All were married
Education status	Half of them have a medical background	Education- higher secondary and junior college
Tribal community	Not Applicable	All belong to the scheduled tribe group. 50% Nuclear family - 44% Joint family

All the stakeholders had different opinions about childhood pneumonia as a cause for concern. Identifying pneumonia cases and administering appropriate antibiotic therapy is the primary strategy to reduce mortality and morbidity caused by pneumonia. The non-availability of common drugs and the lack of skills among health workers in public settings were mentioned as factors affecting community management of pneumonia cases. Families of sick children are forced to travel long distances to reach district medical college hospitals for care. Predisposing factors for pneumonia care include socio-cultural beliefs, delayed care seeking, and nutrition-related practices. There is a lack of clear guidelines for grassroots workers in managing pneumonia cases. Many stakeholders mentioned infrastructure availability and medicines shortage as challenges in providing appropriate care. The study also highlighted that the ANMs were overburdened with administrative work, financial schemes, and Health Management Information System entry. Findings from in-depth interviews revealed opportunities and challenges in implementing IMNCI at the block level and preparedness of healthcare providers for case management of childhood pneumonia. The results also showed the needs of caregivers while managing the illness.

There are better networking opportunities at the regional level, and medical officers at the PHC regularly contact the block-level administration, so a lack of awareness of the difficulties was observed. However, these regional health administrators could not effectively address many contextual issues identified at the health centre level, such as funding and resourcing, training, drug supply, organising health education activities, and addressing the community's concerns. In addition, the selected health centres and health sub-centres have deficit equipment and funding constraints that result in the continuation of deficiencies in infrastructure, training, and medicine supply. The study reports that less importance was given to data management, reporting, monitoring and evaluation, and collaboration initiatives. The grassroots workers had to put in additional efforts due to technological poverty.

UNICEF has defined the primary symptoms of pneumonia as 'cough and fast or difficult breathing due to a chest-related problem' (Pneumonia in Children Statistics - UNICEF DATA, n.d.). Cough was reported as the highest spontaneous symptom, followed by fever, nausea, and vomiting. Food was spontaneously reported as the significant perceived cause of pneumonia, followed by heat-cold humoral climate, and less than 10% could report the correct cause of getting germs/bacteria/ infection. The PROTECT component of the GAPPD framework highlights exclusive breastfeeding for the first six months of life, protecting infants from disease. The present study reported hygiene, frequent hand washing, and adequate nutrition as primary preventive measures, whereas only one caregiver spontaneously reported early and continuous breastfeeding [Figures 1, 2 and 3].

Decision-making regarding treating the child's illness contributes equally to selecting health-seeking options. Private and traditional health facilities were preferred over government facilities. The caregivers also reported branding with a hot rod and massage with oil by "*Choli bai*" as preferred help-seeking measures (Figure 4,5). Hygiene and hand washing were the main reported preventive measures. The study reported very scarce sources of information regarding pneumonia for the respondents. Ten percent of the respondents self-reported that their under-five-year-old children suffered from pneumonia in the past year.

"ASHA workers should have had paracetamol and amoxicillin, but they did not receive them. There is a shortage of grants to buy them. I spoke about this in the meeting but did not get any response. 90% of the drugs are procured at the State level. At the district level, it is provided in sufficient amounts. The procedure may get time." (District level Health Authority)

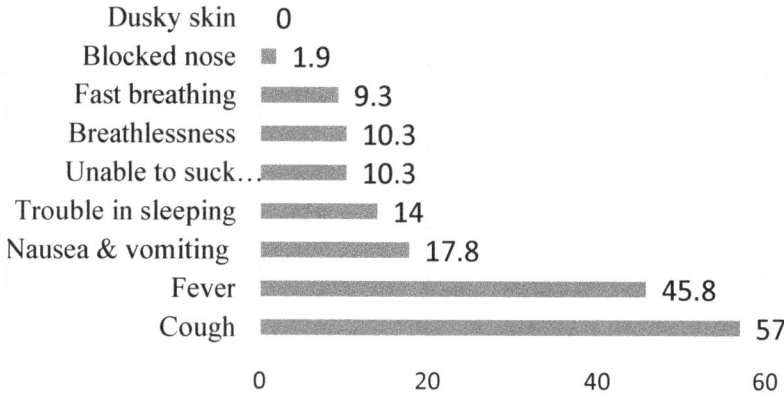

Figure 1 Percentage of caregivers who Reported various symptoms of pneumonia (N=107)

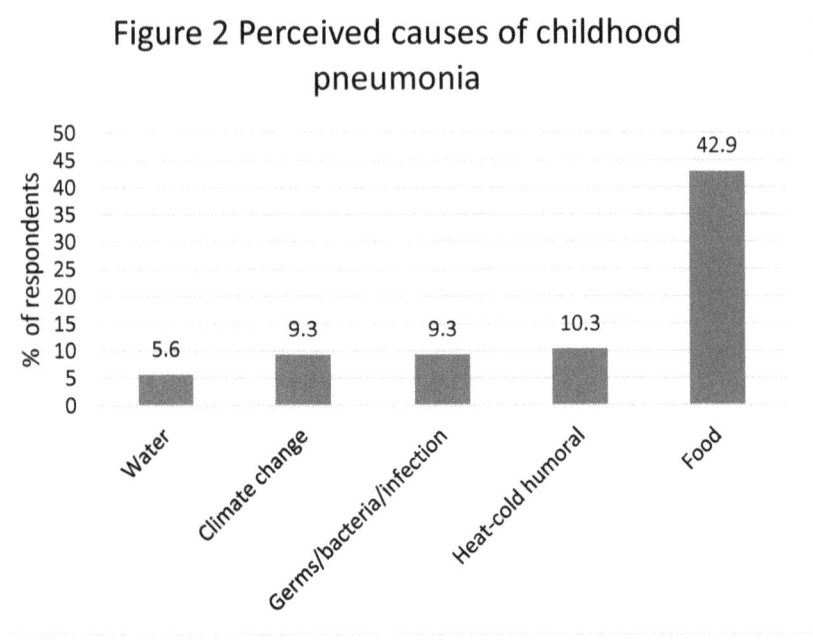

Figure 2 Perceived causes of childhood pneumonia

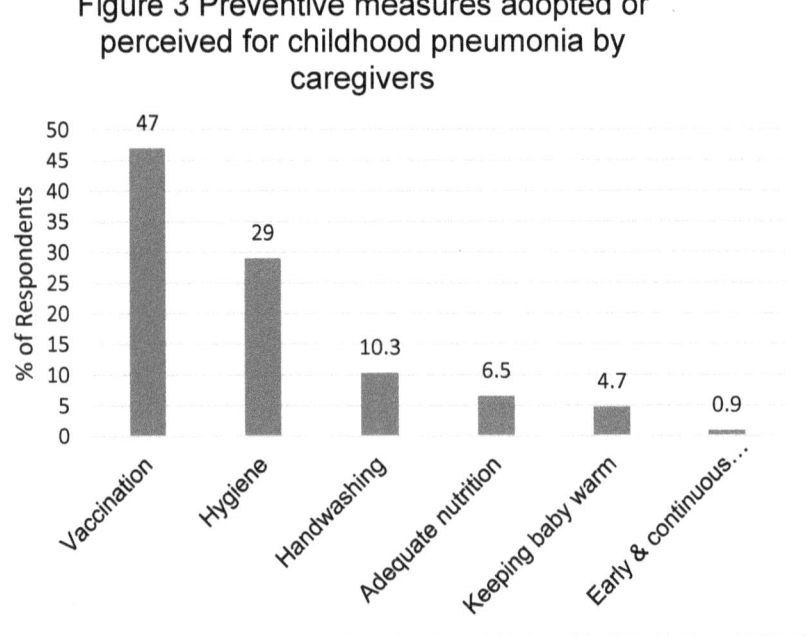

Figure 3 Preventive measures adopted or perceived for childhood pneumonia by caregivers

The IMNCI strategy includes three main components:

- Improvements in the case-management skills of health staff through the provision of locally adapted guidelines on Integrated Management of Neonatal and Childhood illness and activities to promote their use.

- Improvements in the overall health system are required to manage childhood illnesses effectively.

- Improvements in family and community healthcare practices

The community prefers traditional and private facilities over public health facilities because of their easy accessibility. The cycle of analysis is complete, and considering the discussion so far, a complex range of factors mediates the course of policy from its development at the national level to its implementation at the block level. At macro and micro levels, these factors lie on a 'contextual continuum', which is taken up in this where the implications are considered.

> *"In the hilly area, people continue branding on the abdomen of the sick child to cure pneumonia." (Medical Officer, plain area PHC)*

Discussion

The analysis has confirmed that the programme structure has been designed vertically, and the perceived community beliefs about childhood pneumonia, community care practices, availability of infrastructure and resources for pneumonia care, and access to care have not been considered realistically. The IMNCI programme focuses on staff capacity building to provide early and appropriate care and awareness in the community regarding identifying danger signs in the child. The study highlights that the grassroots workers are neither skilled enough to diagnose cases of pneumonia nor the community sufficiently aware of the danger signs in the child. Therefore, findings suggest strengthening the gap between policy and its implementation in a culturally sensitive manner. The suggestions/recommendations are threefold. The first one is enhancing and empowering the voices of the sub-district and district-level officials and administrators, who are the crucial actors in programme implementation.

The second is the link between these administrators and the community, who, although they have the power to bring change, are not provided with the required facilities. The third part is the meaningful involvement of the local community, mainly at a later stage of development, with decision-making power and informed interaction with the designated programme implementation authorities.

The current study reveals that the use of herbs or traditional healing practices (branding near the stomach of the child with a hot rod shown in Figure 4) is preferred over allopath. It indicates the need for intensive anthropological research at the micro level, conducting in-depth inquiry regarding ethnomedicine or alternative medicines so that policy-level changes can be made at the macro level. A study conducted by Beck (Beck, NHM 2018) found that acute respiratory infection (pneumonia) was the second most common problem among children. The study revealed that the home treatment included giving nutmeg (*jaiphal*), clove (*long*) and saffron (*kesar*) in the first stage of the illness. In some areas, faith healers apply a hot iron rod. Using ethnomedicine might provide new insights into human health and the development of indigenous medical knowledge (Bhasin, 2007; Kalita & Kalita, 2014; Kalita & Kalita, N.D.; Kandel et al., 2020). Our study also reports the preference for private and traditional health providers over government health facilities. It could be due to the inadequate presence of public health facilities and the community's easy access to traditional and private health providers. The studies conducted in Kenya and Peru report self-treatment with over-the-counter drugs (Buse et al., 2009; Das et al., 2013). Anthropological research mainly focuses on the use of traditional medicine. Thus, other scientific disciplines should be incorporated to enhance the domain of health care and reassess this part of the cultural practices that have contributed substantially to human health and the development of indigenous medical knowledge and resources (Buse et al., 2009).

Development anthropology provides relevant insights into policy implementation based on field experiences that highlight relevant issues. An anthropological approach aims to view policy/programme from the eyes of these actors and uncover the activities and influences that shape policy decisions and their implementation, effects, and how they play out. The current study provides three perspectives on implementing the IMNCI strategy to control childhood pneumonia. The first one is the absence of voices of sub-district and district-level officials/ administrators who are the critical implementation actors. The second is the grassroots workers, who are the link between these administrators and the community. Although they have the power to bring change, they are not provided with weapons. The third part is the community, whose values and morale structure perceptions. The community perceives childhood pneumonia as an illness related to the stomach rather than the lungs. It is treated by massaging with ground nut oil and branding on the stomach with a heated rod, whereas preventive measures include avoiding certain foods. Grassroots workers and programme implementers are entrusted with deciding what will be suitable for people. Policies can be effectively formulated when we understand what people want and need.

Conclusion

The current study has revealed significant findings that could contribute to new knowledge of health policy implementation in the context of development anthropology. By documenting the challenges of childhood pneumonia management at the block level, the study shows the influence of various contextual factors, highlighting the fundamental impact of socio-cultural factors on practising the policies developed for childhood pneumonia control.

- The influence of programme managers and grassroots workers' actions at every stage of the policy process must be considered while implementing health policies.

- A comprehensive understanding of various dimensions of policy/programme and developing a link between macro and micro levels is essential for understanding how childhood pneumonia prevention programmes get implemented.

- Considering the community's belief in traditional health-seeking practices and relating childhood pneumonia as an illness related to the stomach prevents them from seeking early help from formal healthcare providers. Hence, traditional healers and formal healthcare providers must establish a communication link. Traditional healers need to be sensitised and trained in pneumonia care. There should be a reciprocal relationship between formal health providers (public and private) and informal health providers (traditional healers such as Bhagats, masseuses and herbalists).

- The programmes aimed at the people's development would be successful only if the policymakers, planners, and administrators understood the people, their culture, their needs, and their aspirations. To soothe the relationship between local programme administrations and traditional healers'; anthropologists can help explain the cultural meaning of illness to the health administrators and the importance of medical care to the traditional healers. It is essential that policies be culturally sensitive, and mechanisms for linkage between the levels must be established to allow local voices to be heard and acted upon. Culturally sensitive healthcare has also been described as care in which healthcare providers offer services in a manner that is relevant to patient's needs and expectations (Majumdar et al., 2004). Further, the study envisages the role of an Anthropologist at the Primary Healthcare level/public health system to inform local implementers about the socio-cultural dynamics of health, illness, and disease management.

- Staff training has become an essential aspect of implementing a health programme. However, the training must also be amalgamated, considering the cultural values of the community they serve and the counselling services.

References

Ansari, A. M., Khan, Z., Khalique, N., & Siddiqui, A. R. (2008). Health profile of under-fives in rural areas of Algarh, India. *Ind J Prev Soc Med*, *39*(3). http://medind.nic.in/ibl/t08/i3/iblt08i3p94.pdf

Bhasin, V. (2007). Medical Anthropology: A Review. *Studies on Ethno-Medicine*, *1*(1), 1–20. https://doi.org/10.1080/09735070.2007.11886296

Beck, H. (n.d.). *Perception of health and health-seeking behaviour among the tribal people*. Retrieved February 16, 2023, from https://www.nhm.gov.in/images/pdf/Announcement/Dr_H_Beck.pdf

Buse, K., Mays, N., & Walt, G. (2009). *Making health policy* (Reprinted). Open Univ. Press.

Government of India. (2019). *Child Health & Immunization-Government of India*. Retrieved October 6, 2015, from http://nrhm.gov.in/nrhm-components/rmnch-a/child-health-immunization.html

Government of India. (2019). *Child Health: National Health Mission*. Source: http://nhm.gov.in/index1.php?lang=1&level=2&sublinkid=819&lid=219

Cowling, K., Dandona, R., & Dandona, L. (2014). Social determinants of health in India: Progress and inequities across states. *International Journal for Equity in Health*, *13*(1), 88. https://doi.org/10.1186/s12939-014-0088-0

Das, A., Gupta, R. D., Friedman, J., Pradhan, M. M., Mohapatra, C. C., & Sandhibigraha, D. (2013). Community perceptions on malaria and care-seeking practices in endemic Indian settings: Policy implications for the malaria control programme. *Malaria Journal*, *12*(1), 39. https://doi.org/10.1186/1475-2875-12-39

Guindon, G. E., Lavis, J. N., Becerra-Posada, F., Malek-Afzali, H., Shi, G., Yesudian, C. A. K., & Hoffman, S. J. (2010). Bridging the gaps between research, policy and practice in low- and middle-income countries: A survey of health care providers. *Canadian Medical Association Journal*, *182*(9), E362–E372. https://doi.org/10.1503/cmaj.081165

UNICEF. (2017). What We Do - Health- India. Source: https://www.unicef.org/india/what-we-do/health

Kalita, N., & Kalita, M. C. (2014). Ethnomedicinal plants of Assam, India, as an Alternative source of future Medicine for the Treatment of Pneumonia.

Kandel, B., Thakuri, B., Paudel, S., Sigdel, S., Khanal, P., Sapkota, K., Bhusal, B., Paudel, D., Mahara, S., Gurung, S., Ghimire, S., Subedi, P., Sapkota, P., Ghimire, P., & Tutunga, D. (2020). *Ethnobotanical uses of locally available plants for respiratory diseases by fifteen ethnic groups of Nepal: A review*.

Kulkarni, P. S., & Kurane, A. D. (2023). Parents' Caring Approach for Their Children Suffering from Pneumonia-A Study among Bhil Tribes of Maharashtra. *Indian Journal of Community Medicine, 48*(3), 478. https://doi.org/10.4103/ijcm.ijcm_837_22

Mathew, J. L., Patwari, A. K., Gupta, P., Shah, D., Gera, T., Gogia, S., Mohan, P., Panda, R., & Menon, S. (2011). Acute respiratory infection and pneumonia in India: A systematic review of literature for advocacy and action: UNICEF-PHFI series on newborn and child health, India. *Indian Pediatrics, 48*(3), 191–218. https://doi.org/10.1007/s13312-011-0051-8

Ministry of Health & Family Welfare. (2018). *Child Health Programmes in India.* Source: mohfw.nic.in/WriteReadData/l892s/6342515027file14.pdf

Ministry of Health & Family Welfare. (2014). *India's Newborn Action Plan (INAP)*. Child Health Division, Ministry of Health & Family Welfare, Govt. of India.

Government of India. (2017). *National_health_policy_2017.pdf.* Retrieved May 3, 2022, from https://www.nhp.gov.in/nhpfiles/national_health_policy_2017.pdf

IIPS. *(2019) NFHS-5 Factsheet India.* http://rchiips.org/nfhs/NFHS-5_FCTS/India.pdf

NRHM. (n.d.). *Home-DLHS-4.* Retrieved January 2, 2015, from https://nrhm-mis.nic.in/SitePages/DLHS-4.aspx?RootFolder=%2FDLHS4%2FMaharasthra%2FDistrict%20Factsheets&FolderCTID=0x012000742F17DFC64D5E42B681AB0972048759&View={F8D23EC0-C74A-41C3-B676-5B68BDE5007D}

Chakraborty Rupsa. (2019). Pneumonia deaths in children below five rose by 29.7% in 3 years: Govt data for Maharashtra. *Hindustan Times*, 13 December, 2019.https://www.hindustantimes.com/mumbai-news/pneumonia-deaths-in-children-below-five-rose-by-29-7-in-3-yrs-govt-data-for-maharashtra/story-lj7lc47wuABljUHximFqvK.html

UNICEF. (2019). *Pneumonia in Children Statistics-UNICEF DATA.* (2019). Retrieved July 12, 2022, from https://data.unicef.org/topic/child-health/pneumonia/

WHO. (2017). WHO *India Report*. Retrieved January 2, 2015, from http://www.who.int/countries/ind/en/

Yewale V. (2014). Two Birds, One Stone Approach - Integrated Action Plan for Pneumonia and Diarrhea. *Indian Pediatrics*, 51(12):957–8. DOI: 10.1007/s13312-014-0539-0

12

Risk Factors and Social Determinants of Tuberculosis an Anthropological Study in The Tea Gardens of Assam

C.J. Sonowal

Introduction

Basic Understanding of TB

Tuberculosis (TB) is an airborne disease created by the action of a bacterium called Mycobacterium (M) tuberculosis, also called tubercle bacilli. The airborne particles called droplet nuclei carry these bacteria. Persons with active pulmonary or laryngeal TB disease may generate infectious droplet nuclei when they cough, sneeze, or shout. Such infectious particles may be suspended in the air for several hours, depending on the environment. When a person inhales the droplet nuclei containing M. tuberculosis, transmission occurs.

TB Burden in India

Although India has been engaged in Tuberculosis for over 50 years, TB remains India's deadliest disease. The National Strategic Plan for Tuberculosis Elimination 2017-2025 (NSPTE 2017) shows 2.8 million new cases in 2015, placing India at the top of the most TB-burdened countries. Indonesia, with 1.02 million cases, and China, with 0.92 million cases, follow India. Nevertheless, the incidence of new cases per 100,000 population is 217 in India, placing India in the 24th position among the 30 most TB-burdened countries globally. South Africa has emerged as the most rapidly TB-infected country, with 833 new cases per 100,000 population, followed closely by Lesotho, with 794 new cases per 100,000 population. China, the most populous country globally, has an infection rate of only 67 cases per 100,000 people, occupying 29th place, and Brazil, with 40 new cases per 100,000 people, placed 30th. The estimated TB death in India remains at 480,000 per year.

TB Control in India

The TB control programme in India has been facing intimidating challenges due to various factors besides people's weakened immune resulting from undernourishment, diabetes, indoor air pollution from cook-stoves, or smoking. India is the victim of the TB burden due to decades of unrestrained transmission, leaving hundreds of millions of Indians with latent TB infection, which may reactivate at any time.

The delayed diagnosis and late and inadequate treatment increase the TB transmission risk. There has been evidence of non-adherence to complete treatment among one-third of identified TB patients. The country also bears a significant burden of multi-drug resistant (MDR) TB and extensively drug-resistant (XDR-) TB. A lot of them are undetected and continue to transmit disease.

Although the RNTCP has managed to treat more than 10 million TB patients in India, the TB decline rate does not seem promising to achieve the 2035 "End TB target". Looking at the inadequate decline while continuing the prior effort in TB control, the National Strategic Plan for Tuberculosis Elimination (TSPTE 2017-25) has advocated for a new, comprehensively deployed intervention plan to speed up the rate of decline of incidence of TB. The new strategy is a structure of four integrated strategic pillars: "Detect–Treat–Prevent– Build" (DTPB).

Under the pillar of "Detect", it aims to find all Drug-Sensitive TB and Drug-Resistant-TB cases, emphasising reaching TB patients seeking care from private providers and undiagnosed TB in high-risk populations. Under the pillar of "Treat", it aims to Initiate and sustain all patients on appropriate anti-TB treatment wherever they seek care, with patient-friendly systems and social support. Similarly, under "Prevent", it aims to prevent the emergence of TB in susceptible populations. Finally, under "Build", it tries to build and strengthen enabling policies, empowered institutions and human resources with enhanced capacities.

TB: The Disease of the Poor

WHO (2000) reveals that low and middle-income countries account for more than ninety-five percent of TB-related deaths resulting from a lack of proper sanitation, as people cannot develop better lifestyles. A strong association exists between low GDP per capita income and national TB incidence in non-African countries (Lönnroth et al., 2010). Due to the weakened immune system of HIV patients, TB remains more prevalent in African countries. Out of all TB-related deaths, nearly ninety-five percent of deaths occur in developing countries. Notably, out of these ninety-five percent deaths, more than sixty percent occur in the twenty percent poorest countries. Further, eighty percent of the total TB burden of the world is found in 22 countries. Of these high TB-burdened countries, 15 are low-income (Hanson et al., 2006).

Factors Leading to Exposure to and Infection of TB

Since TB is an airborne disease, exposure to germs is a crucial cause of infection. To get the infection to occur, contact with a person with active TB disease is a necessary risk factor. The risk of exposure and subsequent infection to TB depends on direct and indirect factors. Some directly responsible factors lead to different levels and durations of exposure to droplets containing TB germs. Lönnroth et al. (2010) identify these as 'downstream risk factors'.

Disease Burden and Physical Conditions

How easily a person will get infected with or get exposed to an infected person depends on the extent of the disease burden within the community and how quickly the person with infection is identified and subsequently treated and cured. Besides disease burden, some other congenial physical conditions catalyse or facilitate the possibility of exposure to and infection with infectious droplets of TB. A crowded place with inadequate ventilation increases the possibility of exposure to infectious droplets. Such a physical environment may be anything like a household with many family members and a lack of adequate ventilation, a clinic, workplaces, public transport, and a prison (Rieder, 1999; Menzies & Joshi, 2007). Likewise, the exposure duration depends on how the person concerned is related to those places.

Weaken Defence System of the Hosts

TB germs may remain dormant in an infected person and may or may not exhibit symptoms throughout their lifetime, depending on their defence system.

Impact of Tobacco Smoking

The defence system may turn weak due to tobacco smoke exposure, indoor air pollution from burning solid fuel in a poorly ventilated house, and other air pollution types. Physiologically, such exposure reduces the ability to clear bacilli from a person's airway, leading to an increased risk of infection in exposure to infectious droplets (Rehfuess, 2006; Lin et al., 2007). Tobacco smoke impairs the lung's defence mechanisms against infection, like decreased mucociliary clearance and alveolar macrophages' phagocytic function. Such an impaired immune response in smokers could affect the performance of IFN-y Release Assays (IGRAs) (Altet et al., 2017). Due to these physiological changes and mechanisms, smokers have an increased risk of infection if exposed to *Mycobacterium tuberculosis* (Underner et al., 2012a) and have an elevated risk of active TB if infected (Underner et al., 2012b). Padrão et al. (2018) have identified the threshold risk factors of smoking cigarettes daily for TB. They found that young age smoking is significantly related to TB infection, and a WHO study (2016) also supports it. Similarly, Gopi and Kolappan (2002), Lin (2009) and Amere et al. (2018) also have found an association between increased risk of TB and smoking.

Impact of Malnutrition

The host's defence system also becomes weak due to malnutrition, as has been found by several researchers, and such a weakened defence system may lead to TB infection in a risky environment (Cegielski & McMurray, 2004). Reviewing the studies based on observations in humans and experimental animal studies, Cegielski and McMurray (2004) have indicated a clear-cut relationship between malnutrition and TB incidence. Hoyt et al.'s (2019) study also reveals a similar observation. Edwards et al. (1971) found a four-fold higher risk of TB among men at least ten percent underweight at baseline than men at least ten percent overweight. By assessing the data from the Demographic Health Survey (DHS) 2006 for

India, Oxlade and Murray (2012) found that low BMI had the most potent mediating effect on the association between poverty and prevalent TB. Similarly, Tverdal (1986) reveals a more than five-fold higher risk of TB infection. More direct evidence relating malnutrition to TB is provided by Chan et al. (1997), who point out a link between malnutrition and secondary immunodeficiency, increasing host susceptibility to infection.

The link between malnutrition and TB has been bi-directional. While malnutrition is a possible risk factor for TB infection, TB may also lead to malnutrition in a patient (Ingabire et al., 2019; Feleke et al., 2020). Gupta et al. (2009) have found significantly lower nutritional status in patients with active Tuberculosis than in healthy controls. Jahnavi and Sudha (2010) showed that nutritional supplementation was associated with significant improvements in sputum conversion, cure rates, treatment completion rates, and performance status. Lonnroth et al. (2010) have revealed that TB risk increased by about fourteen percent with each unit reduction in BMI. However, such findings are not without negative results, as shown by Sinclair et al. (2011).

Impact of Alcohol Use

There has been research on the relationship between alcohol use and TB infection worldwide. Alcohol consumption significantly contributes to the tuberculosis burden, with the most severe impacts estimated for the African region (Sameer et al., 2017). Zixin et al. (2017) found an increased TB risk related to a higher amount of alcohol use among smokers. The risk of active Tuberculosis elevates substantially with the alcohol consumption of more than 40 grams of ethanol per day (Lönnroth et al., 2008). This increased risk of infection is also associated with the specific social mixing patterns among alcohol users and the influence on the immune system of alcohol itself and alcohol-related conditions. There has also been a strong association between heavy alcohol use/alcohol use disorders (AUD) and TB (Rehm et al., 2009). Vendhan and Richard (2009) reveal evidence of an increased incidence of pulmonary TB among those who smoke and those who drink.

There is also an indirect impact of alcohol in terms of tuberculosis infection that affects the maintenance of innate and acquired immune systems by alcohol-induced conditions like malnutrition, liver disease, and social drift. Moreover, alcohol consumption may facilitate people to be present in social environments where the risk of spreading tuberculosis infection is high, for instance, in bars, shelters, prisons and social institutions.

Social Determinants of Exposure to and Infection with TB

Poor working-class people are likely to live in crowded and inadequately ventilated houses, they are likely to get exposed to the smoke of solid bio-fuels, they are likely to work in crowded and ill-maintained unhygienic conditions, and they are also more likely to travel by crowded public transport.

Housing Conditions as a Risk Factor for Exposure to Infectious Droplets

Larcombe and Orr (2007) reveal a relationship between TB incidence and housing conditions like high household occupancy density, low air quality, and inadequate ventilation through a study among Canada's First Nations, Inuit, and immigrant populations. The authors point out that in populations that already suffer high TB infection rates, crowded housing and inadequate ventilation increase the risk of transmission and progression to disease among those who share living space. A similar observation has also been made by Clark et al. (2002), who find a significant association between housing density, isolation, income levels, and TB incidence. Similarly, in their study in Tanjungpinang District in Indonesia, Madhona et al. (2016) found a significant correlation between occupancy density, lighting, and humidity with TB incidence. Back home in India, based on National Family Health Survey (NFHS-4) data, Singh et al. (2018) have opined that a contaminated household environment increases the risk of Tuberculosis in India. Further, lower socioeconomic status is also directly related to malnutrition. A concise note on the relationship between malnutrition and TB infection has been made above.

Lower socioeconomic status is also associated with characteristics like a lack of awareness about health care, less power and authority to act on existing healthy behaviour and policy, limited access to the food security program, and better health care. Further, such conditions are also related to risky lifestyles, including tobacco use, excess use of low-quality alcohol, imbalanced dietary habits, unsafe sex leading to HIV-AIDS, and more.

Differential Impacts of Risk Factors and Determinants on Poorer and Richer Populations

Depending upon the community's socioeconomic status, the impact of risk factors and determinants tends to differ (Blas & Kurup, 2010). While the influential and more affluent people are resilient to cope with risk factors and situations, the more impoverished people are stigmatised to live with the risk at the cost of their health. Thus, a similar level of exposure to risk factors may not have a similar effect across different population groups. An increased disease burden within a population group where social exclusion, low income, alcohol abuse, malnutrition, crowded housing, and poor access to health services are prevalent will undoubtedly lead to more infection and disease compared to those free from such burdens.

Further, if one looks at the policy issues, a uniform healthcare strategy for all population groups may result in differential healthcare outcomes due to different socio-cultural and socioeconomic contexts. Even if similar health conditions exist, the consequences will not be the same, mainly because people in advantaged positions possess better healthcare options, job security, and insurance coverage to mitigate loss. In contrast, the more impoverished and disadvantaged people are likely to experience financial loss, job loss, and lesser quality of health care, affecting the health outcome as the consequence of similar health conditions.

The Problem Setting

There have been reports of tuberculosis incidence among the tea gardens of Assam to a great extent. In the Dibrugarh district, forty percent of total TB incidents are found in tea gardens, and considering their percentage share of the district's total population, it is a significant number. Although the tea gardens have healthcare facilities monitored under the Revised National TB Control Program, including DOTS, TB incidence has been recurring. Such incidence leads to the necessity of a complementary approach to the bio-medical regimen of TB cure programs where the focus on and addressing the social determinants may play significant roles. TB burden in tea gardens results from a cyclical process derived from the interaction between pathological and socio-cultural components. The social determinants discussed above have been prevalent in Assam's tea gardens; nevertheless, no detailed study has been conducted on these issues among Assam's tea gardens.

Tea Tribes in Assam refer to the population groups that have been labourers in Assam's tea gardens. British tea planters brought their forefathers from different parts of mainland India. Although their forefathers came from tribal-dominated areas, the tea garden labourers did not have the status of a Scheduled Tribe in Assam. There are approximately 96 different ethnic groups among the tea tribes in Assam. Administratively, their development and welfare responsibilities are partially vested in the Department of Welfare of Plains Tribes and Backward Classes of Assam, Government of Assam. They do not fully come under this department's purview because they are bound by the Tea Company's Plantation Labour Act and many other draconian laws.

From their traditional domain, the ancestors of the present-day tea tribes entered into an agro-industrial environment as labourers, having no independent access to natural resources and any say over their production. They were also generally away from urban contact because they had minimal opportunity and capability to interact with urban life due to strict rules and dire poverty. Thus, confined to a peculiar situation, they retained several age-old beliefs and practices and imbibed crowded industrial labourers' harmful behaviour like alcoholism. While people have encountered the risk of alien diseases, their attachment to traditional practices creates a conflicting situation.

The paper is the outcome of a research study conducted in four tea gardens of Assam, sponsored by the Research Council, Tata Institute of Social Sciences, Mumbai, with the title "Health and treatment seeking behaviour among the tea- tribes of Assam with special reference to the incidence of TB". While preparing the report, it became evident that social determinants related to TB had not been studied and addressed adequately in the state. Though the RNTCP and DOTS have been successful in achieving a positive outcome in treatment, they have been unable to arrest the new incidents occurring in the tea gardens so far. Thus, the primary concern of the paper is to deliberate the issues related to social determinants perceived or established through global research as the responsible factors for the spread of TB. As only the relevant part of the study's complete findings has been used to develop the paper and its objectives, the methodology and objectives set for the study may not appear to fit adequately. The primary difference between the full study report and the paper is the focus of the discussion - the social determinant instead of health and treatment-seeking behaviour.

Objectives

The paper's primary objective is to deliberate the social determinants that increase the risk of exposure to and infection with TB disease. The primary objective may be divided into the following theme-based objectives:

i. To examine, with the help of primary data, the prevalence of risk factors like smoking, alcohol consumption, dietary habits, working conditions, and living conditions among the tea garden population.

ii. To examine, using primary data, people's perceptions and actions regarding causes of illness, diagnosis, treatment preference, adherence to treatment, and awareness, with particular reference to TB.

iii. To discuss in detail the findings using specific literature on health issues in Assam's tea gardens and find out the gap in information on social determinants of TB, specific to Assam's tea gardens, employing the available global literature on the issue.

Material And Methods

The paper focuses on the social determinants of TB using the data derived from a primary field investigation. Secondary data, like literature relating to the tea garden worker population in Assam with particular reference to disease, lifestyle, and living conditions, have been extensively used to substantiate the primary data. The Global literature on TB and social determinants relating to TB has been discussed to find out the gap in information regarding the social determinants of TB in the tea gardens of Assam.

The researcher collected primary data from four tea gardens in the Dibrugarh district, namely, Mankatta, Sessa, Maijan, and North Balijan. These tea gardens were selected using information from the TB control centre at Assam Medical College Hospital, Dibrugarh. The selection criteria for tea gardens and respondents are as follows:

Selection of Tea Gardens

i. Incidences of TB were higher in the selected tea gardens.

ii. Four tea gardens were selected, two each from relatively urban proximity and rural areas.

iii. One tea garden from each locality is registered with the Assam Branch of the Indian Tea Association (ABITA), and one is owned by a more significant business house/company.

Selection of TB Patients

A total of 32 TB incidences from the four selected tea gardens were taken for the study, eight from each tea garden on the following criteria:

i. TB patients with an outcome – death and unsuccessful due to non-adherence.

ii. Relapse cases and/or re-started treatment

iii. Successfully treated and completed cases.

iv. Fresh cases of at least one-month-old.

v. Based on the fulfilment of the above criteria, and depending upon the availability and accessibility, ten males and 22 females were selected for the study.

vi. Age was not a criterion.

Further, 32 caregivers/heads of selected patients' families and ten respondents from each selected garden (20 males and 20 females) were selected.

Reason for Selecting the Stakeholders

Since the study aimed to determine people's health and treatment-seeking behaviour, the selection of patients, caregivers, and the general population was necessary. The general population as a stakeholder was considered important because their perception and action help understand the inherent characteristics and factors influencing or determining the community's health and treatment-seeking behaviour, which is likely to be reflected through a patient's and a caregiver's behaviour. This group was selected to know the people's general perception and actions regarding illness, not as a control group to assess any bio-medical issues concerning selected TB patients.

Separate questions were asked for different categories of stakeholders to assess:

i. The folk concept of illness, causes, progression and curative action

ii. People's knowledge of bio-medical terminology of illness

iii. Day-to-day life, dietary behaviour, work burden, income and poverty, education and awareness and welfare measures include healthcare facilities.

Data Collection and Analysis

A survey schedule was used to assess people's perception of symptoms of various illnesses hypothetically, the folk concept of illnesses, their progression, perceived reason and folk and popular remedial measures. Further, in-depth interviews were conducted with all the selected stakeholders. The patients' explanatory model (Kleinmen, 1975) was created to assess the above queries. Survey data were analysed using the SPSS package, and qualitative data were analysed using the Atlas-ti package.

Ethical Consideration

As a Research Council (TISS) sponsored study, the Institutional Review Board (IRB) examined the research proposal for its scientific quality and ethical issues and cleared it for both. Respondents' Information Sheet and

Informed Consent Forms were prepared according to the guidelines provided by the IRB.

Findings

The paper's findings result from a systematic literature review and the primary data collected from four tea gardens in Dibrugarh District.

Education among the Respondents

The level of education is very low in these tea gardens. Among the 32 patients, fifty-three percent are illiterate, nearly nineteen percent are only primary educated, and another twenty percent are High school educated. No respondent studied beyond class X. Among the caregivers, sixty-one percent are illiterate, twenty-nine percent are primary educated, and only ten percent are high school educated. Among the general respondents, 42.5 percent are illiterate, 37.5 percent are primarily educated, and twenty percent are high school educated. It shows the very backward position of tea tribes in terms of education.

Healthcare Facilities in Tea Gardens

A survey of the healthcare facilities in the four tea gardens under the study reveals that one regular doctor and one or more than one nurse are present in each tea garden hospital. The North Balijan tea garden has 20 health care professionals, the Maijan tea garden has 9, the Sessa tea garden has 7, and the Mancotta tea garden has 5. The Tea Garden Authority provides free medicines, a free ambulance facility, free health check-ups, and a free of cost supplementary diet for Active TB patients. Nevertheless, if the patients opt for private treatment, the garden authority does not provide these facilities.

Under the DOTS system, the tea garden clinic provides medicine for the initial cough and fever symptoms. If it does not subside, they initiate the first stage test for TB, and if found positive, the patient is sent to AMC for further diagnosis. Once the presence of TB is established, the patient is sent back to the garden Hospital or home to take medicine. If the condition worsens, he is kept in the TB ward of AMC for recovery.

Risk Factors Relating to TB Prevalent in Tea Gardens of Assam

Disease Burden in Tea Gardens and the Risk of Exposure to Infectious Droplets of TB

Information collected from the TB control centre in Dibrugarh reveals that the district's tea gardens are burdened with TB a lot. The centre accumulates data on the general population as well as tea gardens. It shows that between 2011 and 2015, 11,997 TB cases were recorded in the Dibrugarh district by the centre, of which 4,789 were recorded in tea gardens alone, indicating a forty percent share of TB cases in the district. While the tea garden population constitutes less than twenty percent of the state, the forty percent share of TB incidence among them is significant for the policy planners. The effect of such a high TB burden in the community has also been reflected in primary data collected from the tea gardens.

The primary data collected from four tea gardens reveals that among the selected TB patients, 34.4 percent had close relatives as TB patients, 28.1 percent had a family member at home as TB patients and 18.8 percent had neighbours as TB patients with whom they used to interact. The remaining 3.1 percent of respondent TB patients had no known exposure. Among the 40 general respondents, 45.0 percent have family members currently having or had TB. Another 12.5 percent have TB patients among their close relatives, whereas 42.5 percent of respondents have no closely related TB patients.

Housing and Workplace Conditions

Primary data reveals that the housing arrangement in tea garden lines is very congested, rooms are small, and there is no proper ventilation facility, especially in bedrooms and kitchen. Forty-seven percent of TB patients have up to five family members; thirty-eight percent of respondents live with up to seven members, whereas nearly sixteen percent of families live with eight or more members. Among the non-patient general respondents, 67.5 percent live with six to seven family members. These data indicate that people mainly live in crowded houses. Such a situation increases the risk of exposure to TB, as indicated by the global research literature. Field data show the incidence of TB cases in the same family one after another, sometimes within the same generation and sometimes across the generations. The workplace of the tea garden workers is not as crowded. Being an agro-based industry, the workers are, to some extent, exposed to pesticides and herbicides. Women were leaf pickers, and men were cleaners and cutters who worked in the open air.

It is important to note that not all TB-infected persons are contagious. A person is contagious only when the infection becomes active with symptoms. An infected person without TB symptoms is non-contagious. TB symptoms may surface very gradually, and people often get confused with symptoms of other diseases for which timely detection and subsequent treatment get delayed. In such a case, people can unknowingly transmit Tuberculosis to others. People with symptomatic TB remain contagious for at least two weeks from starting medication. After that, though the germs may remain in them with symptoms, they are no longer contagious. Such transmission conditions necessitate early detection and treatment to arrest the spread of TB in a risky environment. In a condition with a high TB burden in the community and people living in congested houses without proper ventilation, late detection and treatment have a greater possibility of transmitting the germs to nearby people.

The gap between the Appearance of Symptoms and the Start of Treatment

The study reveals that people usually wait and watch for a few days for a natural cure. After that, they go to the tea garden clinic and take medicine. Sometimes, they bring medicine from the clinic and take it home. Fifty percent of respondents went to a doctor after a week since symptoms first appeared. Another twenty percent of respondents reported to the doctor in 15 days. Nearly twenty-two percent of respondents reported that symptoms appeared after 15 days. These indicate that people mostly prefer to wait and watch and prefer not to go to a doctor as far as possible. The reasons behind this gap are varied. Most respondents thought they were suffering from some usual illness (47%), while thirty-eight percent were waiting for self-cure. Only 12.5 percent of respondents went to the garden doctor to take medicine. Such treatment-seeking behaviour is crucial in the TB control programme in that the infected person remains highly contagious between the appearance of symptoms and 15 days after treatment.

Exposure to Household and Tobacco Smoke

Scientific research indicates that household and tobacco smoke weaken the host immune system in defending against TB germs. The crucial aspect of the TB germ is that exposure to and inhaling TB germ may not lead to an active TB disease in all persons. Scientific evidence reveals that a person's healthy immune system helps defend against the progression of tuberculosis infection into active TB disease, although the person is infected with TB germs. Scientific evidence reveals that less than ten percent of people infected with tuberculosis bacteria develop active tuberculosis disease. Contrarily, people with weakened immune systems are much more susceptible to actually developing active tuberculosis disease after infection. TB bacteria remain dormant in many people and may never develop into an active disease. Scientists have found that HIV-AIDS, malnutrition, exhaustive working conditions, tobacco smoke, and alcohol make a host's immune system weak. Tobacco smoke makes smokers' airways weak enough to clear TB germs while inhaling.

A general observation in the field reveals that the tea garden workers collect firewood from nearby places, including the pruned branches of tea bushes and the dry branches of shade trees planted in the tea gardens. They use these for cooking food. In the winter, they also sit around the fire to warm their body. Thus, people are invariably exposed to household smoke in poorly ventilated houses.

Observation also reveals that smoking *bidi* is quite prevalent among adult males, and many women smoke. The primary data collected from the tea gardens reveal that nearly seven- teen percent of patients have continued smoking even after the detection of TB. Among the patients, nearly sixty-three percent chew tobacco. Among the general population, fifty-eight percent of respondents smoke either *bidi, cigarette,* or both. Besides, a lot of males and females also chew tobacco regularly. This number may be higher as people are reluctant to reveal such behaviour.

Prevalence of Malnutrition among the Tea Garden Population

Global scientific studies have found an association between malnutrition in people and TB, thereby explaining that malnutrition weakens hosts' defence mechanisms against TB. The present study did not include an assessment of the nutritional status of the studied people directly. Instead, the study dealt with a brief survey of people's dietary habits. The study reveals that the people in tea gardens usually take two heavy meals, one in the morning and the other at night. Rice and roti are the two primary food items they eat. Only thirty-four percent of patients reported that they used to take other food supplements like health drinks, milk and eggs. Intake of meat and food supplements is complex due to the cost factor. Their diets are not balanced compared to their workload and are not usually sufficient. Such conditions lead to malnutrition among male and female workers as well. The researcher relied on secondary sources of information, such as research literature, that indicate almost universal malnutrition among the tea garden population in the state.

Use of Alcohol

The people in tea gardens are generally known to be excessive liquor drinkers. They drink both locally made alcohol made of rice (*Hadiya* or *Laupani*) and branded liquor available in the garden shops and vendors. Fermented spirits, locally called Chulai, are also favourite alcoholic drinks for these people. Though several researchers have deliberated on alcohol use among tea garden workers, there is a lack of focused studies relating alcohol to any particular disease, including TB.

Primary data collected from tea gardens reveals that among the population selected for the study (40 respondents), 62.5 percent of people drink liquor, and the number may increase as people are reluctant to reveal it. Adult males spend much of their earnings on liquor. Nearly forty-eight percent of the respondents are habitual drinkers who drink daily. Fifteen percent of the respondents say that they drink twice or thrice a week. People drink till they are inebriated. The study also reveals that some TB patients have been drinking liquor even after being diagnosed with TB. While many of the respondents are tight-lipped regarding their drinking behaviour, considering the environment, one can say that many TB patients indulge in drinking.

The social situation in the tea garden is congenial to drinking liquor. Almost all adult males among the tea garden workers drink liquor. Many families brew liquor at home to sell or consume at home. Besides, branded alcohols are also available in the garden through local shops. There are suppliers of local liquor in the tea gardens. It is also a general belief that having a few liquor pegs reduces tiredness and body pain after a day's work. People take drinking as a means of entertainment and leisure time engagement. There have been frequent hooch tragedy incidents in the tea gardens due to a lack of quality control mechanisms in locally produced liquor.

Social Determinants of TB in Tea Gardens

Poverty and Economic Conditions

Poverty and poor economic conditions have been characteristic features among tea garden workers due to low wage structure and low human capital in terms of education, skill, and awareness to diversify their livelihood. The low wage structure has the colonial legacy continued by the successive Indian tea planters, which have compelled the tea garden workers to reel under everlasting poverty and financial hardship. Based on several records, Dasgupta (1986) observes that the near-starvation wage level was rationalised on the ground that if the planters paid the 'coolies' higher wages, that is, wages above what was considered by the planters as subsistence level, there would be an increase in 'coolie indolence'.

Primary data collected from the selected tea gardens revealed that sixty-six percent of TB patients work there. Others are non-earners. The average minimum payment is INR 115 daily for the tea garden works. Thus, they get around INR 3000 per month on average, which is quite a poor salary for one to get these days. People get food items like rice, dal, wheat flour, medicine, and some free or heavily subsidised dresses. The permanent employees and their family members get health care benefits in tea garden clinics and hospitals. Their meagre income does not allow them to buy nutritious food items or vegetables, which cost a lot. There is a definite compulsion to compromise health owing to economic conditions.

Perceiving Health and Illness and Causes of Illness and Cure

The primary data collected from the selected tea gardens show that thirty-seven percent of patients believe in the cause-effect relationship between supernatural power and illness and misfortune. Forty-seven percent of patients reveal that they have done one or the other rituals during their illness. Contrarily, people have also witnessed the effectiveness of medicines and doctors in curing diseases for which they do not usually wait for a ritual cure. Out of 40 respondents from non-patients, 82.5 percent accept the existence of supernatural power and their effect on human health and well-being. Some sixty percent of respondents believe that the action of spirits, black magic, and evil deeds of people cause illness, and by performing proper rituals and counter-magic, the impact of illness can be reduced or removed. 32.5 percent of families perform rituals at the family level quite often, while 37.5 percent of respondents said they perform rituals very rarely.

Among the 31 selected caregivers, nearly sixty-one percent believe that some ghosts and spirits create illness among people if they are aggrieved or not appeased. Another twenty-nine percent of respondents say they do not believe in ghosts and spirits, though most of their fellow people believe in them. Among the general respondents, nearly 42 percent believe that performing rituals and counter-magic can cure or reduce the effect of illness caused by spirits and human activities like black magic and casting evil eyes. As many as fifty-two percent of respondents say they do not believe in such activities. However, they reveal that their community generally believes in such actions. Thus, based on these views, the tea garden worker community mostly believes in supernatural beings and their influence on the human body and soul. Subsequently, nearly forty-two percent of caregivers informed that they had performed one or the other rituals at the home or community level to better the family and the ill persons. People mostly believe that the actions of supernatural beings cause illnesses. Most of these respondents believe it but cannot pinpoint what type of illness such powers create (58.1%). Another 38.7 percent of caregivers say that chickenpox occurs due to the influence of deities.

In practice, people are more inclined towards modern healthcare facilities around them and think less about spirits' influence. So, they take the diseased person to the hospital irrespective of the type of illness. However, some caregivers opined that performing rituals before taking them to doctors is essential for some illnesses. Contrarily, nearly seventy-seven percent of caregivers deny that one should perform rituals before going to the doctor. In several instances, prolonged illness makes people think of supernatural power and black magic. They invariably perform rituals and counter-magic activities with the help of priests and traditional healers. Such activities are pretty familiar scenes in the tea garden.

Interestingly, people do not think of a total physical cure through rituals and counter-magic. Some of them believe that doctors and modern medicine can cure the physical harm done by such forces. Some people believe that the body cannot respond to a doctor's medicine until the influence of supernatural beings or black magic persists. So, removing the influence of spirits and black magic is essential before one takes the patient to the doctor. So, many people do a ritual before taking the diseased person to the hospital. Nearly fifty percent of respondents believe in this procedure.

Perceived Causes of TB

The study reveals that TB patients are mainly ignorant about what causes TB. As many as eighty-four percent of TB patients have no clear idea of what causes TB. They were mainly tight-lipped about the disease's spread from their family members or close relatives because that would hold those persons responsible. Instead, they tried to falsify the contact as a reason for spreading the disease. In their view, many TB patients do not have any contact with other TB patients. They also opine that illness may occur anytime and in any circumstance. Contrarily, sixteen percent of respondents say that others have infected them. Among the caregivers, 93.5 percent did not have a definite idea of what causes TB. They have a very vague idea about it. Another 42.2 percent of caregivers feel that TB occurs as other diseases occur among them. Among the general respondents, 87.5 percent did not know how people got infected with TB.

By explaining the patient's explanatory model, the study finds that some patients believe their illness is a result of their destiny and bad luck. They accept that some supernatural power or connection is responsible for destiny and bad luck. TB patients also think a cure from TB takes longer due to the back magic inflicted on them. The inquiry also reveals that the course of treatment is directly related to the perceived cause of illness. If the cause of the illness is perceived as supernatural, they will prefer rituals to bio-medical treatment, at least for the initial stage of treatment.

Further, patients are mostly clueless about what triggered their illness. However, with particular uncertainty, few patients think that their drinking habits and hard work when they are weak lead to TB. Some stick to destiny, as well. Some patients believe that their previous illness triggered the incidence of TB in them.

The in-depth interview reveals that people accept TB's severity (fatality) but are not serious about its susceptibility. They have seen TB patients in their neighbourhood, mostly cured after treatment. They have available and easily accessible healthcare facilities. They can- not opt for a different lifestyle and work environment even though they risk getting TB due to the lack of options. It perhaps makes them casual about this fatal disease. It has been manifested in their risky lifestyle. Several patients and non-patient respondents expressed such perceptions. Further, the inability to separate TB symptoms from other respiratory and related diseases worsens the situation, leading to failure in timely detection and subsequent timely treatment.

Knowledge about TB Symptoms among the Patients Before Getting Diagnosed

The interviewed TB patients revealed that doctors and nurses did not inform them about various aspects of TB. The health department has been running awareness campaigns in various ways. The ground reality is that it has hardly reached the targeted people, especially the tea garden population. Relative isolation, low literacy, easy access to doctors and medicines, and the inherent belief system might influence it. As many as seventy-eight percent of patients did not know about TB symptoms before the diagnosis. Twenty-two percent of respondents said their knowledge of TB symptoms was imperfect. Instead, they perceived the illness symptoms as simple cough, fever, or usual illness. The illness' progression led them to further action, like going to doctors and screening for TB. About seventy-five percent of respondent TB patients know TB is fatal if not treated properly. However, only forty-seven percent knew this before being diagnosed with TB. Among the 32 patients, thirty-one percent were informed by fellow patients about the fatality, while doctors told only 9.4 percent. These findings indicate that awareness programs are unable to make people aware of TB.

Discussion

Without denying the success and promising outcomes of the bio-medical TB control regimen, public health professionals and social scientists explicitly express the crucial roles of social determinants in the TB control program. The probability of exposure to infected droplets of TB, getting infected, and the manifestation of the disease depends on factors determined by social conditions in and around people. Based on a literature review and primary data, the study deals with the nature and extent of such determinants in tea gardens and is discussed as follows.

Risk Factors to Exposure among the Tea Garden Workers Population

Disease Burden in Tea Gardens of Assam

Data collected from the TB control centre of Assam Medical College Hospital reveals the high TB burden prevalent in Assam's tea gardens. The effect of high TB burden on the studied population manifests in the field study findings, as it finds multiple TB patients from a single family from the same generation or across the generations at different times. Literature specific to health issues in Assam's tea garden population also supports such findings. For instance, Chelleng et al. (2014) revealed the importance of tracing the family history of Pulmonary TB. Researchers like Deb Nath (2000), Sahoo et al. (2010), Deb Nath and Nath (2014), Khan et al. (2015) and Hazarika and Arakeri (2019) revealed the prevalence of TB and various factors responsible for the spread of TB in tea gardens of Assam.

Physical Surrounding and Risk of Exposure

Some conditions where a person lives or tread determine the risk of exposure to infectious droplets. There is a greater possibility of contact with infectious droplets under specific physical environments, as shown by Rieder (1999) and Menzies and Joshi (2007). Further, the duration of exposure depends on how the person concerned is related to those places.

Besides, disease load in the surrounding congested and overcrowded living or working conditions without proper ventilation is also risky.

Housing Conditions as a Risk Factor for Exposure to Infectious Droplets

The primary data shows that people in tea gardens live in congested and poorly-ventilated houses with many family members. The global literature reviewed indicates that in a high TB disease-burdened condition, late detection and subsequent delay in treating active TB patients may lead to the spread of TB, especially in a crowded environment, as found in tea gardens. The primary data indicate a possibility of TB transmission in the tea gardens of Assam.

Such high household occupancy density, low air quality, and inadequate ventilation have been linked with TB in a study in the Canadian context by Larcombe and Orr (2007), Clark et al. (2002), and Madhona et al. (2016). In India, Singh et al. (2018) also opine that a contaminated household environment increases the risk of tuberculosis. Although the research literature available on tea gardens in Assam does not deal with any such cause-effect relationship, these studies certainly substantiate the findings of primary data by showing the high occupancy of households in tea gardens as shown by researchers like Baruah (2009), Sahoo et al. (2010), Dutta et al. (2011), Dowerah (2013) Bora (2015), Deori and Saikia (2016), Saikia (2017), Boruah (2018), Hazarika and Arakeri (2019) and many more.

Factors Related to Weakened Host Defence System

Impact of Tobacco and Household Smoke

The primary data shows that smoking and chewing tobacco have been prevalent among the tea garden population and the selected TB patients. *Bidi is* a popular item for smokers in the tea gardens. Young people also indulge in smoking tobacco. It has been revealed that parents are least concerned about their children smoking and chewing tobacco at a young age, as it remains a usual practice across genders and generations. Awareness against tobacco use is at its minimum. The earning young generation justifies their smoking habit because it is their earning, and no one has to do anything about it. The following generation also learns and imbibes the practice of tobacco use from their parental generation. Further, the tea garden people use firewood for cooking and heating purposes in an inadequately ventilated house, leading to exposure to tobacco and household smoke pollution.

The global research literature reveals a direct association between tobacco smoking and a weakened host immune system, increasing the risk of getting infected with TB germs. Studies conducted by Underner et al. (2012a, b) and Altet et al. (2017) show smokers were developing a weakened defence system. Similarly, Padrão et al. (2018) have identified the threshold risk factors of smoking cigarettes per day for TB. Researchers like Gopi and Kolappan (2002) and a WHO study (2016) found an association between tobacco smoking and pulmonary tuberculosis development and the activation of latent TB infection (Amere et al., 2018). Further, smoking has a twofold risk of increasing TB, as Hsien-Ho Lin (2009) shows.

It is worth mentioning that no scientific study was conducted among the tea garden worker population establishing the link between exposure to smoke and a weakened host defence system. Among the few available literature, Medhi et al. (2006), Balgir (2009), Sahoo et al. (2010), and Sharma and Bhuyan (2018) reveal that adult males and adolescents, and to a certain extent, women also use tobacco, smoking, and chewing which substantiate the finding so of the primary data. Considering the evidence of exposure to tobacco and bio-fuel smoke in the tea garden population and considering the global evidence, it can be said that tobacco use has increased TB infection and disease risk in tea gardens, and the people in the tea garden are also at such risk due to prevalence of smoking.

Malnutrition and TB

As stated in the findings section, the study did not deal with the tea garden population's malnutrition status and its link with the incidence of TB. Instead, the study briefly inquired about the dietary habits of the people. Thus, the study reveals poor nutrition and food intake compared to the nature of people's work.

The tea garden worker populations, both males and females, are involved in menial and laborious work. They have to work from 8 a.m. till 4 p.m. The labourers sometimes work beyond their usual capacity to fulfil the given target. The reviewed literature and information collected suggest that tea garden workers do not get the minimum wage set by the government for other workers. The meagre earnings put them into poverty, leading them to other related problems like the inability to get adequate nutritious and balanced food, health education, and general well-being.

The supply of subsidised food grain mainly falls short of the requirement of the tea garden population. Further, due to meagre earnings and spending money on alcohol and other non-essential commodities, it worsens. People are seen as habitually less concerned about their diet in terms of good health and following the usual food habits, lacking in required nutrition and quantity. Rampant anaemia among these people, especially women, is related to their food habits, poverty, and work burden.

The global research literature on the link between malnutrition and the risk of infection with TB disease reveals a bi-directional association between the two. While malnutrition creates a congenital condition for TB infection, TB disease itself may lead to malnutrition in patients (Cegielski & McMurray, 2004; Gupta et al., 2009; Hoyt et al., 2019; Ingabire et al., 2019; Feleke et al., 2020). Malnutrition can also lead to secondary immunodeficiency, increasing the host's susceptibility to infection Chan et al. (1997). Furthermore, low BMI had the most substantial mediating effect on the association between poverty and prevalent TB (Oxlade & Murray, 2012).

Although the available research studies specific to tea gardens in Assam do not focus their attention towards any such established link, this literature explicitly indicates widespread malnutrition among the tea garden worker population attributable to the poor economic condition and lifestyle (Sahoo et al., 2010; Chelleng et al., 2014; Deori et al., 2016; Saikia, 2017; Dey, 2019; Borgohain, 2020). Other researchers have revealed that calorie and protein deficiency among these people results from the inadequate intake of essential food constituents (Deb Nath, 2000; Medhi & Mahanta, 2007; Panyang et al., 2018; Konwar et al., 2019). Nevertheless, the discussion points out that the tea garden population is at greater risk of getting infected with TB germs amidst the high disease burden because they live in poverty, do hard physical labour, have low-calorie intake and established malnutrition.

Alcohol Use, Social Underpinning, and TB

Field observation and primary data collected from the field reveal that drinking liquor, mostly in excess, has been a usual way of life among the tea garden population. Even some of the current TB patients also indulge in drinking alcohol. The study also reveals that the social situation and perception of alcohol consumption benefits make the situation congenial for alcohol use in excess.

It is also a general belief that having a few liquor pegs reduces tiredness and body pain after a day's work. People take drinking as a means of entertainment and leisure time engagement. Some people celebrate several rituals and ceremonies with plenty of liquor use. Parents hardly restrict their children from drinking liquor, and they also imbibe the exact behaviour of indulging in drinking following their parents. Among the Christian converts, the use of alcohol is less compared to traditional people. There have been frequent hooch tragedy incidents in the tea gardens due to a lack of quality control mechanisms in locally produced liquor. Excess use of alcohol compounded with the lower quality of alcohol and poor dietary habits makes their immune system weak, and they become vulnerable to fatal diseases like TB.

The available national and international level research evidence shows that a higher level of alcohol consumption is associated with an increased TB risk (Sameer et al., 2017; Zixin et al., 2017). Heavy alcohol use or AUD constitutes a risk factor for the incidence and re-infection of TB, with a higher rate of treatment defaults and the development of drug-resistant forms of TB (Rehm et al., 2009). Social mixing patterns associated with alcohol use hinder TB treatment response (Lönnroth et al., 2008). This evidence suggests that considering the heavy drinking habit of tea garden worker populations, poverty, malnutrition, and lack of awareness about several health aspects pose a grave health concern, including TB incidence. At the level of tea gardens of Assam, research studies reveal widespread use of alcohol in the tea gardens of Assam, substantiating the study's findings (Sharma & Bhuyan, 2016, 2018; Medhi et al., 2006; Sahoo et al., 2010; Bora, 2015).

Linkage between Poverty, Living Conditions, Work, Malnutrition and Unhealthy Habits

It has been evident from the study that the tea garden worker populations are bound to live in the labour lines (colony) as per their service agreement and for their future job security. People are also less concerned about changing their surroundings in terms of cleanliness and hygiene. As their earning is directly related to whether they can fulfil the set daily target of work, the workers have to do their duties even at the cost of their health. They are kept at the income threshold, so everyday work is their compulsion to survive. As mentioned in the findings, this legacy of low payment continues from the colonial regime.

Indeed, income poverty is directly related to malnutrition. However, this is not the only determinant of malnutrition. People's lifestyles and food habits also have significant effects on people's nutritional health. People are hardly concerned about the balanced and nutritional aspects of their food and do not put variation in their diets. The frequency of meals and the gap between meals also have a determining effect on their health. They go to work early with the first meal in the morning and hardly eat anything substantial during the day. They mostly miss the afternoon meal. Black tea with salt has been their refreshing drink between working hours.

Further, they indulge in drinking liquor, and the male adults spend a more significant part of their income on drinking, making the women workers in the family manage the household expenses, including expenses on food. Thus, one can see an unbreakable linkage between the tea gardens' labour administration policy, poverty, living conditions, malnutrition, and unhealthy lifestyles. These increase the risk of exposure to infectious droplets of TB and weaken the host's defence system, which increases the risk of infection and the manifestation of TB disease among the exposed population.

Perception and Action about Health and Treatment

Many tea garden worker populations have mentioned their beliefs and practices related to health and treatment-seeking behaviour, directly or indirectly related to the beliefs in the action or influence of supernatural power, non-material and non-biomedical causes. One can see the blend of traditional beliefs and practices and the use of a bio-medical regimen to treat illness in tea gardens. Such perceptions and actions determine the delay in diagnosis and treatment initiative, adherence, and withdrawal, especially in TB diagnosis and treatment. In the Indian context, several social scientists have explored specific traditional health and treatment-seeking behaviours among the tribes. Several perceptions and actions of the tea garden worker population resemble those perceptions and practices.

Medical anthropologists have established the importance of a global understanding of cultural factors in healthcare practices (Othon, 2011). The influence of local culture on the interpretation of causes and symptoms of illness, which to a great extent, influence the onset of treatment-seeking among people, has been mentioned by several anthropologists (Liefooghe et al., 1997; Yamada et al., 1997; Auer et al., 2000; Banerjee et al., 2000; Ngamvithayapong et al., 2000; Wandwalo& Morkve, 2000; Edginton et al., 2002; Viney et al., 2014). Relating the causes of illness to the effect of supernatural power, wrongdoing, bewitching, and breaking cultural rules of sexual abstinence has been established globally (Pronyk et al., 2001; Eastwood et al., 2004; Viney et al., 2014). These researchers found the perceived causes significant in that people seek treatment patterns based on the cause of illness. Thus, finding no link between causes of illness and modern healthcare practices remains one of the crucial reasons for non-compliance and non-adherence to a particular bio-medical treatment regimen by indigenous people (de Villiers, 1991; Liefooghe et al., 1997; Shrestha-Kuwahara et al., 2017). To some extent, such behaviours are also prevalent among the tea garden population.

There has been very scanty research on the perception and action about health and treatment-seeking among Assam's tea garden worker population. To make TB control programs more inclusive, social sciences researchers will benefit from concrete insight into the inherent folk perception prevalent among the tea garden population about causes of illness, health, and treatment-seeking expectations.

Role of IEC in Awareness Building about TB

Information, Education and Communication (IEC) have been integral parts of the TB control program, where the community participation component has recently been infused in RN-TCP. As per the literature reviews and primary field investigation, any IEC program has minimal impact on the tea garden worker population. Some people learned a few details about TB only after they were diagnosed with the disease. Some people are aware of the disease from other community members, and their information is incomplete.

The study has revealed that people in tea gardens are unaware of TB in terms of its causes, mode of spread, and preventive measures. They are also not well aware of the susceptibility to the disease. Causes of TB, as forwarded by these people, include bio-medical, supernatural, and climatic conditions. They are primarily concerned about sharing TB patients' utensils, as they think it is the mode of transmission.

Differential Impacts of Risk Factors and Social Determinants on Tea Garden Populations

The paper discusses the logic behind the differential impacts of risk factors and social determinants on the population having different socio-political backgrounds mentioned in the paper's introduction. The following is the discussion on the impact of risk factors and social determinants on tea garden populations based on the argument forwarded by Blas and Kurup (2010).

The people of the tea gardens of Assam find themselves at the lowest level of the social and economic domain. Till the 1980s, people used to address them as "coolie", a term given by the British tea planters. Their social status was low, and they were excluded from mainstream Assamese society. They are far lagging in terms of education, economic status, jobs, and skills. They have limited options to come out of their tea garden domain. Lack of awareness about rights and privileges and health and well-being has made them vulnerable to many odds.

Further, political parties use these people as their vote banks. Considering their population, their concentration in certain parts of the state, and their voting behaviour, political parties compete to lure and manage them. Although the tea garden population's importance is immense for political parties, the concerned authorities have done little to improve their condition. They are even devoid of the minimum wage they are supposed to get. There is no denying that a few people from tea gardens became elected MLAs and MPs. However, they are roped into power only to serve the purpose of the political parties. The ordinary people of tea gardens have little or no voice in policy issues. They are dependent on the tea garden authorities and the government.

Exposure to infectious droplets due to high disease burden is likely to affect the tea garden population more in that there is evidence of delayed diagnosis and late treatment seeking due to various reasons mentioned elsewhere in this paper. Malnutrition, rampant among the tea garden population, affects people differently because their work is tedious and laborious. They are the least aware and concerned about the nutritional aspects of their food. Their poorer condition and viewpoints on food and health do not allow them to eliminate the cycle of poverty, malnutrition, and TB infection. Further, researchers have revealed that TB infection leads to malnutrition as well. In such cases, poverty, lack of awareness, ill perception about health, and lack of social security networks, as prevalent among the tea garden worker population, affect them severely, as it is hard for them to get out of the situation.

Smoking is prevalent among the well-to-do population groups, but its consequence differs for the more impoverished and uneducated. People in better socioeconomic positions will cease smoking due to their greater awareness of the effects, susceptibility, and familial and social pressure. In contrast, no such option or conditions are available in tea gardens. Unavoidable exposure to infectious droplets and weakened defence mechanisms of smokers lead people to TB infection and its consequences.

Another crucial aspect is alcohol consumption. Consumption of alcohol is also quite prevalent among the richer and well-to-do population groups. Nevertheless, the quality of alcohol, the nature and extent of drinking liquor, food habits and drinking habits make a differential impact. The people in tea gardens mostly drink locally-made liquor with no quality assurance. There have been hooch tragedies in tea gardens. The branded liquors also have no quality assurance in that local people have sold these without holding proper or no licenses. Further, the tea garden workers perceive alcohol as an energy booster, painkiller, and tiredness killer. Such sort of perceived substitution to regular energy-providing foods deteriorates their health further. Frequent assembling and drinking together in a disease-burdened situation again increases the risk of exposure. Weak health due to irregular diet and excessive drinking increases the risk of developing the disease if a person gets exposed to infectious droplets, which is very likely in tea gardens.

There have also been reports of differential treatment in the health centres by the health care providers and the tea garden workers because there is a general notion among the people outside the tea garden that the tea garden labourers are ignorant, unclean, and uneducated. They are powerless and thus cannot assert their rights. Such perceptions get translated to discriminative actions in some instances, as reported.

Conclusion

Analysis of TB control programs worldwide suggests that for sustainable control of TB, the curative interventions must go hand in hand with preventive interventions likely to reduce people's vulnerability to TB infection and disease. Interventions require the downstream risk factors for vulnerability and more upstream social determinants. The current TB control program addresses the factors leading to inadequate access to quality curative services. Thus, the paper focuses on social determinants and risk factors relevant to TB prevention.

The prospect of controlling TB without addressing the social determinants of TB as preventive measures seems inadequate in that the focused interventions in the tea gardens of Assam have not been able to arrest the spread and incidence of TB. Thus, based on the evidence drawn from the research literature, some broad social determinants of TB have been identified and discussed in detail, highlighting the possible causal pathways through which they increase TB risk.

From the findings and discussion above, it becomes evident that the social determinants prevailing in tea gardens have a direct bearing on the success of TB control programs in that the high disease burden situation that prevails in tea gardens increases the risk of exposure to TB germs as well as infection and the manifestation of TB disease among these people. Therefore, addressing the social determinants (intervention) will help control TB among the tea garden population. Because the tea garden worker populations have a fixed residential location and are concentrated in tea gardens with an almost similar kind of social, economic, and administrative setup, it should be easier to frame a plan to address them. It is also equally essential to point out that amidst the numerous studies on the tea garden population, there is hardly any substantial finding that can reveal a scientifically established link between social determinants and TB incidence.

Recommendations

Following are some recommendations based on the findings and discussion above:

i. An extensive scientific study is required to establish and assess the impact of social determinants on the increased risk of exposure to and infection with TB germs.

ii. IEC should be integrated with community-based agency activities so that people find them a meaningful programme. The issues of malnutrition, tobacco use, alcohol use, and healthy dietary habits must be included in the IEC specific to the tea garden population.

iii. Women's empowerment should be at the core of each of these measures to be taken.

References

Altet N, Latorre I, Jimenez-Fuentes MA, Maldonnado J, Molina I, González-Díaz Y et al. (2017). Assessment of the influence of direct tobacco smoke on infection and active TB management. *PLoS One*, 12(8): e0182998.

Amere GA, Nayak Pratibha, SalindriArgita D, Narayan KMV, Matthew J Magee (2018). Contribution of smoking to tuberculosis incidence and mortality in high- tuberculosis-burden countries. *Am J Epidemiol*, 187(9): 1846–1855. DOI:10.1093/aje/kwy081.

Auer C, Sarol J Jr, Tanner M, Weiss M (2000). Health seeking and perceived causes of Tuberculosis among patients in Manila, Philippines. *Tropical Medicine & International Health,* 5(9): 648–656.

Balgir RS (2009). Health and Morbidity pattern in the Tea Garden Labour communities of North East India: A brief review. In: S Sengupta (Ed.):

The Tea labours of North East India. Delhi: Mittal Publications, pp. 223–236.

Banerjee A, Harries AD, Nyirenda T, Salaniponi FM (2000). Local perceptions of Tuberculosis in a rural district in Malawi. *International Journal of Tuberculosis & Lung Disease*, 4(11): 1047–1051.

Banik P (2015). Food security and migrant workers: A study of tea estates in Assam. *South Asian Journal of Multidisciplinary Studies*, 2(3): 146–57.

Barahi TA, Deori R, Saikia SP (2016). Haemoglobinopa- thies and â-Thalassaemia among the tribals working in the tea gardens of Assam, India. *Journal of Clinical and Diagnostic Research*, 10(12): 19-22. DOI: 10. 7860/JCDR/2016/22010.9002

Baruah Pinuma (2009). A study of health, hygiene and sanitation among the tea garden labours of Assam: A case study in Jamirah Tea Garden. In: S Sengupta (Ed.): *The Tea Labours of North East India*. Delhi: Mittal Publications, pp. 237–248.

Biswas D, Hazarika NC, Hazarika D, Doloi P, Mahanta J (2002). Study on nutritional status of tea garden workers of Assam with special emphasis on Body Mass Index (BMI) and central obesity. *Hum Ecol*, 13(4): 299-302.

Blas Erik, Kurup AS (2010). Equity, Social Determinants and Public Health Programmes. Switzerland, Geneva: WHO.

Bora Borsha Rani (2015). Socioeconomic condition of tea garden workers and its impact on women's health with special reference to Teok Tea Estate. *The International Journal of Humanities & Social Studies*, 3(12): 224–228.

Borgohain Jahnu (2020). Tea garden women, issues of socio-economic status: A study on tea garden women of Sivasagar District, Assam. *Journal of Emerging Technologies and Innovative Research*, 7(3): 1626-1633.

Boruah Pallab Jyoti (2018). Status of water supply, sanitation and hygiene practices: A study on tea garden labourers of Sibsagar District of Assam. *International Journal of Humanities and Social Science Invention*, 7(5): 38–43.

Cegielski JP, McMurray DN (2004). The relationship between malnutrition and Tuberculosis: Evidence from studies in humans and experimental animals. *International Journal of Tuberculosis and Lung Disease*, 8: pp. 286–298.

Chan J, Tanaka KE, Mannion C, Carroll D, Tsang MS, Xing Y, Lowenstein C, Barry RB (1997). Effects of Protein Calorie Malnutrition on Mice Infected with BCG. *Journal of Nutritional Immunology*, 5(1): 11-19, DOI: 10.1300/J053v05n01_03

Chelleng PK, K Rekha Devi, Borbora Debasish, Chetia M, Saikia A, Mahanta J, Kanwar N (2014). Risk factors of pulmonary Tuberculosis in tea garden communities of Assam, India. *Indian J Med Res*, 140(1): 138–141.

Clark Michael, Ribena Peter, Nowgesic Earl (2002). The association of housing density, isolation and Tuberculosis in Canadian First Nations communities. *International Journal of Epidemiology,* 31: 940–945.

Das Gupta R (1986). From Peasants and Tribesmen to Plantation Workers: Colonial Capitalism, Reproduction of Labour Power and Proletarianisation in North East India, 1850s to 1947. *Economic and Political Weekly,* 21(4): 2–10.

de Villiers S (1991). Tuberculosis in anthropological perspective. *South African Journal of Ethnology,* 14(3): 69–72.

Deb Nath R (2000). *Social and Cultural Life of the Labourers in Dewan Tea Garden.* MPhil Dissertation. Sil-char: Assam University.

Deb Nath Ruma, Nath Dipak (2014). Educational vulnerability and risk factors of tea garden workers with special reference to Dewan Tea Garden Village, Cachar, Assam, India. *International Research Journal of Social Sciences*, 3(9): 14-21.

Deori R, Teli AB, Saikia SP (2016). Prevalence of anaemia and role of haemoglobinopathy as an associating factor among the children belonging to the tea garden community of Assam, India. *International Journal of Health Sciences & Research,* 6(9): 196-200.

Dey BK (2019). An enquiry into the living conditions of tea garden workers of Assam: A case study on Fatemabad Tea Estate. *The Research Journal of Social Sciences*, 10(1): 74-84.

Dowerah SS (2013). Health security facilities among the tea garden labourers: A myth or reality: A study on the tea gardens of Dibrugarh District, Assam. *International Journal of Scientific Research*, 2(12): 52–23.

Dutta J, Chetia M, Misra AK (2011). Drinking water quality in six small tea gardens of Sonitpur District of Assam, India, with special reference to heavy metals. *J Environ Sci Eng*, 53(4): 443-450.

Eastwood S, Hill P (2004). A gender-focused qualitative study of barriers to accessing tuberculosis treatment in The Gambia, West Africa. *Int J Tuberc Lung Dis,* 8(1): 70–75.

Edginton M, Sekatane C, Goldstein S (2002). Patients' beliefs: Do they affect tuberculosis control? A study in a rural district of South Africa. *Int J Tuberc Lung Dis*, 6(12): 1075–1082.

Edwards LB, Livesay VT, Acquaviva FA, Palmer CE 1971. Height, weight, tuberculosis infection, and tuberculous disease. *Arch Environ Health*, 22: 106-112.

Feleke BE, Feleke TE, Biadglegne F (20200. Nutritional status of tuberculosis patients, a comparative cross-sectional study. *BMC Pulmonary Medicine.* DOI: 10. 21203/rs.2.10457/v1

Global Network for Right to Food and Nutrition (2016). A Life Without Dignity - The Price of Your Cup of Tea: Abuses and Violations of Human Rights in Tea Plantations in India. Heidelberg FIAN International.

Gopi PG, Kolappan C (20020. Tobacco smoking and pulmonary Tuberculosis. *Thorax,* 57: 964–966.

Goswami M Tulika, Mahanta BN, Gogoi P, Dixit P, Joshi V, Ghos S (2015). Prevalence and determinants of anaemia and effect of different interventions amongst tea tribe adolescent girls living in Dibrugarh district of Assam. *Clinical Epidemiology and Global Health*, 3(2): 85–93.

Goswami M, Das Rekha (2009). Demographic profile of a tea working population of Assam. In: S Sengupta (Ed.): *The Tea Labours of North East India*. Delhi: Mittal Publications, pp. 208-214.

Gupta KB, Gupta R, Atreja A, Verma M, Vishwakarma S (2009). Tuberculosis and nutrition. *Lung India*, 26(1): 1–16.

Hanson C, Floyd K, Weil D (2006). Tuberculosis in the poverty alleviation agenda. In: M Raviglione (Ed.): *TB: A Comprehensive International Approach*. New York: Informa Healthcare, pp. 1147-1164

Hazarika Dharmaraj, Arakeri Shanta V (2019). A study of human development among tea garden community in Dibrugarh District of Assam. *International Journal of Scientific and Technology Research*, 8(8): 1293-1298.

Hazarika MP (2015). Sanitation and its impact on health: A Study in Jorhat, Assam. *International Journal of Scientific and Research Publications*, 5(10): 1–11.

Hoyt KJ, Sarkar S, White L, Joseph NM, Salgame P, Lak- shminarayanan S et al. (2019). Effect of malnutrition on radiographic findings and mycobacterial burden in pulmonary Tuberculosis. *PLoS One* 14(3): e0214011. DOI: https://doi.org/10.1371/journal.pone. 0214011.

Imtiaz S, Shield KD, Roerecke M, Samokhvalov AV, Lönnroth K, Rehm J (2017). Alcohol consumption as a risk factor for Tuberculosis: Meta-analyses and burden of disease. *Eur Respir J*, 50: 1700216. DOI: https://doi.org/10.1183/13993003.00216-2017.

Ingabire GB, Diarmuid DS, Louise CI (2019). More than malnutrition: A review of the relationship between food insecurity and Tuberculosis. *Open Forum Infectious Diseases,* 6(4): 1-10. DOI: https://doi.org/10.1093/ofid/ofz102

Kangjam RD, Mukherjee K, Chelleng PK, Kalita S, Das U, Narain K (2018). Association of VDR gene polymorphisms and 22 bp deletions in the promoter region of TLR2Ä22 (-196-174) with increased risk of pulmonary Tuberculosis: A case-control study in tea garden communities of Assam. *J Clin Lab Anal*, 32: 1-14. DOI: 10.1002/jcla.22562.

Khan AM, Dutta PC, Sarmah K, Baruah NK, Das S, Pathak AK, Sarmah P, Hussain ME, Mahanta J (2015). Prevalence of lymphatic filariasis in a tea garden worker population of Dibrugarh (Assam), India, after six rounds of mass drug administration. *J Vector Borne Dis*, 52: 314–320.

Kleinman AM (1975). Explanatory models in health care relationships. In: *Health of the Family*. Wash- ington, DC: NCIH, 1975, pp. 159–172.

Konwar P, Vyas N, Shah H Shaikh, Gore MN, Choudhury M (2019). Nutritional status of adolescent girls belonging to the tea garden estates of Sivasagar District, Assam, India. *Indian J Community Med*, 44: pp. 238–242. DOI: 10.4103/ijcm.IJCM_357_18.

Larcombe L, Orr P (2007). Housing conditions that serve as risk factors for tuberculosis infection and disease. *Canadian Communicable Disease Report*, 33(9): 1-13.

Liefooghe R, Baliddawa JB, Kipruto EM, Vermeire C, and Munynck AO (1997). From their own perspective: A Kenyan community's perception of Tuberculosis. *Tropical Medicine & International Health*, 2(8): 809–821.

Lin H, Ezzat M, Murray M (2007). Tobacco smoke, indoor air pollution and Tuberculosis: A systematic review and meta-analysis. *PLoS Medicine*, 4(1): e20. DOI: https://doi.org/10.1371/journal.pmed. 0040020.

Lin Hsien-Ho, Ezzati Majid, Chang Hsing-Yi, Murray M (2009). Association between tobacco smoking and active Tuberculosis in Taiwan Prospective Cohort Study. *Am J Respir Crit Care Med*, 180: 475–480.Lodha R, Mukherjee A, Singh V, Singh S, Friis H 2014. Effect of micronutrient supplementation on treatment outcomes in children with intrathoracic Tuberculosis: A randomised controlled trial. *Am J Clin Nutr*, 100(5): 1287–1297. DOI: https://doi.org/10. 3945/ajcn.113. 082255.

Lonnroth K, Williams BG, Cegielski P, Dye C (2010). A consistent log-linear relationship between tuberculosis incidence and body mass index. *Int J Epidemiol*, 39(1): 149-155. DOI: https://doi.org/10.1093/ije/ dyp308.

Lönnroth Knut, Brian GW, Stephanie S, Ernesto J, Christopher D (2008). Alcohol use as a risk factor for Tuberculosis – a systematic review. *BMC Public Health*, 8: 289. DOI: 10.1186/1471-2458-8-289.

Lönnroth Knut, Kenneth G, Castro J, Muhwa C, Singh L, Chauhan K, Floyd P, Glaziou M, and Raviglione C (2010). Tuberculosis control and elimination 2010– 50: Cure, care, and social development. *The Lancet*, 375(9728): 1814-1829.

Madhona R, Zainul I, Fidyah A (2016). Physical environment home and incidence of TB Disease in Tan-jungpinang district. *Advances in Health Sciences Research*, 1: 126-130. DOI: https://doi.org/10. 2991/phico-16.2017.77.

Medhi GK, Hazarika NC, Mahanta J (2007). Nutritional status of adolescents among tea garden workers. *Indian J Pediatr*, 74(4): 343-347. DOI: 10.1007/ s12098-007-0057-3.

Medhi GK, Hazarika NC, Shah B, Mahanta J (2006). Study of health problems and nutritional status of tea garden population of Assam. *Indian J Med Sci*, 60(12): 496-505.

Menzies D, Joshi R, Pai M (2007). Risk of tuberculosis infection and disease associated with work in health care settings. *International Journal of Tuberculosis and Lung Disease*, 11(6): 593–605.

Ngamvithayapong J, Winkvist A, Diwan V (2000). High AIDS awareness may cause tuberculosis patient delay: Results from an HIV epidemic area, Thailand. *AIDS*, 14(10): 1413–1419.

NSPTE (2017). *National Strategic Plan for Tuberculosis Elimination 2017-2025*. Central TB Division, Directorate General of Health Services, Ministry of Health with Family Welfare, New Delhi.

Othon Alexandrakis (2011). Medical Anthropology: The development of the field. *Totem: The University of Western Ontario Journal of Anthropology*, 9(1): 69-80.

Oxlade Olivia, Murray Megan (2012). Tuberculosis and poverty: Why are the poor at greater risk in India? *PLoS One*, 7(11): 1-8, e47533. DOI: https://doi.org/10. 1371/journal.pone.0047533.

Padrão E, Oliveira O, Felgueiras Ó et al. (2018). Tuberculosis and tobacco: Is there any epidemiological association? *Eur Respir J*, 51: 1702121. DOI: https://doi.org/10. 1183/13993003.02121-2017.

Panyang R, Barhai Teli A, Saikia SP (2018). Prevalence of anaemia among the women of childbearing age belonging to the tea garden community of Assam, India: A community-based study. *J Family Med Prim Care*, 7(4): 734–738. DOI: 10.4103/jfmpc.jfmpc_274_17.

Pronyk P, Makhubele M, Hargreaves J, Tollman S, Hausler H (2001). Assessing health-seeking behaviour among tuberculosis patients in rural South Africa. *IntJTuberc Lung Dis,* 5(7): 619–627.

Purkayastha N, Kalita P (2016). Tea garden labourers and their living conditions: A study in Borsillah Tea Estate of Sivasagar District, Assam. *Int J Adv Res*, 4(10): 163-169. DOI: 10.21474/IJAR01/1772.

Rabha B, Goswami D, Dhiman S, Das NG, Talukdar PK, Nath MJ, Baruah Indra, Bhola RK, Singh L (2012). A cross-sectional investigation of malaria epidemiology among seven tea estates in Assam, India. *J Parasit Dis*, 36(1): 1–6. DOI: 10.1007/s12639-011-0070-3.

Rajbangshi PR, Nambiar D (2020). Who will stand up for us? The social determinants of health of women tea plantation workers in India. *International Journal for Equity in Health*, 19(29): 1–10. DOI: https://doi.org/10.1186/s12939-020-1147-3.

Rehfuess E (2006). *Fuel for Life: Household Energy and Health*. Geneva: World Health Organization.

Rehm Jürgen, Samokhvalov AV, Neuman MG, Room Robin, Parry Charles, Lönnroth Knut, Patra Jay- adeep, Vladimir Poznyak, Popova Svetlana (2009). The association between alcohol use, alcohol use disorders and Tuberculosis (TB): A systematic review. *BMC Public Health,* 9: 450. DOI: 10.1186/ 1471-2458-9-450

Rieder H (1999). *Epidemiologic Basis of Tuberculosis Control*. Paris: International Union against Tuberculosis and Lung Disease.

Sahoo D, Konwar K, Sahoo BK (2010). Health condition and health awareness among the tea garden laborers: A case study of a tea garden in Tinsukia District of Assam. *The IUP Journal of Agricultural Economics*, 7(4): 50–72.

Saikia JP (2017). Stories Behind a Hot Cup of Assam Tea: Listening to the Voices of Women Labourers in the Tea Gardens. *Report submitted to the Ministry of Women and Child Development*, Government of India.

Sarma Gadapani (2013). A case study on socioeconomic condition of tea garden labourers –Lohpohia Tea Estate of Jorhat District, Assam. *The Echo*, 1(3): 55–60.

Sengupta Pallav, Sobhana Saho (2014). Health-related morphological characteristics and physiological fitness in connection with nutritional, socioeconomic status, and occupational workload of tea garden workers. *African Health Sciences*, 14(3): 558–563.

Sharma A, Bhuyan B (2016). Livelihood pattern among the Tea garden labours: Some Observations. *Int J Adv Res*, 4(8): 1608–1611. DOI: 10.21474/IJAR01/1369.

Sharma A, Bhuyan B (2018a). A study on health and hygiene practices among the tea garden community of Dibrugarh District, Assam. *Indian Journal of Applied Research*, 8(12): 35–36.

Sharma A, Bhuyan B (2018b). Habit of tobacco and alcohol consumption among adolescents of the tea garden community of Upper Assam. *IAETSD Journal of Advanced Research in Applied Sciences,* 5(3): 435–437.

Sharma A, Sangma CF (2016). Knowledge and attitudes towards tea garden labour with special reference to Tuberculosis of Dibrugarh district, Assam, India. *International Journal of Community Medicine and Public Health*, 3(12): 3584-3587. DOI: http://dx. doi.org/10.18203/2394-6040.ijcmph20164296.

Shrestha-Kuwahara R, Wilce SM, Joseph HA, Carey JW, Plank R, Sumartojo E (2017). Tuberculosis Research and Control: Anthropological Contribution. From <https: //findtbresources.cdc.gov/material/ Anthrop_Contrib.PDF> (Retrieved on 14 October 2017).

Sinclair D, Abba K, Sudarsanam TD, Grobler L, Volmink J (2011). Nutritional supplements for people being treated for active Tuberculosis. *Cochrane Database Sys Rev,* (II). DOI: https://doi.org/10.1002/14651858. CD006086.pub4.

Singh SK, Kashyap GC, Puri P (2018). Potential effect of household environment on the prevalence of Tuberculosis in India: evidence from the recent round of a cross-sectional survey. *BMC Pulm Med,* 18(66): 1–10. DOI: https://doi.org/10.1186/s12890-018-0627-3.

Siroka A, Law I, Macinko J, Floyd K, Banda RP, Hoa NB, Tsolmon B, Chanda-Kapata P, Gasana M, Lwinn T, Senkoro M, Tupasi T, Ponce NA (2016). The effect of household poverty on Tuberculosis. *Int J Tuberc Lung Dis,* 20(12): 1603–1608. DOI: https://doi.org/10. 5588/ijtld.16.0386.

Sudha CH, Jahnavi G (2010). Randomised controlled trial of food supplements in patients with newly diagnosed Tuberculosis and wasting. *Singapore Med J,* 51(12): 957-962.

Timung Jogo, Sarmah Juliana (2013). Nutrition, health and hygienic practice of women tea plantation workers of Assam. *Asian Journal of Home Science,* 8(2): 421-424.

Tverdal A. (1986). Body mass index and Tuberculosis. *Eur J Respir Dis,* 69(5): 355-362.

Underner M, Perriot J, Peiffer G, Ouedraogo G, Meurice JC, Gerbaud L. (2012a). Smoking and active Tuberculosis. *Rev Mal Respir,* 29(8): 978-993. DOI: 10.1016/j.rmr. 2012.04.007.

Underner M, Perriot J, Ouedraogo G, Meurice JC, Trosi- ni-Desert V, Peiffer G, Dautzenberg B. (2012b). Tobacco smoking and latent tuberculous infection. *Rev Mal Respir,* 29(8): 1007-1016. DOI: 10.1016/j.rmr.2012.06.006.

Vendhan Gajalakshmi, Richard Peto. (2009). Smoking, drinking and incident tuberculosis in rural India: population-based case–control study. *International Journal of Epidemiology,* 38: 1018–1025, doi: 10.1093/ije/dyp225.

Viney AK, Penelope J, Tagaro M, Fana S, Linh NN, Kelly P, Harley D, Sleigh A. (2014). Tuberculosis patients' knowledge and beliefs about Tuberculosis: a mixed methods study from the Pacific Island nation of Vanuatu. *BMC Public Health,* 14: p. 467. DOI: https://doi.org/10.1186/1471-2458-14-467.

Wandwalo E, Morkve O (2000). Knowledge of disease and treatment among tuberculosis patients in Mwanza, Tanzania. *Int J Tuberc Lung Dis,* 4(11): 1041–1046.

WHO. (2000). The Stop TB Initiative, The Economic Impact of Tuberculosis. *Ministerial Conference Amsterdam.*

WHO. (2016). Global Tuberculosis Report 2016. Gene- va, World Health Organization. From <www.who. int/tb/publications/global_report/en/> (Retrieved on 10 October 2016).

Yamada S, Caballero J, Matsunaga D, Agustin G, Magana M. (1997). Attitudes regarding Tuberculosis in im- migrants from the Philippines to the United States. *Fam Med*, 31(7): 477–482.

Zixin SA, Bin Eng Chee C, Wang Yee-Tang, Yuan Jian- Min, Koh Woon-Puay. (2017). Alcohol drinking and cigarette smoking in relation to risk of active tuberculosis: Prospective cohort study. *BMJ Open Resp Res,* 4(1): e000247. DOI: 10.1136/bmjresp-2017- 000247.

13

Influence of Biosocial Factors on Fertility and Child Mortality: An anthropological study among the Kabui Naga of Manipur, India

D.K. Limbu
C. Kamei
A. Haloi

Introduction

Anthropological Demography

Generally speaking, fertility and child mortality studies are the core areas of demographic interest. However, these areas are closely related to human culture and natural phenomena, the relationship of which is one of the primary domains of anthropological exploration. This is the entry-point reason for anthropology to be included in this heavily demographic domain. Anthropological demography is a speciality that uses anthropological theory and methods to understand demographic phenomena in current and past populations better. Its genesis and ongoing growth lie at the intersection between demography and socio-cultural anthropology and with their efforts to understand population processes, mainly fertility, migration, and mortality. It is mainly concerned with the dynamic forces defining population size and structure and their variation across time and space (Bernardi, 2007). Kertzer and Fricke (1997) characterise the relationship between anthropology and demography as "long, tortured, often ambivalent, and sometimes passionate" and recognise that anthropological demography is mainly the result of the demographic community's opening up to anthropological insights into population processes. However, the majority of anthropologists still hesitate to learn and adopt demographic techniques. Some of the essential basic points which may be mentioned regarding the relationship between fertility and mortality rates in developing nations are:

1. The primary cause of the current rapid population growth in many nations of the world is the decline in the death rate.

2. Another general pattern has been for urban birth rates to decline first, resulting characteristically in a differential between urban and rural birth rates for the same region (Cowgill, 1963)

From an evolutionary point of view, demographic parameters like fertility and mortality are critical to understanding the genetic makeup of a population. It is theoretically believed that natural selection, one of the major evolutionary forces, is operating on the human population through differential fertility and mortality (Crow, 1958; Johnston, 1973). Similarly, other demographic parameters like population size, mating patterns, admixture rate, migration, etc., are beneficial for understanding the biological characteristics of the population.

The demographic pattern of developing countries is characterised by the co-existence of high fertility and high infant and child mortality (Saksena et al., 1984). Therefore, studies on fertility and mortality are of significant concern in developing countries, where governments, along with non-government organisations and world bodies, are trying to address the problem by researching the determinants of fertility and infant and child mortality in third-world countries. There are many factors of fertility and child mortality in human populations, and biological, behavioural, and socio-demographic factors operate separately as well as in conjunction with each other. These include factors like age at menarche, age at marriage, the present age of women, infant mortality, caste, type of family, religion, place of residence, income, educational level, employment status, occupation, sex preference of a child, lactation, etc. The response of vital statistics to change in the environments of specific populations, as well as the implications of the response for the survival of the children, especially in developing countries (Mosley & Chen, 1984), emphasised the importance of ascertaining biosocial and socio-demographic correlates of fertility and mortality. Biosocial studies pertain to or entailing the interaction or combination of social and biological factors or the social phenomenon that is affected by biological factors.

The infant and child mortality rate constitutes an important demographic indicator. In developing countries, mortality rates tend to be somewhat higher in rural areas than in cities (Chandrasekhar, 1967; World et al., 1967; Peterson, 1969). Infant mortality can be seen as the outcome of a complex process that involves socio-economic, demographic, environmental and biological variables. Socio-economic variables influence biological variables, which finally determine morbidity and mortality. The present study attempts to determine whether any factors might exist in the Kabui Naga populations of the Tamenglong sub-division and Imphal West district of Manipur.

The Tamenglong sub-division is the remotest Kabui Naga inhabited area of the Tamenglong district of Manipur, where most villages lack health centres or schools and have poor transport and communication facilities. The majority of the people are cultivators with low incomes and education. Considering these factors, we have selected the villages from the Tamenglong sub-division for the present study. On the other hand, Imphal West district is a fast-developing district in the valley with better education, income, health facilities, transport and communication facilities, etc. With this view in mind, the Kabui Nagas living in Imphal are expected to have become more literate and wealthier and have better access to medical services. As fertility and infant and child mortality rates decline with the increase in the educational level of mothers, income, better access to medical services, etc., consequently, they are expected to become more health conscious and thereby take better care of their children than those living in the remote villages. Thus, this study will test the following central hypothesis:

"The higher the level of socio-economic development, the lower the fertility and infant and child mortality."

The objectives of the study are:

1. To find out various bio-social factors influencing fertility and infant and child mortality in the study population.

2. To compare the rural and urban Kabui Naga in relation to fertility and infant and child mortality.

Review of Literature

Reddy and Sudha (2010) conducted a study to find out the influence of bio-social factors on fertility among Setti Balija of Southern Andhra Pradesh. The study showed that the low-income group shows higher fertility and mortality than the middle and high-income groups. The age at marriage showed that women of early marriage will have higher rates of prenatal as well as postnatal mortality. The net survivorship of offspring is also related to the age at marriage. Dey and Goswami (2009) studied the fertility differentials of married couples in the Northeastern States of India in relation to their different socio-demographic characteristics by using NFHS-2 data. They observed a positive association between fertility and child mortality. It was found that couples who had lost three or more children had, on average, seven or more ever-born children, and even education failed to prevent higher fertility associated with child loss. Duration of breastfeeding has also been found to be positively correlated with fertility. The study revealed that mother's education and age at marriage had a significant effect on reducing fertility. The study also indicates that, even without the use of family planning methods, increasing the level of education and age at marriage and providing opportunities for women to work outside the home can go a long way in reducing fertility. Amonker and Brinker (1997), in their study, tried to investigate the relationship between the level of socio-economic development and infant and child mortality in India. The study suggests that higher levels of population literacy, education of women, urbanisation, and child immunisations, as well as lower levels of underweight children under four years, lead to a decline in infant and child mortality.

Verma (2002) studied the socio-cultural correlates of infant mortality among the Baigas of Mandala District of Madhya Pradesh. His study reveals that illiteracy of parents, parents engaged in agriculture-related practices, and persons married in blood relations had experienced high infant mortality, which may be attributed to their belief in the indigenous unhygienic methods of delivery, primitive method of cutting the cord, discarding the colostrum, etc. Improvement in socio-economic status is generally considered to be essential for improvement in children's health conditions, thereby reducing infant and child mortality. Rustein (2000) supported this finding and suggested that such a trend in infant and child mortality is no doubt associated with an improvement in socio-economic status along with the improvement in a number of factors like nutritional status, environmental health conditions, breastfeeding and the use of health services.

Oppong (1983) observed that occupation, particularly women's occupation, is believed to exert a significant influence on fertility and mortality. It has been argued that women whose work is more independent enjoy a more egalitarian marital relationship, which allows them to exercise more control over fertility decisions. Kost and Amin,1992; and Bicego and Boerma, 1993, further observed in their studies that economic variables like household income and occupation are negatively associated with fertility in many developing countries.

According to Caldwell, 1980; Bharati and Dastidar, 1990, mass education, which tends to emphasise modernisation and secular attitudes, is the only means to enhance child survival and reduce mortality as well as fertility. Driver (1963), who studied the differential fertility in central India, observed that fertility declines drastically with the increasing level of a mother's education. In rural India, female education is justifiable as an end in itself because it results in improved marriage prospects and provides women with the skills to better care for and educate their children (Purfield, 2006). Pant (1991) carried out a study on the effect of education and household characteristics on infant and child mortality in urban Nepal. His study showed that the effect of education without resources might not be an important factor in lowering infant and child mortality. Both education and resources could be complementary, and access to both of these may improve child survival in Nepal. However, Adsera and Menendez (2011), in their study on fertility changes in Latin America, found that the relationship between fertility rates and unemployment was not homogeneous across groups of women. They found a strong association between adverse economic circumstances and delayed motherhood among women who were urban, more educated and came from younger cohorts. The association between unemployment and the transition to second or third births was, on the other hand, somewhat more robust for the least educated and recent cohorts. At the same time, no significant differences were observed by place of residence. They found that as easy access to family planning is extended to the entire population and as increasingly educated Latin American women aim to secure more stable jobs, childbearing patterns may become even more tied to the economic fortunes of a country. Khan and Khan (2010), in their study on the fertility behaviour of women in Punjab, Pakistan, reported that the husband's education, income, age at marriage, number of living children, number of sons, household income, and urbanity of the household are significant determinants of contraceptive prevalence among women.

Simmons (1985) summarised the effects of the individual variables considered in various research studies. He has found a strong relationship between women's education and fertility. Women's labour-force participation, sex preference, availability of family-planning services, general environment and population programmes and policies were found to have a medium effect on fertility. In contrast, infant mortality, per capita income, income distribution, and preferred number of children only had a weak effect on fertility. Rosenzweig and Schultz (1982) reported that the education of a mother is strongly and positively correlated with the survival rate of her children in Columbia. They observed that the least educated mothers are the most affected in terms of their reduced fertility and increased child survival rates. The United Nations (UN, 1985) study outlines several conceptual frameworks on the relationship between women's employment and fertility. The significant finding of the study was that the relationship between women's occupation and fertility appears to be strong in countries at higher levels of socioeconomic development, particularly in countries with vital family planning programmes and where women's status is relatively higher as measured by age at marriage and educational attainment. Husain (1970) has suggested that parents with higher educational status are likely to limit their family size as they are more aware of the socio-economic and well-being of their children. Agarwala (1972) has also observed the differential fertility by educational level. However, he is of the opinion that education plays more roles only when mothers are educated up to matriculation or more.

Dabral and Malik (2005) conducted a study on the Gujjars and found that women's age has the most significant effect on fertility and family planning acceptance. They also observed that women's education is also an essential determinant of these variables as fertility increases with higher infant mortality. Gulati (1969) and Das Gupta (1974) clearly showed in their studies that the age at marriage is higher in urban areas than in rural areas, and educated men and women marry later than uneducated ones. Mosley (1983) observed that a higher risk of infant death is biologically associated with childbearing at a very young age. He further pointed out that maternal age is associated with a higher frequency of anomalies, while both extreme ages are associated with a higher risk of birth trauma. Age at marriage also influences prenatal and postnatal mortality. Khongsdier (2005), in his study on the prenatal and postnatal mortality of War Khasi of Meghalaya, reported that the mean number of live births decreases with the increase in age at marriage of the mothers. Maitra (2004) examined the effect of socio-economic characteristics on age at marriage and total fertility rates in Nepal using a household-level dataset. The estimated results showed that an increase in age at marriage significantly reduced the total fertility of women. An increase in the number of children who died had a statistically significant effect on total fertility (child replacement effect). The estimation results also emphasised the role of female education in reducing total fertility and increasing the age of marriage. Moreover, the female educational effect had a strong inter-generational effect on age at marriage, and this effect was more substantial than the effect on male educational attainment. Khiloni (2009) reported that age at marriage, the mother's education and economic status have an impact on fertility among the Anal women of Lambung village in Chandel district of Manipur. Khongsai (2012), in a study conducted on bio-social determinants of fertility and child mortality among the Khongsai Kukis of Manipur, found that the mother's age, occupation, type of house, size of family, mother' education, type of family, birth interval has a significant influence on the fertility and child mortality of the Kukis. Yadav and Badari (1997) analysed the age of effective marriage and fertility in India.

They reported that age at marriage can still play an important role in the reduction of fertility in some states of India, such as Uttar Pradesh, Bihar and Rajasthan.

Chandrasekhar (1959) reported that urbanisation is another characteristic of socio-economic development that has been found to have a profound influence on mortality. Infant and child mortality rates vary among groups within a country as much as they vary among countries. Throughout the developing countries of the world, conditions of life in rural areas for infants and children are very often worse than they are in cities. The lower crude death rate and infant mortality rate in urban areas is attributable to better sanitary conditions, protected drinking water, and easy availability of medical facilities. Chaudhury et al. (2000) reported that lower infant and child mortality rates in Bangladesh are found in urban areas compared to the rural areas. Kabir and Uddin (1997), in their study on the fertility transition in Bangladesh, reveal that the slight change in overall fertility may be attributed partly to the change in age at first marriage and partly to the increased use of contraception. This is due to the greater availability of health care services and higher income and educational levels in urban areas.

Majumder (1991) observed that preceding birth interval, subsequent pregnancy and breastfeeding duration each have an independent influence on early mortality risk in Bangladesh. It was found that within a specific interval, the risk of dying decreases with an increase in the duration of breastfeeding and also with an increase in the time between the index birth and the subsequent pregnancy. It was noted that for every disease category studied, breastfed babies had lower morbidity rates than bottle-fed babies (Wray, 1978). Forste (1994) examined in detail the effects of breastfeeding practices and birth spacing on infant and child survival in Bolivia. She found that birth spacing, lactation, antenatal care, and mothers' education improved the chances of the survival of the infant and child. Sahu et al. (2015) observed that among the Scheduled Tribes in rural India, birth interval, household wealth, and region were found to be significantly associated with infant and child mortality. The hazard of infant mortality was found to be highest among births to mothers aged 30 years or more as compared with births to mothers aged 20-29 years. The hazard of under-five mortality was higher among four or more birth orders compared with the first birth order. The risk of infant death was higher among male children than among female children, while male children were at 30 per cent less hazard of child mortality than female children. Literate women were at 40 per cent less hazard of child death than illiterate women. Fotso et al. (2013), in their study conducted in Nairobi to see the relationship between birth spacing and child mortality, found that in infancy, a preceding birth interval of less than 18 months is associated with a two-fold increase in mortality risks (compared with lengthened intervals of 36 months or longer), while an interval of 18–23 months is associated with an increase of 18%. During the early childhood period, children born within 18 months of an elder sibling are more than twice as likely to die as those born after 36 months or more.

Nanda (2005), in a study on the demography and ethnography of fertility behaviour among the non-industrial population in India, shows that longer perceived ideal birth intervals have been consistently associated with lower fertility. Singh (2003) studied the patterns of mortality of two isolates of Bhoksa tribesmen settled in different ecosystems of the state of Uttaranchal, i.e., Tarai and foothill areas. The study indicates that the Bhoksas of the Tarai region have lower mortality than the Bhoksas of the foothill areas, which may be due to their greater degree of adaptation to the environment. Infant and pre-reproductive mortality are higher as compared to that of the other ages in both groups. A heavy toll of mortality is caused either by delivery infection or by communicable diseases. Kapoor (2009) reported a strong influence of female work participation, female literacy and female labourers in agricultural work on the infant mortality rate in India. It was observed that the infant mortality rate could be reduced by improving the quality of female capital. The increase in the participation of male workers outside of agriculture has also been observed to reduce infant mortality rates indirectly.

Klaauw and Wang (2011), in their study on Child mortality in rural India from the second National Family and Health Survey (NFHS), undertaken in 1998 and 1999, found that socioeconomic and environmental characteristics have significantly different impacts on mortality rates at different ages. These are particularly important immediately after birth. The parameter estimates indicate that child mortality can be reduced substantially, particularly by improving the education of women, providing safe water, and reducing indoor air pollution caused by dirty cooking fuels. Adak (1996) reported that among the Khasis of Shillong, the infant mortality rate has a strong correlation with the mother's age at marriage, the mother's education, and family size, and also correlates with persons who conducted the delivery. The study further observed that there is a more significant percentage of infant or early childhood mortality among mothers with no lactation, mothers without immunisation and medical check-ups before delivery and mothers who used non-boiled drinking water at the household level.

Sengupta and Chakravarty (1995), in their study on family type, fertility and mortality among the Ahoms of Assam, observed that there is a higher total fertility rate as well as foetal wastage in the nuclear family as compared to the joint family.

Singh (2006), in his study conducted on ethnic variation in fertility patterns among four communities of Manipur, reported an inverse relationship between fertility and the educational level of the mother. It was observed that live births decrease with an increase in the educational level of mothers. The study further showed a higher number of children among mothers who are engaged in manual labour work, particularly among those mothers who are engaged in agriculture.

Ladusingh and Singh (2006) examine the relevance of socio-cultural and environmental factors in explaining child mortality in Northeast India. Using data from the Indian National Family Health Survey, they observed that lack of hygiene in the household and poor women's engagement in physically demanding agriculture-based work contributes to a higher risk of child mortality. Unlike in other parts of India, female children have the edge over boys in childhood survival and living with a paternal grandmother tends to lower the risk of child death in the first five years of life. Community education is found to be the dominant factor outside the household that has a significant effect on child mortality.

From the above review of literature, it can be observed that a number of studies have been carried out across the globe in the area of fertility and infant and child mortality. However, it can also be observed that the factors which influence both fertility and mortality are many and vary from one population to another. Moreover, since most of the studies are aimed and conducted at a macro-level based on a regional and state-wise survey, there is a chance that the underlying minute, though important, bio-social factors might influence the demography of a particular community or a tribe might be either missed out or ignored for various reasons. Therefore, there is an imperative need to undertake a micro-level in-depth study.

Materials And Methods

The Kabui (Rongmei) Naga: The population under study

The Kabui Naga, also known as the Rongmei, is one of the indigenous Naga tribes living in Manipur, Nagaland, and Assam of North-East India. Kabui or Rongmei is one of the tribes that form the 'Zeliangrong' tribe, which is constituted of the Zemei, Liangmei, and Rongmei tribes. The term is a combination of the prefixes of their respective ethnonym, Ze+Liang+Rong = Zeliangrong (Kamei, 2004), which stands for Zemei, Liangmei and Rongmei.

Kabuis in Manipur are concentrated in Tamenglong, Nungba, and Taoshem Subdivisions; they are also found in Sadar Hills and Loktak Project, as well as in the districts of Imphal West, Imphal East, Thaubal, and Bishnupur. They are also found in the neighbouring districts of Senapati and Churachandpur.

Linguistically, the Kabuis belong to the Tibeto-Burman family. According to philologists like Dr. G.A. Grierson (1903), the Zeliangrong people speak a language related to the Bodos of Assam and have been grouped under a Sub-family of Naga-Bodo within the Tibeto-Burman languages. Racially, the Kabuis are Mongoloid, a group of southern Mongoloids who migrated southward across the Himalayas in the prehistoric period to Northeastern India and Southeast Asia. Many Naga traditions point to Makhel in North Manipur as their homeland and a point of migration during their migration from Southwest China to Burma and island Southeast Asia, and then Northward movement back to Manipur, and then to northern Manipur before branching out to their respective tribal habitats (Kamei, 2004). They are emotionally attached to their customs and traditions, which have a rich cultural heritage. This has been reflected in the form of folk dances, music, arts and crafts. They are conservative and culture-conscious people. All the cultural activities are the same among the cognate tribes of the Zeliangrong, except for minor variations in dialects, culture, beliefs, etc.

Economy

The main occupation of the Kabuis is agriculture. Some of their essential crops include rice, maize, soya bean, pumpkin, gourd, ginger, chilli, groundnut, potatoes, brinjal, etc. Rice is the staple food. Though agriculture is the primary source of livelihood, livestock farming plays a prominent role in their economy. Most of the Kabui houses domesticate animals. Piggery and poultry are also given equal importance. They rear animals for requirements to be used during Genna, public functions, festivals and marriage feasts. Apart from agriculture and farming, cottage industries like weaving and dying are done by women folks (Kamei. 2014).

The present study is a comparative study on the bio-social factors influencing fertility and infant and child mortality among the rural and urban Kabui Naga populations of Manipur. Tamenglong's subdivision and Imphal's town represent rural and urban areas. A cross-sectional method was used for this study. For the present study, three villages, namely Langkhong, Khongjaron Khunthak and Duigailong of Tamenglong district and three localities from Lamphelpat sub-division of Imphal West district of Manipur, namely Neikanlong, Tarung and Guigailong were selected. These study areas were selected using the purposive sampling method.

Data were collected from 434 ever-married women aged 15-49, of whom 174 were from the Imphal West district, and 260 were from the Tamenglong sub-division of Manipur. Data were collected using an interview schedule, which consisted of questions related to demographic and bio-social factors. A house-to-house survey was conducted for data collection, which involved interaction with the head and other members of the family.

Types of Data Collected:

Demographic data: individual household records, fertility records, mortality records, occupation, and mothers' education, which are further classified as illiterate, primary level, secondary level, and higher secondary and above. Data on socio-economic factors comprised of family size, types of family, education, occupation and income. Data on monthly income of the family were classified into three categories:

Above 75th percentile (≥ Rs. 15001) = High income group

50th to 75th percentile (Rs. 9351 to Rs. 15000) = Middle-income group

Below 50th percentile (≤ Rs. 9350) = Low-income group

Biological determinants include the mother's age at marriage, the birth interval, causes of death, and reproductive history data.

All data were processed and analysed using SPSS 16 software, with the level of significance set at 5%. The coefficient of correlation(r) was tested to find an association between two continuous variables. At the same time, the differences in more than two means were determined using a one-way analysis of variance (ANOVA).

RESULTS

The two critical demographic variables, i.e., fertility and child mortality, are greatly influenced by a host of bio-social factors, which work together in a number of ways. These factors include age at menarche, maternal age, age at marriage, age at first childbirth, education, religion, economic conditions, adoption of family planning methods, etc. However, the effect of these factors on fertility and mortality varies from population to population. This study is an attempt to understand the influence of selected bio-social factors on fertility and infant and child mortality among the Kabui Naga of Tamenglong sub-division and Imphal West of Manipur.

Table 1 shows fertility rates by age group of the Kabui Naga women. It is observed that the highest number of mothers in both the Tamenglong sub-division (43.84%) and Imphal West district (43.67%) belong to the age group 25-34 years. There is an increase in the mean number of live births per mother with the increase in the mother's age. It varies from 1.46 ± 0.10 to 5.76 ± 0.41 among mothers of the age groups ≤ 24 years and ≥ 45 years, respectively, in the Tamenglong sub-division, while the same is observed to vary from 1.23 ± 0.13 to 3.59 ± 0.38 respectively in Imphal West district. The ANOVA test shows a statistically significant difference in the mean number of live births with respect to the mother's age group in both the study areas (Tamenglong: F= 42.431, p<0.001; Imphal: F= 19.382, p<0.001).

Table 2 shows the infant and child mortality by mother's age. In the Tamenglong sub-division, the percentages of infant mortality are 5.30%, 3.70%, 3.50% and 3.22% among the mothers belonging to the age groups ≤24, 25-34, 35-44 and ≥45 years, respectively. This reveals that infant mortality is inversely correlated with the age group of the mothers (r= 0.10, p>0.05), though it is not statistically significant. The child mortality shows a positive and significant correlation with the age of the mothers (r= 0.30, p<0.01). In Imphal West district, not a single infant mortality is recorded among mothers of the age group ≤ 24 years, while it is observed to be 1.18%, 3.20% and 1.70% among mothers of the age groups 25-34, 35-44 and ≥45 years respectively. Infant mortality shows a positive correlation with the mother's age; however, it is statistically not significant (r= 0.14, p>0.05). No child mortality was observed among the mothers of the age groups 25-34, 35-44 and ≥45 years, respectively. In the present population, child mortality shows a positive and significant correlation with the mother's age (r= 0.23, p<0.01). The above table, therefore, reveals that the mother's age is an essential factor which influences child mortality among the Kabui Naga populations of both the Tamenglong sub-division and Imphal West district.

Table 3 shows fertility by age at marriage among the Kabui Naga women, which have been divided into three groups. ≤ 19 years, 20-23 years, and ≥ 24 years. In the Tamenglong subdivision, the highest percentage of women (44.23%) got married at the age of ≤19 years, whereas in Imphal West, the majority of them (39.65%) got married at the age of ≥24 years. In the Tamenglong sub-division, the mean number of live births decreases with the increase in the mother's age at marriage. The mean number of live births varies from 3.47±0.18 to 2.88±0.27 in the age group between ≤ 19 and ≥ 24 years. In Imphal West district, the mean numbers of live births vary from 3.33±0.27 in ≤ 19 years to 1.96±0.13 in ≥24 years. The ANOVA test shows that the difference in the mean number of live births with respect to the mother's age at marriage is not found to be statistically significant in the Tamenglong sub-division. However, it is significant in the Imphal West district (Tamenglong: F=2.001, p>0.05; Imphal: F= 12.809, p<0.01

Table 4 shows the infant and child mortality by age at marriage of the Kabui Naga women. In Tamenglong, infant mortality decreases with an increase in the mother's age at marriage, the percentages being 4.76%, 3.55% and 1.62% who got married at ≤19 years, 20-23 years and ≥24 years, respectively. Infant mortality shows a negative correlation with the mother's age at marriage, though it is statistically not significant ($r = -0.11$, $p > 0.05$). Child mortality in the study population increases with the increase in the mother's age at marriage, which varies from 1.25% to 2.77% among mothers who got married between the age -groups ≤19 years and ≥24 years, respectively. However, it is not statistically significant ($r = 0.06$, $p > 0.05$).

In Imphal West district, the percentages of infant mortality were found to be 1.42%, 9.61% and 0.75% among the mothers who got married at age ≤19 years, 20-23 years and ≥24 years, respectively, while child mortality was 2.14%, 5.76% and 1.50% in the age-groups ≤19 years, 20-23 years and ≥24 years respectively. The coefficient of correlation shows a negative relationship between the mother's age at marriage and infant and child mortality, although they are not statistically significant (Infant: $r = -0.07$, $p > 0.05$; Child: $r = -0.07$, $p > 0.05$).

Table 5 shows fertility by age at first childbirth among the Kabui Naga women. From the above table, it is observed that in the Tamenglong sub-division, the mean numbers of live births decrease with an increase in the mother's age at first childbirth. It decreased from 4.18±0.38 among mothers who were < 18 years old to 3.24±0.27 among mothers who were 24+ years old at the time of their first childbirth. A similar result was also observed in the Imphal West district, where the mean number of live births decreased from 3.85±0.93 in the age group of <18 years to 2.10±0.12 among mothers whose age at first childbirth was 24+ years. The ANOVA test shows that the difference in the mean number of live births with respect to the mother's age at first childbirth is statistically significant in both the study areas (Tamenglong: $F= 12.745$, $p<0.01$; Imphal: 13.453, $p<0.01$).

Table 6 shows infant and child mortality by mother's age at first childbirth. In the Tamenglong sub-division, infant mortality was found to be highest (5.97%) among the mothers whose age at first childbirth was < 18 years, followed by 18-24 years (3.84%) and least found in 24+ years (1.61%).

The correlation between infant mortality and mother's age at first childbirth is not significant in the Tamenglong sub-division (r= -0.07, p>0.05). Similarly, child mortality was also found to be highest (1.49%) among the mothers whose age at first childbirth was <18 years, followed by 18-24(1.46%) years; however, it again increased to 2.68% among the 24+ years. There is a positive relationship between child mortality and mothers' age at first childbirth; however, it is statistically not significant (r= 0.65, p>0.05). In the Imphal West district, no single infant mortality was observed among mothers whose age at first childbirth was <18 years. The highest percentage of infant mortality was found among the women who were 18-24 years (2.66%) at the time of their first childbirth, followed by the 24+ years. A negative association was observed between infant mortality and the mother's age at first childbirth; however, it was not significant statistically (r= -0.03, p>0.05). It is further observed that child mortality decreases with an increase in the mother's age at first childbirth. The highest percentage of child mortality was found among the mothers whose age at first childbirth was < 18 years (7.40%). There is a negative relationship between child mortality and the mother's age at first childbirth in the Imphal West district; however, it was not found to be statistically significant (r=-0.06, p>0.05).

Table 7 shows the regression of age at marriage of the Kabui Naga mothers on independent variables. It is observed that of all the selected independent variables, urban/rural residence (Tamenglong/Imphal) and maternal occupation have significant influence on age at marriage. The coefficient of correlation (B) is 1.688±0.449, p<0.01 for urban/rural residence (Tamenglong/Imphal) and 0.739±0.192, p<0.01 for maternal occupation. Thus, place of residence and maternal occupation play significant roles in influencing the age of marriage in the study population.

Table 8 shows fertility by birth interval among the Kabui Naga women. The highest percentage of women (54.19%) in the Tamenglong sub-division and the Imphal West district (74.21%) have a birth interval of 24-35 months. In the Tamenglong sub-division, there is no consistency in the mean number of live births with respect to the birth interval. The mean number of live births was found to be the highest (3.92 ± 0.15) among the mothers who have maintained a birth interval of 24-35 months and the lowest (3.53±0.57) among the<24 months. In Imphal, the mean number of live births increases with the increase in the duration of the birth interval. It increased from 2.00±0.00 to 3.31±0.21 among the mothers who maintained a birth interval of <24 months and >35 months, respectively. The ANOVA test shows that the difference in the mean number of live births with respect to the birth interval is statistically significant only in the Imphal West district (F= 10.854, p<0.01).

Table 9 shows the infant and child mortality by birth interval among the Kabui Naga women. In the Tamenglong sub-division, infant mortality is found to be the highest (7.54%) among the mothers who maintained a birth interval of <24 months, followed by >35 months (4.06%). Infant mortality was found to be lowest (3.45%) among the mothers who had a birth interval of 24-35 months. Child mortality is found to be highest (1.97%) among those mothers who maintained a birth interval of 24-35 months, followed by < 24 months (1.88%) and the lowest (1.16%) in >35 months. Birth interval in this population is positively correlated with infant mortality. However, it is statistically not significant (r=0.11, p>0.05). Similarly, there is a positive correlation between birth interval and child mortality; however, it was not found to be statistically significant (r= 0.08, p>0.05). In Imphal West, infant mortality is recorded as highest (50.00%) among those mothers who maintained a birth interval of <24 months, followed by >35 months (3.77%). The lowest percentage of infant mortality (1.07%) is observed among those mothers who maintained a birth interval of 24-35 months. Child mortality is found to be highest (2.14%) among those mothers who had a birth interval of 24-35 months, followed by > 35 months and lowest in<24 months. Birth interval and infant mortality are positively correlated and found statistically significant in the Imphal West district (r= 0.15, p<0.05); however, with respect to child mortality, it is found statistically not significant in the Imphal West (r=0.11, p>0.05).

In Table 10, regression of birth interval among the Kabui Naga women on independent variables is given. From the above table, it is observed that of all the selected independent variables, only maternal occupation has a significant influence on birth interval. For maternal occupation, the coefficient of correlation (B) is 0.094±0.043, p<0.01. Thus, maternal occupation has a significant influence on increasing the birth interval among Kabui Naga women.

Table 11 shows fertility by type of family in the study population. In the Tamenglong sub-division, the mean number of live births per mother was found to be higher in a nuclear family (3.74±0.15) than the joint family (2.43±0.22), while in Imphal West, it is 2.60±0.13 and 2.11±0.19 in a nuclear family and joint family respectively. The ANOVA test shows that the difference between the mean number of live births between the nuclear and the joint family is found to be statistically significant in both the study areas (Tamenglong: F= 24.171, p<0.01; Imphal: F= 4.258, p<0.05).

Table 12 shows the infant and child mortality by type of family among the Kabui Naga. The above table reveals that in the Tamenglong sub-division, infant mortality is slightly higher (3.94%) in the joint family than in the nuclear family (3.61%). In contrast, Imphal West shows higher infant mortality (2.23%) in nuclear families than in joint families (0.89%). There is a negative correlation between the two. However, it is statistically not significant (Tamenglong: $r = -0.04$, p>0.05; Imphal: $r = -0.08$, p>0.05). In the Tamenglong sub-division, the percentage of child mortality is higher (1.80%) in the nuclear family compared to the joint family (1.47%). A similar trend is also seen in Imphal West, where child mortality is higher in nuclear families (2.23%) compared to joint families (0.89%). A negative correlation was found between child mortality and types of families in both study areas. However, both are not found to be significant (Tamenglong: $r = -0.06$, p> 0.05; Imphal: $r = -0.07$, p>0.05).

Table 13 shows the fertility rate of Kabui Naga mothers by educational level. It is observed that in the Tamenglong sub-division, the mean number of live births decreases with an increase in the educational level of the mothers. The highest fertility (4.84±0.25) is recorded among illiterate mothers and the lowest (2.21±0.21) among those who have studied up to higher secondary and above. A similar trend is also observed in Imphal West, where the mean number of live births is found to be highest (3.42±0.41) among the illiterate mothers and lowest (1.94±0.11) among the higher secondary and above-educated mothers. The ANOVA test shows that the differences in the mean number of live births with respect to the educational level of mothers are highly significant in both the study areas (Tamenglong: $F = 26.022$, p< 0.01; Imphal: $F = 10.437$, p<0.01

Table 14 shows infant and child mortality by educational level of the Kabui Naga mothers. In the Tamenglong sub-division, there was no consistency in Infant mortality with respect to the mother's education. The highest infant mortality (4.92%) was found among those mothers who have attained a secondary level of education, and no infant mortality is observed for those who have studied up to higher secondary and above. No consistency is observed in child mortality with regard to mothers' educational level. Highest among the illiterate mothers. No significant correlation is observed in both infant mortality and child mortality with respect to mothers' educational level (Infant: $r = -0.16$, $p<0.01$; Child: $r = -0.16$, $p<0.01$). In Imphal West, infant mortality is found to be highest among illiterate mothers (3.07%) and lowest among primary-level educated mothers (1.16%). Child mortality is found to be highest among mothers who have studied up to the primary level (4.65%), while no child mortality is recorded among illiterate mothers. No significant correlation was found between infant mortality and mothers' education ($r = -0.07$, $p>0.05$). The same is also true for child mortality and mothers' education ($r = -0.07$, $p>0.05$). Thus, infant and child mortality are highly influenced by mothers' education in the Tamenglong sub-division but not in Imphal West.

Table 15 shows fertility by household income among the Kabui Naga. In this table, the household monthly income is divided into three categories, viz., the Low-income group (LIG), the Middle-income group (MIG) and the High-income group (HIG). It may be noted that households having an income of $\leq$ Rs. 9350, Rs. 9351 - Rs. 15000 and $\geq$ Rs. 15001 were categorised as LIG, MIG and HIG, respectively. In the Tamenglong sub-division, the highest mean number of live births (3.83±0.24) is observed in MIG and the lowest in LIG (2.91±0.17). In Imphal West, the highest mean number of live births is observed in HIG (2.64±0.17) and lowest in MIG (1.78±0.20). The ANOVA test shows that the differences in the mean number of live births with respect to household income are statistically significant in both the study areas (Tamenglong: $F = 5.535$, $p<0.01$; Imphal: $F = 4.238$, $p< 0.05$). The findings of the present study reveal that income is one of the critical factors that influence fertility in the present population.

Table 16 shows infant and child mortality by household income. In the Tamenglong sub-division, infant mortality decreases as the household income increases, i.e., highest among the Low-income group (6.08%), followed by the Middle-income group (1.97%) and lowest among the High-income group (1.70%). In Imphal West, infant mortality is found to be highest among the Low-income group (2.95%), followed by the High-income group (1.49%). Interestingly, not a single infant mortality was found in the Middle-income group. A negative and significant correlation between infant mortality and household income was observed in the Tamenglong sub-division. In Imphal West also, the correlation was found to be negative; however, it was not statistically significant (Tamenglong: $r = -0.129$, $p<0.05$; Imphal: $r = -0.075$, $p> 0.05$). In reverse to infant mortality, in the Tamenglong sub-division, the percentage of child mortality increases as the household income increases, i.e., highest among the High-income group (3.82%) followed by the Middle-income group (1.18%) and Lowest in the Low-income group (0.79%). In Imphal West, the percentage of child mortality is found to be highest among the Low-income group (2.39%), followed by the High-income group (1.99%). There is a positive correlation between child mortality and household income in the Tamenglong sub-division. In Imphal West, child mortality and household income are negatively correlated, though statistically found not significant (Tamenglong: $r = -0.19$, $p< 0.01$; Imphal: $r = -0.01$, $p> 0.05$). Thus, household income shows a significant influence on infant and child mortality in the Tamenglong sub-division only but not in Imphal West.

Discussion

In the recent past, there has been an increase in research on fertility and infant and child mortality in tribal populations of northeast India. Each society has its own distinct culture and practices, which may directly or indirectly influence fertility, mortality, and health status. Accordingly, the bio-social factors influencing the above demographic traits and health status may vary from population to population.

The findings of the present study reveal that the mean number of live births decreases with an increase in the mother's age in Kabui Naga women of both the study areas. In Tamenglong, infant mortality decreases, and child mortality increases with the increase in the mother's age. In Imphal West, no specific pattern was observed with respect to infant mortality, but child mortality was found to increase with an increase in the mother's age.

Therefore, this study confirms that a mother's age at marriage is an essential factor in influencing the survival of both infants and children. Birth spacing, which is an essential factor associated with fertility and mortality, is found to be inversely related to fertility in the present study. However, the effect of birth spacing on fertility is found to be statistically significant only in Imphal West. This finding is also in accord with the findings of other studies (Khongsai, 2012; Syngkon, 2013).

In both study areas, fertility is higher in nuclear families. The effect of family types on infant and child mortality does not show statistical significance in the study areas. This finding holds, as reported by Haloi and Limbu (2012) and Syngkon (2013). Education is an essential factor in reducing fertility and mortality through hygienic practices that lead to increased child survival (Cochrane et al., 1980; Das Gupta, 1990). In the present study, fertility is negatively associated with the educational level of the mother. This finding conforms with earlier studies (Maheo, 2004; Bhasin & Nag,2007; Uddin *et al.*, 2000; Haloi & Limbu,2012; Khongsai, 2012; Syngkon, 2013).

Among the Kabui Naga women in both study areas, no particular trend is observed in their fertility pattern in relation to household income. In the Tamenglong sub-division, infant mortality decreases with the increase in household income; a positive and significant correlation is found between child mortality and household income. In the Imphal West district, a negative correlation is observed between infant and child mortality and household income, though it is statistically not significant. It may be noted here that in India, many studies have been carried out to understand the role of income in relation to fertility, and the majority of them have highlighted that fertility decreases as income increases as beyond that particular level of income, there appears to be a tendency for fertility to decline. This tends to suggest that minimum economic propensity may be essential for the decline in fertility.

Conclusion

India has the largest population in the world and is diverse in many areas, including socio-cultural practices, demographic characteristics, economic characteristics, etc. Tribal populations are no different in this regard. Various studies have reported vast differences in the rate of fertility and mortality even within the country, which may be attributed to a host of bio-social factors.

The present findings reveal that maternal age, age at first birth, family size, maternal education, and household income are the biosocial factors that have a significant influence in reducing fertility among Kabui Naga women. It has been observed that the influence of various biosocial factors on fertility and infant and child mortality is more robust in the Tamenglong sub-division than in Imphal West. The present study also shows that the rural-urban differences with respect to fertility and infant and child mortality rates can be reduced by improving women's education, income, healthcare practices, etc. People should be made aware of the fact that a healthy mother can have a healthy child, which will eventually lead to a healthy nation.

Policy implications

The government, together with the NGOs, has a vital role to play here. Conducting workshops with the help of health personnel can go a long way in helping people update their knowledge to check fertility and infant and child mortality. Also, maternal education needs to be stressed to make any awareness programme more effective for attaining a healthy population.

References

Adak, D.K. (1996). Infant and Early Childhood Mortality among the Khasis of Shillong (Meghalaya): Bio-cultural Observations. In: F.A. Das (ed). *Communities of North-East India.* New Delhi: Mittal Publication.

Adsera, A &A. Menendez. (2011). Fertility changes in Latin America in periods of economic uncertainty. *Population Studies,* 65(1):37–56.

Agarwala, S.N. (1972). *India's population problem.* Bombay: Tata McGraw-Hill Publication House.

Amonker, R.G. and G.D. Brinker. (1997). Determinants of Infant and Child Mortality in India. *International Review of Modern Sociology.* 27(2):1-22.

Bernardi, L. (2007). An introduction to Anthropological Demography. *Max Planck Institute for Demographic Research Working Paper, WP 2007-031, Germany*. Retrieved from http://www.demogr.mpg.de/papers/working/wp2007-031.pdf.

Bicego, T.G. & J.T. Boerma. (1993). Maternal education and child survival: A comparative study of survey data from 17 countries. *Social Science and Medicine*, 36:1207-1227.

Bharati, P. & M.G. Dastidar. (1990). Maternal Education, fertility and mortality in a Bengali Population sample. *Journal of Indian Anthropological Society*, 25(1):90–93.

Bhasin, M.K. & S. Nag. (2007). Demography of the Tribal groups of Rajasthan: 2. Levels of Differentials and Trends in Fertility. *Anthropologist*, 9(1): 39–46.

Caldwell, J. C. (1981). Perspectives of Fertility and Mortality in Africa. In Population Dynamics: Fertility and Mortality in Africa. Proceedings of the Expert Group Meeting of Fertility and Mortality Levels and Trends in Africa and their policy implications, Monrovia, Liberia, 1979.United Nations Economic Commission for Africa.

Chandrasekhar, S. (1959). *Infant mortality in India1901-1955.*London: George Allen and Unwin Ltd.

Chaudhury, B. S., I.K. Rahman and M.A. Maleque. (2000). Impact of some biosocial variables on infant and child mortality. *Demography India*, 29(2):211–221.

Crow, J.F. (1958). Some possibilities for measuring selection intensities in man. *Hum. Biol.* 30:1-13.

Dabral, S. and S. L. Malik. (2005). Demographic study of Gujjars of Delhi: IV. Maternal and child health care practices. *Journal of Human Ecology*, 17 (2): 1-12.

Das Gupta, M. (1990). Death clustering, mother's education and the determinants of child mortality in rural Punjab, India. *Population Studies*, 44:489-505.

Dey, S & S. Goswami. (2009). Fertility Pattern and Its Correlates in North East India. *Journal of Human Ecology*, 26(2): 145–152.

Driver, E. O.1963. *Differential Fertility in Central India.* Princeton: Princeton University Press.

Forste, R. (1994). The effects of breast-feeding and birth spacing in infant and child mortality in Bolivia. *Population Studies,* 48 (3): 497–511.

Fotso, J.C., J. Cleland, B. Mberu, M. Mutua and P. Elungata. (20130. Birth Spacing and Child Mortality: An Analysis of Prospective Data from the Nairobi Urban Health and Demographic Surveillance System. *J. Biosoc Sci.,* 45(6):779-798.

Grierson, G.A. (1903). *Linguistic Survey of India.* Vol.III. Tibeto-Burman Family.Part II: Calcutta.

Gulati, S. C. (19690). Impact of literacy, urbanisation and sex ratio on age at marriage in India'. *Artha Vijnana,* 2(4).

Hussain, I.Z. (1970). Education Status and Differentia Fertility in India. *Social Biology,* 17:132-139.

International Institute of Population Sciences (IIPS). (20000. Knowledge of Family Planning Methods. *National Family Health Survey-2, 1998-1999.* Bombay: Population Research Centre.

Haloi, A. and Limbu, D. K. (2012). Impact of Socio-Economic Factors on Fertility among the Assamese Muslims of Dadara and Agyathuri Villages of Kamrup District, Assam. *J. Indian Anthrop. Soc.* 47: 211-216.

Hill, K. (1991). Approaches to the Measurement of Childhood Mortality: A Comparative Review. Source: *Population Index,* Vol. 57, No. 3 (Autumn, 1991), pp. 368-382. Published by: Office of Population Research. Stable URL: *http://www.jstor.org/ stable/3643873.*

Johnston, F.F. & K.M. Kensinger. (1971). Fertility and mortality differentials and their implications for micro-evolutionary change among the Cashinahua. *Hum. Biol.* 43: pp. 356–364.

Kabir, M. and, M. Uddin. (1997). Fertility Transition in Bangladesh: Trends and Determinants. Asia Pacific Journal, 2(4): 53-72.

Kamei, G. (2004). The History of the Zeliangrong Nagas from Makhel to Rani Gaidinliu. New Delhi: Spectrum Publications.

Kamei, B. (2014). A Way of Life of the Zeliangrong Nagas in Manipur with Special Reference to the Rongmei (Kabui) Tribe. *International Journal of Social Science and Humanity*, 4(2):151–154.

Kapoor, S. (2009). Infant Mortality in India: District-Level variations and correlations. The University of California, Riverside, USA.

Kertzer, D. and T. Fricke. (1997). Toward an Anthropological Demography'. In: Kertzer, D and T.T. Fricke, (ed). *Anthropological Demography Towards a New Synthesis*. Chicago: University of Chicago Press: 1-35.

Khan, T. and R.E.A. Khan. (2010). 'Fertility Behaviour of women and their household characteristics: A case study of Punjab, Pakistan. *Journal of Human Ecology*, 30(1):11-17.

Khiloni, L. (2009). Fertility performance of the Anal women of Lambung Village, Chandel district, Manipur. *The Anthropologist*, 11(4):277–280.

Khongsai, L. (2012). Bio-Social Determinants of Fertility and Child Mortality among the Khongsai Kukis of Manipur. *Unpublished Ph.D. Thesis, Department of Anthropology*, North-Eastern Hill University, Shillong.

Khongsdier, R. (1995). Prenatal and postnatal mortality in the War Khasi of Meghalaya. *Journal of Human Ecology*, 6(3): 201-204.

Khongsdier, R. (2005). *Demographic Genetics of an Indian Population*. Itanagar & New Delhi: Himalayan Publishers.

Klaauw, B.V.D. and L. Wang. (2011). Child mortality in rural India'. *Journal of Population Economics*, 24(2):601-628.

Kost,K.and S.Amin. (1992). 'Reproductive and socioeconomic determinants of child survival: Confounded, interactive and age-dependent effects. *Social Biol*. 39:139-150.

Ladusing, L. & C. H. Singh. (2006). Place, Community Education and Child Mortality in North-East India. *Population, Space and Place*, 12: 65–76.

Maheo, L. M. (2004). The Mao Naga Tribe of Manipur –A Demographic Anthropological Survey. New Delhi: Mittal Publications.

Maitra, P. (2004). Effect of Socioeconomic Characteristics on Age at Marriage and Total Fertility in Nepal. *Journal of Health, Population and Nutrition*, 22(1):84–96.

Majumder, A. K. (1991). Breast-feeding, birth interval and child mortality in Bangladesh. *Journal of Biosocial Science*, 23 (3): 297-312.

Mosley, W. H. & C. H. Chen. (1984). Child survival strategies for research. *Population and Development Review*, New York: The population council.

Nanda, S. (2005). Demography and Ethnography of Fertility Behaviour: A Study of Non-Industrial Population in India. *Journal of Human Ecology*, 18(4):301–302.

Oppong, C. (1983). 'Women's role, opportunity costs, and fertility'. In Bulatao, R.A. and R. Lee (eds.): *Determinants of Fertility in Developing Countries. Vol. II*, London: Academic Press.

Pant, P. D. (1991). Effect of education and household characteristics on infant and child mortality in urban Nepal. *Journal of Biosocial Science*, 23 (4): 437–443.

Peterson, W. (1969). *Population*. Second Edition. New York: MacMillan.

Purfield, C. (2006). 'Mind the Gap-Is Economic Growth in India Leaving Some States Behind?'. *IMF Working Paper, No.06/103*, Washington DC: International Monetary Fund.

Reddy, K.S.N. & G. Sudha. (2010). Factors Affecting Fertility and Mortality: Case Study among the Setti Balija Community of Andhra Pradesh'. *The Anthropologist*, 12(4):271–275.

Rosenzweig, M.R. and T.P. Schultz. (1982). Child mortality and fertility in Colombia: Individual and Community effects. *Health Policy Education*, 2(3-4):305-348.

Rustein, S.O. (2000). Factors associated with trends in infant and child mortality in developing countries during the 1990s. *Bul. WHO*, 78:1256-1270.

Sahu, D., S. Nair, L. Singh., B.K. Gulati, & A. Pandey. (2015). Levels, trends and Predictors of infant and child mortality among the Scheduled Tribes in rural India. *Indian J Med Res,* 141:709-19.

Saksena, D., J. Srivastava and E. Lehler. (1984). Impact of child mortality and socio-demographic attributes on family size: Some data from urban India. *Journal of Biosocial Science*, 16: 119-126.

Sengupta, S. & K. Chakravarty. (1995). Family type, fertility and mortality: A study among the Ahoms of Assam. *Journal of Human Ecology,* 6 (3): 197–200.

Simmons, G.B.1985. 'Research on the Determinants of Fertility'. In Ghazi Farooq and George Simmons(eds.): *Fertility in Developing Countries: An Economic Perspective on Research and Policy Issues.* London: Macmillan, pp.67–108.

Singh, S.J. (2006). Ethnic Variations in Fertility Patterns among Four Communities of Manipur. *Journal of Human Ecology*, 20 (1): 1–9.

Singh, U.P. (2003). Trends of mortality among Bhoksa tribe of Uttaranchal. *The Oriental Anthropologist,* 3:1.

Sinha, V.C. & E. Zacharia. (1984). *Elements of Demography.* New Delhi: Allied Publishers Private Ltd.

Syngkon, H. (2013). Status and determinants of Child mortality among the Pnars of Jaintia Hills District, Meghalaya. *Unpublished Ph.D. Thesis, Department of Anthropology, North-Eastern Hill University, Shillong.*

U.N. (1985). Socio-economic Differentials in Child Mortality in Developing Countries. Sales No.E.85. XIII.7.

Verma, A. (2002). Socio-cultural correlates of infant mortality in a primitive tribe. *Journal of Human Ecology*, 13(3):203–207.

Yadav, S.S. and V.S. Badari. (1997). Age at effective marriage and fertility: An analysis of data for North Kanara. *The Journal of Family Welfare*, 43(3): 61-66.

Uddin, M.J., M.Z. Hossain and M, Ullah. O. (2000). Child mortality in a developing country: a statistical analysis. *Journal of Applied Quantitative Methods*, 4(3): 270–283.

United Nations, (2001). Road Map Towards the Implementation of the United Nations Millennium Declaration - *Report of the Secretary-General*, 6 September 2001.

WHO? (1967). *International Classification of Diseases.* Geneva: World Health Organization.

Wray, J.D. (1978). Maternal nutrition, breastfeeding and infant survival. In: W.H. Mosley (ed.), *Nutrition and Human Reproduction*, pp.197–229.New York: Plenum Press.

Table 1: Fertility by age group among Kabui Naga mothers

Age group (years)	TAMENGLONG			IMPHAL		
	No. of mothers	Mean no. of live births	(±) SE	No. of mothers	Mean no. of live births	(±) SE
≤24	52(20.00)	1.46	0.10	31(17.81)	1.23	0.13
25-34	114(43.84)	3.12	0.14	76(43.67)	2.24	0.14
35-44	73(28.07)	4.27	0.30	50(28.73)	3.14	0.22
≥45	21(8.07)	5.76	0.41	17(9.77)	3.59	0.38
F-statistics	42.431, p<0.001			19.382, p<0.001		

(Figures in parentheses indicate percentages).

Table 2. Infant and child mortality by age group

Age group (years)	No. of live births	Infant mortality	Child mortality	Total
TAMENGLONG				
≤ 24	76	4(5.30)	0(0.00)	4(5.30)
25-34	352	13(3.70)	0(0.00)	13(3.70)
35-44	314	11(3.50)	10(3.18)	21(6.68)

≥ 45	124	4(3.22)	5(4.03)	9(7.25)
Coefficient of correlation (r)		0.10	0.30**	0.23**
IMPHAL				
≤ 24	38	0(0.00)	0(0.00)	0(0.00)
25-34	170	2(1.18)	1(0.60)	3(1.80)
35-44	157	5(3.20)	3(1.91)	8(5.10)
≥ 45	60	1(1.70)	4(6.70)	5(8.33)
Coefficient of correlation (r)		0.14	0.23**	0.26**

(Figures in parentheses indicate percentages, ** $p<0.01$)

Table 3. Fertility by age at marriage

Age at marriage (years)	TAMENGLONG			IMPHAL		
	No. of mothers	Mean no. of live births	(±) SE	No. of mothers	Mean no. of live births	(±) SE
≤ 19	115 (44.23)	3.47	0.18	42 (24.13)	3.33	0.27
20-23	81 (31.15)	3.48	0.23	63 (36.20)	2.41	0.16
≥ 24	64 (24.61)	2.88	0.27	69 (39.65)	1.96	0.13
F-statistics	2.001, $p>0.05$			12.809, $p<0.01$		

(Figures in parentheses indicate percentages).

Table 4. Infant and child mortality by age at marriage of mothers

Age at marriage (years)	No. of mothers	No. of live births	Infant mortality	Child mortality	Total
TAMENGLONG					
≤19	115(44.23)	399	19(4.76)	5(1.25)	24(6.01)
20-23	81(31.15)	282	10(3.55)	5(1.77)	15(5.33)
≥24	64(24.61)	185	3(1.62)	5(2.70)	8(4.32)
Coefficient of correlation (r)			-0.11	0.06	-0.06
IMPHAL					
≤19	42(24.13)	142	2(1.42)	3(2.14)	5(3.57)
20-23	63(36.20)	150	5(9.61)	3(5.76)	8(15.38)
≥24	69(39.65)	133	1(0.75)	2(1.50)	3(2.25)
Coefficient of correlation (r)			-0.07	-0.07	-0.10

(Figures in parentheses indicate percentages).

Table 5: Fertility by age of mother at 1st childbirth

Age at 1st childbirth (years)	TAMENGLONG			IMPHAL		
	No. of mothers	Mean no. of live births	(±) SE	No. of mothers	Mean no. of live births	(±) SE
≤ 18	32	4.18	0.38	7	3.85	0.93
18-24	160	3.41	0.15	95	2.76	0.15
24+	57	3.24	0.26	65	2.10	0.12
F-statistics	12.745, p<0.01			13.453, p<0.01		

(Figures in parentheses indicate percentages).

Table 6: Infant and Child mortality by age of mother at 1st childbirth

Age at 1st childbirth (years)	No. of mothers	No. of live births	Infant mortality	Child mortality	Total
TAMENGLONG					
<18	32	134	8(5.97)	2(1.49)	10(7.46)
18-24	160	546	21(3.84)	8(1.46)	29(5.31)
24+	57	186	3(1.61)	5(2.68)	8(4.30)
Coefficient of correlation (r)			-0.07	0.65	-0.02
IMPHAL					
<18	7	27	0(0.00)	2(7.40)	2(7.40)
18-24	95	263	7(2.66)	4(1.52)	11(4.18)
24+	65	135	1(0.74)	2(1.48)	3(2.22)
Coefficient of correlation (r)			-0.03	-0.06	-0.07

(Figures in parentheses indicate percentages).

Table 7: Regression of age at marriage of the mothers on independent factors

Parameters	Coefficient of regression (B) and its standard Error (SE) B ±SE	t-value	p-value
Rural/Urban Residence	1.688±0.449	3.762	Significant at 1%
Maternal education	0.285±0.206	1.386	Insignificant
Paternal occupation	0.610±0.242	2.520	Insignificant
Maternal occupation	0.739±0.192	3.854	Significant at 1%

Paternal education	-0.291±0.251	-1.158	Insignificant
Household income	0.241±0.261	0.920	Insignificant
constant	16.479±1.095	15.051	Significant at 1%

Table 8: Fertility by Birth Interval

Birth intervals (in months)	TAMENGLONG			IMPHAL		
	No. of mothers	Mean no. of live births	(±SE)	No. of mothers	Mean no. of live births	(±SE)
<24	15 (5.24)	3.53	0.57	1 (0.78)	2.00	0.00
24-35	155 (54.19)	3.92	0.15	95 (74.21)	2.94	0.13
>35	45 (15.73)	3.82	0.23	32 (25.00)	3.31	0.21
F-statistics	2.366, p>0.05			10.854, p>0.01		

(*Figures in parentheses indicate the percentage)

Table 9: Infant and child mortality by birth interval

Birth interval (in months)	No. of live births	Infant mortality	Child mortality	Total
TAMENGLONG				
<24	53	4(7.54)	1(1.88)	5(9.43)
24-35	607	21(3.45)	12(1.97)	32(5.27)

>35	172	7(4.06)	2(1.16)	9(1.16)
Coefficient of correlation (r)		0.11	0.08	0.13
IMPHAL				
<24	2	1(50.00)	0(0.00)	1(50.00)
24-35	280	3(1.07)	6(2.14)	9(3.21)
>35	106	4(3.77)	2(1.88)	6(5.66)
Coefficient of correlation (r)		0.15*	0.11	0.17*

(Figures in parentheses indicate percentages* $p<0.05$)

Table 10: Regression of mean birth interval of the mothers on independent factors

Parameters	Coefficient of regression (B) and its B±SE	t-value	p-value
Residence (Tamenglong/Imphal)	-0.015±0.102	-0.145	Insignificant
Maternal education	-0.120±0.047	-2.535	Insignificant
Paternal education	-0.136±0.054	-2.515	Insignificant
Maternal occupation	0.094±0.043	2.170	Significant at 1%
Paternal occupation	-0.025±0.057	-0.449	Insignificant
Household income	0.071±0.060	1.186	Insignificant
Size of family	-0.003±0.061	-0.053	Insignificant
Constant	1.971±0.249	7.928	Significant at 1%

Table 11: Fertility by types of family

Types of family	TAMENGLONG			IMPHAL		
	No. of mothers	Mean no. of live births	(±SE)	No. of mothers	Mean no. of live births	(±SE)
Nuclear	177 (68.07)	3.74	0.15	120 (68.96)	2.60	0.13
Joint	83 (31.92)	2.43	0.22	54 (31.03)	2.11	0.19
F-statistics	24.271, p<0.01			4.258, p<0.05		

Table 12: Infant and child mortality by types of family

Types of family	No. of live births	Infant mortality	Child mortality	Total
TAMENGLONG				
Nuclear	663	24 (3.61)	12(1.80)	36(5.42)
Joint	203	8(3.94)	3(1.47)	11(5.41)
Coefficient of correlation (r)		-0.04	-0.06	-0.06
IMPHAL				
Nuclear	313	7(2.23)	7(2.23)	14(4.47)
Joint	112	1(0.89)	1(0.89)	2(1.78)
Coefficient of correlation (r)		-0.08	-0.07	-0.11

(*Figures in parentheses indicate percentages)

Table 13: Fertility by educational level

Educational levels	TAMENGLONG			IMPHAL		
	No. of mothers	Mean no. of live births	(±) SE	No. of mothers	Mean no. of live births	(±) SE
Illiterate	69(26.5)	4.84	0.25	19(10.9)	3.42	0.41
Primary	78(30.0)	3.37	0.21	26(14.9)	3.31	0.36
Secondary	56(21.5)	2.54	0.20	44(25.3)	2.52	0.21
Higher Secondary and above	57(21.9)	2.21	0.21	85(48.9)	1.94	0.11
F- statistics	26.022, p<0.01			10.437, p<0.01		

(*Figures in parentheses indicate percentages)

Table 14: Infant and child mortality by educational level

Educational levels	No. of live births	Infant mortality	Child mortality	Total
TAMENGLONG				
Illiterate	334	13(3.89)	10(2.99)	27(8.08)
Primary	263	12(4.56)	2(0.76)	14(5.32)
Secondary	142	7(4.92)	1(0.70)	8(5.63)
Higher Secondary and above	127	0(0.00)	2(1.57)	2(1.57)
Coefficient of correlation (r)		-0.16**	-0.16**	-0.46**

IMPHAL				
Illiterate	65	2(3.07)	0(0.00)	2(3.07)
Primary	86	1(1.16)	4(4.65)	5(5.81)
Secondary	111	2(1.80)	2(1.80)	4(3.60)
Higher Secondary and above	163	3(1.84)	2(1.22)	5(3.06)
Coefficient of correlation (r)		-0.07	-0.07	-0.38

(*Figures in parentheses indicate percentages** $p<0.01$)

Table 15: Fertility by monthly household income

Income groups	TAMENGLONG			IMPHAL		
	No. of mothers	Mean no. of live births	(±) SE	No. of mothers	Mean no. of live births	(±) SE
Low-income group (LIG)	130(50.0)	2.91	0.17	66(37.93)	2.56	0.19
Middle-income group (MIG)	66(25.4)	3.83	0.24	32(18.4)	1.78	0.20
High-income group (HIG)	64(24.6)	3.66	0.29	76(43.7)	2.64	0.17
F- statistics	5.535, $p<0.01$			4.238, $p<0.05$		

Table 16: Infant and child mortality by monthly household income

Income groups	No. of live births	Infant mortality	Child mortality	Total
TAMENGLONG				
Low-income group (LIG)	378	23 (6.08)	3(0.79)	26(6.87)
Middle-income group (MIG)	253	5(1.97)	3(1.18)	8(3.16)
High-income group (HIG)	235	4(1.70)	9(3.82)	13(5.53)
Coefficient of correlation (r)		-0.12*	0.19**	-0.00
IMPHAL				
Low-income group (LIG)	167	5(2.99)	4(2.39)	9(5.38)
Middle-income group (MIG)	57	0(0.00)	0(0.00)	0(0.00)
High-income group (HIG)	201	3(1.49)	4(1.99)	7(3.48)
Coefficient of correlation (r)		-0.07	-0.01	-0.05

(Figures in parentheses indicate percentages *p<0.05 **p<0.01)

14

Impact of Supplementary Food and Socio-economic Predictors on Nutritional Status of Children Attending Anganwadis in Bilaspur, Chhattisgarh, India

Manisha Ghritlahre
Mahua Chanak
Subal Das
Kaushik Bose

Introduction

According to the World Health Organization (WHO), a healthy child is the wealth of a nation. India, a developing country, covers 40.0% of undernourished children worldwide. Undernutrition predominantly occurs due to insufficient availability of proper food, early age at marriage and first birth, gestational age, delivery mode, height (cm) and weight (kg) of the children, lack of breastfeeding, family size, low birth weight, open defecation and low socio-economic condition of the family (Khan & Nalli, 2018). Malnutrition is more prevalent, especially in central India, such as Chhattisgarh and Madhya Pradesh (Dakshayani & Gangadhar, 2015).

In India, many recent studies have shown a high malnutrition rate in preschool children's nutritional status (Purohit, 2017). The government of India initiated the Integrated Child Development Service (ICDS) scheme on 2 October 1975 under the national nutritional policy to reduce malnutrition and break the vicious cycle of morbidity and mortality among children below six years old. It has become the world's most extensive programme for early and proper childhood growth and development

(Joseph, 2014). ICDS service provides a vast network of ICDS centres, known as "Anganwadi", which is derived from the Hindu word "Angan" (Surwade et al., 2013, pp. 107-10).

The literal meaning of Angan is the courtyards of a house where children can play and get supplementary food and preschool education (ICDS Report, 2009). Other than these, Anganwadi provides immunisation, health check-ups, referral services, and health and nutrition education for the betterment of children (Sharma et al., 2006). It is a childcare centre located within the village and is run by one trained female person called an Anganwadi worker (Bhattarai et al., 2017). She is a community-based front-line voluntary worker of the ICDS programme (Ahmad et al., 2020). Her primary work is to support the family, particularly mothers, to ensure adequate health and nutrition care, early recognition and timely treatment of infirmities (Das et al., 2020). It serves the highly vulnerable and underprivileged sections of backward and remote areas of the nation and provides services at the doorsteps of the beneficiaries to ensure their maximum involvement (Chudasama et al., 2016).

Nutrition also improves their ability to learn, communicate, think analytically, socialise effectively and adapt to new environments and people. Growth and development are continuous processes which begin at conception and end at maturity. Poor health of children alters their nutritional status. This poor nutritional status of the child leads to the development of infectious diseases and, finally, malnutrition, which may lead to permanent physical and mental impairment (Sheila et al., 2014). The nutritional status is determined by a complex interaction between internal and external factors: internal factors like age, sex, nutrition, behaviour, physical activity and diseases and external environmental factors like food safety and cultural, social and economic circumstances (Thurstan et al., 2020). Given the above background, the study's objective was to assess the impact of supplementary food provided by ICDS and the socio-economic status of parents on the nutritional status of studied children.

Material and Methods:

The study was based on a cross-sectional method and was conducted on 780 children (392 girls and 388 boys) from 50 ICDS Centers from 5

Tehsils out of 8 Tehsils in Bilaspur. The participants' ages (years) ranged from 2-5 years in Bilaspur, Chhattisgarh, India. A stratified random sampling technique has been adopted for data collection. Anthropometric measurements, socio-demographic profiles, supplementary food, and other basic facilities provided by ICDS Centers were collected from Anganwadi workers. The age (years) of the children was collected from the "Jaccha-Baccha" card. A questionnaire schedule has opted for the collection of data. Data were collected after obtaining the necessary approval from the competent authorities. Height and weight were recorded from each participant by the first author (M.G) following standard techniques (Lohman et al., 1988).

Technical measurement errors were found to be within reference values (Ulijaszek & Kerr, 1999) and thus not incorporated in statistical analyses. The estimated sample size of the studied children was calculated by the formula $n = (z^2pq)/d^2$ (Cochran, 1977). Following the World Health Organization (WHO, 2006), age- and sex-specific -2 z-scores have been considered to define undernutrition. Three indicators of undernutrition have been used: stunting (low height-for-age), also referred to as chronic malnutrition; underweight (low weight-for-age), referred to as acute malnutrition; and wasting (BMI-for-age), referred to as acute malnutrition (WHO, 2010). According to WHO (1995), a population experiencing (5-9%) of undernutrition are classified as Low prevalence; (10-19%) as medium prevalence; (20-39%) as high prevalence; and (40% and above) is categorised as very high prevalence. All statistical analyses were performed using the Statistical Package for Social Science (SPSS/PC-Version 23), such as percentages, frequency, chi-square test, and regression. Statistical significance has been set to a value of $p < 0.05$.

Results

Table 1 shows the overall combined age and sex composition of the studied children. Out of 780 children, boys constitute 388 (49.7%), and girls constitute 392 (50.2%), respectively. For the age group of 2 years, boys constitute 75 (19.3%), and girls constitute 75 (19.1%), respectively. For the age group of 3 years, boys constitute 99 (25.5%), and girls constitute 90 (23.0%), respectively. For the age group of 4 years, boys constitute 125 (32.3%), and girls constitute 113 (28.8%). Similarly, for the age group of 5 years, boys constitute 89 (22.9%), and girls constitute 114 (29.1%), respectively.

Table 2 shows the descriptive statistics and mean difference in anthropometric variables among the studied children. It is clear from the table that there is a significant mean positive sex difference in mean weight (t-value = 0.022; df = 148; p = 0.009), height (t-value = -0.427; df = 148; p = 0.001), and BMI (t-value = 0.512; df = 148; p = 0.051) at the age of 2 years. Similarly, there is a significant mean positive sex difference in mean weight (t-value = 0.896; df = 187; p = 0.003), height (t-value = -1.592; df = 187; p = 0.050), and BMI (t-value = 0.794; df = 187; p = 0.012) at the age of 3 years.

Table 3 shows the age and Sex-Specific prevalence of stunting and their relationship among studied children. Overall, out of 780 children, 48.7% of children had been found stunted. The highest prevalence of stunting was found among the age of 3 years in the case of both sexes (35.3% of boys and 25.5% of girls), and the least prevalence was found in the age of 2 years among boys (14.6%) and girls (12.0%). Similarly, the highest prevalence of moderate stunting was found among the age two years for boys (41.3%) and four years for girls (30.7%) and the least prevalence was observed for the age of 3 years amongst boys (28.8%) and girls (13.3%). It is clear from the above table that there is a significant relationship between boys and girls at age three years (x^2 = 12.352; df=2; p = 0.002) and four years (x^2 = 4.381; df=2; p = 0.021) concerning their height-for-age.

Table 4 shows the age and Sex-Specific prevalence of underweight and their relationship among studied children. It shows that out of 780 children, a total of 46.3% of them had been found to be underweight. It has been observed that severely underweight was found to be highest at the age of 3 years in the case of boys (21.2%) and four years in the case of girls (16.8%), and the lowest prevalence was observed at the age of 4 years in case of boys (12.0%) and five years in case of girls (7.8%). Similarly, the highest prevalence of moderately underweight has been observed at the age of 3 years for boys (50.5%) and girls (45.5%), and the lowest prevalence was observed at the age of 4 years among boys (24.8%) and five years among girls (23.6%). It is clear from the above table that there is a significant relationship between boys and girls at age 3 ($x^2 = 6.185$; df=2; p=0.045) years concerning their weight-for-age.

Table 5 shows the age and Sex-Specific prevalence of wasting and their relationship among studied children. It was observed that out of 780 children, a total of 28.8% of children were wasted. It was found that the highest prevalence of severely wasted was among the age of 3 years in boys (21.2%) and two years in girls (13.3%), and a lower prevalence of severely wasted was found at the age of 5 years among both sexes (7.8% of boys and 3.5% of girls) Similarly, the highest prevalence of moderately wasting was observed at the age of 2 years in boys (38.6%), and girls (36.0%) and the lowest had been found at the age of 5 years among boys (7.8%) and four years among girls (5.3%). The highest prevalence of overweight was found at the age of 5 years among boys (6.7%) and three years among girls (8.8%), and the lowest prevalence was observed at the age of 2 years in the case of boys (1.3%) and five years in case of girls (3.5%) respectively. It is clear from the above table that there is a significant relationship between boys and girls at the age of 2 years ($x^2=$ 14.056; df=5; p=0.026), three years ($x^2= 23.328$; df=4; p = 0.000), and four years (10.102; df=2; 0.034) with respects to their BMI-for-age.

Table 6 shows the relationship between receiving supplementary food by ICDS children with weight-for-age, height-for-age and BMI-for-age among the studied children. Stunting, underweight, and wasting were found to be higher among children who were not receiving supplementary food regularly than those who were receiving food regularly. It was observed that those children who were not regularly receiving supplementary food were more severely stunted (32.1%) than those who attended regularly and exhibited moderately stunted (23.9%). A similar study conducted in Aligarh ICDS children found that 68% of the children who were not taking regular food were observed to be stunted (Alim & Jahan, 2012). Dropout of children occurred due to irregular opening of the ICDS centre; helpers do not go home daily, it is far from home, and the unwillingness of children. Approx. 20.7% of the children had been found underweight due to not regularly taking supplementary food. Around 16.4% and 19.6% of the children were found to be severely and moderately wasted, respectively. Most parents were engaged as wage labourers or cultivators, so children also used to be with them all the time instead of attending Anganwadi. Time is an important consideration when it comes to regular attendance at Anganwadi centres. Regular attendance by children increases their chances of participating in educational programmes, getting access to healthcare services, and receiving nutrition supplements, all of which can improve their nutritional status. The longer children have access to Anganwadi services, the more significant the potential impact on their nutritional well-being. Providing ongoing support over an extended period can help children recover from malnutrition and maintain a healthy nutritional status. It is clear from the table that there is a significant relationship between receiving supplementary food by ICDS children with height-for-age (17.57; df=2; 0.01), weight-for-age (20.98; 22.963; df-2; 0.000), and BMI-for-age (27.90; df=5; 0.000) respectively.

Table 7 deals with the linear regression analysis with age (as an independent variable) to record the impact of age on anthropometric and derived (dependent) variables recorded separately. The dependent variables are weight and height. Moreover, it was clear from the table that age had a significant impact on the anthropometric measurements used. Height (dependent variable) showed the highest significance, and adjusted R^2 indicated the variance to be 58.7%, followed by weight (dependent variable). Adjusted R^2 indicated a variance of 55.7%. It is clear from the table that for height and weight, the p-value is 0.000, which is less than 0.05; hence, it shows a significant association between independent and dependent variables.

Table 8 shows the association of socio-demographic predictors for height-for-age by stepwise binary logistic regression. It is clear from the table that out of the 12 variables used to see the association between height for age and the variables mentioned above, five variables, such as sex (p = 0.000), Mother's education (p = 0.026), number of siblings (p = 0.009), Birth order (p = 0.000), and Breastfeeding (p = 0.054), had a significant relationship with height-for-age among the studied children.

Table 9 shows the association of socio-demographic predictors for weight-for-age by stepwise binary logistic regression. It is clear from the table that out of the total 11 variables used to see the association between weight for age and variables mentioned above, only eight variables, such as sex (p = 0.011), father's education (p = 0.000), father's occupation (p = 0.000), family income (p= 0.040), socio-economic status (p = 0.002), number of siblings (p = 0.000), birth order (p = 0.000), and breastfed (p = 0.000), showed significant association with weight-for-age among the studied children.

Discussion

Education is one of the most important things to the family's socioeconomic standing. There is a clear correlation between parental education and the nutritional status of their children, as seen by the proportion of malnutrition reduction in children of educated parents compared to those of ignorant parents. Literate parents are more likely to have access to and comprehend knowledge of good nutrition, such as the significance of a balanced diet, sensible serving sizes, and the dietary requirements of kids of various ages. Poor feeding practices and food choices may result from the ignorance of these parents. In order to address child malnutrition, it is essential to comprehend health-related information such as growth charts, dietary guidelines, vaccination schedules, nutritional recommendations, deworming medication, colostrum feeding for newborn babies, and sending nutritional rehabilitation centres based on Anganwadi workers' recommendations. Parents without formal education may find it more difficult to get healthcare, education, and trustworthy sources of nutrition-related information for their children. Poor feeding practices and food choices could result from the ignorance of these parents. To address children's malnutrition, it is essential to comprehend health-related information such as growth charts, dietary guidelines, vaccination schedules, nutritional recommendations, deworming medication, colostrum feeding for newborn babies, and sending nutritional rehabilitation centres based on Anganwadi workers' recommendations. Parents with less education may have less access to healthcare, educational resources, and trustworthy sources of nutrition-related information for their children.

About 66.0% of the Anganwadi centres had separate buildings meant for them, whereas 20% of the rental houses and 14% of the centres were run at the workers' homes (14.0%). It showed they needed separate buildings with all basic facilities such as room for children seating, store room for keeping all food items, kitchen and toilet. For rent, Anganwadi workers get only Rs. 200 per month from the government, and they pay more than

Rs. 500 per month for rent to run their centres. They complained that running Anganwadi centres on rent or at home was very difficult due to a lack of space for seating, playing and eating altogether at a time. Almost 78.0% of the Anganwadi centres had pucca buildings, while 22.0% of the Anganwadi centres had kaccha buildings. Thirty-six Anganwadi centres were open for four hours, followed by twelve Anganwadi centres open for five hours. It was observed that 90.0% of the Anganwadi centres opened for 5-6 days a week, while 10.0% of the Anganwadi centres opened for 3-4 days a week. Most of the registered children (67.0%) were attending Anganwadi regularly, while 32.7% of the children were not attending Anganwadi regularly. It was observed that in 28.0% of the Anganwadi centres, food was cooked daily as per the menu, while in 72.0% of the Anganwadi centres, food was cooked as per the menu. It was attributed to a delayed supply of raw food from the Self-Help Group. Some of the centres were found to lack kitchen space.

The present study revealed that about 66.0% of the Anganwadi workers knew correctly about the use of weighing machines. In comparison, 34.0% of the Anganwadi workers had incorrect knowledge because they did not check the zero error in the weighing machine or were not acquainted with using the digital weighing machine properly. It had been observed that 74.0% of the Anganwadi centres had weighing machines in functional condition, whereas weight machines in 26.0% of the Anganwadi centres were non-functional. Due to battery issues or weighing machine damage, they could not monitor growth regularly. Only 54.0% of Anganwadi centres weighed children every month, while the rest were found to weigh children every three months. The recommended calorie consumption is 635 kcal/per meal/child. Approximately 47.0% of the Anganwadi workers had correct knowledge of providing supplementary calories to children every day. In comparison, 26.0% of the Anganwadi workers were unaware of it. Another study conducted among children from Telangana found that 26.0% of the workers were unaware of supplementary nutrition (Harikrishna et al., 2020).

Most of the Anganwadi workers had correct knowledge of different colours (red, yellow and green) present in the MUAC strip, while 16.0% of the Anganwadi workers did not possess correct knowledge. All Anganwadi centres get the WHO (2006) recommended growth chart for assessing the health status of children; 80.0% of the Anganwadi workers were found to have correct knowledge of growth chart reading, whereas 20% of the workers were found with incorrect knowledge, and they used to take help of other Anganwadi workers to fill it. The main reason that was pointed out was the lack of skills among Anganwadi workers in filling out growth charts. A similar result was observed in the study of Bhattarai et al. (2017), which demonstrated that 21.8% and 21.1% of the Anganwadi workers had incorrect knowledge of colours present in the MUAC Strip and the flattened growth line on the growth chart.

There is a complicated interaction of circumstances between the presence of children and the amenities available in Anganwadi centres rather than a straightforward cause-and-effect relationship. In India, Anganwadi centres are community-based daycare facilities that offer a variety of services, such as health care, nutrition, and early childhood education. Children's attendance at Anganwadi centres is primarily dependent on their location. Parents are more inclined to send their kids to a centre if it is conveniently located in the neighbourhood. Travel time can be cut via proximity. One primary motivator for parents to send their kids to Anganwadi centres is the provision of wholesome meals and snacks. Offering high-quality, well-balanced meals to children fosters greater attendance since parents view it as a source of healthy nourishment for their kids. Early childhood education and educational resources might draw in parents who place high importance on their kids' growth. These facilities can provide a fun and secure learning environment, which may persuade parents to bring their kids there on a regular basis. Immunisations and routine physical examinations are among the essential healthcare treatments offered by some Anganwadi centres. The fact that these services are offered may encourage parents to enrol their kids. Children's attendance can be significantly impacted by their knowledge and comprehension of the services provided at Anganwadi centres, such as the availability of clean drinking water, a safe, clean, and hygienic atmosphere, and sanitation facilities. Parents are more willing to send their kids to these centres if they are aware of their advantages. The choice to enrol a kid in an Anganwadi centre can occasionally be impacted by the parents' job schedules and domestic duties. It is noteworthy that the existence of children in Anganwadi centres is also impacted by more general factors such as socioeconomic status, cultural norms, and the success of central and local government outreach and communication initiatives. In order to promote children's attendance, it is imperative to take into account a wide range of criteria and customise the services offered by Anganwadi centres to the unique requirements and conditions of the communities they cater to. In order to stay hydrated and avoid waterborne illnesses like dysentery, cholera, and diarrhoea, it is imperative to have access to clean drinking water. Intestinal lining damage and decreased nutrition absorption in children are two consequences of waterborne diseases. Malnutrition and malabsorption may result from this. All Anganwadi centres are expected to have drinking water facilities, but it was observed that only 68.0% of the Anganwadi centres had drinking facilities while 32.0% of Anganwadi centres did not. Except for seven Anganwadi centres, the rest of the centres had no water filters in their centres. Anganwadi helpers used to go to other places to fetch water for cooking and drinking for the children. It was observed that 72.0% of the Anganwadi centres had a toilet in their centres while 28.0% of centres did not have this facility; out of these 72.0% centres, only 44.0% of the Anganwadi centres had a toilet in working condition while 56.0% of the centres had a toilet in non-working condition and opted for open defecation that might lead to severe illnesses and infections. Better waste disposal and sanitation facilities, such as functional toilets, contribute to a decrease in the transmission of illnesses and infections. As a result, there are fewer illnesses and absences from school or other activities, which can benefit a child's development and growth. Regarding mats or chairs, 88.0% of the centres had mats for seating, while only 12.0% of the Anganwadi centres had benches for children.

Every month, all mothers are called to the Anganwadi centres to impart awareness regarding nutritional health; however, due to engagement in wage labour or cultivation, they cannot attend, which is one of the reasons for the lack of awareness. The choice to put wage-labour ahead of children's health is not taken in a vacuum; it is impacted by a number of intricate and frequently unavoidable variables. For basic necessities like food, shelter, and medical care, families frequently rely on the income of parents, especially mothers. In times of financial hardship, parents may feel compelled to prioritise earning a living in order to support their family.

Mothers could not have access to sufficient support networks that would enable them to manage job and childcare duties, such as extended family, childcare providers, or social safety. Without this kind of assistance, women might feel pressured to put wage jobs first. Mothers find it challenging to fit their work around their children's demands when their jobs have rigid work schedules, especially if they do not influence their work schedules. There may not be as many job options for mothers in some areas or economic situations. This may put them in a position where they have to accept any job that comes up, regardless of whether it fits their preferences for juggling work and family obligations. Mothers may put their children's long-term financial security ahead of their own wage labour. They could think that by working and making money, they will be able to give their kids greater chances later on. Some moms find it challenging to bring their young children to work for extended periods, so they enrol them in Anganwadi centres, where these centres would take care of them. It is critical to address this matter with compassion and understanding, acknowledging that moms who find themselves in similar situations frequently have to make tough choices. In the end, helping moms in these circumstances can be advantageous for their families as well as society at large.

The study revealed that half of the mothers had partial knowledge of Anganwadi services, like food distribution. At the same time, only 33.8% of the women knew about all services provided by Anganwadi centres, like preschool education, vaccination, and supplementary food. It was found that 66.9% of the mothers were satisfied with the working pattern of Anganwadi workers, like the regular opening of Anganwadi centres, food quality and caretaking of children, whereas 33.1% of the mothers were not satisfied with the working pattern of Anganwadi workers. Poor rapport building by the Anganwadi workers with mothers and children can also be a significant factor in undernutrition. The perceived or actual low quality of services provided at Anganwadi centres is one of the leading causes of discontent. Anganwadi centres could not have the necessary infrastructure, such as hygienic and secure premises, enough space for kids to play, and working restrooms. Concerns regarding the environment's hygienic conditions and safety can arise from inadequate infrastructure. Mothers' satisfaction is significantly influenced by the Anganwadi centres' location and accessibility. Mothers are discouraged from using centres that are too remote from their neighbourhood, are hard to get to or have irregular hours. Some mothers may not receive adequate information about the advantages of the services offered at Anganwadi centres, or they may not be fully aware of them. Underutilisation and discontent may result from this; anganwadi centres must be easily accessible, especially in remote and underprivileged locations. The geographic distribution of the centres and their outreach programmes to reach outlying or marginalised communities should be examined in the investigation. It is crucial to comprehend the elements that affect mothers' degree of participation in the programmes and their level of satisfaction with Anganwadi services. Analyses can be used to pinpoint obstacles to involvement and provide methods for raising parent involvement. The Anganwadi workers often do not get enough time to spend with children due to engagement in other work such as surveys, polio camping, census work, election work, or some other work related to the village. Further, they must prepare at least 22 registers to maintain all records. Since the honorarium was not satisfactory, it resulted in their effectiveness and efficiency in performing their duties.

Conclusion

The current study was carried out on 780 ICDS children, of which 388 (49.7%) were boys and 392 (50.2%) were girls. According to the current study, the prevalence of underweight, wasting, and stunting is 46.3%, 28.8%, and 48.7%, respectively. It illustrates the dire state of undernutrition among the kids. Education ranks second in importance only to the family's socioeconomic standing. There is a clear correlation between parental education and the nutritional status of their children, as seen by the proportion of malnutrition reduction in children of educated parents compared to those of ignorant parents. Good hygiene practices are encouraged by adequate sanitation facilities, which include having access to soap and clean water for handwashing. Maintaining clean hands improves general health and nutrition by lowering the chance of contamination and the spread of germs. Childhood stunting can result from long-term exposure to contaminated water and unsanitary conditions. One type of malnutrition, known as stunting, is characterised by stunted growth and development. A sufficient supply of clean water and sanitary facilities can aid in lowering the incidence of stunting. Children who suffer from iron deficiency anaemia might get parasitic diseases like hookworm as a result of poor sanitation and contaminated water sources. Anaemia may have an impact on general health and cognitive development. The choice to put wage-labour ahead of children's health is not taken in a vacuum; it is impacted by a number of intricate and frequently unavoidable variables. For basic necessities like food, shelter, and medical care, families frequently rely on the income of parents, especially mothers. Nutrition surveillance should be done continuously, and special attention should be given to vulnerable groups such as the poorest and the most severely malnourished children. Even after providing nutrition supplements to the preschoolers in Anganwadis, their nutritional status is not at par with the standard reference values for the age mentioned above range and a need-based diet is recommended to be provided to severely and moderately acute malnourished children. Proper training should be given to the supervisors and ICDS workers for proper care and education of the minors. Efforts should be taken to supply food with better quality and variety. More attention should be given to prompt medical care in case of reaction after immunisation, monitoring of children/women for completing immunisation course and follow-up of immunisation. Evaluating the success of the services offered at Anganwadi centres requires ongoing monitoring and assessment of the nutritional status of the children. It aids in determining whether more support is required or progress has been made. Anganwadi centres can modify their offerings to suit the children's evolving requirements based on continuous assessments. For instance, the centre might think about changing the kinds or length of nutrition supplements given if a child's nutritional condition is not getting better. Malnutrition can be avoided in the first place with the help of early intervention and continuous care over time. Malnutrition can be avoided in part by using Anganwadi centres to address nutritional deficiencies and encourage a healthy diet. Children who did not get supplemental food on a daily basis showed more severe stunting (32.1%) compared to those who went regularly and showed moderate stunting (23.9%). Time is a crucial component in analysing and improving the nutritional health of children in Anganwadi centres. A child's nutritional status may be impacted by the length of their involvement in these centres, how frequently they visit, and whether or not they receive nutrition supplements. A child's nutritional well-being can be enhanced and maintained with a steady, long-term support process that necessitates the monitoring, appraisal, and gradual adaptation of services. The impact of these centres is mainly determined by the socioeconomic situation of the families utilising Anganwadi services. A new analysis should look at the relationship between socioeconomic characteristics and the effectiveness of the services offered. To find areas for development, Anganwadi programmes must be continuously monitored and evaluated. A new analysis ought to take into account the procedures for gathering, evaluating, and using data to support choices and programme modifications.

Acknowledgements

The authors are thankful to the Anganwadi workers, children and their parents and caretakers of the children for allowing us to collect data, for the homely atmosphere and their support during data collection. One of the authors (MG) collected data for partial fulfilment of her Ph.D. degree. Financial assistance has been received by MG (UGC Letter No.: 688 (NET-JUNE 2014) dated 12.02.2015).

Reference

Ahmad, D., Afzal, M., & Imtiaz, A. (2020). Effect of socio-economic factors on malnutrition among children in Pakistan. Future Business Journal, 6(1), 30. DOI https://doi.org/10.1186/s43093-020-00032-x

Alim, F., and Jahan, F. (2012). Assessment of Nutritional Status of Rural Anganwadi Children of Aligarh under the ICDS (Integrated Child Development Services) and Rural Health. *Studies on Home and Community Science*, 6(2): 95-98. https://doi.org/10.1080/09737189.2012.11885372

Bhattarai, P., Walvekar, P. R., and Narasannavar, A. (2017). Knowledge of Anganwadi workers regarding different components provided by integrated child development scheme: A cross-sectional study. *Indian Journal of Health Science Biomedical Research*, 10, 241-244. DOI: 10.4103/kleuhsj.kleuhsj_51_17

Chudasama, R. K., Patel, U. V., Thakrar, D., Mitra, A., Oza, J., et al. (2016). Assessment of nutritional activities under integrated child development services at Anganwadi centres of different districts of

Gujarat from April 2012 to March 2015. *International Journal of Health Allied Sciences,* 5:93-8. DOI: 10.4103/2278-344X.180420.

Dakshayani, B., and Gangadhar, M., R. (2015). Nutritional status of Hakkapikki and Iruliga- Tribal children in Mysore District, Karnataka. *Indian Journal of Research Anthropology,* 1(1), 15–24.

Das, S. R., Prakash, J., Krishna, C., Iyengar K., Venkatesh, P., and Rajesh, S., S. (2020). Assessment of Nutritional Status of Children between 6 Months and 6 Years of Age in Anganwadi Centers of an Urban Area in Tumkur, Karnataka, India. *Indian Journal of Community Medicine,* 45(4), 483–486. DOI: 10.4103/ijcm.IJCM_523_19Harikrishna,

B. N., Jothula, K. Y., Nagaraj, K. and Prasad, V. G. (2020). The utilisation of Anganwadi services among preschool-age children in rural Telangana: a cross-sectional study. International Journal of Research and Review. 2020; 7(6): 162-167.

Joseph, J. E. (2014). ICDS scheme to the growth development in preschoolers: A systematic review of the literature. *International Journal of Public Health Science,* 3(2), 87-94. http://doi.org/10.11591/ijphs.v3i2.4679

Khan, Q., H., Arora, G., and Nalli, S. (2018). Nutritional status of 1-5 years children in the urban slum area of Jagdalpur city, Bastar region, Chhattisgarh. *International Journal of Community Medicine and Public Health,* 5(3), 1172-1176. http://dx.doi.org/10.18203/2394-6040.ijcmph20180779

NIPCCD. (2009). Research on ICDS: An Overview (1996-2008) Volume 3. National Institute of Public Cooperation and Child Development. 5, Siri Institutional Area, Hauz Khas, New Delhi – 110016

Sharma, B., Mitra, M., Chakrabarty, S., & Bharati, P. (2006). Nutritional status of preschool children of Raj Gond, a tribal population in Madhya Pradesh, India. *Malaysian Journal of Nutrition,* 12(2), 147–155.

Surwade, J. B., Mantri, S. B., & Wadagale, A. V. (2013). Utilisation of ICDS scheme in urban and rural areas of Latur district with special reference to pediatric beneficiaries. *International Journal of Recent Trends Science and Technology,* 5, pp 107-10.

Thurstan S et al. (2020). Boys are more likely to be undernourished than girls: a systematic review and meta-analysis of sex differences in undernutrition. *BMJ Global Health,* 5: e004030. doi:10.1136/bmjgh-2020-004030.

Sheila, C., Kalita, A., Mondal, S., & Malik, R. (2014). Impact of community-based maintenance programme on undernutrition in rural Chhattisgarh State, India. *Food and Nutrition Bulletin,* 35(1), 83–91. https://doi.org/10.1177/156482651403500110

World Health Organization. (2006). Child growth standards: length/height-for-age, weight-for-age, weight-for-length, weight-for-height and body mass index-for-age: methods and development. World Health Organization, Geneva. 1-312.

World Health Organization (1995). The Use and Interpretation of Anthropometry: Technical Report, Series 854. Geneva. WHO.

World Health Organization (2010). Nutrition Landscape Information System (NLIS) Country Profile Indicators Interpretation Guide, WHO Document Production Services, Geneva, Switzerland 1–38.

Table 1: Age and sex composition of the studied children

Age (Years)	Sex	Frequency	Percentage
2	Boys	75	19.3
	Girls	75	19.1
3	Boys	99	25.5
	Girls	90	23.0
4	Boys	125	32.3
	Girls	113	28.8
5	Boys	89	22.9
	Girls	114	29.1
	Total	780	100.0

Table 2: Descriptive statistics of anthropometric and derived variables among the studied children.

Age (Years)	Sex (N)	Weight (kg)		Height (cm)		BMI (kg/m²)	
		Mean	SD	Mean	SD	Mean	SD
2	Boys (75)	9.57	0.93	81.13	3.86	14.5	1.36
	Girls (75)	9.45	1.25	81.48	5.60	14.4	1.63
	t value	0.022*		-0.427*		0.512*	
3	Boys (99)	10.87	1.13	85.77	4.47	14.76	1.17
	Girls (90)	11.04	1.49	86.89	5.22	14.6	1.47
	t value	0.896*		1.592*		0.794*	
4	Boys (125)	12.98	1.65	94.35	6.23	14.5	1.26
	Girls (113)	12.61	1.65	94.50	5.85	14.1	1.54
	t value	1.743		-0.187		2.429	
5	Boys (89)	14.46	1.967	100.01	6.89	14.47	1.55
	Girls (114)	14.26	1.773	100.10	6.78	14.28	1.80
	t value	0.765		-0.090		0.776	

N= Number of children; Significance At *=P<0.05

Table 3: Age and sex-specific prevalence of height-for-age and their relationship among studied children.

Age (Years)	Sex (N)	Height For-Age						Chi-Square (χ^2)
		Severely Stunted		Moderately Stunted		Normal		
		N	%	N	%	N	%	
2	Boys (75)	11	14.6	31	41.3	34	45.3	2.580
	Girls (75)	09	12.0	22	29.3	43	57.3	

3	Boys (99)	35	35.3	28	28.8	36	36.3	12.352**
	Girls (90)	23	25.5	12	13.3	55	61.1	
4	Boys (125)	31	24.8	32	25.6	62	49.6	4.381**
	Girls (113)	18	15.9	35	30.7	60	53.0	
5	Boys (89)	19	21.3	29	32.3	41	46.0	2.466
	Girls (114)	16	14.0	29	25.4	69	60.5	

Table 4: Age and sex-specific prevalence of weight-for-age and their relationship among studied children

Age (Years)	Sex (N)	Weight-For-Age						Chi-Square (χ^2)
		Severely Underweight		Moderately Underweight		Normal		
		N	%	N	%	N	%	
2	Boys 75)	13	17.3	29	38.6	33	44	2.736
	Girls (75)	8	10.6	26	34.6	41	54.6	
3	Boys 99)	21	21.2	50	50.5	28	28.8	6.185*
	Girls (90)	10	11.1	41	45.5	39	43.3	
4	Boys (125)	15	12.0	31	24.8	79	63.3	0.594
	Girls (113)	19	16.8	32	28.3	66	58.4	
5	Boys (89)	10	11.3	23	25.8	56	62.9	7.892
	Girls (114)	09	7.8	27	23.6	78	67.5	

Table 5: Age and sex-specific prevalence of BMI-for-age and their relationship among studied children

Age (Years)	Sex (N)	BMI-for-age								Chi-Square (χ^2)
		Severely Wasted		Moderately Wasted		Normal		Over Weight		
		N	%	N	%	N	%	N	%	
2	Boys (75)	13	17.3	29	38.6	32	41.3	1	1.3	14.056*
	Girls (75)	10	13.3	27	36.0	33	44.0	5	6.6	
3	Boys (99)	19	21.2	31	31.3	43	43.3	4	4.0	23.328*
	Girls (90)	4	4.4	14	15.5	64	71.1	8	8.8	
4	Boys (125)	12	9.6	14	11.2	92	73.7	7	5.6	10.102*
	Girls (113)	5	4.4	6	5.3	97	85.6	5	4.2	
5	Boys (89)	7	7.8	7	7.8	69	77.5	6	6.7	7.169
	Girls (114)	4	3.5	20	17.5	86	75.6	4	3.5	

N= Number of children; Significance At *=P<0.05, **=P<0.01.

Table 6: Relationship of receiving supplementary food by ICDS children with weight-for-age, height-forge and BMI-for-age among the studied children

Category	Height-For-Age						Chi-Square (χ^2)
	Severe Stunting		Moderate Stunting		Normal		
	N	%	N	%	N	%	
Regularly	100	19.0	170	32.3	255	48.5	17.57*
Occasionally	82	32.1	61	23.9	112	43.9	

Category	Weight-For-Age						Chi-Square (χ^2)
	Severe Underweight		Moderate Underweight		Normal		
	N	%	N	%	N	%	
Regularly	48	9.1	217	41.3	260	49.5	20.98**
Occasionally	53	20.7	97	38.0	105	41.1	

Category	BMI-For Age										Fischer Exact
	Severe Wasting		Moderate Wasting		Normal		Over weight		Obese		
	N	%	N	%	N	%	N	%	N	%	
Regularly	41	7.8	63	12.0	391	74.4	29	5.5	1	0.1	27.903***
Occasionally	42	16.4	50	19.6	152	59.6	10	3.9	1	0.3	

N= Number of children; Significance at *=P<0.05, **=P<0.01, ***=P<0.001

Table 7: Regression Analysis: Impact of Age (Independent Variable) on anthropometric measurements among the studied children

Dependent variable	B	SEB	Beta	t	Sig.	Adjusted R2
Weight(kg)	6.229	0.197	0.747	31.654	0.000	0.557
Height(cm)	67.843	0.739	0.766	91.849	0.000	0.587

Where, refers to regression coefficient. SEB refers to the standard error of B.

Beta refers to the estimated regression coefficient. Sig. Mean levels of significance.

Table 8: Association of socio-demographic predictors for height-for-age by stepwise binary logistic regression

	Variable	B	SE.	Wald	df	Sig.	Exp (B)
Step 7a	Sex	0.539	0.148	13.255	1	0.000	1.714
	Mothers Education	0.171	0.077	4.986	1	0.026	1.187
	Number of siblings	0.267	0.103	6.788	1	0.009	1.306
	Birth order	-0.327	0.093	12.328	1	0.000	0.721
	Breastfed	-0.350	0.189	3.439	1	0.054	0.704
	Constant	-0.789	0.419	3.540	1	0.060	0.454

Table 9: Association of socio-demographic predictors for weight-for-age by stepwise binary logistic regression

	Variables	B	SE.	Wald	df	Sig.	Exp(B)
Step 4[a]	Sex	0.398	0.156	6.528	1	0.011	1.489
	Fathers Education	0.623	0.139	20.200	1	0.000	1.864
	Fathers' occupation	0.739	0.191	14.993	1	0.000	2.094
	Family Income	0.415	0.202	4.230	1	0.040	1.514
	Socio-economic status	-0.276	0.088	9.767	1	0.002	0.759
	Number of siblings	0.432	0.111	15.019	1	0.000	1.540
	Birth order	-0.474	0.101	21.872	1	0.000	0.623
	Breastfed	-1.337	0.216	38.403	1	0.000	0.263
	Constant	-0.957	0.534	3.219	1	0.073	0.384

15

Socio-economic and Reproductive Determinants of Fertility among the Mising Tribe in Dhemaji district of Assam

Dr. Chandika Roy
Milanjyoti Borgohain

Introduction

Fertility is one of the three most important factors affecting a population's growth, structure, and makeup. Healthy women contribute to more educated and productive societies, and assuring women's control over their reproduction contributes to economic growth and prosperity. Fertility rates may be connected to the amount of money spent on maternal health and education for women, which may have a long-term impact on the workforce and productivity (Lal et al., 2021). The welfare and health of an individual, family, society, and nation depend significantly on the size of a family. High fertility rates are a crucial factor in rapid population expansion. On a broader scale, population growth may harm a nation's economic performance since it may put more strain on its already constrained infrastructure and financial resources (Ahinkorah et al., 2021).

High population growth and high fertility may increase maternal and pediatric disorders and mortality. The critical factor in reproductive trends is fertility preference, which is also impacted by several interconnected factors such as age, marital status, income, level of education, and parity. Several factors have been discovered to have significant effects on fertility preferences, including socioeconomic position, education, maternal age, the total number of children ever born, infant mortality, and the views of important individuals (Chandiok et al., 2016; Ahinkorah et al., 2021).

Global data shows that indigenous populations have inferior health and social outcomes than non-Indigenous populations. Tribal people in independent countries are those whose social, cultural, and economic conditions distinguish them from other national communities. Their status is regulated wholly or partly by their customs or traditions or special laws or regulations. The tribes are India's most socioeconomically disadvantaged social group, with low literacy and terrible economic and living conditions (Sridevi et al., 2022).

Marital status is a cultural variable, and cultural ideals influence the age at which couples marry. Marriage, in most communities, signifies the beginning of exposure to conception. Several studies have found that indigenous women are younger when they marry. Marriage at a younger age increases the duration of sexual or reproductive life and, consequently, the likelihood of having more children. In tribal societies, this inverse relationship between female age at marriage and fecundity has been observed (Mahanta, 2016). Maternal health is a crucial factor in the progress of any nation, as it contributes to the development of equality and the alleviation of poverty. The preservation and welfare of mothers are not only crucial in their regard but also pivotal in addressing significant broader economic, social, and developmental issues (Das & Purkayastha, 2023).

Biological, economic, social, and psychological factors influence birth and fertility rates. Economic condition is a crucial factor determining the number of children in a family since raising children is a concern for non-affluent families (Golub et al., 2023). Tribal women and children are particularly susceptible to vulnerability compared to men, as women have encountered numerous interconnected challenges such as early marriage, malnutrition, and limited access to education. Women, particularly those in their reproductive years, are more susceptible to several health issues, such as anaemia, hypertension, malnutrition, and high-risk pregnancies. The reasons for the challenging circumstances in tribal communities include limited access to healthcare facilities, communication barriers, inadequate infrastructure in the healthcare system, and a shortage of educated healthcare workers (Chandana & Kumar, 2020). The Maternal Mortality Ratio is a significant metric for assessing the calibre of healthcare services within a nation. India has achieved significant advancements in decreasing maternal mortality rates during the past twenty years. In 1990, India had a high Maternal Mortality Ratio (MMR) of 600 deaths per hundred thousand live births, resulting in nearly 150,000 women dying every year during childbirth (Das & Purukayastha, 2023).

Since independence, the government has taken steps to improve the impoverished conditions of tribal communities in an effort to end social exclusion and integrate them into mainstream society. However, these development initiatives have resulted in significant failure and have not been able to reach the target populations with the success that is desired thus far (Bharali & Mondal, 2021).

The present study attempts to identify the reproductive and social determinants influencing the fertility pattern among Mising women in the Dhemaji district of Assam.

The rationale of the study:

The reproductive health status of tribal groups in India is much inferior in comparison to the general population (Bharali & Mondal). The health of a woman needs to be addressed because their health is significantly impacted by various socio-demographic factors such as low income, lack of education, early marriages, poor diet, and lack of decision-making skills (Chandana & Kumar, 2020). Fertility is the primary determinant in demographic research. It denotes the total number of births per one thousand women annually between the age range of 15 to 44 years who are of childbearing age. Fertility refers to the exact count of children born to women (Das & Purukayastha, 2023). Many researchers have established a correlation between increased fertility rates and the reduction of poverty, migration, bad living conditions, communication, infrastructure, and a hierarchical social structure (Mazumder & Mukherjee, 2018).

Since attaining independence, the government has undertaken numerous endeavours to ameliorate the impoverished circumstances of tribal communities so as to eradicate social exclusion and facilitate their integration into mainstream society. However, these development projects have been a disappointing failure and have thus far not succeeded in achieving the intended outcomes among the target populations (Bharali & Mondal). This study is an attempt to study the relationship between socio-economic conditions and fertility behaviour among the Mishing people and also to find out the fertility determinants and reproductive profile of the same.

Objectives

a) To study the relation of socio-economic condition on fertility behaviour of the Mising people

b) To study the fertility determinants and reproductive profile of Mising women.

Material And Methods

Study area and study population

The area selected for the present study is the Dhemaji district of Assam. This district was chosen for the study because of the availability of an adequate number of subjects and the cooperation extended by the community. It also helps ease accessibility to the study area. The district has a total population of 686133 lakh, made up of 351249 lakh men and 334884 lakh women, according to the 2011 census. There are 176 people per square kilometre, and about 66% of people are literate (Assam portal). Dhemaji and Jonai are the two sub-divisions of the district, which is composed of the following five blocks: Dhemaji, Sissiborgaon, Morkongselek tribal development block, Bordoloni, and Machkhowa. The district comprises 1150 revenue villages (Assam portal).

The study was conducted among the Mising population in Dhemaji District, Assam. The population selected for the present study is evenly distributed throughout the District. A few villages have been selected from two blocks, namely Dhemaji and Bordoloni blocks, for this study. These villages are selected due to the concentration of the Mishing population and accessible communication. Table 1 shows the names of the villages selected for the study and the number of households from the respective villages.

Table 1: Name of the village and number of households

Sl. No.	Name of the village	Name of the Development Blocks	No. of households
1	Mainapara Mising Gaon	Dhemaji	57
2	Malbhug Mising Gaon	Bordoloni	42
3	Rajakhana Mising Gaon	Bordoloni	60
4	Siga Mising Gaon	Bordoloni	52
5	Murkhongselek Mising Gaon	Bordoloni	60
6	Laipulia Mising Gaon	Dhemaji	80
	TOTAL	-	351

For the present study, six villages were selected based on PPS Sampling (Probability Proportional to Population Size). An effort has been made to find a way to obtain the required information from the respondents of different villages with populations made up of numerous clusters of communities that vary in size.

Among these villages, 351 households were randomly selected for the study. It was ensured that only one married woman (in the age group 15-49 years of age) was considered from each household. Thus, 347 married women of reproductive age (15 to 49) constitute the sample for the present study.

About the Mising tribe

The Misings are the second largest officially recognised tribe in Assam. Misings people predominantly reside in the Brahmaputra valley districts. Because they mainly reside in river valley locations, their villages relatively lack health care and education facilities (Mahanta, 2016). Tribal communities have low levels of literacy, an inferior economic status, and deeply rooted traditional healthcare ideas. The Mising community faces economic backwardness due to the absence of permanent cultivable land and infrastructure amenities, which serve as the root cause of the problem (Roy, 2023). The Mising community has a poor literacy rate, with illiteracy being more common among women. In the social hierarchy,

Mising women are in a far lower position than men. Tribal women have to overcome numerous obstacles, such as early marriage, starvation, and ill health. During pregnancy, they experience anaemia, hypertension, and other dangers in their reproductive lives (Roy, 2023).

Data collection

Data collection was carried out for qualitative and quantitative data to the objectives of the present study. The data for the present study were collected using two structured schedules.

The first schedule, the census schedule, was designed to collect information on the type of family, educational status, occupation, and educational and occupational status of their husbands. The second schedule was prepared to obtain information on fertility, mortality, family planning, an exact number of live births, living children, fetal wastage, stillbirth, age at death, type of delivery, place of delivery, duration of breastfeeding, postpartum sterility period, age at menarche, age at marriage, first conception and age at menopause were collected through this schedule. The data were collected mainly through open-ended interviews.

Secondary data are those that have already been collected by someone else and have already been passed through the statistical process. Secondary data may either be published or unpublished. Both primary and secondary data are used for the present study.

Findings And Discussion

General Characteristics of The Participants

Socio-demographic characteristics such as the present age of the participants, type of family, education qualification, occupational status, marital status, spouse's age, spouse's occupation, monthly income of the family and others have been recorded, consolidated and presented in the tables.

Table: 2 Distributions of participants by type of family

Type of family	No.	%
Nuclear family	243	70.03
Joint family	104	29.97
Total	347	100

Table 2 shows that most participants live in a nuclear family (70.03 percent).

Educational status

Education significantly impacts fertility rates, especially in tribal societies (Mahanta, 2016). The impact of women's education on fertility has been attributed to several factors, including more decision-making autonomy, increased understanding of reproduction and contraception, and higher earning capacity (Bongaarts& Hodgson, 2022).

Table 3 Educational Status of the Women Respondents:

Educational status	**No.**	**%**
No formal education	120	34.58
Primary	82	23.63
Middle	58	16.71
High School	41	11.82
Higher Secondary School	26	7.49
Graduation	12	3.46
Post-graduation	08	2.31
Total	347	100.00

Table 3 presents the educational status of the participants. It shows that the Majority (34.58 percent) do not have any formal education.

Educational status of their husbands

Table: 4 Distributions of participants by the educational status of their husbands

Educational status of husbands	No.	%
No formal education	96	27.67
Primary	72	20.75
Middle	66	19.02
High School	50	14.41
Higher Secondary	32	9.22
Graduate	20	5.76
Postgraduate	06	1.73
Professional	05	1.44
Total	347	100.00

Table 4 presents the participants' husbands' educational status. The majority (27.67 percent) of the men did not have formal education.

Occupational Status

Table 5 Distributions of Participants on Occupational Status

Occupation	No.	%
Cultivation	145	41.79
Govt. Jobs	12	3.46
Private jobs	18	5.19
Housewives	138	39.76
Daily wagers	10	2.88
Self-employed	24	6.92
Total	347	100

Table 5 shows the occupation status of the participants. The table shows that the majority (41.79 percent) of women are engaged in agricultural work. However, most participants are housewives (39.76 percent), followed by self-employed women.

Occupational Status of Husbands

Table: 6 Distributions of participants on occupational status of the husbands

Occupation	No.	%
Agriculture	202	58.21
Govt. Job	48	13.83
Private job	31	8.93
Petty Businessmen	38	10.95
Daily wagers	24	6.92
Contractor	04	1.15
Total	347	100.00

Table 6 presents the occupation status of the husbands of the Mising women who participated in the study. The majority (58.21 percent) are involved in agricultural work, followed by government jobs (13.83 percent) and petty business (10.95 percent).

Fertility determinants:

The present age and live births

Table 7: Distribution of live births according to age group

The present age of women (in years)	No.	Live births		
		No.	%	Mean
15-19	18	16	1.26	1.00
20-24	66	120	9.47	2.00
25-29	73	246	19.42	2.96
30-34	62	252	19.90	4.06
35-39	61	218	17.20	4.04
40-44	43	242	19.10	5.76
45-49	24	173	13.65	5.24
Total	347	1267	100	3.62

Table 7 shows the present age-wise distribution of Mising women concerning the number of live births. Average fertility was found to be increasing with the present age of women. The mean number of live births was slightly higher for the age group 40-44 years in the present study population.

Age at Menarche

The age at which a woman reaches menarche is an essential factor determining her reproductive status because the childbearing period begins only after menarche. Numerous factors, including genetic factors, socioeconomic conditions, general health and lifestyle, nutritional status, seasonality, physical activity, and altitude levels, influence the age of onset of menarche (Chandiok et al., 2016).

Table 8 Distribution of participants on age at menarche

Age at menarche	No.	%
12	13	3.75
13	44	12.68
14	72	20.75
15	111	31.99
16	80	23.05
17	21	6.05
18	06	1.73
Total	347	100
Mean ± SD	14.85 ± .99	

Table 8 shows the distribution of Mising women according to age at menarche. The mean age at menarche is 14.85 ± .99 years.

Age at marriage

Table 9 Distribution of participants according to age at marriage

Age at marriage	No.	%
>9 or ≤ 12	08	2.31
>12 or ≤ 15	46	13.26
>15 or ≤ 18	176	50.72
>18 or ≤ 21	78	22.48
>21 or ≤ 24	35	10.09
>24	04	1.15
Total	347	100
Mean ± SD	19.50 ± 2.48	

The above table (9) shows the distribution of Mising women according to age at marriage. The mean age at marriage is 19.50 ± 2.48 years.

Age at first conception

Table 10: Distribution of participants on age at first conception

Women's age at first pregnancy (years)	No.	%
≤ 15	11	3.17
>15 or ≤ 18	121	34.87
>18 or ≤ 21	143	41.21
>21 or ≤ 24	50	14.40
>24	22	6.34
Total	347	100
Mean ± SD	20.39 ± 2.41	

The above table (10) shows the distribution of Mising women according to age at first pregnancy. The mean age at first conception is 20.39 ± 2.41 years.

Conceptions and Live-births

Table 11 Distribution of participants on no. of conception and live births

No. of Pregnancies	No.	%	No. of live births	No.	%
1 – 2	76	21.90	1 -2	101	29.11
3 – 4	131	37.75	3 – 4	133	38.33
5 – 6	102	29.39	5 – 6	81	23.34
>6	38	10.95	>6	32	9.22
Total	347	100.00	Total	347	100.00
Mean ± SD	3.47 ± 1.61		Mean ± SD	3.30± 1.40	

Table 11 shows the distribution of Mising women according to the number of conceptions and live births. In the present study, the mean number of pregnancies and live births is 3.47 ± 1.61 and 3.30± 1.40, respectively.

Abortions and Stillbirths:

Table 12 Distribution of participants on several abortions and stillbirths

No. of spontaneous abortions	No.	%	No. of Induced Abortions	No.	%	No. of Stillbirths	No.	%
1	41	65.08	1	21	100	1	36	66.67
2	14	22.22	T*, T**	21 (347)	100	2	11	20.37
3	08	12.70	Percentage*	6.05 %		3	07	12.96
T*, T**	63 (347)	100				T*, T**	54 (347)	100
Percentage*	18.16%					Percentage*	15.56%	

T* = Total number of women who had abortions

T** = Total number of women

Percentage* = percentage of women who had abortions

Table 12 shows the distribution of Mising women according to no. of abortions and stillbirths. It is clear from the table that 18.16 percent, 6.05 percent, and 15.56 percent had spontaneous abortions, induced abortions and stillbirths, respectively.

Duration of breastfeeding

Breastfeeding practices are essential for child survival and maternal health and have been found to affect fertility significantly. Breast milk provides essential nutrients and protects the child against infections, thus reducing morbidity and mortality. The World Health Organization (WHO) has recommended that infants be given only breast milk up to four to six months of age.

Table 13 Distribution of participants on the duration of breastfeeding

Duration of breastfeeding in months	No.	%
≤ 6	-	-
>6 or ≤ 12	29	29.59
>12 or ≤ 18	44	44.89
>18 or ≤ 24	25	25.51
>24	-	-
Total	98	100.00
Mean ± SD	16.45 ± 5.08	

Table 13 shows the distribution of Mising women according to the duration of breastfeeding. The mean duration of breastfeeding is found to be 16.45 ± 5.08 among the Mising women.

Child Survival and Infant Mortality:

Table: 14 Distribution of participants on no. of children surviving and no. of infants' death

No. of children surviving	No.	%	No. of infant death	No.	%
1 – 2	133	38.33	1	52	63.41
3 – 4	100	28.82	2	16	19.51
5 – 6	59	17.00	3	05	6.10
>6	55	15.85	4	05	6.10
Total	347	100.00	5	03	3.66
Mean ± SD	2.81 ± 1.48		T*, T**	82 (347)	100.00
			Percentage		23.63%

Table 14 shows the distribution of participants' concern in the number of children surviving and no. of infant deaths. The mean number of children surviving is 2.81 ± 1.48 in the present study. At the same time, 23.63 percent of the women have infant deaths.

Age at menopause

Table 15: Distribution of participants on age at menopause

Age at menopause	No. of women	%
40	-	-
41		-
42	-	-
43	-	-
44	4	19.0
45	8	38.1
46	6	28.6
47	3	14.3
48	-	-
49	-	-
Total	21	100.00
Mean ± SD	45.38 ± .97	

Table 15 shows the distribution of Mising women's age at menopause. The mean age at menopause is 45.38 ± .97 years. The table clearly shows that only a few (21) women attained menopause during the study; others are in their peri-menopause or pre-menopause stage.

Family planning

The present study found that most (91.93 percent) participants adopted family planning methods. Of all the methods, oral contraceptive pills (OCP) are commonly used by the participants in the present study. Other preferred methods are sterilisation, condoms, and others. The educated people have better knowledge of family planning and have favourable attitudes towards it, which results in higher adoption of contraceptives (Sharma, 2016).

Conclusion

This study concludes that most participants live in a nuclear family and do not possess any formal education. They are mainly housewives; others are self-employed, such as petty business. Besides, their husbands mainly engage in agricultural work because they do not have formal education. Regarding the fertility of the Mising women, it is found that average fertility is directly proportionate with the present age of the women. Determinants of fertility such as menarche, marriage, and conception show that most women attained menarche at 14-16 years, marriage at 15-18 years and first conception at 18-21 years. In the present study, the mean number of pregnancies and live births is 3.47 ± 1.61 and 3.30 ± 1.40, respectively. The mean breastfeeding duration is 16.45 ± 5.08 among the Mising women in the present study. The mean age at menopause is $45.38 \pm .97$ years among the menopausal women in the present study. Oral contraceptive pills (OCP) are more commonly used by the participants in the present study than other methods.

Acknowledgement

The authors thank all the participants for participating in the study and sharing their valuable information.

Authors' contribution

Both MB and CR conceptualised and designed the study. MB collected the data and completed the data entry, coding, analysis and interpretation. CR participated in writing the first draft of the manuscript. Both MB and CR critically revised the manuscript for final approval for submission.

References

Ahinkorah, B. O., Seidu, A., Armah-Ansah, E. K., Ameyaw, E. K., Budu, E., & Yaya, S. (2021). Socio-economic and demographic factors associated with fertility preferences among women of reproductive age in Ghana: evidence from the 2014 Demographic and Health Survey. *Reproductive Health, 18*(1). https://doi.org/10.1186/s12978-020-01057-9

Bongaarts, J., & Hodgson, D. (2022). Socio-Economic Determinants of Fertility. In *Springer eBooks* (pp. 51–62). https://doi.org/10.1007/978-3-031-11840-1_4

Chandiok, K., Mondal, P. C., Mahajan, C., &Saraswathy, K. N. (2016). Biological and Social Determinants of Fertility Behaviour among the *Jat* Women of Haryana State, India. *Advances in Library and Information Science (Online)*, *2016*, 1–6. https://doi.org/10.1155/2016/5463168

Golub, R., Ivkov-Dzigurski, A., &Simeunović, V. (2023). Determinants of Fertility Intentions of the Women in Bosnia and Herzegovina-An Example from the Semberija Region. *Behavioral Sciences*, *13*(5), 417. https://doi.org/10.3390/bs13050417

Lal, S., Singh, R., Makun, K., Chand, N., & Khan, M. S. (2021). Socio-economic and demographic determinants of fertility in six selected Pacific Island Countries: An empirical study. *PLOS ONE*, *16*(9), e0257570. https://doi.org/10.1371/journal.pone.0257570

Mahanta, A. (2016). Impact of Education on Fertility: Evidence from a Tribal Society in Assam, India. *International Journal of Population Research*, 2016, pp. 1–7. https://doi.org/10.1155/2016/3153685

Sreedevi, A., Vijayakumar, K., Najeeb, S. S., Menon, V., Mathew, M., Aravindan, L., Anwar, R., Sathish, S., Nedungadi, P., Wiwanitkit, V., & Raman, R. (2022). The pattern of contraceptive use, determinants and fertility intentions among tribal women in Kerala, India: a cross-sectional study. *BMJ Open*, *12*(4), e055325. https://doi.org/10.1136/bmjopen-2021-055325

Bharali N, Mondal N. Association of Age at Marriage, Early Childbearing, Use of Contraceptive Methods and Reproductive Health Consequences Among Mishing Tribal Women of Assam, Northeast India. *Online J Health Allied Scs*. 2021;20(3):2

Chandana KR, Kumar R. Health status of tribal women of Bhadradri Kothagudem district in Telangana state. Int J Health Sci Res. 2020; 10(1):53–62.

Roy, C. A comparative study on post-menopausal health among the Bengali and the Mishing women of Lakhimpur district, Assam. 2023, https://dhemaji.gov.in/portlets/dhemaji-at-a-glance

16

Differentials In Hypertension and Anaemia Burden Between the Workers in Abandoned and Operational Tea Plantations: An Anthropological Study in Alipurduar, West Bengal

Akash Mallick
Subrata K. Roy

Introduction

Background of the Study

In exchange for goods or services, income plays a significant role in the health and well-being of humans and is directly or indirectly related to human survival. It helps to achieve fundamental needs (food, clothing, and shelter) and can also be utilised for other essentials, such as education, health care, and others (Souma, 2002). Therefore, in times of financial hardship or loss of income, it is not easy to maintain financial stability and become physically and mentally healthy (Fryer & Fagan, 1993). Therefore, in the life of a working individual, the unexpected loss of income due to unexpected job loss, not due to their fault, is considered one of the most detrimental events (Bentolila & Ichino, 2002) because they experience lower economic output and poor lifestyles. Individuals from a poor socio-economic background become worst affected due to unemployment as they additionally experience economic insecurity, family conflicts, and deteriorating health conditions (Clark & Oswald, 2002; Frey & Stutzer, 2002). Over time, people without employment (in terms of job loss) face income volatility, adopt unhealthy lifestyles, including habits of smoking and alcohol drinking (Falba *et al.*, 2005; Arcaya *et al.*, 2014), exhibit food insecurity and compromise with dietary intake (Lee *et al.*, 2001; Mohammad et al., 2006; Kendzor *et al.*, 2012), develop various physical health problems such as undernutrition, hypertension, anaemia and hyperlipidaemia (Gallo *et al.*, 2004; Strully, 2009; Strandh *et al.*, 2014), and eventually death (Gerdtham & Johannesson, 2003; Voss *et al.*, 2004). Therefore, job loss significantly disrupts the socio-economic well-being of individuals and creates social burdens by affecting the labour force, and above all, compromises public health (Gregg *et al.*, 2004; Martikainen *et al.*, 2007; Adsera, 2011; Del Bono *et al.*, 2012).

The present chapter emphasises a similar situation related to the tea plantations of Northern West Bengal, mainly covering the area of the Dooars tea region of the Alipurduar district. Over the decades, the Dooars tea industry of West Bengal has produced and exported quality tea from the country and all over the world (Asopa, 2007; Kumar *et al.*, 2008; Arya, 2013). Many indigenous and marginalised labourers, skilled and unskilled, found employment in the Dooars tea gardens (Roy *et al.*, 2005; Borgohain, 2013). The tea plantation labourers of the Dooars tea region largely depend upon the sustainability and productivity of the tea gardens. In contrast, the Dooars tea region also remains vibrant due to the activity of the thousands of tea garden labourers (Kumar *et al.*, 2008). The issue of mass involuntary unemployment among the tea labourers of the Dooars tea region of West Bengal was, therefore, unanticipated. In the past decade, the authorities have abandoned many tea gardens without prior notice to the labourers and without providing sufficient reasons (Asopa, 2007; Dutraj, 2014). As a result, production stopped, and many tea garden labourers lost their jobs and their primary source of income. The issue has given complete uncertainty to thousands of labourers and their families, who are at stake in their survival. The present unemployment issue at the Dooars tea gardens has primarily affected the way of living of the tea garden labourers (Biswas *et al.*, 2005; Rudra, 2018; Roy & Biswas, 2018).

Review of Literature

Some literature indicates that individuals with job loss primarily exhibited increased smoking habits and consumed alcohol more frequently (De Vogli & Santinello, 2005; Kendzor *et al.*, 2012; Schunck & Rogge, 2012). In similar studies, increased smoking and alcohol consumption were observed in older unemployed individuals (Griffin *et al.*, 2003), especially among unemployed males (Ahmad *et al.*, 2005; Moore *et al.*, 2005). It is quite understandable that if a job loss or persisting unemployment affects the consumption of alcohol and smoking, it may indirectly affect the blood pressure level of the concerned people. Moreover, it has also been observed that unemployment plays a decisive role in determining the pattern and intensity of dietary intake and physical activity among individuals, regardless of other determinants (Morikawa *et al.*, 2008; Chakrabarty & Bharati, 2010; Balieiro *et al.*, 2014; Roudsari *et al.*, 2017). Among the unemployed individuals, total expenditure on food was also significantly low, the pattern and intensity of diet were compromised, and the nutritional quality of food decreased alarmingly, followed by skipping meals (Letsie, 2009; Antelo *et al.*, 2017). Several studies reassuringly found that unemployed individuals were less physically active, especially in work-time and leisure-time activity, compared to employed individuals, which is intuitively understandable (Mohammad et al., 2006; Pharr *et al.*, 2012; Xu, 2013; Gough, 2017; Colman & Dave, 2018). It is certain that with low physical activity and low food intake, there is a greater possibility among unemployed persons to develop high blood pressure and high anaemia.

The rapidly growing burden of hypertension in association with malnutrition has provided researchers with an opportunity to explore the health traits at a more extensive spectrum (Anstey & Christensen, 2000; Horwich *et al.*, 2002; Datta Banik, 2007), especially in low and middle-income countries (Kalaivani, 2009). Several studies have found a significant relationship between unemployment and blood pressure (Kasl & Cobb, 1970; Janlert *et al.*, 1992). In support, several studies showed that unemployed individuals exhibited a comparatively higher level of blood pressure compared to employed individuals (Janlert, 1997; Weber & Lehnert, 1997), and the prevalence of hypertension was significantly higher among the unemployed individuals (Brackbill *et al.*, 1995; Koziel *et al.*, 2010; Zagodzon *et al.*, 2014). Haemoglobin level is also considered an important marker of health and nutritional status. Several internal and environmental factors regulate it, yet it is not found to show any direct association with job loss. Studies showed a strong but indirect association between unemployment and low haemoglobin levels among jobless individuals (Luo *et al.*, 2011; Sia *et al.*, 2019) and observed a greater prevalence of anaemia among jobless individuals compared to employed individuals (Morrone *et al.*, 2010; Agulia *et al.*, 2018). However, findings on haemoglobin levels and unemployment are scarce.

Rationale of the Study

The review does not claim to be exhaustive. However, it indicates the significance of exploring the present issue of a double burden of hypertension and anaemia among the labourers of abandoned tea plantations of the Dooars region in the context of job loss. In light of the review, it may be hypothesised that the labourers are perhaps at a greater risk of suffering from livelihood issues and may develop adverse health conditions like high blood pressure (hypertension) and low haemoglobin level (anaemia) after losing their jobs due to financial hardship and food insecurity. There is hardly any study that addresses the issue from an anthropological point of view or a public health perspective.

Objectives of the Study

The present study primarily aimed to assess the effects of unemployment/job loss on the physical health condition in terms of blood pressure and haemoglobin level of the tea plantation labourers of an abandoned tea garden in Dooars. The study compared the aspects mentioned above between one abandoned and one operating tea plantation with the assumption that the situations would be different between labourers of these two tea plantations. In this view, the objectives of the study were:

i. To find out the differences in physical health status between the labourers of abandoned and operating tea plantations in terms of Blood pressure and Haemoglobin level,

ii. To find out the prevalence of hypertension and anaemia in these two plantations and,

iii.   To find out the potential factors behind hypertension and anaemia.

Materials and Methods

Study Population

The present study was restricted to a single ethnic group, the Oraons. The highest number of Oraons are found in Jharkhand state of India, followed by Chhattisgarh state and West Bengal (Census of India, 2011). In West Bengal, Oraons are the second-largest scheduled tribe population after the Santals and have scattered colonies in several districts with a total population of 6, 43,510 including 322,933 males and 320,577 females. In West Bengal, the highest concentration of Oraons is found in the Jalpaiguri district (including the present Alipurduar district) with a total population of 3, 68,413 including 183,985 males and 184,423 females (West Bengal District Gazetteers, 1981). Historically, the Oraons belonged to the Dravidian linguistic group of southern India. They have their native language, the 'Kurukh', but currently speak in the 'Sadri', a fusion of Bengali, Hindi, and Nepali languages. Hand-made bread (Chapati) is one of the preferred staple foods, along with rice and pulses. They prefer animal-sourced foods and especially have a passion for eating pork. In almost every Oraon household, a homemade liquor, known as 'Handia', is brewed by fermenting rice into a bowl or pitcher. The study was restricted to the Oraon population only to eliminate possible ethnic/genetic effects on the health traits.

Study Area

The present study was conducted in two separate tea gardens of the Dooars foothill region of Alipurduar district, West Bengal, namely, Birpara tea garden, under Madarihat-Birpara block and Tasati tea garden, under Falakata block. The tea gardens are adjacent and situated within 15 km. from the nearest railway station, Dalgaon. The first plantation was abandoned, and the second was fully operating. The Dooars area was chosen purposively per the present study's objective. In the recent decade, many, but not all, tea gardens in the Dooars area were declared Abandoned without any prior notice by the tea garden authorities. Hence, the area was an ideal mixture of both the experimental (abandoned tea garden) and control (operating tea garden) groups to fulfil the objectives of comparing health traits between the two groups (who are occupied in the tea garden and who have lost their jobs from tea garden).

Data Collection

The fieldwork was conducted in abandoned and operating tea gardens from November 2018 to December 2018. The data were collected by visiting each home. The individual health traits of study participants were obtained by meeting with them individually. The purpose of the study was explained to every participant, and written consent was obtained before any data was collected. The informed consent was either signed by them or thumb impressions were taken (especially for women who could not read or write). The study was approved by the Indian Statistical Institute's Ethics Committee for Protection of Research Risks to Humans (Ethical clearance number: ISI-IEC/2018/10/01).

Data Types

A total enumeration of all the households in the selected gardens was attempted to generate demographic data, except for very few households because of their absence during the survey. The data included parameters like age, sex, marital status, place of birth, and clan of all household members. Data were collected from the household head with a pre-tested household survey schedule (Mozumdar *et al.*, 2014). In the absence of a household head, the information was obtained from some elderly individuals. The age of the individuals was cross-checked and verified by other household members along with the reference of the voter's list or some local or national events since many of the individuals lacked birth records.

Socio-economic data were collected from the household head of the family (in most cases) using a pre-tested schedule. The data included economic condition regarding monthly household expenditure on food, dress, house type and toilet facilities, drinking water and cooking fuel source, and educational and occupational status.

Both systolic blood pressure (SBP) and diastolic blood pressure (DBP) were measured using standard instruments, and data were collected by a single investigator following a standard protocol (Pickering *et al.*, 2005).

Individuals were measured after resting for 15 minutes in a sitting position on the left upper arm by an auscultatory method using an inflatable cuff, a mercury sphygmomanometer and a stethoscope. The Korotkoff phase II (appearance) and phase V (disappearance) were recorded for SBP and DBP, respectively. Two subsequent measurements within 10-minute intervals were obtained, and the average value of the two measurements was used for the analysis. The participants were advised to avoid using any substance (smoking, alcohol intake) for at least 1 hour before the measurement.

The study participants' Haemoglobin (Hb) levels were assessed with a portable HemoCue® Hb201 instrument. The instrument followed a modified azide methemoglobin reaction method to assess Hb levels (Von Schenck et al., 1986). The blood sample was collected by finger pricking with a sterilised lancet, and the first drop of blood was discarded. Subsequent blood drops were filled into the micro-cuvette and placed into the portable HemoCue, which provided the study participants' Hb level (g/dl).

Data Classification

All the data were presented separately for abandoned and operating tea garden labourers. Data on health traits were classified following standard cut-off values, as shown in Table 1.

Data Analysis

In the present study, demographic and socio-economic data were both continuous (age, monthly per capita expenditure) and categorical (sex, marital status, educational status, house type, toilet facility in the household). Blood pressure and haemoglobin level measurements were continuous data as well. Several variables were converted into different categorical variables for convenience in data analysis. Descriptive statistics like mean ($\bar{X}$) and standard deviation (SD) are calculated for continuous data. A chi-square test was performed to understand the association between traits for non-parametric data presented as categorical variables. A comparison was made using t-statistics (Student's t-test) for parametric data to find out the mean differences between study groups. Binary logistic regression analysis was performed to understand the association between health traits and their different concomitants. The stepwise backward method in logistic regression was preferred as the analysis removed the least useful predictors, one at a time, until only the significant predictors remained. All the statistical analyses were carried out using PASW 18.0.

Findings

Table 2 shows the socio-demographic characteristics of the study participants. A total of 234 individuals participated in the abandoned tea plantation, among which 48.29% were males and 51.71% were females. From the operating tea plantation, 214 individuals participated, 106 of whom were males and 108 females. The mean age of participants in the abandoned tea garden (40.88±12.99) was higher than the Operating tea garden (39.37±14.89). A considerable number of households in both the abandoned tea garden (22.22%) and Operating tea garden (18.22%) had no sanitation facility in the households. In the abandoned tea gardens, 73% of the households used dry leaves and wood as cooking fuel. The proportion was significantly lower in the Operating tea garden (67.76%). Around 32% of the individuals in the abandoned tea garden were non-literate compared to 39% in the Operating tea garden.

Table 3 shows descriptive statistics of SBP and DBP of both Abandoned and Operating tea garden labourers of either sex. Among males, mean age values were similar between the study groups. The mean values of SBP and DBP between the study groups did not differ significantly and were within the normal range. Among females, mean age values were similar between the study groups. The mean values of SBP and DBP between the study groups did not differ significantly.

Table 4 shows the prevalence of hypertension level (The hypertension level of the study participants was determined based on JNC-VIII classification of blood pressure level) of the Abandoned and Operating tea garden labourers in either sex. Among males, 26.21% of Abandoned and 23.58% of Operating tea garden labourers were hypertensive, while a higher percentage (47.17%) of Operating tea garden labourers were pre-hypertensive than the Abandoned tea garden labourers (33.98%). Among females, 31.40% and 30.58% were pre-hypertensive and hypertensive in Abandoned tea gardens. In comparison, only 19.45% and 24.07% were hypertensive in the Operating tea garden, respectively. Comparing females of Abandoned tea gardens with Operating tea gardens showed a significant difference in hypertension.

Table 5 shows the descriptive statistics of Hb level in Abandoned and Operating tea garden labourers of either sex. In males, the mean Hb level between the study groups did not differ significantly. In females, the mean Hb values in both the study groups and in either sex were below the normal level. The anaemia status of the study participants was determined based on the WHO (2011) classification of haemoglobin level.

Table 6 shows the prevalence of anaemia in the labourers of both Abandoned and Operating tea gardens in either sex. In males, most of the labourers in Abandoned tea garden (71.68%) and Operating tea garden (68.93%) were anaemic. Also, among females, most of the labourers in abandoned tea gardens (88.70%) and operating tea gardens (81.31%) were anaemic. There was no significant difference in the anaemia category for either sex when comparing the labourers of the abandoned tea garden with the operating tea garden.

Table 7 shows the relationship between the selected health status (in terms of hypertensive and anaemic status) of the Oraon labourers and selected socio-economic variables. The result of binary logistic regression shows that the selected health status (in terms of hypertension and anaemic status) was significantly determined by several factors.

Regarding the model of hypertension, the Odds ratios (OR) explain that individuals tend to become hypertensive with the advancement of age. Also, females were less likely to be hypertensive compared to males. Compared to individuals with higher secondary educational attainment, non-literate individuals were more likely to be hypertensive. It further explains that higher educational attainment will make individuals less vulnerable to hypertension. Regarding the model of anaemia, the Odds ratio (OR) explains that with the advancement of age, individuals tend to become anaemic. All other groups were more likely anaemic than individuals with higher secondary educational attainment. It further explains that individuals with higher educational attainment will be less susceptible to anaemia.

Discussion

The present study was conducted in the tea gardens of the Dooars region of Alipurduar district, West Bengal, given the mass unemployment issue in the area due to rapid tea garden closures. In recent decades, many tea gardens were declared abandoned without prior notice, and consequently, a large number of tea garden labourers lost their jobs (unemployed) and their earnings were stopped. However, the unemployment issue of the tea garden labourers has not been adequately addressed. It was assumed that the Abandoned tea garden labourers would show poor economic and health conditions compared to Operating tea garden labourers.

Based on the study objectives, the present cross-sectional study was conducted in two tea gardens in the Alipurduar district. Birpara (an Abandoned tea garden) and Tasati (an Operating tea garden) are nearby. The study was restricted to a single ethnic group, the Oraons (homogenous tribal community), to eliminate genetic/ethnic effects (if any) on data. Before the study, institutional ethical approval and written consent from participants was obtained. It was assumed that health conditions would differ between Abandoned and Operating tea garden labourers. Therefore, comparisons were planned between the study groups (Abandoned vs. Operating).

Here, we will briefly recapitulate the salient findings following the study's objectives and interpret them with the existing body of literature. A set of acronyms and symbols are used in this section, which needs explanation, e.g., Abandoned tea garden (ATG) and Operating tea garden (OTG) and for the study participants, males ($\male$) and females ($\female$).

The labourers of ATG showed mean values of SBP ($\male$ - 122.35 mmHg and $\female$ - 125.55 mmHg) and DBP ($\male$ - 80.05 mmHg and $\female$ - 78.93 mmHg) comparatively similar to OTG, the mean values of SBP ($\male$ - 126.28 mmHg and $\female$ - 119.66 mmHg) and DBP ($\male$ - 80.13 mmHg and $\female$ - 76.69 mmHg) (Table 4.3.1). The prevalence of hypertension (HYP) in males of both the study groups was more or less similar (ATG - 26.21% vs. OTG - 23.58%). In females, a comparatively higher percentage of ATG females were found hypertensive (ATG - 31.40% vs OTG - 19.45%) (Table 4.3.2).

The male labourers of ATG showed similar mean haemoglobin levels (12.10 g/dl) to those of OTG (12.06 g/dl). In females, the mean haemoglobin value of ATG labourers (10.33 g/dl) showed a statistically significant difference from the mean haemoglobin value of OTG labourers (10.78 g/dl). The prevalence of anaemia in the males (ATG – 71.68% and OTG – 68.93%) and of the females (ATG – 88.70% and OTG – 81.31%) of both the study groups were similar.

Some socio-demographic factors significantly predicted the health parameters (blood pressure and haemoglobin level). The findings showed that a tea garden labourer would likely be hypertensive with age increment. The males, non-literate individuals, and individuals with W/D/S status were also more likely to be hypertensive than their counterparts. Also, the significant predictors of anaemia (low haemoglobin level) were only age and educational status. It showed that increased age increases the likelihood of anaemic tea garden labourers. Also, tea garden labourers with lower educational status had a significantly higher chance of being anaemic.

The present study assumed that ATG labourers would have significantly higher blood pressure than OTG labourers. Contrary to this, the ATG and OTG labourers showed 'normal' systolic and diastolic blood pressure levels, irrespective of sex. However, Meneton et al. (2014) and Soliman and colleagues (2017) observed conflicting results where they found elevated blood pressure levels among unemployed individuals due to significantly low physical activity. In support of the findings, the study groups showed similarity because of similar food consumption levels and physical activity (rigorous). The prevalence of hypertension in both study groups was similar, a notable finding that only validates the work of Agyemang (2006).

On the other hand, several studies have found that hypertension was more prevalent in the unemployed group (Nygren *et al.*, 2015; Adeniyi *et al.*, 2016; Zhao *et al.*, 2018). It is to be noted that the prevalence rate in both groups included older individuals in the populations who generally are less physically active and exhibit elevated blood pressure. Also, in the present study, age played a significant role in determining hypertension, along with sex and educational status. These findings were in line with the findings of Zhao *et al.* (2018) on education with Soliman *et al.* (2017) on sex but not with Nygren *et al.* (2015) and Man *et al.* (2019).

Even though the haemoglobin levels of both the ATG and OTG labourers were found to be entirely below the WHO-recommended cut-off value, they showed similarities. In the present study, almost all participants, irrespective of sex and employment status, were anaemic. The prevalence rate exceeded the latest national rate of anaemia (NFHS-4). The decreased haemoglobin levels among the tea labourers were possibly due to nutritional deficiency (Chowdhury & Roy, 2019), especially among the females who consumed low amounts of iron-rich food. It was observed that unemployment/job loss did not affect their haemoglobin level because both the study groups maintained similar dietary practices. The finding contrasted with some earlier studies (Mattiason *et al.*, 1990; Ahenkorah *et al.*, 2016; Lamba *et al.*, 2019; Gupta *et al.*, 2020). The findings also depicted that only age and educational status were the significant concomitants of anaemic status among the tea garden labourers. The works of Malakar and Roy (2016), Abdo *et al.* (2016), and Little *et al.* (2018) validate the finding, proposing that with an increase in age and low education, the risk of being anaemic increases significantly due to changes in food intake. Moreover, Cappellini and Mottaa (2015), Ganesan & Saravanabavan (2018), and Aguila *et al.* (2018) argued that the relationship between unemployment and anaemia largely depends on the intake of iron, folate, and vitamin C. However, the present study did not explore the level of intake of nutrients among tea garden labourers, thereby suggesting further research is needed.

Conclusion

Unemployment is one of the most uncomfortable occasions, affecting a working individual's economic and emotional stability. It is generally followed by income off and, thus, restricts one's ability to fulfil basic needs and affects one's health conditions. In the long term, unemployed individuals become relatively poor and sometimes succumb to death. At the population level, unemployment is crucial in changing demographic measures such as fertility, mortality and small- to large-scale migration. However, at the individual level, the effects of unemployment are numerous, starting from increasing health-abusive behaviours such as smoking and alcohol drinking, compromised dietary habits and low physical activity to the occurrence of various ailments among the unemployed individuals. A good piece of literature has also found that unemployment is directly or indirectly associated with poor psychological health, physical health status, and the deteriorated quality of life among unemployed persons, especially from the socio-economically deprived sections of society.

The issue of unemployment has harvested a great deal of attention from economists, sociologists, and psychologists worldwide. However, it never has been addressed from an anthropological viewpoint, keeping the public health perspective in mind. There was a dearth of knowledge on the relationship between unemployment and health parameters like blood pressure and haemoglobin level. There is no doubt that the present work is pioneering for its systematic and holistic nature of investigation. The present study adds some significant evidence to the literature on the indigenous people of India, who are rapidly experiencing unemployment in several regions. There are also some possible future research directions the present study was limited to following. The issue should also be addressed from a psycho-social perspective using more advanced tools and methods. As a note, the study's cross-sectional nature perhaps did not yield significant results because the present research started two years after the garden was Abandoned. Taking a longitudinal approach would have been better to address it from the beginning. There may be several other concomitants related to unemployment, health and coping strategies, which were not explored simultaneously in the present study. Last but not least, it was necessary to consider a larger sample size to unearth more evidence. Future rigorous studies should avoid the lacuna to reveal more worthy findings.

Nonetheless, the study is limited to drawing any conclusive statement due to some study limitations. The study may have yielded significant results if a longitudinal approach was conducted in a large sample size. Still, the findings raise significant public health concerns regarding tea garden labourers, one of the most socio-economically deprived and marginalised occupational groups. Further rigorous studies must be warranted to provide better insights into the present issue and help accomplish crucial public health implications.

Acknowledgements

The authors are indebted to the study participants for their voluntary participation and to the Indian Statistical Institute for their financial and logistical support.

Authors' contribution

SKR conceptualised and designed the study. AM collected the data and completed the data entry, coding, analysis and interpretation. Both SKR and AM participated in writing the first draft of the manuscript. SKR critically revised the manuscript for final approval for submission.

References

Abdo, N., Douglas, S., Batieha, A., Khader, Y., Jaddou, H., Al-Khatib, S., & Ajlouni, K. (2019). The prevalence and determinants of anaemia in Jordan. *Eastern Mediterranean Health Journal*, 25(5), 341-349.

Adeniyi, O. V., Yogeswaran, P., Longo-Mbenza, B., & Goon, D. T. (2016). Uncontrolled hypertension and its determinants in patients with concomitant type 2 diabetes mellitus (T2DM) in rural South Africa. *PloS one*, 11(3), e0150033.

Adsera, A. (2011). Where are the babies? Labour market conditions and fertility in Europe. *European Journal of Population/Revue européenne de démographie*, 27(1), 1-32. doi:10.1007/s10680-010-9222-x

Aguila, D. V., Gironella, G. M. P., & Capanzana, M. V. (2018). Food intake, nutritional and health status of Filipino adults according to occupations based on the 8th National Nutrition Survey 2013. *Malaysian Journal of Nutrition*, 24(3), 333–348.

Agyemang, C. (2006). Rural and urban differences in blood pressure and hypertension in Ghana, West Africa. *Public health*, 120(6), 525–533.

Ahenkorah, B., Nsiah, K., & Baffoe, P. (2016). Socio-demographic and obstetric characteristics of anaemic pregnant women attending antenatal clinic in Bolgatanga Regional Hospital. *Scientifica*, 2016, 1-8. http://dx.doi.org/10.1155/2016/4687342

Ahmad, K., Jafary, F., Jehan, I., Hatcher, J., Khan, A. Q., Chaturvedi, N., & Jafar, T. H. (2005). Prevalence and predictors of smoking in Pakistan: results of the National Health Survey of Pakistan. *European Journal of Preventive Cardiology, 12*(3), 203–208.

Anstey, K., & Christensen, H. (2000). Education, activity, health, blood pressure and apolipoprotein E as predictors of cognitive change in old age: a review. *Gerontology, 46*(3), 163–177.

Antelo, M., Magdalena, P., & Reboredo, J. C. (2017). Economic crisis and the unemployment effect on household food expenditure: The case of Spain. *Food Policy, 69*, 11-24.

Arcaya, M., Glymour, M. M., Christakis, N. A., Kawachi, I., & Subramanian, S. V. (2014). Individual and spousal unemployment as predictors of smoking and drinking behaviour. *Social Science & Medicine, pp. 110*, 89–95.

Arya, N. (2013). Indian tea scenario. International Journal of Scientific and Research Publications, 3(7), 1–10.

Asopa, V. N. (2007). *Tea industry of India: The cup that cheers has tears* (Working Paper No. 2007-07-02). Ahmedabad: Indian Institute of Management.

Balieiro, L. C. T., Rossato, L. T., Waterhouse, J., Paim, S. L., Mota, M. C., & Crispim, C. A. (2014). Nutritional status and eating habits of bus drivers during the day and night. *Chronobiology International, 31*(10), 1123–1129.

Bentolila, S., & Ichino, A. (2008). Unemployment and consumption near and far away from the Mediterranean. *Journal of Population Economics, 21*(2), 255-280.

Biswas, S., Chokraborty, D., Berman, S., & Berman, J. (2005). *Nutritional Survey of Tea Workers on Closed, Re-Opened, and Open Tea Plantations of the Dooars Region, West Bengal, India*. West Bengal Agricultural Workers' Association & International Union of Food Workers and the American Jewish World Service.

Brackbill, R. M., Siegel, P. Z., & Ackermann, S. P. (1995). Self-reported hypertension among unemployed people in the United States. *BMJ*, *310*(6979), 568.

Cappellini, M. D., & Motta, I. (2015). Anaemia in clinical practice-definition and classification: Does haemoglobin change with ageing? *Seminars in Hematology*, 52(4), 261-269.

Census of India. (2011). CD Block-wise primary census abstract data (PCA). Office of the Registrar General & Census Commissioner, India. Retrieved from http://www.censusindia.gov.in/pca/Searchdata.aspx

Chakrabarty, S., & Bharati, P. (2010). Adult body dimension and determinants of chronic energy deficiency among the Shabar tribe living in urban, rural and forest habitats in Orissa, India. *Annals of Human Biology*, *37*(2), 150–168.

Chowdhury, T. K., & Roy, S. K. (2019). Prevalence of anaemia and associated factors among Oraon females of North 24 Parganas, West Bengal, India. *Anthropological Review*, *82*(1), 15–27. https://doi.org/10.2478/anre-2019-0002

Clark, A. E., & Oswald, A. J. (2002). A simple statistical method for measuring how life events affect happiness. *International Journal of Epidemiology*, *31*(6), 1139-1144.

Colman, G., & Dave, D. (2018). Unemployment and health behaviours over the business cycle: a longitudinal view. *Southern Economic Journal*, *85*(1), 93-120.

Datta Banik, S. (2007). Age-sex and diurnal variation of blood pressure in different nutritional states among the adult Telegas of Kharagpur in West Bengal, India. *Collegium antropologicum*, *31*(3), 717-722.

De Vogli, R., & Santinello, M. (2005). Unemployment and smoking: Does psycho-social stress matter? *Tobacco control*, *14*(6), 389-395.

Del Bono, E., Weber, A., & Winter-Ebmer, R. (2012). Clash of career and family: Fertility decisions after job displacement. *Journal of the European Economic Association*, *10*(4), 659–683.

Dutraj, S. (2014). *Livelihood Shift among the Tribal Tea Garden Workers: Determinants and Consequences.* (Unpublished doctoral dissertation). Sikkim University, Gangtok.

Falba, T., Teng, H. M., Sindelar, J. L., & Gallo, W. T. (2005). The effect of involuntary job loss on smoking intensity and relapse. *Addiction, 100*(9), 1330-1339.

Frey, B. S., & Stutzer, A. (2002). What can economists learn from happiness research? *Journal of Economic Literature, 40*(2), 402-435.

Fryer, D., & Fagan, R. (1993). Coping with unemployment. *International Journal of Political Economy, 23*(3), 95–120.

Gallo, W. T., Bradley, E. H., Falba, T. A., Dubin, J. A., Cramer, L. D., Bogardus Jr, S. T., & Kasl, S. V. (2004). Involuntary job loss as a risk factor for subsequent myocardial infarction and stroke: findings from the Health and Retirement Survey. *American Journal of Industrial Medicine, 45*(5), 408–416. doi:10.1002/ajim.20004

Ganesan, J., & Saravanabavan, V. (2018). Nutritional problems of anaemia disorders among the tea plantation labourers in Nilgiris district– a geo medical study. *International Journal of Research Studies in Science, Engineering and Technology,* 4(4), 360-1366.

Gerdtham, U. G., & Johannesson, M. (2003). A note on the effect of unemployment on mortality. *Journal of Health Economics, 22*(3), 505-518. doi:10.1016/S0167-6296(03)00004-3

Gough, M. (2017). A couple-level analysis of participation in physical activity during unemployment. *SSM-population health, pp. 3,* 294–304.

Gregg, P., Machin, S., & Manning, A. (2007). Mobility and Joblessness. In: D. Card, R. Blundell & R. B. Freeman (Eds.), *Seeking a Premier Economy: The Economic Effects of British Economic Reforms, 1980-2000* (pp. 371–410). University of Chicago Press.

Griffin, K. W., Botvin, G. J., Scheier, L. M., Doyle, M. M., & Williams, C. (2003). Common predictors of cigarette smoking, alcohol use, aggression, and delinquency among inner-city minority youth. *Addictive behaviors, 28*(6), 1141–1148.

Gupta, A., Ramakrishnan, L., Pandey, R. M., Sati, H. C., Khandelwal, R., Khenduja, P., & Kapil, U. (2020). Risk factors of anemia amongst elderly population living in high-altitude regions of India. *Journal of family medicine and primary care*, 9(2), 673-682.

Horwich, T. B., Fonarow, G. C., Hamilton, M. A., MacLellan, W. R., & Borenstein, J. (2002). Anaemia is associated with worse symptoms, greater impairment in functional capacity and a significant increase in mortality in patients with advanced heart failure. *Journal of the American College of Cardiology*, 39(11), 1780-1786.

James, P. A., Oparil, S., Carter, B. L., Cushman, W. C., Dennison-Himmelfarb, C., Handler, J., et al. (2014). Evidence-based guideline for the management of high blood pressure in adults: Report from the panel members appointed to the Eight Joint National Committee (JNC 8). *JAMA*, 311, 507–520.

Janlert, U. (1997). Unemployment as a disease and disease of the unemployed. *Scandinavian Journal of Work, Environment & Health*, pp. 23, 79–83.

Janlert, U., Asplund, K., & Weinehall, L. (1992). Unemployment and cardiovascular risk indicators data from the MONICA survey in Northern Sweden. *Scandinavian Journal of Social Medicine*, 20(1), 14-18.

Kalaivani, K. (2009). Prevalence & consequences of anaemia in pregnancy. *Indian Journal of Medical Research*, 130(5), 627-33.

Kasl, S. V., & Cobb, S. (1970). Blood pressure changes in men undergoing job loss: A preliminary report. *Psychosomatic Medicine*, 32(1), 19–38.

Kendzor, D. E., Reitzel, L. R., Mazas, C. A., Cofta-Woerpel, L. M., Cao, Y., Ji, L., ... & Wetter, D. W. (2012). Individual and area-level unemployment influences smoking cessation among African Americans participating in a randomised clinical trial. *Social science & medicine*, 74(9), 1394-1401. doi: 10.1016/j.socscimed.2012.01.013

Kozieł, S., Łopuszańska, M., Szklarska, A., & Lipowicz, A. (2010). The negative health consequences of unemployment: the case of Poland. *Economics & Human Biology*, 8(2), 255-260.

Kumar, P., Badal, P. S., Singh, N. P., & Singh, R. P. (2008). Tea industry in India: Problems and prospects. *Indian Journal of Agricultural Economics, 63*(1), 84–96.

Lamba, R., Agarwal, A., Rana, R., & Agarwal, V. (2019). Prevalence of anemia and its correlates among the elderly population of an urban slum in Meerut. *Journal of the Indian Academy of Geriatrics,* 15(3), 109–114.

Lee, J. S., & Frongillo Jr, E. A. (2001). Nutritional and health consequences are associated with food insecurity among US elderly persons. *The Journal of Nutrition, 131*(5), 1503-1509.

Letsie, D. (2009). *Experiences, Coping and Well-being of Unemployed People in the North-West Province.* (Unpublished Doctoral dissertation). North-West University, Potchefstroom.

Little, M., Zivot, C., Humphries, S., Dodd, W., Patel, K., & Dewey, C. (2018). Burden and determinants of anemia in a rural population in south India: A Cross-Sectional Study. *Anemia,* 2018, 1-9. https://doi.org/10.1155/2018/7123976

Malakar, B., & Roy, S. K. (2016). Prevalence of Anaemia and Age-Related Changes in Haemoglobin Level of the Santal Labourers of Birbhum District, West Bengal, India. *North Bengal Anthropologist,* 4, 154-163.

Man, R. E., Gan, A. H. W., Fenwick, E. K., Gan, A. T. L., Gupta, P., Sabanayagam, C., ... & Lamoureux, E. L. (2019). Prevalence, determinants and association of unawareness of diabetes, hypertension and hypercholesterolemia with poor disease control in a multi-ethnic Asian population without cardiovascular disease. *Population Health Metrics,* 17(1), 1–10.

Martikainen, P., Mäki, N., & Jäntti, M. (2007). The effects of unemployment on mortality following workplace downsizing and workplace closure: a register-based follow-up study of Finnish men and women during economic boom and recession. *American Journal of Epidemiology, 165*(9), 1070-1075.

Mattiasson, I., Lindgärde, F., Nilsson, J. A., & Theorell, T. (1990). Threat of unemployment and cardiovascular risk factors: a longitudinal study of quality of sleep and serum cholesterol concentrations in men threatened with redundancy. *British Medical Journal*, 301(6750), 461-466.

Meneton, P., Kesse-Guyot, E., Méjean, C., Fezeu, L., Galan, P., Hercberg, S., & Ménard, J. (2015). Unemployment is associated with high cardiovascular event rates and increased all-cause mortality in middle-aged, socially privileged individuals. *International Archives of Occupational and Environmental Health*, 88(6), 707-716.

Mohammad Ali, S., & Lindström, M. (2006). Psycho-social work conditions, unemployment, and leisure-time physical activity: a population-based study. *Scandinavian Journal of Public Health*, 34(2), 209-216.

Moore, A. A., Gould, R., Reuben, D. B., Greendale, G. A., Carter, M. K., Zhou, K., & Karlamangla, A. (2005). Longitudinal patterns and predictors of alcohol consumption in the United States. *American Journal of Public Health*, 95(3), 458–464.

Morikawa, Y., Miura, K., Sasaki, S., Yoshita, K., Yoneyama, S., Sakurai, M., ... & Nakagawa, H. (2008). Evaluation of the effects of shift work on nutrient intake: a cross-sectional study. *Journal of Occupational Health*, 50, 270-278.

Morrone, A., Nosotti, L., Piombo, L., Scardella, P., Spada, R., & Pitidis, A. (2012). Iron deficiency anaemia prevalence in a population of immigrated women in Italy. *The European Journal of Public Health*, 22(2), 256-262.

Mozumdar, A., Das, B. M., & Roy, S. K. (2014). Life table analysis of a small sample of Santal population living in a rural locality of West Bengal, India. *Anthropological Review*, 77(2), 233-248.

Nygren, K., Gong, W., & Hammarström, A. (2015). Is hypertension in adult age related to unemployment at a young age? Results from the Northern Swedish Cohort. *Scandinavian Journal of Public Health*, 43(1), 52-58.

Pharr, J. R., Moonie, S., & Bungum, T. J. (2012). The impact of unemployment on mental and physical health, access to health care and health risk behaviors. *International Scholarly Research Notices*, 2012, pp. 1–7. doi:10.5402/2012/483432.

Pickering, T. G., Hall, J. E., Appel, L. J., Falkner, B. E., Graves, J., Hill, M. N., ... & Roccella, E. J. (2005). Recommendations for blood pressure measurement in humans and experimental animals: Part 1: Blood pressure measurement in humans: A statement for professionals from the Subcommittee of Professional and Public Education of the American Heart Association Council on High Blood Pressure Research. *Hypertension*, *45*(1), 142–161.

Roudsari, A. H., Vedadhir, A., Amiri, P., Kalantari, N., Omidvar, N., Eini-Zinab, H., & Sadati, S. M. H. (2017). Psycho-socio-cultural determinants of food choice: A qualitative study on adults in the social and cultural context of Iran. *Iranian Journal of Psychiatry*, *12*(4), 241.

Roy, N. C., & Biswas, D. (2018). Closed Tea Estates: A Case Study of the Dooars Region of West Bengal, India. *Vision*, *22*(3), 329-334. doi: 10.1177/0972262918788231

Roy, S. K., Mozumdar, A., & Kar, S. (2005). Effect of skill on work productivity and physical body dimensions of the Oraon tea garden labourers of the Jalpaiguri district, West Bengal, India. *Anthropologischer Anzeiger*, *4*, 449-460.

Rudra, D. (2018). Case Analysis III: Closed Tea Estates - A Case Study of the Dooars Region of West Bengal, India. *Vision*, *22*(3), 339–341. doi: 10.1177/0972262918788230

Schunck, R., & Rogge, B. G. (2012). No causal effect of unemployment on smoking? A German panel studies. *International Journal of Public Health*, *57*(6), 867-874.

Sia, D., Miszkurka, M., Batal, M., Delisle, H., & Zunzunegui, M. V. (2019). Chronic disease and malnutrition biomarkers among unemployed immigrants and Canadian-born adults. *Archives of Public Health*, *77*(1), 1-10.

Soliman, E. Z., Zhang, Z. M., Judd, S., Howard, V. J., & Howard, G. (2017). Comparison of risk of atrial fibrillation among employed versus unemployed (from the Reasons for Geographic and Racial Differences in Stroke Study). *The American Journal of Cardiology*, 120(8), 1298–1301.

Souma, W. (2002). Physics of personal income. In H. Takayasu (Ed.), *Empirical Science of Financial Fluctuations* (pp. 343–352). Springer.

Strandh, M., Winefield, A., Nilsson, K., & Hammarström, A. (2014). Unemployment and mental health scarring during the life course. *The European Journal of Public Health*, *24*(3), 440-445. doi:10.1093/eurpub/cku005

Strully, K. W. (2009). Job loss and health in the US labour market. *Demography*, *46*(2), 221-246.

Von Schenck, H., Falkensson, M., & Lundberg, B. (1986). Evaluation of "HemoCue," a new device for determining hemoglobin. *Clinical chemistry*, *32*(3), 526-529.

Voss, M., Nylén, L., Floderus, B., Diderichsen, F., & Terry, P. D. (2004). Unemployment and early cause-specific mortality: a study based on the Swedish twin registry. *American Journal of Public Health*, *94*(12), 2155-2161.

Weber, A., & Lehnert, G. (1997). Unemployment and cardiovascular diseases: a causal relationship? *International Archives of Occupational and Environmental Health*, *70*(3), 153-160.

West Bengal District Gazetteers. (1981). *Jalpaiguri District*. Government of West Bengal, Calcutta.

World Health Organization (WHO). (2011). Haemoglobin concentrations for the diagnosis of anaemia and assessment of severity. Vitamin and Mineral Nutrition Information

Xu, X. (2013). The business cycle and health behaviours. *Social Science & Medicine*, pp. 77, 126–136. http://dx.doi.org/10.1016/j.socscimed.2012.11.016

Zagożdżon, P., Parszuto, J., Wrotkowska, M., & Dydjow-Bendek, D. (2014). Effect of unemployment on cardiovascular risk factors and mental health. *Occupational medicine*, *64*(6), 436-441.

Zhao, L., Sun, W., Wang, J., Wu, J., Zhang, Y., Liu, Y., & Liu, B. (2019). Differences in the treatment and control of hypertension in urban and rural residents of the northeastern region of the People's Republic of China: a cross-sectional study. *Clinical and Experimental Hypertension*, 41(4), 366–372.

Table 1. Classification of the variables used in the present study

Variables	Male	Female	Reference
Blood pressure	Normal		JNC-VIII, 2014
	SBP <120 & DBP <80 mm.Hg		
	Pre-hypertensive		
	SBP 120-139 & DBP 80-89 mm.Hg		
	Hypertensive		
	SBP ≥140 & DBP ≥90 mm.Hg		
Haemoglobin level	Normal		WHO. 2011
	≥13.00 g/dl	≥12.00 g/dl	
	Anaemic		
	<13.00 g/dl	<12.00 g/dl	

Table 2. Socio-demographic characteristics of the study participants

Socio-demographic variables		Abandoned tea plantation (n=234)	Operating tea plantation (n=214)
Sex	Male	113 (48.29)	106 (49.53)
	Female	121 (51.71)	108 (50.47)
Age (in years)		40.88±12.99	39.37±14.89
Sanitation facilities in household	Yes	182 (77.78)	175 (81.78)
	No	52 (22.22)	39 (18.22)
	Wood	173 (73.93)	145 (67.76)

Types of cooking fuel	Wood and LPG	61 (26.07)	69 (32.24)
Educational status	Non-literate	75 (32.05)	84 (39.25)
	Up to Primary	63 (26.92)	44 (20.56)
	Above primary	96 (41.03)	86 (40.19)

Note: Figures in parenthesis are percentages *Mean ± SD.

Table 3. Descriptive statistics of blood pressure level of the study participants of abandoned and operating tea gardens in either sex

Male ($n=209$)							
Variables	Abbr.	Abandoned TG ($n=103$)		Operating TG ($n=106$)		t-value ($df=207$)	p-value
		Mean	SD	Mean	SD		
Systolic blood pressure (mm. Hg)	SBP	122.35	17.34	126.28	15.55	1.727	0.086
Diastolic blood pressure (mm. Hg)	DBP	80.05	11.77	80.13	11.58	0.052	0.959
Female ($n=229$)							
Variables	Abbr.	Abandoned TG ($n=121$)		Operating TG ($n=108$)		t-value ($df=227$)	p-value
		Mean	SD	Mean	SD		
Systolic blood pressure (mm. Hg)	SBP	125.55	24.12	119.66	25.03	1.844	0.071

| Diastolic blood pressure (mm. Hg) | DBP | 78.93 | 12.39 | 76.69 | 14.42 | 1.269 | 0.206 |

*Significant at 0.05 level

Table 4. Distribution of the study participants of Abandoned and Operating tea gardens based on the classifications of blood pressure level

Male (n=209)						
Blood pressure category (JNC-VIII)	Abandoned TG (n=103)		Operating TG (n=106)		χ^2 (df=2)	p-value
	n	%	n	%		
Normal (SBP<120 and DBP<80)	41	39.81	31	29.24	4.071	0.131
Pre-hypertension (SBP=120-139 and/or DBP=80-89)	35	33.98	50	47.17		
Hypertension (SBP≥140 and/or DBP≥90)	27	26.21	25	23.58		
Female (n=229)						
	Abandoned TG (n=121)		Operating TG (n=108)		χ^2 (df=2)	p-value
	n	%	n	%		
Normal (SBP<120 and DBP<80)	46	38.02	61	56.48	8.210*	0.016

Pre-hypertension (SBP=120-139 and/or DBP=80-89)	38	31.40	21	19.45		
Hypertension (SBP≥140 and/or DBP≥90)	37	30.58	26	24.07		

*Significant at 0.05 level

Table 5. Descriptive statistics of the haemoglobin level of study participants of Abandoned and Operating tea gardens in either sex

Male (n=216)						
Variable	Abbr.	Abandoned TG (n=113)		Operating TG (n=103)		t-value (df=214)	p-value
		Mean	SD	Mean	SD		
Haemoglobin level (g/dl)	Hb	12.10	1.57	12.06	1.99	0.147	0.883
Female (n=222)						
Variable	Abbr.	Abandoned TG (n=115)		Operating TG (n=107)		t-value (df=220)	p-value
		Mean	SD	Mean	SD		
Haemoglobin level (g/dl)	Hb	10.33	1.58	10.78	1.69	2.070*	0.040

*Significant at 0.05 level

Table 6. Distribution of the study participants of Abandoned and Operating tea gardens based on the classifications of haemoglobin level

Anaemic status (WHO, 2011)	Male (n=216)				χ^2 (df=2)	p-value
	Abandoned TG (n=113)		Operating TG (n=103)			
	n	%	n	%		
Non-anaemic (≥13.00 g/dl)	32	28.32	32	31.07	0.195	0.659
Anaemic (<13.00 g/dl)	81	71.68	71	68.93		
	Female (n=222)					
	Abandoned TG (n=115)		Operating TG (n=107)		χ^2 (df=2)	p-value
	n	%	n	%		
Non-anaemic (≥12.00 g/dl)	13	11.30	20	18.69	2.390	0.122
Anaemic (<12.00 g/dl)	102	88.70	87	81.31		

*Significant at 0.05 level

Table 7. Concomitants of the nutritional status (in terms of Hypertension and Anaemia) of the adult Oraon labourers

Selected characteristics		Stepwise binary logistic regression (Backward method)			
		Blood pressure category† (Hypertensive)		Hb level category† (Anaemic)	
		OR (95% CI)	p	OR (95% CI)	p
Age		**1.058*** (1.041-1.075)	0.001	**1.067*** (1.007-1.130)	0.028
Sex	Male	Reference group			
	Female	**0.599*** (0.407-0.881)	0.009	-	-
Status of tea garden	Operating	Reference group			
	Abandoned	-	-	-	-
Educational status	Non-literate	**2.192*** (1.144-4.200)	0.018	**5.304*** (2.600-10.820)	0.001
	Primary	2.122 (0.885-5.090)	0.092	2.435 (0.953-6.223)	0.063

| | Above primary | 1.160 (0.589-2.287) | 0.667 | **2.343*** **(1.151-** **4.770)** | 0.019 |

*Significant at 0.05 level.

†Reference categories: 'Non-hypertensive' for Blood pressure; 'Non-anaemic' for Haemoglobin.

# 17

Health Care Practises Among the Deshi Muslims: An Anthropological Investigation in Dhubri District Assam, India

Suraiya Prodhani
Arifur Zaman

Introduction

Health encompasses the physical, mental, and emotional well-being of an individual. It is the outcome of the interplay among an individual's genetics, surroundings, and sociocultural factors. WHO (World Health Organization) defined health as "a state of complete physical, mental and social well-being, and not merely the absence of diseases and infirmity" (cited in Park, 2015:523). Anthropological knowledge is crucial for recognising health requirements and for developing suitable medical care and public health strategies in societies. Medical anthropology is the field of anthropology that focuses on understanding beliefs, behaviours, and customs related to health, illness, and healing. Caudill (1953) provided a thorough assessment of the initial significant anthropological contributions to medical issues. Subsequently, there has been a significant shift in the scenario, leading to a notable rise in the contributions of anthropologists and other social scientists in the field of medicine and allied areas (e.g., Polgar, 1962; Scotch, 1963). Culture significantly impacts the health of a specific population. Each human community possesses its unique understanding of health and the preventative and healing methods associated with it. Health perceptions differ between cultures, communities, and regions. Health is closely connected to healing, which is commonly viewed as the process of restoring the well-being of the body and mind (Zaman, 2021, p. 16). Cultural impacts on healing vary and can be seen in different ways across cultures. Health is a critical requirement for both indigenous and modern communities. Indigenous communities have unique healing practices that are closely connected to their local healthcare system. Indigenous health can be understood in two main ways: as a cultural complex encompassing material objects, tools, techniques, knowledge, ideas, and values and as a component of social structure and organisation involving relationships between different groups, classes, and categories of individuals (Zaman, 2017, p. 1).

In traditional cultures, individuals mainly depend on natural resources such as wild roots, herbs, plants, and animal parts to recover from illness. They have developed native healing methods to protect their health from various illnesses. They utilise the benefits of modern Medicare provisions in rural tribal areas while also preserving their traditional Medicare system. In traditional societies, people attribute disease and illness to demons and deities. Rural communities also have the belief that evil gazes, breaches of taboos, sorcery, and similar practices hinder good health. Traditional communities depend on ethnomedicine and village medicine men to address the condition. Many anthropologists and sociologists are interested in the healthcare systems of primitive communities. Traditional health care systems around the world have been studied by Rivers (1924), Clement (1932), Field (1937), Spencer (1941), Ackerknecht (1942, 47), Elwin (1964), Lieban (1973), Choudhuri (1986, 1990), Lyall and Stack (1997), Medhi (1994, 1995), Kumar, Murthy and Upadhaya (1998), Hostettmann, Marston, Ndjoko and Wolfender (2000), Rates (2001), Gurib-Fakim(2006), Kar and Borthakur(2007), Sikdar and Dutta (2008), Hynniewta and Kumar(2008), Flatie, Gedif, Asres, and Gebre-Mariam. (2009), Zaman (2011; 2021;2022), Dey and De (2012), Lokho (2012), Singha, Patel and Kanungo (2012), Teron and Borthakur (2012, 2013), Singh, Borthakur and Phukan (2014), Chakraborty (2019), and others.

The study will encompass the Deshis, an indigenous Assamese Muslim community in Assam, India, as well as many facets of healthcare practices. Ethnographic studies on the Deshi people's healthcare methods are scarce. They utilise the benefits of modern Medicare provisions in rural tribal areas while also upholding their traditional Medicare system. The Deshis, an indigenous Assamese Muslim community in Assam, India, will be part of the study, which will also include many elements of healthcare procedures.

The People

Muslims in Assam have played a crucial and constructive role in shaping and advancing Assamese society and culture from the historical past to the present. They are dispersed throughout the state, especially in the Brahmaputra valley, due to a combination of the socio-economic and cultural interface, centring the Assamese culture. Assam boasts a diverse and vibrant culture due to the presence of several races and tribes since ancient times, which have contributed to the unique Assamese culture and civilisation through their rituals, traditions, and ways of life. Muslims constitute the largest minority community in Assam, accounting for 34.22% of the total population. Social academics often overlook the native Deshi Muslims residing in the western region of Assam for generations. The indigenous people of Assam, originally from Koch, Mech, Garo, Bodos, etc., have cultural similarities in areas such as dietary preferences, clothing styles, marital customs, and language. Hunter (1897) referred to these converted Muslims as 'Musalman Koch' in his work 'A Statistical Account of Assam'. Studying the physical structure, language, arts, rituals, and traditions of the Deshi Muslims reveals that they are individuals who have converted from ethnic groups such as Koch-Rajbongshi, Nath-Kalita, or Kaibarta.

Over 11.2 million Muslims are residing in Assam, with 4.2 million being indigenous Muslims. The other Muslims are of East Bengali descent. The indigenous Muslims include Deshi, Goria, Moria, Syed, and Julha. The Deshis mainly reside in the western part of Assam, specifically in the former Goalpara District, albeit being spread out in various areas of Assam. In addition, Deshi Muslims reside in certain villages in Barpeta, Chirang, and Kokrajhar, as well as in the broader area of Boko-Balijhar in the Kamrup (R) District. Out of the 42 indigenous Muslims, around 16 are Deshis. Distinguishing between the native Deshi Muslims and the migrating eastern Bengali Muslims is quite challenging. The increased presence of eastern Bengali Muslims compared to indigenous Muslims in eastern Assam is a significant element contributing to the identity issue among the Deshi people - the history of conversion dates back around one thousand years.

The conversion of faith in the year 1205 AD is supported by unambiguous historical evidence. In 1205 AD, Mohammad Bin Bakhtiyar Khilji enlisted a Mech commander to assist him in invading Tibet. The Mech chief and Bakhtiyar Khilji developed a cordial friendship, leading to the Mech leader's conversion to Islam. Minhaj-al-Siraj, a Persian historian, documented his journey with Bakhtiyar Khilji in his work 'Tabkat-e-Nashiri' and referred to the Mech chieftain as 'Ali Mech'. Ali Mech is the ancestor of the 'Deshi people'. In 1460 AD, King Chakradhwaj turned to Islam after being influenced by Ismail Gaj.

Consequently, hundreds of tenants abandoned their religion and embraced Islam as their new faith. Later on, the 'Peer' and 'Darbesh' who arrived with the Muslim invaders captivated the locals with their powerful religious speeches, humble living, and discriminatory actions, leading many to convert to Islam. King Bishya Singha, the founder of the Koch dynasty and his descendants adhered to secular religious ideas. The Hindu ruler did not prohibit his subjects from converting to Islam by renouncing Hinduism. Conversely, he offered land and financial aid to build mosques, dargahs, and other religious structures.

Consequently, a significant number of Koch-Rajbongshi individuals readily converted to Islam. Due to historical circumstances, even though the Deshis come from many tribes that converted to Islam, the majority of them have Koch-Rajbongshi ancestry. Dutta (1973), a prominent scholar of folk culture, suggested that some Deshi Muslims may be descendants of early Muslim settlers who chose to remain in the region. Most likely, these strangers married local women before establishing themselves here.

Conversely, the majority of the others' ancestors were early converts from the local area. This is evident from their physical characteristics, behaviours, and traditions. The local Muslims identify themselves as Desi and refer to the Muhammadans from east Bengal as Bhatiya.

Objectives

This study aims to explore the health beliefs of indigenous Deshi Muslims, prevalent diseases in the area, general health practices, especially those concerning pregnant women and children, and the availability of modern medical services in the region, along with any recent changes in healthcare access for the study population.

Methodology

A study was conducted to assess the important features of healthcare practices in two villages, Srigram Part IV and Saslapara, located in the Bilasipara region of Assam's Dhubri District. Data for the study was collected periodically between July and September 2022 and December 2022 to July 2023. Two hundred residences from both villages were surveyed, comprising 623 individuals, with 296 (47.51%) males and 327 (52.48%) females. The current study selected participants at random, including children under five, moms with at least one child in that age group, and pregnant women. Most of the data was collected from older adult women in the villages and experienced midwives knowledgeable about pregnancy and healthcare procedures. Detailed documentation was made regarding the medical properties of many herbs and plants, including their names, parts used, animal components, preparation methods, dosages, administration routes, and therapeutic applications for specific illnesses or disorders. Extensive personal interviews, in-depth talks, and case studies were conducted with two traditional practitioners and some village people to document their exceptional medical practices. Information regarding current medical facilities in the hamlet was gathered from the primary health centre and its staff, which included a detailed interview with the village's prominent health care advocate, the ASHA.

Table 1: Distribution of population According to Sex

Total No. of Households	Male Population		Female Population		Total Population	
	No	%	No	%	No	%
200	296	47.51	327	52.48	623	100

Table 1 shows the distribution of the total population of the studied Villages according to Sex. During the time of the survey using the

household survey schedule, it was found that among the 200 households, the total population was 623. Out of which, 296 were males, with a percentage of 47.51%, and 327 were females, with a percentage of 52.48%. However, it can be noticed that the number of males is significantly less than the number of females.

Results

A blend of traditional indigenous beliefs and Islamic teachings shapes the Deshi Muslims' conception of health. Indigenous Deshi Muslims of Assam often take a holistic approach to health, seeing the health of the body, mind, and spirit as interconnected. They consider good health to include physical, mental, and spiritual dimensions. Here are some essential features of their health concept:

Traditional Healing Practises:

Traditional healing practices founded in indigenous culture play an essential role in the community's views on health. They may use indigenous preventive measures in conjunction with traditional herbal treatments, rituals, and practices to cure various ailments. These practices frequently include the use of natural components such as herbs, roots, and other plant-based treatments, as well as some magical-religious practices performed by medicine men.

Table 2 gives an idea of how the Deshi Muslims of the study villages use medicinal plants to combat disease and illness.

Table 2: Medicinal use of plants among the Deshis of the study villages

Sl. No.	Name of Plant		Plant part used	Form of medicine	Integral disease
	Local	Botanical			
I	II	III	IV	V	VI
1	Nefafu	Clerodendrum colebrookianum	Leaf	The raw and dry leaf	High blood pressure
2	Kapah	Gosypium herbaceum	Root; Leaf	extracted juice; paste of leaf	To create and accelerate labour pain, snake bite

359

Sl. No.	Name of Plant		Plant part used	Form of medicine	Integral disease
	Local	Botanical			
3	Pate gaja	Bryophyllum pinnatum	Leaf and root	extracted juice	Burning
4	Lewa	Myriopteron extensum	Stalk	a piece of stalk	Inserted through genitalia for abortion
5	Kuhiar	Saccharum officinarum	Stem	extracted juice	Jaundice.
6	Modhuriam	Psidium guyava	Tender leaves	Paste of leaves with honey, tender leaves	Bruiser or ulcer, blood dysentery
7	Mahaneem	Azadirachta indica	Bark, leaf, and twig	Powdered dried leaves or water extracted after boil	Skin diseases
8	Dhuna	Canarium bengalense	Resin	Powdered dry	Fracture
9	Silikha	Terminalia chebula	Fruit	Powder of dried fruit	Acidity, constipation, cough, fever, piles, stomach pain
10	Tulakhi	Ocimum sanctum	Leaf	Juice extracted from leaves	Cough, fever, skin diseases
11	Dimoru	Ficus hirta	Leaf	leaves	applied externally as a bandage to treat

Sl. No.	Name of Plant		Plant part used	Form of medicine	Integral disease
	Local	Botanical			
					swelling of the neck or throat
12	Amlakhi	Phyllanthus embilica	Fruit	Powder of dried fruit	It is used to cure Dysentery and is also applied at the mouth of the uterus to cure excessive bleeding during menstruation.
13	Bel	Aegle marmelos	Fruit, leaf	(i)Juice of fruit (ii)paste of the leaf	(i)The juice extracted from wood apples is used to treat nasal bleeding, sweating; (ii) leaf paste is consumed with warm water to get relief from excessive bleeding during menstruation
14	Kachu	Colocasia antiquorum	latex	Fluid	Ear ache
15	Athia kal	Musa balbisinia	Inflorence Latex	curry of inflorence; fluid latex	Iron deficiency; Diarrhoea
16	Ada	Zingiber officinale L.	Rhizome	The juice extracted is mixed with or without honey	Cough and cold

Sl. No.	Name of Plant - Local	Name of Plant - Botanical	Plant part used	Form of medicine	Integral disease
17	Bhebeli lota	Paederia foetida	leaf	Paste of the leaf	applied externally to cure rheumatic pain.
18	Era	Ricinus communis L.	Leaf	Juice extracted from leaves	Cure acidity, body pain
19	Jamalakhuti	Costus speciosus	Rhizome	extracted paste	jaundice, pneumonia.
20	Dalim	Punica grantam	Root	extracted juice	Stop excessive bleeding during pregnancy
21	Haladhi	Curcuma domestica	Rhizomes	extracted juice	To cure severe pain in the abdomen after childbirth, bleeding
22	Anaras	Ananas comosus	Tender leaves	(a) Decoction of extracted juice (b) Juice extracted from a paste of the leave	(a) Upset stomach (b) Worm infection and vomiting in children
23	Salkuwari	Aloe barbadensis	Leaf	(a) Leaf-gel	(a) The pure gel of Aloe-vera is applied on the scalp to treat alopecia

Sl. No.	Name of Plant		Plant part used	Form of medicine	Integral disease
	Local	Botanical			
					(b) Used in affected areas to cure burns.
24	Laijabari	Drymoglossum heterophyllum	Leaf	Leaf paste	The paste of the leaves is used to treat jaundice.
25	Bihlangani	Portulacea oleraca	Leaf	Leaf paste	Paste of these leaves is used externally to treat skin diseases and pneumonia.
26	Bar Manimuni	Centella asiatica	Leaves	Raw leaf, curry	Leaves are consumed to treat jaundice and gastric problems.

It has already been mentioned that the Deshis of the study areas have elaborate knowledge about the use of varieties of plant parts for the treatment of different ailments and diseases. In addition, they also have integral knowledge about the use of animal parts as well as mineral objects, which constitute a significant portion of their ingredient for *materia medica* needed for medicare purposes. The local medicinal experts of the study villages utilise animal bi-products as well as ingredients obtained from the bodies of animals and birds for therapeutic purposes.

Table 3 contains a list of some of the fauna, such as reptiles, avians, Pisces, etc., parts of which are used in the therapeutic measures of the Deshis.

Table 3: Medicinal use of faunal parts among the Deshis of the study villages

Sl. No	Fauna Used	Diseases/ Ailments
1	Dry Fish	Body pain, Malaria, diabetes, obesity
2	Catla Fish	Arthritis, For joint bone pain
3	Garfish	The part of the body where a person feels pain is tightly wrapped with cloth, and the teeth of garfish (khata fish) pierce that part of the body to bring out the impure blood.
4	Pigeon	Curry for liver diseases and Low blood pressure
5	Cow	Cow trotters' soup for calcium deficiency and immunity booster
6	Honey bee	Honey is applied orally in cases of cough, cold, eye disease, or tongue flexibility in babies.

Traditional Medicare and Taboos during Pregnancy

The majority of Deshi Muslim pregnancies are unplanned. They consider it a divine favour. When a lady becomes pregnant, she first informs her husband and then the rest of the family. They regard childbirth as a natural process and engage in a variety of home tasks during the pregnancy. Cohabitation was prohibited for Deshi women in the villages surveyed during pregnancy. After the first child was born, 23 miscarriages were discovered among them. Traditional beliefs among women in a Deshi Muslim community are that vomiting, loss of appetite, and stoppage of menstruation are symptoms of pregnancy, which is typical in many civilisations around the world. The shift among Deshi women from depending exclusively on traditional beliefs to obtaining medical care during pregnancy is a positive trend. The first pregnancy of a woman was discovered at the age of 12 years, and the last pregnancy was reported at the age of 37. During pregnancy and delivery, traditional birth attendants provide care. They are referred to as Dhai or Dhaiani in Deshi. Pregnant women are not permitted to enter a residence where someone has died, are not permitted to visit the wharf (river bank), and are not permitted to leave the house at midday. During 'Sankranti (the sun's transit from one zodiac to another), pregnant women are not permitted to go outside at night. During pregnancy, they should eat more healthy foods and avoid lifting heavy objects.

The Deshis believed that sicknesses and diseases were caused by wicked spirits, hostile souls, or deities. They were also affected by the effects of black magic. The 'Kabiraj,' a traditional healer, may treat the sickness induced by black magic. By chanting 'Suras' and writing it on paper, place it in a little copper box and jam it with wax, which is known as 'Tabeej'. This safeguards against evil spirits and black magic. Tabeej from a traditional healer is to be worn around the neck or belly, and pregnant women or children should avoid visiting profane or unholy locations during this period. Because low blood sugar can cause dizziness, Deshi people believed that enchanted sugar and water by the 'Maulana' (religious leader) could relieve dizziness. The pregnant woman's husband was barred from killing a snake or a frog.

Prohibited Food During Pregnancy

Most of the women in the studied village suffer from anaemia and Iron deficiency, which are the main factors in the perinatal death of the child. For the prevention of cold and cough, a special soup was made with *Baska tita* (*Justicia adhatoda L*), basil (*Ocimum sanctum*), jaggery, black pepper and honey for pregnant women. In the first trimester, they do not consume papaya, pineapple, or tamarind as they consider that it would cause abortion. Some prohibited foods during pregnancy which lead to miscarriage or spontaneous abortion are as follows:

i. *Khar* (alkali)- typically made from the ashes of banana peel, is strictly prohibited as it increases blood pressure and reduces the nutrients found in the food.

ii. *Sidol* is a sun-dried paste made from crushed dry fish, mustard oil, garlic, and taro stems.

iii. Papaya, pineapples, brinjal, and eggs were prohibited to prevent miscarriage.

iv. Eating *Mola carplet* (moa fish) fish is restricted during pregnancy.

v. Fused bananas and other fruits were prohibited as they caused twin pregnancies.

The Deshi women of the study village take extreme care of their diet during pregnancy. Eggs are considered hot food, so they are avoided for the first three months for fear of bleeding. Women are also restricted from taking twin fruits to avoid the birth of twins. However, the birth of twins is welcomed and considered auspicious.

Rites Observed During Pregnancy

In the seventh month of pregnancy, the Deshi woman of the researched village celebrates *Sat khoa* (ceremony of seven food items), a pregnancy rite. Only in their mother's home do the women carry out the ritual. On a big bronze platter, the mother received seven various kinds of food, including fruits, vegetables, meats, fish, sweets, pithas (traditionally prepared rice cakes), and *sidol* (sun-dried fish paste). Due to the fact that it contains all wholesome and nourishing elements, this ceremony is advantageous for both the mother and the kid.

Vaccination and Health Checkups

A modern healthcare professional advises that pregnant women visit the doctor at least once a month during the first two trimesters, twice a month during the third trimester, and once a week in the final few days. Deshi women seek prenatal treatment because modern healthcare campaigners, particularly ASHA (Accredited Social Health Campaigners) and community health authorities, encourage it. The following table, which was examined based on the information acquired from 150 mothers taken into consideration for the current study, reflects the village's current situation.

Table 4: Antenatal Health Care Received

Nature of Health Care	No. of Expectant mothers	Percentages
Folic Acid Iron Tablets	70	46.66
T.T. vaccine	113	75.33

| Regular health checkups | 86 | 57.33 |

Table 4 shows that the women in the studied community receive all of the crucial antenatal care that is required for pregnant women. Vaccination was done in the case of 75.33% expectant mothers. The next step in treating iron deficiency during pregnancy is to take iron and folic acid tablets. Only 46.66% of expectant mothers were found to take iron and folic acid supplements. The majority of the women in the hamlet under study, therefore, were found to have iron deficiencies. Only 57.33% of women visited a doctor for routine health examinations. A woman in the Deshi community receives a vaccination during pregnancy, according to the table mentioned above. However, relatively few people in the community take folic acid or iron supplements or make regular visits to a doctor.

Traditional Practices Followed on Childbirth:

Dai, also known as *Dhaiyani,* is a local traditional birth attendant who offered essential healthcare services to Deshi women throughout pregnancy and on delivery at their homes in the hamlet under the study. When the expectant mother started experiencing labour pain, she would be taken to the bedroom and made to lie down on the floor with her face towards the west. A strong rope is securely fastened to a pole in the room, allowing the woman to hold it with both hands to exert pressure by pulling it towards her to facilitate quick delivery. The *Dhai* then would secure a rope around the pregnant woman's abdomen, extending to her navel and below her chest. The midwife would carefully manipulate the position of the baby in the pregnant woman's womb and massage the perineal area. *Dhai* assesses the expected time of delivery by checking the birth canal with her fingertips. If she could insert her finger into the distal phalanx, the delivery would be delayed. If the midwife could efficiently perform a procedure on the middle phalanx of her finger, the delivery process would last approximately 30 minutes. A new blade is used to cut the umbilical cord. The *dhai* would induce hair and garlic in the delivering mother's mouth to induce vomiting and separate the placenta. The placenta would be interred or positioned under a container. Both the baby and the mother would be cleaned with warm water after birth. She would administer the colostrum to the newborn immediately after delivery.

Dhai does not expect reciprocation for the services she provides. Nevertheless, she would receive cash or kinds as gifts offered by the family of the newborn. The midwife remains with the mother for 3 to 4 days. The *dhai's* extensive experience indicates that a male foetus is located in the left ovary, while a female foetus is located in the right ovary. If the birth took place at a hospital, the ASHA and nurses would offer crucial healthcare services. Health experts frequently conduct home visits in the community.

Poati was the name bestowed upon a recently delivered mother. After childbirth, they provide the mother with cooked sticky rice, known as *jau bhat* and *kali jeera* (black cumin seed). During the initial 41 days, the postpartum woman is forbidden from leaving her home or engaging in employment. For a month, the mother and infant receive massages using a mixture of garlic and black cumin seed blended with warmed mustard oil.

Table 5: Place of Childbirth among the Deshi Muslim community

Place	No. of Mothers	Percentage (%)
Home	44	29.33
Hospital	114	76
Total	150	100

Table 5 contains information gathered from the 150 mothers interviewed who had a child within the last five years. The table shows that as modern medical facilities have advanced, 76% of the women delivered their children in hospitals, while the remaining 44 mothers (29.33%) gave birth to their children at home.

Food for the Infants

For at least two years from birth, the majority of Deshi children in the current study were fed on their mothers' milk. The start of a second pregnancy is one of the many reasons why breastfeeding abruptly stops. This phenomenon is referred to as "pregnancy-induced lactation suppression." The following are some of the causes of

Deshi lactating mothers' sudden cessation of milk production:

i. **Pregnancy**: When a woman becomes pregnant while she is still breastfeeding, her body undergoes hormonal changes that can decrease her milk supply and eventually stop production altogether.

ii. **Insufficient Milk Supply:** Some women may experience insufficient milk supply from the beginning, which can make breastfeeding difficult.

iii. **Baby's Refusal to Suckle:** The baby refuses to breastfeed or frequently stops breastfeeding for any reason, which reduces milk production.

iv. **Maternal Illness or Medications:** Certain illnesses in the mother or medications taken affect milk production.

v. **Weaning:** Intentional weaning or a gradual reduction in breastfeeding sessions also leads to the cessation of milk production.

TABLE 6: Weaning Practices Followed by Lactating Mothers

Measures Used	No of Mothers	Percentage (%)
No Measures taken	108	72
Use of a bitter substance	35	23.33
Use of pepper	07	4.66
Total	150	100

Table 6 shows the number of lactating mothers who use various methods to stop breastfeeding. It shows that 23.33% of mothers use bitter substances on their nipples to keep their babies away from breastfeeding, whereas 4.66% of women use pepper to wean the kid. However, 72% claim that no steps were taken to stop the infant from consuming breast milk. Weaning is a smooth and steady process of childcare practices among the persons being studied.

Traditional Healing Practices

A person with rheumatic pain typically seeks out a local *Kobiraj or Oja* (traditional healer) to help them insert a *Gull* within one of their legs. Making a hole in one of the legs with a hot iron bar and inserting a little piece of circular polished Neem tree wood is how one builds a *gull*. A white, spotless cloth is used to cover and tightly bind the area where the Gull is placed. Every morning, cold water is used to clean the area thoroughly where the *Gull* is placed. Drinking charmed water provided by the *Kobiraj* (traditional healer) is the traditional therapy for measles and chickenpox. The *kobiraj* must take a glass of water and use a sickle to steer up the water while seated facing west in order to access the charmed water. While reciting hymns, the *kobiraj* also blows air from his mouth into the glass of water.

The Deshi people believe that pregnant women who have labour pain prior to delivery should be given an herb called Mariyam tree to put around their arms or necks to facilitate easy delivery. The root of a medicinal plant known locally as *Bhutani Gas* (Ghost Tree), which is used as a local treatment for people who suddenly experience back or shoulder pain after getting out of bed early in the morning and are unable to sit, stand, or walk properly, can get a quick relieve from such pain. By turning the plant's root three times and facing west, the root can be dug out from the ground. The root must be thrown away after use, either on the house's roof or in some other location.

Birth Control Measures

The Deshis of the research village frequently uses traditional birth control methods and coitus-interrupting behaviours. They do employ specific, but relatively few, forms of contraception. On the contrary, they had more children because they thought that having more children would aid them in carrying out agricultural chores. However, at the moment, the married couple is aware of family planning practices that they learn about from sources like social media, periodicals, doctors, and other experts. Males utilise condoms for contraception, while ladies use oral contraceptive tablets such as Oral L, Choice, Sukhi, and others.

Table 7: Sources of Information on Family Planning Measures

Sources of information	No. of women	Percentage
Medical staff	26	21.66
Neighbour	10	8.33
Media	55	45.83
Book	03	2.5
ASHA	26	21.66
Total	120	100

Table 7 reveals that 120 of the 150 women under the study, 87.5%, were aware of family planning. Of those, 26.6% first came to know about family planning from healthcare personnel, and 8.33% came to know it through their neighbours. Another 45.83% came to know from ASHA and the media (T.V. and radio), 2.5% from literature, and the remaining 21.66% from ASHA employees.

Customs and Traditions for the Wellbeing of Children

The Deshis commonly practise the rice-feeding ceremony, known as *bhat mukhot dia*, which is typically held when the kid is between six and ten months old, depending on their gender. Girls are given their first food in odd months, whereas boys are given their first food in even months. The term *Kajal fota* refers to a little circular black mark on a child's forehead that is believed to protect them from the evil eye. To protect the newborn from evil spirits, the mother sets a broom in front of the door and a knife (*katari*) under the pillow. The baby's pillow is filled with mustard seeds to help shape the baby's head into a round or round form. In order to protect herself and the infant from the evil actions of the demon or ghost, the mother places a matchstick in her braid. To ward off evil spirits, branches of the jujube tree are placed at both entryways. *Akhika* is a traditional ceremony where a goat or cow is offered to Allah to ensure the child's future well-being. After 40 days, the child's hair begins to shed. Hairs are separated and measured during *Akhika*, and an equal value of silver or gold is donated to the needy. After six months, the child was provided with a supplementary meal called luthuri, made from ground rice mixed with hot water and milk. Various veggies like masurdal, moongdal, papaya, and potatoes were simmered in khichri along with salt, oil, and water for 20 minutes. It contains protein, iron, and calories. Semolina is boiled with water, milk, and jaggery to prepare *suji halwa*, a classic dessert.

Modern Strategies to Improve Nutritional Status

Poshan Abhiyaan is a government programme that aims to eliminate stunting, undernutrition, anaemia, and low birth weight in young children with pregnant and nursing mothers in the study region. According to the health report gathered from the community health officer of the investigated region, the child death rate has decreased compared to past years.

Islamic Teachings:

As members of Islam, the Indigenous Deshi Muslims of Assam incorporate Islamic teachings into their understanding of health. They believe that good health is essential for completing religious commitments and living a decent life. Cleanliness, hygiene, and self-care are all emphasised in Islamic teachings as fundamental components of healthy living.

Conclusion

Traditional practitioners are familiar with most of the community's diseases and health issues. They identify and diagnose diseases by making general observations of the patient, considering symptoms stated by the patient, and drawing on personal knowledge in treating human disorders. They were found to possess detailed and precise descriptions of the disease's characteristics and associated symptoms. Magico-religious practices serve as both curative and preventive health care measures. While lacking scientific validity, these beliefs significantly influence the mindset of the patient and their family members. The people adhere to established standards of conduct to prevent anger from evil spirits and deities since they believe in their existence. Various illnesses and conditions, believed to be the result of evil spirits or malicious deities, can be prevented by performing magico-religious and spiritual rituals conducted at the appropriate time and with precision. Upon examination, it was found that Desi Muslims often do not view modern medicine as a viable answer to their problems, as they believe it cannot offer a lasting remedy. People choose modern medication along with conventional therapy for all other illnesses. The therapeutic and healing options for diseases and disorders vary.

References

Acherknecht, E. (1942b). Primitive medicine and culture pattern. *Bulletin of the History of Medicine 12*:545-74.

Acherknecht, E. (1947). Primitive surgery. *American Anthropologist, 49*:25-45.

Acherknecht, E. (1942a). Problems of primitive medicine. *Bulletin of the History of Medicine 11*:503-21.

Chakraborty, S. (2019). Health, illness and therapeutics: A study on power healing among the Lepcha. In S. Sengupta and J. Bora (Eds.). *Spectrum of Anthropological Perspectives of Northeast India*. Gyan Publishing House, New Delhi: pp. 235–250.

Choudhuri, Buddhadeb (Ed.). (1986). *Tribal Health-Socio Cultural Dimensions*, Inter India Publications, New Delhi.

Choudhuri, Buddhadeb (Ed.). (1990). *Cultural and Environmental Dimensions on Health*, Inter India Publications. New Delhi.

Choudhury, B. (1986). Medical Anthropology in India with Special Reference to Tribal Population, in *Tribal Health: Sociocultural Dimensions*, B. Choudhury (Ed.). P.P., 1-11. New Delhi: Inter India Publications.

Clements, F., E. (1932). Primitive concepts of disease. *American Archaeology and Ethnology, 32*:185-252.

Dey, A., De, J.N. (2012). Traditional Use of Plants against Snakebite in Indian Subcontinent: A Review of the Recent Literature. *Afr. J. Trad. Complm. Altern. Med. 9(1)*: 153 – 174.

Dutta, B. (1973). A study of the folk culture of the Goalpara district of Assam. P.14

Elwin, V. (1964). *Philosophy for NEFA,* Shillong.

Field, M.J. (1937). *Religion and Medicine of the Ga People,* Oxford University Press, London.

Flatie, T., Gedif T., Asres K., Gebre-Mariam, T. (2009). Ethnomedical survey of Berta ethnic group Assosa Zone, Benishangul-Gumuz regional state, mid-west Ethiopia. *J. Ethnobiol. Ethnomed.* 5:14.

Gurib-Fakim, A. (2006). Medicinal plants: traditions of yesterday and drugs of tomorrow. *Molec. Aspects Med.* 27:1–93.

Hostettmann, K., Marston, A., Ndjoko, K., Wolfender. J. L. (2000). The potential of African medicinal plants as a source of drugs. *Curr. Org. Chem.* 4:973–1010.

Hunter, W. W. (1879). *A Statistical Account of Assam Volume II.* London: Trubner & Co.

Hynniewta, S.R., Kumar, J. (2008). Herbal remedies among the Khasi traditional healers and village folks in Meghalaya. *Indian J. Trad. Knowl.* 7(4): 581 – 586.

Kar, A., Borthakur, S.K. (2007). Wild vegetables sold in local markets of Karbi Anglong, Assam. *Indian J. Trad. Knowl.* 6(1): 169 – 172.

Kumar, K.; Murthy, A.R. & Upadhyay, O.P. (1998). Plants used as antidotes by the tribals of Bihar. *Ancient Sci. Life 17(4)*: 268 – 272.

Lieban, R. W. (1973). Medical Anthropology. In J.J. Honigman (Ed.) *Handbook of Social and Cultural Anthropology*, Rand McNally College Publishing Company, Chicago: 1031–1072.

Lokho, A. (2012). The folk medicinal plants of the Mao Naga in Manaipur, North East India. *Intrn. J. Sci. Res. Publ. 2(6):* 1 – 8.

Lyall, Sir Charles, Edward, Stack. (1997). *The Karbis.* Guwahati, Spectrum Publications.

Medhi, Birinchi K. (1994). Health culture in a Kaibarta Village. The Bulletin of the Department of Anthropology, Gauhati University, Vol. VIII: 39-45.

Medhi, Birinchi K. (1995). Ethnomedicine: A study among the Mishings in a rural context. *The Bulletin of the Department of Anthropology, Gauhati University, Vol. IX:* 61-68.

Park, K. (2015). Preventive medicine in obstetrics, paediatrics, and geriatrics. In *Textbook of Social and Preventive Medicine* (16th ed). Jabalpur: Bhanot Publisher.

Polgar, S. (1962). Health and Human Behaviour: Areas of Interest Common to the Social and Medical Sciences, Current Anthropology, 3: 159–205.

Pool, R. (1986). Belief concerning the avoidance of food during pregnancy and the immediate postpartum period in a tribal area of rural Gujarat, India. *The Eastern Anthropologist* 39(3): 251–257.

Rates, S. M. K. (2001). Plants as a source of drugs. *Toxicon 39*:603–613.

Rivers, W.H.R. (1924). *Medicine, Magic and Religion,* Harcourt, Brace, New York.

Scotch, N. (1963). *Medical Anthropology,* in Biennial Review of Anthropology, S.J. Seigal (Ed.), Stanford, Stanford University Press: 30-38

Sikdar, M., Dutta, U. (2008). Traditional Phytotherapy of the Nath people of Assam. *EthnoMed.* 2(1): 39 – 45.

Singh, Bikrama, Borthakur, S. K., Phukan, S. J. (2014). A Survey of Ethnomedicinal Plants Utilised by the Indigenous People of Garo Hills with Special Reference to the Nokrek Biosphere Reserve (Meghalaya), India. *Journal of Herbs, Spices & Medicinal Plants, 20:1,* 1-30.

Singha, M.K.; Patel, D.K., Kanungo, V.K. (2012). Medicinal plants used as antidotes in the northern part of Bastar district of Chhattisgarh. *J. Ecobiotech.* 4(1): 58 – 60.

Spencer, D.M. (1941). *Disease, Religion and Society in the Fiji Islands,* Monograph of the American Ethnological Society, New York.

Teron, R., Borthakur, S.K. (2012). Traditional knowledge of herbal dyes and the cultural significance of colours among the Karbis Ethnic Tribe in Northeast India. *Ethnob. Res. Appl. 10*: pp. 593 – 603.

Teron, R., Borthakur, S.K. (2013). Folklore claims some medicinal plants as an antidote against poisons among the Karbis of Assam, India. *Pleione* 7(2): 346 – 356.

Zaman, A. (2011). Women health care among the Tiwas of Assam: a study in continuity and change. *Bulletin of the Department of Anthropology,* Dibrugarh University, *Vol.-39*:125-135.

Zaman, A. (2017). Aspects of Health Care Measures of New Born Among the Tai Phakes of Upper Assam, India. *Current Trends Biomedical Engineering & Biosciences.* 6(4): 1–10.

Zaman, A. (2021). Maternal and child health care among the rural hill Karbis of Assam, India. *Man in India, 101 (1-2)*: pp. 15–36.

Zaman, A. (2022). An Investigation on the Effects that the Local Flora and Fauna Have on the Health Care Practices among the Hill Karbis of the East Karbi Anglong District in the Indian State of Assam". *Antrocom J. of Anthropology, p. 18-2b*: pp. 627–637.

www.ingramcontent.com/pod-product-compliance
Lightning Source LLC
LaVergne TN
LVHW061538070526
838199LV00077B/6832